CREATIVE 3-D DISPLAY AND INTERACTION INTERFACES

CREATIVE 3-D DISPLAY AND INTERACTION INTERFACES

A Trans-Disciplinary Approach

Barry G. Blundell and Adam J. Schwarz

WILEY-INTERSCIENCE

A JOHN WILEY & SONS, INC., PUBLICATION

Published by John Wiley & Sons, Inc., Hoboken, New Jersey.
Published simultaneously in Canada.

For general information on our other products and services or for technical support, please contact our Customer Care Department within the United States at (800) 762-2974, outside the United States at (317) 572-3993 or fax (317) 572-4002.

Wiley also publishes its books in a variety of electronic formats. Some content that appears in print may not be available in electronic format. For more information about Wiley products, visit our web site at www.wiley.com.

Library of Congress Cataloging-in-Publication Data:

Blundell, Barry, 1956-
   Creative 3-D display and interaction interfaces: a trans-disciplinary
approach/Barry G. Blundell, Adam J. Schwarz.
   p. cm.
Includes bibliographical references and index.
ISBN-13 978-0-471-48271-0 (cloth: alk.paper)
ISBN-10 0-471-48271-4 (cloth: alk.paper)
   1. User interfaces (Computer systems). 2. Human-computer interaction. 3. Three-dimensional display systems. 4. Computer vision. I. Schwarz, Adam J., 1969- II. Title.

QA76.9.U83B58 2005
005.4′37--dc22   2005013734

Printed in the United States of America

10 9 8 7 6 5 4 3 2 1

Il est amer et doux, pendant les nuits d'hiver
D'écouter, près du feu qui palpite et qui fume,
Les souvenirs lointains lentement s'élever
Au bruit des carillons qui chantent dans la brume.[1]

Charles Baudelaire
La Cloche Fêlée, in "Les Fleurs du Mal" (Spleen et Idéal)

[1]A translation is provided at the end of the Acknowledgments.

CONTENTS

PREFACE

Digital systems . . . should augment human intelligence,
not automate it.[1]

The techniques most commonly used to interact with the computer are based on pioneering research carried out some 30 or more years ago. Certainly, the keyboard and mouse, coupled with the flat-screen display employing the event-driven interface (characterized by, for example, icons and menus), have provided a versatile and almost universal means of effecting human–computer interaction. However, as our usage of computers has evolved, it has become increasingly evident that for some applications, the conventional interface is by no means optimal, and is frustrating our communication with the digital world. In fact, perhaps for the first time since the early 1970s, hardware innovation is lagging behind software development.

For many years, alternative interface paradigms have been the subject of extensive research. A range of display techniques have been prototyped and developed. These offer to support nonpictorial depth cues (such as stereopsis) and thereby interface more naturally with the human visual system. Furthermore, many different types of interaction tool have been researched—some of which can provide haptic feedback to the user, while others are able to support bimanual interactive activity. Unfortunately, simply increasing the number of "channels" via which we can communicate with the digital domain, and extending the bandwidth of these channels, is not automatically advantageous. Major gains can, however, be brought about by the synergy that may be catalysed when we bring these "channels" together in an appropriate way and achieve interaction by means of natural human action, thereby reducing effort and promoting the richness of human creativity.

To date, much of the effort devoted to the development of new forms of displays that can support nonpictorial cues has been quite naturally directed towards the new visualization opportunities that they may offer. However, it represents only one aspect of their usefulness. Of equal importance is the way they can advance the interaction process, and this forms a pivotal theme in this book. Our premise is that a display should not be viewed in isolation but rather as a crucial component within an integrated multi-sensory interface, through which we can readily make optimal use of computer technologies. The successful development of such

---

[1]From Smith and Alexander [1999].

interfaces is extremely challenging and requires an in-depth understanding of a broad range of disciplines (including, for example, physics, computer science, the creative arts, engineering, biology, cognitive psychology etc.). Researchers must not only understand the fundamental technologies and techniques that are employed in the implementation of digital systems, but they must also comprehend a wide variety of aspects of the human cognitive processes and sensory systems. Furthermore, before systems can be properly developed, researchers must have a fundamental understanding of the nature of the applications for which the systems may be used. All too often, developers have produced systems that do not readily match human sensory requirements, and which have been developed using a bottom-up, rather than an application-driven, top-down, design strategy. Naturally, this is a recipe for disaster since only by good fortune will such systems meet the needs of end users.

In writing this book, we have sought to adopt a trans-disciplinary approach, which brings together a range of subject matter that would seldom be integrated within today's graduate or postgraduate research curricula. We encompass not only areas of science and technology that are essential to the development of advanced computer interfaces but also discuss the human visual and haptic systems and provide an insight into aspects of artistic depiction techniques. Throughout the book we underpin our discussions by reference to historical milestones in both the arts and the sciences and emphasize the substantial benefits that may be derived from the coalescence of traditional disciplines. We have attempted to frame our discussions in such a way as to make them accessible to students as well as to researchers who specialize in other areas, and to this end, we have when possible simplified our use of terminology, minimized reliance on acronyms, and endeavored to present the necessary mathematics in an approachable way. An extensive set of references is provided at the end of the book, together with a general bibliography. We hope that these citations will provide the interested reader with a sound basis for selecting additional reading.

In the late eighteenth century Samuel Taylor Coleridge and fellow poet William Wordsworth coined the phrase "suspension of disbelief," in connection with the impact that their verse could have on human imagination (see Section 1.5). This term is frequently used today in the context of creative media. From our perspective, it represents an important concept because of the augmented sense of realism that may be derived from creative display and interaction technologies. It was in connection with the concept of a "suspension of disbelief" that Coleridge wrote "The Rime of the Ancient Mariner." With this in mind we present a short verse from this poem at the beginning of each chapter, together with an image from Gustave Doré's accompanying illustrations. Verse and image are presented in random order (they do not necessarily relate to each other), and in doing this we seek to highlight the fact that both Coleridge's verse and Doré's imagery impact strongly on our imagination in equal measure—irrespective of the different medium through which the underlying ideas are conveyed.

Naturally, given the limited space available, it has only been possible to include in this work a small sample of the vast amount of related research. Despite the careful effort that has been applied to its authorship during 2 years of preparation, it is likely that this book will contain omissions and some mistakes. Please therefore let us know of areas in which errors have been made or of research that should be included in future editions.

For details of a resource pack that supports various material discussed in this book, please contact the author at the e-mail address given below.

We sincerely hope that this book will be of interest to you. Its preparation has been both a pleasure and a privilege.

BARRY G. BLUNDELL

E-mail: barry.blundell@physics.org
April 2005 France

ACKNOWLEDGMENTS

He holds him with his glittering eye –
The Wedding-Guest stood still,
And listens like a three years' child:
The Mariner hath his will.

My interest in the area of novel three-dimensional (3-D) display technologies dates back to days when as a student I spent long, pleasurable hours perusing dust-covered books and journals in the silent basement of the old John Rylands Library at the University of Manchester. Occasionally within these works (which in the main had not seen daylight for many decades), I would come across some long-forgotten gem in connection with some aspect of science or technology. Descriptions of generally forgotten electromechanical, 3-D display systems were particularly fascinating. However, it was not until I moved to the University of Canterbury in New Zealand that I had the opportunity to set up a laboratory within which I had the freedom to undertake the research of my choice: What could have been better than to carry out basic research into new types of 3-D computer display systems? Soon a vibrant laboratory was founded, attracting students and others who often possessed strongly individual (and sometimes rather eccentric) characters. Largely unfettered by today's bureaucratic safety procedures and other forms of current entropy, a variety of prototype display systems were rapidly created and evaluated.

It was during those early days (when building prototypes from scrap components and employing vacuum systems together with instrumentation that would have been better situated in a museum) that I received much encouragement from the late Professor Richard Bates and from Professor Arthur Williamson. Regularly, when passing by late at night, Professor Bates would call into my laboratory to ask some curt (and mentally challenging) question. Invariably, before leaving he would quietly add some terse but strongly encouraging and memorable remark. It was Professor Williamson who initially supported the work and facilitated the first real funding, and it was he who continually emphasized that research must be interesting—it must be fun. It took time to appreciate the importance of his assertion. Perhaps without these two great scholars, it would have been impossible to surmount the many difficulties faced at the outset. Of course, at that time and unlike today, interdepartmental assistance within universities was the norm, free from paperwork and surreal accounting procedures. There were therefore many people within the university who contributed to the early research work, and because a book represents the sum of many parts, they indirectly contributed to the creation of this book.

Early funding was provided personally by a number of remarkable New Zealanders, often on an ad hoc basis. Subsequently, and for some years, Richard Wood facilitated the development of prototype systems and provided a visionary insight into the potential of new forms of computer interface. Our long conversations were a source of great inspiration, and it is a privilege to have known him. It was while I was still at the University of Canterbury, some 10 years ago, that I had the good fortune to begin corresponding with Professor Rüdiger Hartwig. He has continued to provide invaluable advice and wise encouragement. I am also indebted to him for the literature and citations that he has supplied to assist in the production of this work and for his excellent sketch of the Kaiser Panorama (Figure 6.2(d)).

Professor John Willmott CBE, Dr. John Baker, Dr. Scott Hamilton, Professor Peter Walker, Professor Al Lewit, Professor Lynn Rosenthal, Robert Craig, and Dr. Basil Kerdemelidis all deserve special thanks for their indirect support in connection with this book. I have had the good fortune to meet many remarkable scholars (including the above, and those previously alluded to); these are the people who have (knowingly or otherwise) played a pivotal part in shaping my outlook. In looking back at those I have mentioned, I note at least one common factor: They are, or were, all great teachers, unstinting in the time given selflessly to their students.

I suppose that Quintus should take a considerable degree of direct responsibility for the inception of this book. In 2000, we were once again enjoying a contented New Zealand lifestyle, when one late autumn day my wife made the first reference to Quintus. Of course, he was not referred to at that time by name, but rather in a more abstract way—an embryonic life form. Despite the odds, he eventually emerged to take his first look at planet Earth, and at the tender age of 4 months, he catalysed our return to Europe. Once more, and quite unexpectedly, I found myself again in France living amid the parklands that had formed the backdrop for the previous book published with John Wiley in 2000. During my walks in that peaceful countryside, this book began to make the transition from abstract form to physical entity.

At John Wiley, Val Moliere, the book's editor since its first proposal, gave invaluable assistance and demonstrated great patience, as I never envisaged the problematic circumstances that would lead us to being in France for such a length of time, nor was the preparation of this work intended to take longer than a year. She was most ably assisted by Kirsten Rohstedt, and later by Emily Simmons. Recently, George Telecki and Whitney Lesch have taken on these roles, and they too deserve my thanks. Kellsee Chu has managed production most ably, and Dean Gonzalez has done some excellent work with the figures and illustrations.

In January of this year it seemed as though the book's completion was in sight and consequently I began to mail permission requests to publishers of scientific works and to various owners of the artwork that was to be reproduced in Chapter 4. Certainly I never envisaged the difficulties associated with this task, and I thank Alys most sincerely for taking over a responsibility that exceeded my patience. Today, some publishers require significant fees for the reproduction of even the simplest diagram, irrespective of originality. Consequently, various diagrams and images have had to be removed from the manuscript. Fortunately, some publishers and holders of artworks have been very understanding, waiving major fees and requirements for multiple free copies of the finished book. Many other authors have also been most helpful, and in this respect, I should particularly like to thank Professor Nicholas Wade (University of Dundee) who was kind enough to provide the Chimenti images reproduced in Appendix A; Professor Michael Land (University of Sussex), who provided Figure 2.1(b); and Professor Dale Purves (Duke University Medical Center), for Figure 2.2. Other images were provided by Dr. Francesco Buranelli (Director, Vatican Museums); Professor Steven Westland (University of Leeds); Ms. Christina Ellas (MIT Press Journals); Ms. Vivien Adams (National Gallery, London); Dr. Mark Ashdown (University of Tokyo); Ms. Karen Lawson (Royal Collection Enterprises, Windsor Castle); Professor Vinesh Raja (University of Warwick); Dr. Gregg Favalora (Actuality Systems Inc.); Dr. Ingrid Kastel (Albertina, Vienna); Professor I. Sutherland who gave informal permission in connection with Figure 8.8; Laura Wolf (Electronic Visualization Laboratory, Chicago) for Figure 8.9 (and caption); and Dover Publications who gave informal advice about copyright and allowed us to use the Gustave Doré images from their excellent edition of "The Rime of the Ancient Mariner." Many thanks also to Chris West, Martin Price and Lynn Cooling for providing library resources.

In France, I would like to thank M. Joël Souchal and Mlle Laëtitia Caboco in Chambon-sur-Voueize, who gave us access to the treasures of the Abbatiale Ste-Valérie, some images from which are reproduced in Chapter 4. In this quiet and idyllic setting, there are far too many people to mention personally, but I would particularly like to thank M. and Mme. Guy and Maite Beaufils for their warmth, friendship, and generosity; indeed, they represent the finest spirit of this region. Also

Mme. and Mlle. de V for continuing to open their home and splendid parklands to us (never forgetting the latter's aid to the weary and stranded traveler). Thanks also to Jean-Pierre for his friendship and camaraderie and to Jeanine who calmly accepts the chaos in her life that our presence entails.

I greatly value the friendship of Rosemary Russo, Iwan Pekerti, and Dorothy Moras, who I would never have been fortunate enough to meet had I not perused, years ago, those dusty publications in that library basement. Thanks also to all the other friends and colleagues in many lands who have eased my way down the thorny path toward the third dimension through their encouragement and understanding.

My sincere thanks go to all my family, especially Jandy, Alys, and Quintus (not forgetting Giotto and Alberti). Without their encouragement, this book would not have been realized. Jandy has spent a great deal of time working on it; I trust her work is justified by my contribution. Her skills have been invaluable, and Jandy's determination in the face of many difficulties to complete this work has been a source of great inspiration to me. Alys has demonstrated admirable perseverance in researching sources for permissions and helping with a myriad of activities. Quintus, too, should be thanked for his creativity; he derives much pleasure from driving trucks across my computer keyboard and gleefully pressing the power switch to "off." Uncanny judgment in one so young.

Finally, thanks to our three patient spaniels, Milo, Jasper, and Fenix, who have faithfully spent many long hours under this table. Unfortunately, both Milo and Fenix have had to go long haul. Jasper keeps watch.

BARRY BLUNDELL

Courcelle

A Translation of the earlier quotation:

Bittersweet it is, during the winter's evenings
By the fire as it glows and smokes,
To listen to the distant memories rising slowly,
To the sound of the carillons singing out in the mist.

The authors wish to acknowledge permissions received to reprint artworks and images from the following institutions:

Albrecht Dürer, "Draughtsman Drawing a Recumbant Woman"; © 2005 Albertina, Vienna

Giotto, "Pentecost"; © 2005 National Gallery, London

Leonardo da Vinci, "Deluge"; The Royal Collection © 2005 Her Majesty Queen Elizabeth II

Leonardo da Vinci, "The Skull Sectioned"; The Royal Collection © 2005 Her Majesty Queen Elizabeth II

Leonardo da Vinci, "The Infant and Womb"; The Royal Collection © 2005 Her Majesty Queen Elizabeth II

Leonardo da Vinci, "Study of drapery"; © 2005 Musée du Louvre, Paris

Peter Paul Rubens, "The Judgement of Paris"; © 2005 National Gallery, London

Raphael, "The School of Athens"; © 2005 Vatican Museums

Unknown artist, "Man of Sorrows"; © 2005 National Gallery, London

GLOSSARY OF ABBREVIATIONS

1-D   = one-dimensional
2-D   = two-dimensional
3-D   = three-dimensional
AABS = axis-aligned bounding box
ADT   = abstract data type
CAD   = computer aided design
CCD   = charge-coupled device
CFF   = critical flicker frequency
CNS   = central nervous system
CRT   = cathode ray tube
CT   = computed tomography
DOF   = degree of freedom
FA   = fast adapting
HMD   = head-mounted display
HPO   = horizontal-parallax only
IHOP = ideal haptic interaction point
IVR   = immersive virtual reality
LCD   = liquid crystal device
LGN   = lateral geniculate nucleus
MRI   = magnetic resonance imaging
OBB   = oriented bounding box
PC   = personal computer
PET   = positron emission tomography
SA   = slowly adapting
SLM   = spatial light modulator
PSF   = point spread function
VR   = virtual reality

1 The Nature of the Quest

I looked upon the rotting sea,
And drew my eyes away;
I looked upon the rotting deck,
And there the dead men lay.

1.1 INTRODUCTION

During the course of the last two decades of the twentieth century, the stylish desktop personal computer became a *de facto* standard. Automated low-cost, mass-production techniques have facilitated its proliferation to practically every part of our world, and despite some misgivings, it has generally been welcomed in almost every area of human endeavor. Indeed, it is difficult to imagine how we managed without such technology, and when teaching today's students, we must

Creative 3-D Display and Interaction Interfaces: A Trans-Disciplinary Approach, by Barry G. Blundell and Adam J. Schwarz
Copyright © 2006 John Wiley & Sons, Inc.

continually bear in mind that for this generation computers have always been readily available and are taken for granted. A world without desktop computers, Microsoft products, Internet access, and wireless connectivity is unknown to them.

Here, we might say, lies a remarkable and unparalleled success story of technological achievement. On the other hand, it is interesting to stand back for a moment and speculate on the number of hours per week that we now spend bound to our computers, attempting to convey our emotionally driven thought processes via imprecise communication skills to machines that operate solely upon logic and are utterly oblivious to the richness of human dialogue.

We are, however, remarkably adaptable and adept at problem solving, especially when it is possible to apply prior experience to new situations. This human skill greatly assists our interaction with computer systems, but in a growing number of situations, as software complexity increases, we encounter a lack of useful affordances, which can erode the value of our wealth of experience. Seemingly straightforward tasks become needlessly complicated and consequently frustrating. Often we blame ourselves, but in truth, the underlying cause frequently stems from deficiencies in the human–computer interface. As computer applications advance, it is increasingly evident that in some situations human creativity is in fact being inhibited by the standard computer interface, which imposes needless complexity on tasks that could, in principle, be undertaken more readily via alternative interface techniques.

Consider the time we waste each day attempting to identify the command sequences needed to accomplish a task, or maybe the time spent waiting for a response to a given interactive operation.[1] Even cursory consideration highlights the vital nature not only of the interface between our human communication channels and the machine but also of the machine's ability to conform to our expectations of "real-time" response. Has the human–computer interface truly been optimized, or is there room for improvement? Can further advancement be achieved through fine-tuning existing techniques, or is a radical change needed? The indications are that for *certain* applications there is a need to move forward and augment conventional approaches with radically new hardware and software solutions. This result is hardly surprising because much of the architectural and software detail of today's machines was determined years ago, possibly as the result of some now largely forgotten incident in corporate warfare. Indeed, the evolutionary development of today's computers has not always been governed by the survival of the strongest and best technologies and techniques but frequently by the fortunes of industry.[2] We shall return to this discussion shortly.

This book focuses on aspects of the human–computer interface and especially areas that involve the visualization of complex data (three-dimensional (3-D) in

---

[1]See the excellent text by Jef Raskin [2000] for some interesting discussion.

[2]In an article by Stan Liebowitz and Stephen Margolis [1996], the history of the QWERTY keyboard is discussed. As they indicate, this embellished story is often used to *"argue that market winners will only by the sheerest of coincidences be the best of the available alternatives."* There are, of course, many economists who would contest this.

form) together with our interaction with such data. In this context we explore issues relating to the depiction of data in ways that not only support the provision of additional depth cues but also provide an image depiction region (or image space) that moves away from the conventional two-dimensional (2-D) tableau. This latter consideration is especially important because it makes possible a range of alternative interaction techniques, and throughout the book, we emphasize the synergy between display and interaction interfaces. We therefore focus on two issues that we believe should drive the development and application of alternative display paradigms:

- Their potential to advance the visualization process
- Their ability to support new interaction tools and techniques

In the next section we describe the general characteristics of the display and interaction systems that form the basis for our subsequent discussions. We refer to these (admittedly rather arbitrarily) as "creative" interfaces—a title that is by no means formalized and is of our own choice. "Innovative systems," or some other title, would be equally appropriate.

Although it seems best to introduce the nature of creative interfaces (and thereby define the focus of this book) as soon as possible, it is equally important to place these interfaces in context. In Section 1.3, we provide some brief background discussion relating to the evolution of computing systems, and in Section 1.4, we discuss issues concerning the conventional display and interaction paradigms. Here we identify various strengths and weaknesses of the conventional display, deferring discussion on traditional interaction tools until Chapter 5. Having laid some foundations for the scope of the material presented in this book, and having placed the material in context, we consider in Section 5 areas in which the traditional interface may be nonoptimal and discuss how creative systems may augment the human–computer interaction process. We focus on three areas, which we refer to as augmented realism, augmented information content, and creative design.

Subsequent sections of this chapter introduce other relevant material along with further terminology that we will employ. Section 1.6 introduces some elementary computer graphics techniques and describes the nature of volumetric data sets. Section 1.7 provides a display model that defines several of the key sub-systems of a display, and in Section 1.8, we discuss various general factors that have hampered the widespread adoption of creative 3-D displays.

In short, this chapter is intended to lay some foundations for our subsequent discussions. Here we begin our voyage of discovery, and before leaving the harbor, we should be clear about the nature of our quest. During this voyage, we will make visits to different lands and briefly gain an insight into local geography, history, and culture. However, we will not stay long in any one place for we must make best use of the available time. Hopefully, we will return from this voyage with a knowledge of the diversity of the skills that exist and need to be brought together in order to effectively develop creative interfaces to the digital world. Later, we can peruse at our leisure, literature that will provide us with greater detailed understanding.

1.2   CREATIVE DISPLAY AND INTERACTION PARADIGMS

In this section, we loosely describe the features exhibited by systems that we consider to lie within the scope of this book. We should emphasize from the outset that there is no formal definition of "creative" interfaces; the attributes we mention in connection with such systems are defined by the authors.

The phrase "creative 3-D display systems" may conjure up techniques such as immersive virtual reality (IVR) systems, head-mounted displays (HMDs) containing stereoscopic imaging hardware, or futuristic holographic approaches. There are, however, various other classes of creative display, and many of these have been the subject of research activity for a considerable time. The operation of these displays is usually not reliant on recent major technological breakthroughs, and in some cases, the fundamental principles of operation have been known for many years. Consider, as an example, the image projection system incorporated within an IVR HMD so as to enhance the realism of a 3-D scene or structure through the inclusion of the binocular parallax depth cue (see Section 2.6.2). This approach, whereby each eye receives a slightly different view of a computer-generated image so that differences in the two views provide a sense of *relief*, is based on the stereoscope, which was pioneered by Wheatstone and Brewster as long ago as the mid-nineteenth century (see Section 6.3). It seems that first stereoscope employing electronic displays was prototyped in the 1940s, and this implementation is briefly discussed in Section 8.4.1.

Some classes of creative display do not require the use of special viewing apparatus. The classic example of one such implementation is known as the Lenticular approach (based on the work of F. E. and H. E. Ives in the first half of the twentieth century). In one form, a Lenticular faceplate comprising a set of cylindrical lenslets is located on the outer surface of a conventional display (see Sections 6.5.2 and 8.3.1). A stereopair is then interleaved in such a way that, for example, portions of the left view lie under even-numbered lenslets, and those of the right view reside beneath odd-numbered lenslets. The lenslets then direct the appropriate image to each eye.

Volumetric systems (see Sections 6.5.3 and 8.5) have also undergone a long period of gestation. A patent filed in 1912 by Luzy and Dupuis (see Blundell and Schwarz [2000]) describes what is perhaps the first proposed volumetric embodiment, and at the close of the Second World War, there was a resurgence of interest in this area concerning the application of volumetric display technology to the visualization of radar data [Parker and Wallis 1948, 1949].

Clearly, therefore, the general principles of operation of the majority of creative display systems are not new. Consequently, the date when they were first proposed is of no relevance in distinguishing these systems from the conventional techniques used in our day-to-day human–computer interaction processes. Similarly, because various classes of creative display draw on and extend the technologies employed in the implementation of conventional systems, hardware considerations do not necessarily provide the best means of distinguishing between the two. For the purposes of this book, we will differentiate between conventional and creative display technologies by assuming that in the case of the latter there exists a degree of uncertainty in one or more of the four areas indicated in Figure 1.1.

1. *Display System Architecture*: Any display consists of several well-integrated sub-systems incorporating a diverse set of technologies (see Section 1.7). In the case of many creative 3-D displays, a degree of uncertainty currently exists over the technologies that should be brought together in their implementation to achieve optimal performance. By contrast, the architectural arrangement and technologies used in the production of conventional flat-screen display systems are now reasonably well defined.

2. *Physical Form and Visual Attributes*: The optimal physical form and visual characteristics of conventional display systems are well established and have been continually refined over the course of the many years, during which these systems have been produced. However, in the case of creative 3-D systems, much research still needs to be undertaken to optimize the physical form of the image space and determine optimal visual attributes of the display. This research is of particular importance if the ensuing systems are to be usefully employed across the broadest spectrum of applications *without undue compromise in performance.*

3. *Interaction Opportunities*: The manner in which we interact with the computer via the conventional screen is now well established through the use of the event-driven user interface employed in conjunction with the mouse, touch screen, or joystick, etc. However, as we will discuss, creative 3-D display technologies offer to facilitate the interaction process by means of techniques

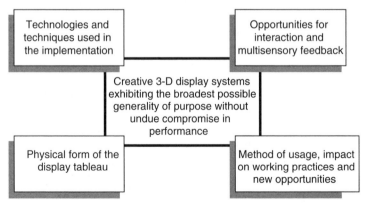

Figure 1.1: Creative 3-D display systems will be defined as having the ability to satisfy the binocular parallax (and possibly motion parallax) depth cues and for one or more of the four areas indicated, we assume that a considerable amount of further research needs to be undertaken. (Diagram © 2005 A.R. Blundell.)

that have not yet been fully explored. Specifically, creative displays provide an image space that is three-dimensional. This is the region that an image may physically occupy or from which the image appears to emanate. In Chapter 5, we discuss aspects of the image space in some depth and consider the mapping that exists between this region and the interaction space (this is the region in which interaction may be affected).

4. *Impact in the Workplace*: Finally, although the role and impact of the conventional display on working practices has in general been assessed, relatively little is known with certainty about the benefits that may ultimately be derived from creative 3-D display systems and associated interaction tools (especially when we include the possibility of effectively supporting two-handed (bi-manual) interaction).

Any display with a graphics capability, an ability to support various depth cues including binocular parallax (see Section 2.6.2), and which exhibits one or more of the above characteristics will, for our purposes, be loosely defined as a creative 3-D display technology.

1.3 A LITTLE HISTORY

The best way to predict the future is to invent it.[3]

By the end of the 1960s, practically all major architectural ingredients that form the basis of today's computer systems were understood and in use. However, at that time, few could have predicted the technological revolution that was poised to take place, and now, over 30 years later, it is impossible to guess with any accuracy where it will lead us. There can be few other scientific or technological break-throughs that have gained such widespread adoption, application, and acceptance in so short a time. Clearly, to have any chance of guiding development and so working toward the future, we need to fully appreciate the factors that have led to the proliferation of computers in practically every area of human endeavor. We must also attempt to properly comprehend their increasingly pivotal (and complex) role in the human creative processes.

Despite the dominance of computers in our day-to-day lives, the average user has difficulty in defining their essential characteristics. As long ago as the nineteenth century, Charles Babbage appreciated the potential of a machine that could operate via a set of predefined instructions. He also foresaw the power that could be derived from a machine that could not only follow a sequence of instructions but also select different sequences of instructions for execution (according to results computed previously, or because of changing input conditions) and moreover repeatedly execute a sequence of instructions (until the existence of some condition). In short, some 150 years ago, Charles Babbage formulated and understood (to a remarkable extent) the potential power of a machine that could execute instructions in sequence, by

[3]A slogan said to have been popular at Xerox PARC [Johnson et al. 1989].

selection, and by repeated iteration. He defined the essence of the programmable computer and distinguished it from the calculating machine. Furthermore, he was well aware of the need to store results in short-term memory (temporary variables) and issue them in printed form at the end of execution. Despite a lifetime of effort and progress made in the implementation of parts of his Analytical Engine, he, sadly, could not fulfill his vision [Swade 2000]. Following a visit to Charles Babbage a few years before his death, John Fletcher Moulton, a Cambridge mathematician, wrote,

> *In the first room I saw the part of the original Calculating Machine, which had been shown in an incomplete state many years before and had even been put to some use. I asked him about its present form. 'I have not finished it because in working at it I came on the idea of my Analytical Engine, which would do all that it was capable of doing and much more. Indeed the idea was so much simpler that it would have taken more work to complete the calculating machine than to design and construct the other in its entirety, so I turned my attention to the Analytical Machine'. After a few minutes' talk we went into the next workroom where he showed and explained to me the working of the elements of the Analytical Machine. I asked if I could see it. 'I have never completed it', he said, 'because I hit upon the idea of doing the same thing by a different and far more effective method, and this rendered it useless to proceed on the old lines'. Then we went into the third room. There lay scattered bits of mechanism but I saw no trace of any working machine. Very cautiously I approached the subject, and received the dreaded answer. 'It is not constructed yet, but I am working at it, and will take less time to construct it altogether than it would have taken to complete the Analytical Machine from the stage in which I left it'. I took leave of the old man with a heavy heart.* (Quoted in [Swade 2000]).

And so the visionary who was probably the first person to understand the power of the programmable computer failed to achieve his purpose, and after his death in 1871, many years were to pass before the true significance of his work was properly understood.

The history of computer development is, of course, well documented and many fascinating books abound on the subject. Our purpose is not to review this history (and with limited space we could certainly not do this justice) but rather to briefly focus on a few of the events that have taken place in relatively recent times.

In the early 1980s, the dominant role played by larger centralized installations (mainframes) and minicomputers that could support many users interfaced via terminals was challenged by desktop machines. These machines became known as personal computers (PCs) or workstations. The latter were high-end professional systems offering relatively high-performance processing, support for virtual memory, multitasking, high-performance graphics, network communications, security, and so on. Over time, the PC could offer similar features. Economies in manufacture due to volume sales (coupled with low-cost applications software) led to its domination of the market today.

With the advent of the desktop machine, users no longer needed to compete for processing resources. For each user, performance was guaranteed and was determined only by the individual's hardware and software configuration. Overheads were reduced as there was no longer a need to implement the increasingly complex algorithms necessary to ensure the equitable sharing of mainframe computer resources between users. At around the same time, the traditional text-based computer interface, as typified by mechanical teletypes, dumb terminals, and screeds of computer paper generated by line-printers, quickly became a thing of the past. This was largely made possible by the replacement of vector graphics terminals (and associated hardware) that could generally be afforded only by professional users with low-cost raster-scanned bitmap displays.[4] Low-cost graphical depiction of computer-processed data consequently became possible and offered to greatly assist the user in the visualization process. Interaction devices such as the light pen and mouse became standard (the mouse was in fact first prototyped in around 1964; see Section 5.2), which thus enabled users to circumvent the keyboard and work directly with the graphical interface. Concepts refined years before for use in mainframe computer architectures (such as virtual memory, cache memory, and multitasking) were quickly taken on board.

Much of the research undertaken in connection with the development of today's desktop machines took place at the Xerox Palo Alto Research Center (Xerox PARC). In 1971, Xerox PARC licensed from the Stanford Research Institute the right to incorporate the mouse in their computer designs, and by 1972, they had produced the Alto (see Figure 1.2), which provided a 600 by 800-pixel bitmapped graphics display, mouse, etc. [Johnson et al. 1989]. Subsequently the Xerox 800 series workstation was developed.[5] This represented an advance, being essentially an office automation product that facilitated *distributed* personal computing. Johnson et al. [1989] write: "*Star's designers assumed that the target users were interested in getting their work done and not at all interested in computers. Therefore an important design goal was to make the 'computer' as invisible to the users as possible.*" Great care was taken in the design of the event-driven user interface, which incorporated windows, icons, and so on. Furthermore, this system made available to the user a WYSIWYG document editor and other tools that we take for granted today. Machines could be easily networked over Ethernet, therefore facilitating the distributed computing paradigm. In 1981, the 8010 Star Information System appeared (this was the same year that IBM introduced their much less expensive PC). It was not a great commercial success, nor was a similar machine (Lisa) that was released by Apple in 1983, one year before the appearance of the Macintosh. Johnson et al. [1995] wrote in connection with the Star, "*Often the technological trailblazer only paves the way for a second or third product to be successful. Perhaps Xerox was simply too early; the 'knowledge worker' market did not exist in 1981.*" They go on to discuss various other potential reasons including price, lack of an open architecture policy, and the fact that the direct

---

[4]In fact, although the term "bitmap" is commonly used in this context, this strictly applies to systems in which each pixel is represented by one bit (and is therefore illuminated or otherwise). In the case in which each pixel has associated with it a number of bits (defining grayscale, color, etc.), then it is more accurate to use the term "pixmap." [Foley et al. 1997]. Consequently, in this text, we shall generally use the term "pixmap."

[5]This is often referred to as the Xerox Star. However, "Star" was originally used as a name for the software system rather than for the workstation itself.

Figure 1.2: The Xerox Alto computer. This machine was developed at Xerox PARC and was operational in 1972. Employing a bitmapped display (supported by some 50 Kb of display memory) and a mouse, this machine pioneered today's event-driven user interface. The 600 by 800-pixel monitor is oriented in portrait mode to better support word-processing activities. Subsequent machines such as the Apollo 100 permitted the monitor to be physically placed in either landscape or portrait mode. (Reproduced by permission from Johnson et al., "The Xerox Star: A Retrospective," *IEEE Computer,* **22** (9), (1989); © 1989 IEEE.)

manipulation interface (e.g., using a mouse for selection operations) may not be optimal for all situations.[6] In their excellent book, *Fumbling the Future*, Douglas Smith and Robert Alexander [1999] discuss the failure of Xerox to commercially exploit the remarkable Alto and so market the PC much sooner. Certainly, their failure to do so cannot be explained by insurmountable technical problems.

By the mid-1980s, a hardware configuration not greatly dissimilar to that employed in current desktop machines had come into being, prices had fallen, and the global proliferation of these computers took place at a remarkable rate.

From the mid-1980s, corporate warfare within the computer industry intensified and led to companies disappearing, seemingly overnight. Takeovers resulted not only in the acquisition of commercially exploitable technologies but also enabled industry to suppress technologies that posed a threat. In parallel, the development of standards became an increasing focus of attention together with a demand for backward compatibility. Consequently there was a reduction in the diversity of

---

[6]In connection with this discussion see an interesting publication by Edwin Hutchins et al. [1986].

types of workstation, hardware and software had to conform to standards (which because of their complexity are often outdated before their release), and new products had to retain the characteristics of their predecessors. In fact, the need to conform to standards together with the requirement for backward compatibility have, in terms of hampering computer advancement, perhaps been the two most significant difficulties faced by the computer industry.

New innovations particularly in the area of communications and the Internet have greatly impacted on the computer paradigm, but these have tended to extend the application of computer technology, rather than replacing basic approaches that were in place 20 years ago. Today's desktop systems are fundamentally based on an architecture that essentially came into being during a very short period in which the architecture gradually evolved, not solely as a consequence of scientific research, but as a result of corporate strategies. Advances in hardware and software were not often determined by merit alone but through the influence of tremendous commercial forces, by conformance to standards (often dictated by the largest players in the computer world), by price, and by a need to ensure that the new would work alongside the old.

Despite recent rapid advances in the development of thin screen displays, the Cathode Ray Tube (CRT) continues to play a dominant role in the human–computer interface. More than 100 years have passed since the first implementation of this remarkable device (for interesting reading in this area, see Abramson [1987]). Not only has it played a pivotal role in the depiction of televised and computer-generated information, but in passing, it is interesting to note that hybrid devices provided early computers with the means of storing binary data and rapidly switching electronic signals.[7] In the next section, we briefly consider some attributes of the conventional display that have enabled it to gain such widespread acceptance. Subsequently, we discuss several areas in which the shortcomings of the flat-screen approach are becoming increasingly apparent and are negatively impacting on the way in which we visualize and interact with computer systems.

1.4   THE CONVENTIONAL INTERFACE: WORKING IN FLATLANDS

> It is now more than a century and a half since the days of which we have been speaking...Even in times of crisis it is the things of the "spirit" (in the French sense) that count most, and this spirit is perhaps best imparted by great teachers. . . .like Carnot, one should never lose heart, no matter how disillusioning the political or intellectual outlook may be.[8]

With the exception of some specialized applications, the flat screen dominates in our interaction with computer technologies.[9] To place alternative 3-D display paradigms

---

[7]In connection with the latter, see Blundell and Schwarz [2000].
[8]Boyer [1991].
[9]As we will discuss shortly, the flat screen also forms the basic display element in most creative 3-D technologies.

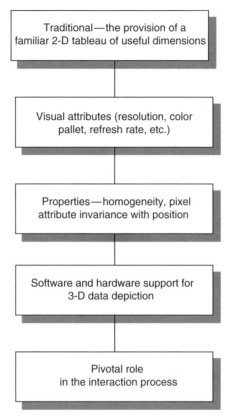

Figure 1.3: Here we illustrate some of the key issues that have led to the almost universal adoption of the traditionally CRT-based flat-screen display. This list is by no means exhaustive and omits many factors such as cost/performance and the flexibility of the technology to match ever-increasing performance specifications. (Diagram © 2005 A.R. Blundell.)

in context, it is instructive to consider why this approach continues to play such a pivotal role. Figure 1.3 illustrates some factors relating to the widespread adoption of the conventional approach to information depiction. Below we consider each of these factors briefly in turn.

1. *The Traditional*: From the outset, the use of a flat screen formed a natural extension to traditional working practices. Through pictorial methods employed by both artist and engineer, rapidly advancing computer graphics techniques have enabled images to exhibit an ever greater degree of realism. Although the foundations of computer graphics techniques had been put firmly in place before the 1960s (see Sections 1.6.1 and 8.4), the first integrated interactive computer graphics system is generally attributed to Sutherland [1963]. Nevertheless, for many years, graphics terminals represented an expensive luxury, and for most computer users, mechanical

teletypes and visual display units—whose capabilities were limited to the depiction of alphanumeric characters—represented the primary means of effecting human–computer interaction. As we have seen, it was not until the early 1980s and the advent of the desktop computer that software and hardware support for graphical information depiction and interaction became commonplace. The flat-screen display then provided an electronic tableau that could mimic traditional drawing media, and it was only natural that existing design practices should be ported across to this new environment. The engineer could put to one side the A0 paper, pencil, eraser, and drafting table and take advantage of the features offered by digital technology.

In point of fact, the traditional approach of depicting mechanical and other engineering objects and structures by means of orthogonal views dates back more than 200 years. This drafting technique is attributed to the mathematician, Gaspard Monge (1746–1818). In a chapter dealing with mathematical history during this time, Carl Boyer [1991] describes the period as follows:

> *The eighteenth century had the misfortune to come after the seventeenth and before the nineteenth. How could any period that followed the "Century of Genius" and which preceded the "Golden Age" of mathematics be looked upon as anything but a prosy interlude?*

Boyer sees this period as one in which the foundations were laid for the subsequent "... *explosive proliferation of mathematics during the succeeding century.*" Gaspard Monge was a strong proponent of the French revolution, and during this traumatic period of change, he lectured in various areas of mathematics. One course that he presented focused on descriptive geometry (then known as stereotomy), and this included topics such as shadow, perspective, topography, and aspects of surface geometry. Based on his teaching, Monge produced a textbook entitled *Geometrie Descriptive* [1989], and it was here that he discussed his double orthographic projection technique, which provided 2-D elevation and plan views of 3-D objects and had obvious applications for the advancement of military engineering. The text was consequently viewed as containing classified material, and its publication was somewhat delayed. Gaspard Monge became a great follower of Napoleon Bonaparte but lost both his position and status after his exile. Without a doubt, Gaspard Monge significantly advanced engineering design techniques, and through his inspired teaching in descriptive and differential geometry, he may be said to have significantly contributed to the techniques widely employed in today's computer graphics systems.

2. *The Visual*: Support for bitmap and pixmap raster scanned displays, rather than the more expensive vector graphics terminals, denoted a major advance. Since then visual characteristics such as resolution, refresh rate, and the color pallet of the display have advanced, and these now well match basic requirements of the human visual system (see Sections 2.5 and 2.6). The CRT provided the vehicle by which our requirements were properly

assessed, and the development of thin-panel display technologies has been greatly facilitated by knowing (in advance) target specifications.[10] This consideration is important as it contrasts with creative 3-D display and interaction system research. Workers in these areas have no definitive model of the target for which they should strive, and the optimal results of their quest have often still to be defined. Similarly, we generally do not know with any certainty how creative systems will impact on working practices.

3. *Homogeneity*: This is an essential attribute of the conventional display and is generally taken for granted. Consider a geometric object depicted at a certain location on a conventional flat screen, which is subsequently shifted to a different place. We expect the number and spatial distribution of pixels from which it is formed to remain essentially invariant (we neglect aliasing). In short, we expect that it will remain the same size and shape. Should this not be the case, the screen would no longer provide a predictable tableau and its usage would be severely restricted. Homogeneity is possible as the screen provides a matrix of uniformly spaced pixels (although the spacing is different in the vertical horizontal directions and so the conventional display does not form an isotropic tableau). Moreover, all pixels are the same size and there is no variation in the range of properties that may be ascribed to them. As indicated in Sections 6.5.3 and 8.5, inhomogeneity, and variation in voxel attributes denote major problems in the implementation of many AutoQ displays, and unless carefully considered, this can lead to serious problems in the application of these systems. Other creative implementations exhibit similar problems as a consequence of variations in image space isotropy, specifically in the third dimension.

4. *Interaction*: When considering factors that have led to the widespread acceptance of conventional display systems, we should not underestimate the synergy existing between the display and the interaction techniques. The introduction of the event-driven graphical menu system coupled with the mouse and/or touch screen has greatly facilitated an interaction process that had previously been almost exclusively reliant on keyboard input. This advance placed the user within an environment in which the conventional display plays a pivotal role. However, as discussed in Section 1.5, for certain applications, strengths originally associated with this approach are now being gradually eroded.

Until quite recently, the electronic computer display was almost universally based on the CRT, and for the first time, we see alternative (thin-panel) displays rapidly challenging this traditional approach. The CRT has indeed proven to be highly adaptable and there still remains considerable scope for its advancement, especially in the area of "intelligent" large screen displays, provided that investment is made in furthering this type of technology. However, given the current focus on thin-panel displays, it is likely that opportunities may be lost in further CRT development. For an example of

---

[10]For a slightly dated but still useful text in this area, see the book edited by Lucien Biberman [1973].

an alternative approach to the implementation of the CRT, see van den Brink and Willemson [2003].

1.5 INHIBITING THE HUMAN–COMPUTER INTERACTION PROCESS

> A moment later the couple went off –
> he, trained on some textbook
> that had blunted his capacity for wonder,
> she inert and insensitive to the thrill of the infinite.[11]

For many applications, the conventional flat-screen display and associated interaction tools, such as the keyboard and mouse, serve us well and provide a convenient (although perhaps at times frustrating) interface with the digital world. However, in the case of certain activities, there is a growing realization that the conventional approach may be nonoptimal and could in fact be inhibiting rather than augmenting the human–computer interaction process—perhaps even restricting the benefits that we can derive from the computer. For example, in a most interesting and comprehensive publication, Gregg Favalora, Won Chun, and co-workers at Actuality Systems Inc. write:

> *There is an obvious and demonstrable need for true 3-D displays. Rapid improvements in contemporary sensor, communication, storage and computation technology enable the broad dissemination of an unprecedented wealth of data to minds working in fields as diverse as oil and gas visualization, medical imaging, command and control, and entertainment. In effect, the availability of data has far outstripped the capabilities of contemporary 2-D displays. The constriction of the visual bottleneck will continue to increase due to the grossly incommensurate scaling between information technologies and display technologies; 2-D display bandwidth has essentially reached a plateau. [Chun et al. 2005]*

Although fine-tuning the existing interface may, in the case of some applications, lead to short-term improvements, ultimately it is likely that we will need to consider the adoption of radically new approaches. Hinckley et al. [1998][12] begin an excellent publication (which forms a focus for some discussion on the subject of bi-manual interaction in Chapter 9) as follows:

> *The current paradigm for graphical user interfaces (GUIs) has been dubbed the 'WIMP' (Windows, Icons, Menus, and Pointer) interface. Many WIMP graphical interaction techniques were originally designed for computers which, compared to modern machines, had low-powered processors and impoverished black-and-white displays) ... Yet as computing technology becomes ubiquitous and the capabilities of processors, displays, and input devices continue to grow, the limitations of the WIMP interface paradigm become increasingly apparent. To get past this 'WIMP plateau', devising new interface metaphors*

---

[11]Umberto Eco [2001].
[12]Reproduced with permission from Hinckley et al. [1998].

will not be enough. We need to broaden the input capabilities of computers and improve the sensitivity of our interface designs to the rich set of human abilities and skills.

In the sub-sections that follow, we will consider several indicative areas of application that illustrate weaknesses of the traditional display and interaction paradigms. These weaknesses are intended to highlight the need to thoroughly investigate (and properly evaluate) alternative techniques.

1.5.1 Augmented Realism: Suspension of Disbelief

Realism is of particular importance in, for example, 3-D applications such as those involving the visualization of mechanical or structural designs, some areas of education, and of course, computer games. Clearly the use of the term "realism" does not necessarily relate to realistically mimicking the physical world, especially, for example, when we are discussing entertainment, or situations in which we seek to teach scientific principles by changing basic laws of nature. However, in such cases, we rely on the recipient entering willingly into the experience and augmenting synthetic images with their imagination, which can then lead to the viewer becoming completely absorbed or immersed within a digitally generated environment. The expression "suspension of disbelief" is often used in this context. The phrase represents an essential ingredient of cinema, theater, and literature. It is by no means new (although sometimes referred to as such), and the poet, Samuel Taylor Coleridge, may have been the first to coin the term in the late 1700s, as recorded in his *Biographia Literaria* (first published in 1817) [Coleridge 1985].[13] Writing

---

[13]"During the first year that Mr. Wordsworth and I were neighbours, our conversations turned frequently on the two cardinal points of poetry, the power of exciting the sympathy of the reader by a faithful adherence to the truth of nature, and the power of giving the interest of novelty by the modifying colours of imagination. The sudden charm, which accidents of light and shade, which moon-light or sun-set diffused over a known and familiar landscape, appeared to represent the practicability of combining both. These are the poetry of nature. The thought suggested itself (to which of us I do not recollect) that a series of poems might be composed of two sorts. In the one, the incidents and agents were to be, in part at least, supernatural; and the excellence aimed at was to consist in the interesting of the affections by the dramatic truth of such emotions as would naturally accompany such situations, supposing them real. And real in this sense they have been to every human being who, from whatever source of delusion, has at any time believed himself under supernatural agency. For the second class, subjects were to be chosen from ordinary life; the characters and incidents were to be such, as will be found in every village and its vicinity, where there is a meditative and feeling mind to seek after them, or to notice them, when they present themselves.

In this idea originated the plan of the 'Lyrical Ballads'; in which it was agreed, that my endeavours should be directed to persons and characters supernatural, or at least romantic, yet so as to transfer from our inward nature a human interest and a semblance of truth sufficient to procure for these shadows of imagination that willing ***suspension of disbelief*** for the moment, which constitutes poetic faith. Mr. Wordsworth on the other hand was to propose to himself as his object, to give the charm of novelty to things of every day, and to excite a feeling analogous to the supernatural, by awakening the mind's attention from the lethargy of custom, and directing it to the loveliness and the wonders of the world before us; an inexhaustible treasure, but for which in consequence of the film of familiarity and selfish solicitude we have eyes, yet see not, ears that hear not, and hearts that neither feel nor understand. With this view I wrote the 'Ancient Mariner.'"

much earlier, Shakespeare, although he did not use the expression "suspension of disbelief," showed that he was well aware of the relevance of this type of concept as applied to live theater. In the Prologue to Henry V, he writes:

Piece out our imperfections with your thoughts;
Into a thousand parts divide one man,
And make imaginary puissance;
Think when we talk of horses, that you see them
Printing their proud hoofs i' the receiving earth;
For 'tis your thoughts that now must deck our kings,
Carry them here and there; jumping o'er times,
Turning the accomplishment of many years
Into an hour-glass: for the which supply,
Admit me Chorus to this history;
Who prologue-like your humble patience pray,
Gently to hear, kindly to judge, our play.

Suspension of disbelief leads an audience to become engrossed—individuals lose themselves within a world created by others. Cruz-Neira et al. [1992] writing in the context of virtual reality, succinctly describe suspension of disbelief as "*the ability to give in to a simulation—to ignore its medium.*" The audience may become so engrossed by content, for example, that they overlook poor quality props and unconvincing cinematic effects. The level of immersion may be such that for a time they put their real surroundings to one side and exist within an arti- ficial, or perhaps we should say virtual, world.

In the context of this book and the human–computer interface in general, we begin by considering suspension of disbelief as having two key components (we will introduce a third component shortly). These are illustrated in Figure 1.4 and will be referred to as the "experience" and the "audience." The former will be assumed to comprise "content" and "presentation." In literature, theater, and film, for example, "content" would refer to the underlying story or message. The term may equally well apply to the opportunities offered by software packages such as those used for design or visualization. "Presentation" refers to the manner in which the content is conveyed to an audience and is influenced by the nature of the interface existing between the experience and the audience. For example, thea- trical presentations (the theatrical interface) generally cannot compete with the film industry (cinematic interface) in terms of the scale of the special effects that can be offered to an audience, and similarly the author of a nonillustrated fictional novel (text interface) must rely exclusively on human imagination. Clearly, outstanding content may be negated by a poor, nonharmonious presentation style that continu- ally distracts the audience from the content.

The "experience" as a whole must be conducive to a suspension of disbelief, and at the same time, the audience must at least be willing to submit to the experience. Lying between these two facets of the immersion process is the "interface," and we may view this as a virtual window through which we view a world created by others. This window may take the form of the pages within a book, a theatrical stage, a radio, a television screen, an artist's canvas, or indeed a computer interface.

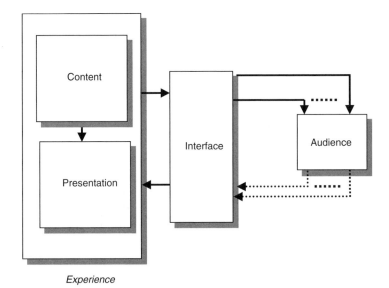

Experience

Figure 1.4: Augmented realism requires a suspension of disbelief that can in principle enhance the degree of immersion experienced by an audience. For our purposes, we will assume that the experience comprises the "content" (e.g., a plot or story) and the "presentation" (e.g., the written expression of the story). This is paralleled in some types of software system (e.g., a computer game). The "interface" provides the window to the "experience" and may for example be illustrated by a cinema screen or simply the pages within a book. Unobtrusive computer interfaces that can support natural bidirectional communication are sometimes difficult to achieve (depending on the nature of the application) and are a goal of creative 3-D display system researchers. (Diagram © A.R. Blundell.)

It defines the human senses that may participate in the experience. The window should be unobtrusive, and in noninteractive situations, immersion and suspension of disbelief will often enable an audience to transcend this barrier.

In this context, Hutchins et al. [1986], whose publication we referred to earlier, talk of a concept of "distance," which they refer to as "*gulfs between a person's goals and knowledge and the level of description provided by the systems with which the user must deal.*" They refer to distance as comprising two components: the "gulf of execution" and the "gulf of evaluation." The former is said to concern the mapping between a user's goals and the physical system, whereas the latter maps the computed response back to the user. They indicate:[14]

> *The Gulf of Execution is bridged by making the commands and mechanisms of the system match the thoughts and goals of the user as much as possible. The Gulf of Evaluation is bridged by making the output displays present a good Conceptual Model of the system that is readily perceived, interpreted and evaluated. The goal in both cases is to minimize cognitive effort.*

---

[14]This article is especially interesting as it was written not long after the general introduction of the event-driven interface.

Interaction is a fundamental ingredient of computer-based activities, and so in Figure 1.4, we show the interface as supporting bidirectional throughput. Here the interface enables the audience to obtain multisensory input from the experience and also to interact with it by means of various interaction paradigms. The interface should properly integrate with the relevant human sensory systems and should support interaction activities in a natural and intuitive manner. Not surprisingly, creating such an interface is extremely challenging.

Consider a simple word-processing task. When using my computer for this type of activity, I lose touch with my surroundings for hours at a stretch. We all share the experience of looking up from our computer screen and reaching for the nearby cup of coffee, only to find what had been hot seemingly moments before now sits before us cold, tasteless, and with a dead fly floating on its surface. Such an immersion experience implies that the interface to the word processor provides a harmonious, unobtrusive, and intuitive environment for our activity. However, when undertaking a word-processing task, we tend to limit our use of the available facilities to those that are easily remembered and therefore employed intuitively and without conscious thought. On the other hand, if we decide to use a new facility or one that has not been used for some time, our attention must turn toward the software interface, which can easily disrupt task immersion, returning us to our physical surroundings, and that cold cup of coffee.

Creative 3-D display techniques offer to enhance realism not only through support for binocular disparity and perhaps immersion but also through any new interaction opportunities that they may offer. This latter consideration is of particular importance in, for example, a computer games application in which suspension of disbelief is paramount. Although a display paradigm may in itself reinforce a suspension of disbelief, the appropriateness of the interface must also be considered with great care. An ill-matched, nonintegrated, and/or cumbersome interaction interface is likely to negate the benefits derived from any additional visualization opportunities offered by the display.

Irrespective of the nature of the experience or interface window, from an audience's (or a computer user's) perspective, imagination is pivotal to the suspension of disbelief. The augmentation of realism does not (or rather should not) seek to undervalue or replace the need for human imagination, as this is one of our most powerful mental facilities. For some applications, maximum benefit may be derived by working with and extending the imagination processes, and when considering the development of systems targeted at applications in which we seek to augment realism, we should always consider with care the impact of such systems on the imagination. It is, after all, with the help of our imagination that we truly achieve a suspension of disbelief.[15] As illustrated in Figure 1.5, we consider imagination as the third essential ingredient needed to support this concept.

The games and entertainment industries represent highly lucrative sectors, and in applications such as these, suspension of disbelief is essential. Consequently, they

---

[15]Frederick Brookes emphasizes the importance of imagination in the brief paragraph quoted in Section 6.9.

Figure 1.5: Here we illustrate the three key components that we assume support the suspension of disbelief. Even in the case of an appropriate experience and interface window, imagination remains a pivotal ingredient. Creative systems should not strive to minimize the need for human imagination but should build on it.

are likely to drive display developments, and other key areas of science, education, and medicine that could benefit from the realism offered by new display and inter- action paradigms may well have to wait for these technologies to be passed down to them. This paradox is well expressed by Frederick Brooks who writes in the Foreword to the excellent text by Grigore Burdea [1996]:

> *Virtual worlds, or synthetic environments, technology holds great promise for medi- cine, for design, for training, and for science. It is ironically sadly characteristic of our culture that these promising uses will be enabled, if at all, as byproducts of our desire to be entertained. God help us.*

1.5.2 Augmented Information Content

It may seem that conventional display systems, when used in conjunction with image processing and computer graphics software, are satisfactory for professional 3-D visualization applications. This may be the case in many areas of usage, but in certain applications, creative approaches may represent a significant advance—not as a consequence of the realism that they offer, but rather through their ability to augment the information content of the visual scene. In fact, at times and in some applications, augmented realism may detract from the performance of the visual interface. Consider a volumetric display system (see Sections 6.5.3 and 8.5) that is to be applied to the depiction of real-time radar data pertaining to objects in flight (either for Air Traffic Control or in a military situation). In principle, the volumetric display would enhance the visualization process by clearly showing the spatial separation of the airborne objects and by enabling a plurality of observers to simultaneously view the display without any significant restriction in viewing angle. Each object could, for example, be represented as a simple icon accompanied by a vector(s) expressing its past and predicted flight trajectory. Additional text could be assigned to each icon to provide information relating to speed, etc. Alternatively, depicting each object more realistically would enhance the degree of realism. Aircraft could be drawn to resemble the associated aircraft type. Adding contrails and perhaps the plumes of smoke ejected by a missile could give additional realism. However, it is readily apparent that enhancing realism in this way provides no additional information to the operator and is quite likely to have a negative impact by cluttering the image space with unnecessary information content.

In general terms, augmented realism and augmented information content represent two different aspects of a display's ability to effectively enhance the human–computer interface, and certainly in most professional applications, it is the information content, rather than the realism, that is critical. In certain situations, displays that properly support binocular disparity and/or that permit images to be depicted in alternative ways may enhance the information content, or simply facilitate the ease with which information may be derived from an image scene.

It is convenient to loosely distinguish between situations in which either enhanced object clarity or enhanced spatial clarity are of primary relevance. For our purposes, enhanced object clarity may be considered to involve the display of 3-D objects and/ or structures that do not easily lend themselves to the processes of depiction and manipulation via conventional means. For example, object clarity is important when we need to visualize (and perhaps manipulate) a geometrically complex mechanical component, or a sheet of material that has been curved in a complex and nonuniform manner. Object clarity may relate to static or dynamic scenes.

Spatial clarity is of primary relevance in, for example, the air traffic control application mentioned above and in medical applications such as stereotactic neurosurgery that involves the depiction of the 3-D "web" of capillaries within the brain (see Figure 1.6). In the case of the visualization of airborne objects, the operator must view dynamic data sets, and the ability to correctly interpret and respond to events in real time is paramount. In the case of stereotactic neurosurgery, key objectives may be:

• To provide greater insight into the spatial form of the vessels within the brain.
• To allow complex data to be visualized and interpreted more readily.
• To increase the accuracy of the interpretation process through the simplification of spatial information.

1.5.3   Creative Design

Currently, application program manufacturers do not offer a new release of software containing fewer features than its predecessor! Consequently, each new

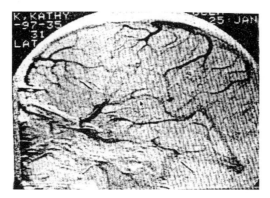

Figure 1.6: Stereotactic digital subtractive angiography. This shows the form of the venous system in a portion of the brain. During surgical operations, probes must be inserted with great care so as to avoid damage to these blood vessels. The visualization of such a 3-D structure is indeed difficult when conventional display technologies are used. (Reproduced by permission from Gildenberg, P. and Tasker, R., *Textbook of Stereotactic and Functional Neurosurgery*, McGraw-Hill (1998); © 1998 The McGraw-Hill Companies.)

release of an applications program offers additional features, and so contains more menu options. Naturally, as the extent of a software interface increases, so does the scope of the menu system, and to prevent undue screen erosion by the menu system, increasing reliance is placed on a hierarchical implementation of the user interface. Unfortunately, navigation may then become increasingly difficult (nonintuitive). In such cases, the simplicity that was originally offered by the event-driven menu system in its earlier years is gradually being reduced. Furthermore, screen erosion remains an issue, and if care is not exercised in the design of the interface, the extent of useful working space in which the user may perform creative tasks (such as word-processing and design activities) will be overly restricted. As discussed below, various approaches are commonly adopted by interface designers to alleviate these problems (see also the brief discussion of the Toolglass interface (which provides an alternative solution) presented in Section 9.2).

For example:

1. *Scaling*: This allows the breadth of the interface to be increased without necessarily increasing its depth. The size of items such as icons within the interface is often reduced, thus enabling more options to be depicted within the same area. Unfortunately, text labeling may then become difficult, and it is now common to find icons whose functionality is indicated pictorially. The difficulty of comprehending the functionality of such icons is exacerbated by the extent of their usage across a range of appliances (e.g., computer software, digital cameras, video cameras, TV remote controls, kitchen whiteware,

etc.). Quite different icons may denote tasks that are similar; there is no standardization.[16]

2. *Hierarchical Implementation*: In this case, rather than increasing the interface breadth, the hierarchical depth of the interface is increased. This may result in navigation difficulties and is likely to increase the number of selections that must be made to accomplish a particular task.

3. *Configurable Interface*: This approach allows groups of less frequently used (and functionally related) menu items to be "hidden" until such time as they are required. Unfortunately, as we all know, when a hidden item (or one that has been put somewhere for safe keeping) has eventually to be retrieved, we may experience problems recalling where it was placed!

All too often, therefore, we are left to navigate without appropriate affordances through menu systems where functionality is indicated by symbols and brief help messages that are frequently cryptic. Although this problem is exacerbated by software vendors who continue to fail to direct sufficient attention to good interface design, underlying problems may be a result of the inherent nature of the interface paradigm. In short, in the case of more complex software, achieving simplicity through the conventional approaches to interface implementation may simply not be possible.

The degree of difficulty experienced by the user (and the obtrusiveness of the interface) often relates to the nature of an application. For example, consider a creative 3-D design task that involves the construction of an object, structure, or animated film character. The operator will generally carry out this process within the confines of orthogonal perspective views. Tasks that are inherently 3-D in nature must therefore be carried out within the 2-D "flatland" described so well by Abbott in the entertaining and satirical stories set within a 2-D world inhabited by geometrical shapes [Abbott 1884] and more recently by Tufte [1990]. In one of his books, Edward Tufte begins a chapter entitled "Escaping Flatland" in the following way:

> *Even though we navigate daily through a perceptual world of three spatial dimensions and reason occasionally about higher dimensional arenas with mathematical ease, the world portrayed on our information displays is caught up in the two-dimensionality of the endless flatlands of paper and video screen. All communication between the readers of an image and the makers of an image must now take place on a two-dimensional surface. Escaping this flatland is the essential task of envisioning information – for all the interesting worlds (physical, biological, imaginary, human) that we seek to understand are inevitably and happily multivariate in nature. Not flatlands.*

In flatlands, tasks can often no longer be carried out intuitively, based on our real-world 3-D experience.[17] Thus, a computer interface may become obtrusive as the

---

[16]The author (BGB) recently purchased a camcorder. Only one button was labeled in text (ON/OFF). In my enthusiasm to try out the appliance and given my dislike for instruction booklets (written in ten languages), I frantically pressed this button. Finally, unable to obtain any response I sadly consulted the instructions (convinced by this time that the appliance was defective). However it turned out that the actual power (ON/OFF) button was labeled by a cryptic icon, and the button labeled "ON/OFF" served to turn on or off the special digital effects.

operator focuses on the interaction process rather than on the creative design task. Undertaking tasks that are inherently 3-D within the confines of 2-D space can greatly increase task complexity, which in turn augments the complexity of the software interface. For tasks that are performed frequently, this is unlikely to be a problem as we can rely on our memory. However, despite our natural skills in problem solving when faced with new tasks, we are often provided with few affordances, and navigation through the hierarchical layers of a menu system can become problematic.

Creative 3-D display and interaction interfaces offer to simplify the design process by permitting tasks that are inherently 3-D in nature to be carried out within a 3-D design space. In principle, it is then possible to undertake tasks in a more intuitive and direct manner (especially if, where appropriate, bi-manual interaction is supported), which results in a simplified interface structure. Furthermore, the aesthetic results of the creative process may be discerned more readily. The development of interaction hardware that closely matches the characteristics of the display paradigm is paramount for this type of application (for further reading see Blundell [2006]).

1.6 GRAPHICS ISSUES

> The world is wide
> On every side
> New wonders we can find
> And yet for each man
> Space extends
> No farther than the mind[18]

Various computer graphics techniques are used in the depiction of a 3-D scene on a conventional flat 2-D display. Techniques such as ray-tracing algorithms, illumination models, and more recently volume rendering have, in recent years, been the subject of immense research interest. A goal is to represent the "pictorial" depth cues (see Section 2.6.1) as realistically as possible. Although this book focuses on approaches that invoke the additional, nonpictorial depth cues, the methods of rendering used in conventional computer graphics provide a basis for 3-D techniques that employ several monocular projections so as to create a 3-D image space. For this reason, we very briefly summarize the basics of standard computer graphics rendering as this will provide a foundation for subsequent discussions in Chapter 8, where we examine the rendering process in the context of other forms of 3-D display technologies. Subsequently, we consider the nature of volumetric (voluminous) data. For more details on conventional surface and volume graphics techniques, see standard texts in computer graphics, for example, Foley et al. [1994], Watt [2000] (others are listed in the General Bibliography section), and Chen et al. [2000] (which deals specifically with volume data).

---

[17]The stories written by Abbott are recommended to the interested reader as they highlight many aspects of life in a 2-D space. (Life—but not as we know it . . . .)

[18]Anonymous. Taken from Satava and Sackier [1998].

1.6.1   Projection Geometry for a Single View

A perspective projection is used to depict an image on a 2-D surface so that it appears "realistic" and undistorted. This technique ensures that the pictorial depth cues are represented correctly and that the geometry of the image is the same as would be observed from a single eye when viewing the natural scene. In fact, as discussed in Chapter 4, the rules for perspective projection were laid down in systematic form many centuries ago and are synonymous with the Renaissance.

The geometry for a single-point perspective projection is illustrated in Figure 1.7. The important elements are the point(s) within the 3-D space being depicted, the display screen that acts as a window onto this space, and the position from which the space is viewed. Let us assume that the screen lies in the x, y plane, and that the direction of positive z is into the screen. For simplicity, we assume that the viewpoint lies on the z-axis at position (0, 0, 0). Given that the distance between

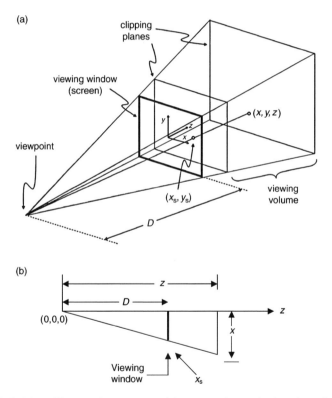

Figure 1.7: In (a), we illustrate the geometry of the perspective projection. Once the viewpoint and viewing plane (window) are defined, the coordinates of any point (x, y, z) in the viewing volume (image space) can be transformed into screen coordinates (x_s, y_s) simply by reference to similar triangles. This transformation is illustrated in (b), where we show a plan view. The ratio of z to D determines the ratio of x to x_s. Often, near and far clipping planes (illustrated in (a)) are defined so as to limit the extent of the image space.

the viewpoint and the screen is D, then a straight line from a point (x, y, z) in the image space to the viewing position will intersect the screen at a point (x_s, y_s) given by

$$x_s = \frac{xD}{z}, \qquad y_s = \frac{yD}{z}. \tag{1.1}$$

In this way, a set of points within the 3-D space can be mapped into 2-D screen positions corresponding to the calculated viewpoint.[19] Note also that this projection through a "virtual window" (an artist's canvas, or computer screen) to a single point defines a finite range of viewing angles; objects that lie outside this range (and hence are not visible) need not be rendered.

In the early 1960s, Ivan Sutherland undertook pioneering work in the area of computer graphics and image creation. The first CRT-based displays able to depict 3-D images in perspective were, however, prototyped some years earlier. Otto Schmitt [1947] describes one such system. In this interesting and comprehensive publication, he writes:

> *It is the purpose of this report to point out how easily the underlying principles of projective and perspective drawing and of stereoscopic photography can be applied to cathode-ray presentation so as to convert raw electrical data directly into vividly recognizable three-dimensional pictures.*

In Section 8.4.1, we return to this publication in connection with Schmitt's work in the development of what was probably the first immersive electronic 3-D display system. MacKay [1949a and b] provides further interesting discussion in this area, and in Figure 1.8(a) and (b), we illustrate two of his 3-D images. An essential difference between the work carried out by these early pioneers and Sutherland's research activity concerns the nature of the process by which perspective was achieved. Although Sutherland carried out the computation in the digital domain, the earlier systems used analog techniques to achieve the same goal. In Figure 1.9, we illustrate an image reported by Carl Berkley [1948]. In a later publication, MacKay [1960] describes improved transformation techniques that enable, for example, image rotation, and although the computation is carried out using discrete solid-state components, the circuits remained nondigital.

1.6.2 Surface Rendering

The most common representation of a virtual scene for computer graphic rendering takes the form of the surfaces of various objects, and typically these surfaces are approximated by a mesh of flat polygonal faces. Objects can be captured to different degrees of detail depending on the number and size of polygons used; indeed, the

---

[19]In the case that a right-handed coordinate system is used (i.e., so that increasing positive z is in the direction of the observer), then the equivalent equations are:

$$x_s = \frac{xD}{D-z}, \qquad y_s = \frac{yD}{D-z}.$$

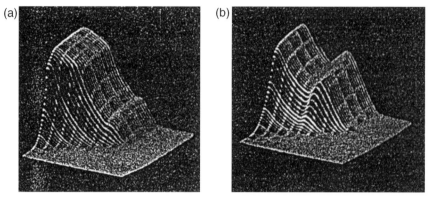

Figure 1.8: In (a) and (b), we illustrate 3-D perspective images reported by D.M. MacKay in his 1949 article (see text for details). These images form part of an image sequence showing stages of *"the development of a secondary emission 'valley' in the characteristic surface of a tetrode."* The computation was carried out using analog signals. (See also the work of Otto Schmitt [1947], mentioned in Section 1.6.1 in connection with perspective displays, and in Section 6.4.1 in connection with an electronic stereoscopic approach.) This represents what was probably the first immersive 3-D display system. (Reproduced by permission from MacKay, D.M., "Protective Three-Dimensional Displays, Part I," *Electronic Engineering* (1949); © 2005 CMP Information Ltd.)

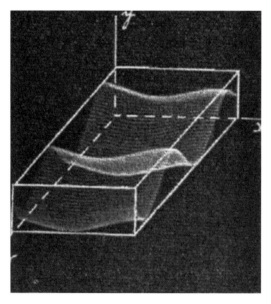

Figure 1.9: Here we reproduce a perspective image reported by Carl Berkley [1948]. As with the images shown in Figure 1.8, computation was carried out by means of analog techniques. (Reproduced by permission from Berkley, C., "Three-Dimensional Representation on Cathode-Ray Tubes," *Proc. I.R.E.* (1948); © 1948 IEEE.)

polygon density can alter within an object and often increases in more highly curved regions.

To render a view on the 3-D scene, the reflection of light from the virtual objects, as seen from the selected viewpoint relative to the scene, is simulated. Lines representing light rays are traced from the viewing plane into the 3-D scene. In this way, we can build a synthetic 2-D picture simulating the view on the virtual scene. The most computationally expensive part of the ray-tracing procedure is generally the collision detection phase, which determines whether the ray has intersected an object within the scene. As discussed in Chapter 7 in the context of collision detection in haptic rendering, this process can be speeded up by enclosing objects in "bounding volumes" (often spheres or boxes); testing for ray intersections with constituent polygons is then only necessary if it intersects the bounding volume.

Ray reflection from ideal planar surfaces is simply calculated by the principle of equal angles of incidence and reflection. The orientation of each polygon relative to the light source and the viewing plane allows the resultant pixel intensity on the screen to be calculated. Rays can be traced for each vertex of the polygon and then interpolated to generate values corresponding to points inside the polygon. This process provides a degree of smoothness to the resulting view and reduces the visibility of the polygonal boundaries. Several shading algorithms have been developed to simulate more realistically the appearance of surfaces under direct or indirect illumination. In particular, specular and diffuse reflections are often incorporated; for example, the Phong shading technique includes both of these along with the contribution from ambient lighting (see, for example, Foley et al. [1994]).

1.6.3 Working with Volumetric Data

In this subsection, we focus on volumetric (volume) data because this often forms the underlying type of data most suited for use with various display and interaction paradigms discussed in this book.

Data of this type can be derived from physical measurement, or it may be computer generated, and are voluminous—describing properties *throughout* an associated volume. Volumetric data take the form of a set of scalar values defining one or more properties at discrete "points" within a 3-D space that we will denote as R^3. Consider a function (F) whose domain and range are subsets of such a space. This function is referred to as a vector field and associates a vector $F(x, y, z)$ with each point in its domain (x, y, z) [Adams 1991]. The vector field can be represented in terms of its three scalar-valued components:

$$F(x, y, z) = F_1(x, y, x)\mathbf{i} + F_2(x, y, z)\mathbf{j} + F_3(x, y, z)\mathbf{k}, \qquad (1.2)$$

where $\mathbf{i}, \mathbf{j}$, and $\mathbf{k}$ are orthogonal unit vectors and each component of the function $F(x, y, z)$ denotes scalar fields [e.g., $F_1(x, y, z)$]. Volume (or volumetric) data correspond to a set of scalar fields. When this set is obtained from physical measurement or computer simulation, the underlying data take the form of a set of samples (v) that corresponds to a set of discrete locations in a space and is therefore not continuous.

A continuous function may be obtained by interpolation between samples—the simplest approach being to make a nearest-neighbor approximation such that the function takes on the value defined by the closest sample [Chen et al. 2000]. This simple approach is known as the zero-order interpolation technique and results in a constant value being assumed around each sample position. The form of this region is naturally determined by the geometric spacing of the data points. When such data are obtained from a physical measurement, samples rarely lie on regular lattice positions defined within R^3, and so the volumetric data set is likely to exhibit anisotropic and nonhomogeneous characteristics as far as data point positioning is concerned.

In the case of volumetric data corresponding to a physical measurement, each member of the data set has associated attributes indicating quantities such as material density, temperature, or intensity of electromagnetic radiation at a particular location in a 3-D space. Spacing between samples determines the Nyquist frequency and hence the maximum frequencies within the scalar field that can be properly reconstructed [Foley et al. 1997]. In the case of medical scans, for example, the transition from flesh to bone denotes an abrupt change in density, and this transition is characterized by high spatial frequency components in the scalar field. The distribution of the volumetric data points in such a region will therefore determine the degree of aliasing and consequently how well this transition in matter can be defined.

Volumetric data sets tend to be very large, and of course doubling the linear dimensions of a cubic region (and maintaining a uniform data point representation) results in an eightfold increase in data. As a consequence of the sheer scale of data, the processing of tasks tends to be computationally demanding. We will loosely use the expression "volume rendering" to describe the processing of the volumetric data set for depiction on a display system. The result of this process is an image data set, the form of which will be highly influenced by the type of display to be used.

Most display paradigms employ a basic image element known as the "pixel" for image formation. For example, the conventional raster scanned pixmap display employs a 2-D matrix of such pixels for the formation of the visible image. Typically, a screen may comprise approximately 1000 by 800 of these regularly spaced elements, each of which has associated attributes. Each screen pixel is mapped to an associated address in video memory (the frame buffer) where these pixels' attributes (e.g., color) are stored. In the case of conventional (and various forms of creative 3-D) displays, the final image is created by setting the attributes of each pixel. Consequently, the output from the graphics pipeline (whatever the type of data being processed) must be an array of pixel attribute values that are mapped into the frame buffer.

For systems that employ conventional computer graphics techniques, image components are generally stored as a set of high-level primitives, rather than as point form data. To maximize efficiency, the decomposition of such primitives into the point form pixel values is undertaken in the final stages of processing. However, when dealing with volumetric data sets taken from physical measurement, image primitives are not directly available to us and we must either manipulate individual data set values directly or find a means of converting members of the data set into image components that can be specified and manipulated at a higher level. Ultimately, after graphical manipulation, it is necessary to decompose these primitives into point form data that may be mapped to the display system.

The elements comprising the point form volumetric data set are frequently referred to as "voxels." This term is also used in different contexts. For example, a voxel is often viewed as being the 3-D equivalent of the pixel (being a volume rather than a picture element). In our case, the voxel represents the fundamental unit from which an image is constructed (see Section 6.5.3). These image elements are derived from the source volumetric data and correspond to the output from the graphics pipeline rather than to the source point form volumetric data that may be the input to the pipeline. In short, the voxels within the volumetric data set will be processed and generate voxels that may be depicted on a display, either directly or after a process of scan conversion. Clearly, the use of the term "voxel" in different contexts can cause confusion. Although we follow other literature and refer to the source volumetric data elements as voxels, to ensure clarity in our discussions, we will distinguish between these and the basic elements from which various types of 3-D image are constructed, by referring to the latter as "image voxels." More specifically, we will make use of the expression "image voxel" in the following contexts:

1. As the basic element used in the creation of visible images that occupy three physical dimensions (for example, volumetric displays (see Section 6.5.3 where, in this context, we define the nature of the image voxel more specifically)).

2. Some display techniques give rise to images that *appear* to occupy a 3-D space (for example, stereoscopic systems). In such cases we consider it appropriate to consider the image as consisting of a set of image voxels, despite the fact that pixels are often responsible for the underlying creation of the image, and the nature of the 3-D image originates from the way in which we view these pixels.

In summary, image voxels represent the basic particles that we use to describe and characterize certain aspects of various types of 3-D image. Speculating on future developments in medicine, Satava and Sackier [1998] consider the association of additional data with each voxel. In this context, they write:[20]

> *This information and more is stored in each pixel of the patient's representative image (a "medial avatar") such that the image of each structure and organ (e.g., the liver) stacks up into a "deep pixel" containing all the relevant information about the structure. Each pixel contains anatomic data as well as biochemical, physiological, and historical information, all of which can be derived directly from the image and not have to be sought in volumes of written medical records or through a prolonged database search.*

A fundamental technique used in volume rendering is the semitransparent gel approach, in which each voxel in the data set is assigned an opacity and color

---

[20]In terms of the terminology used in this book, in this passage, you should read "pixel" as "voxel."

value. Rays are then cast through the data set from behind toward the viewing plane, being modified as they traverse the data by the properties of each voxel they encounter (ray-casting). More generally, further optical properties such as reflection and scattering models can be assigned, and external illumination as in surface rendering can be incorporated [Max 1995].

1.7 DISPLAY SUB-SYSTEMS

As may be seen in Figure 1.10, a display may be considered in terms of either three, four, or five sub-systems. The lower three sub-systems depicted in the diagram are generally common to all displays, whereas the re-imaging projection sub-system is found only in certain architectures. Should this sub-system be

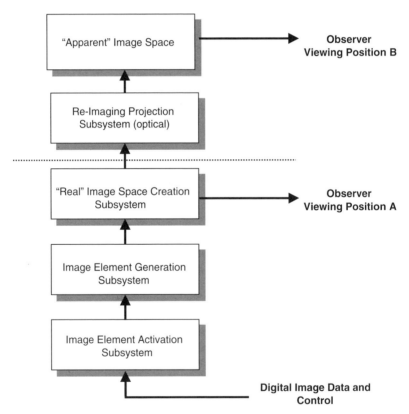

Figure 1.10: Creative 3-D display technologies may consist of up to five sub-systems. Some approaches may use only the lower three sub-systems, whereas others may require all five. The topmost (Apparent Image Space) is not strictly a sub-system as this space is defined by and derived from the Re-Imaging Projection sub-system. However, for convenience, it is included as a sub-system in its own right (see text for more details). (Diagram © Q.S. Blundell.)

present, it will give rise to an apparent image space. The apparent image space is therefore a consequence of the re-imaging projection sub-system and so does not have any self-defined attributes. In this sense, it is therefore not a sub-system, although for convenience and simplicity we will consider it as such. This approach enables us to discuss the characteristics of the apparent image space separately from those of the re-imaging sub-system. However, it is important to bear in mind that the former is a result of the latter and does not physically exist in its own right.

The display sub-systems are highly interdependent, and their operation and performance must be considered not only from an individual standpoint, but also in terms of their interaction. We now briefly consider each sub-system in turn:

1. *Real Image Space Creation*: This relates to the physical techniques brought to bear in order to provide a region where visible images may be depicted. By way of analogy, this sub-system may be compared with the surface selected by an artist for creative expression. Given a particular tableau (paper, canvas, etc.) of suitable dimensions, the artist must consider appropriate methods of expression (oils, water colors, pen, etc.). Conversely, given a particular method of expression, the artist may seek an appropriate tableau. So it is with the real image space creation sub-system—although this relates only to the region in which electronically generated images are to be depicted. The other sub-systems responsible for the production of the visible image (the image element generation and image element activation sub-systems) are likely to impact on its form and implementation. The inclusion of the word "real" is intended to distinguish this sub-system from the apparent image space, and we emphasize that it is here that the light corresponding to an image scene is generated. In certain display paradigms, this light may correspond to the final image and so may be viewed directly (from position A, as indicated in Figure 1.10). Alternatively, the re-imaging projection sub-system may modify (or direct) the light in some way before viewing (from position B).

2. *Image Element Generation*: This sub-system denotes the physical process that gives rise to the emission of light. Continuing with the analogy used in (1), the artist may choose to use certain pigments or charcoal. In this case, the underlying physical process giving rise to the visible image will be the interaction of ambient light with these materials. In the case of, say, a conventional flat-screen display based on CRT technology, the image space takes the form of a 2-D surface and the phosphor coatings are used for the production of the visible image. Thus, the process of cathodoluminescence denotes the image generation sub-system, and it is this phenomenon that is responsible for the emission of light from the screen.

3. *Image Element Activation*: This sub-system is responsible for driving the image element generation sub-system. Returning to the example of the artist's work, this sub-system would be represented by the external lighting

that illuminates and thereby makes the work visible. In the case of the conventional CRT-based display, this sub-system takes the form of the three electron beams that, under computer control, address the phosphor coatings and stimulate the production of visible light.

As indicated, the three sub-systems are highly integrated within the display, and the choice of one is likely to limit the opportunities available to us for the implementation of the others. For example, if we choose to use electron beams for image element activation, then there are only certain physical phenomenon that will respond to this stimulus by emitting visible light. In turn, the use of a small number of electron beams indicates that the display will probably be sequentially addressed, and this will impact on the maximum size of the real image space creation sub-system.

The re-imaging projection sub-system is necessary only in the case of certain display techniques. It represents any components through which light originating within the real image space creation sub-system travels during its transmission to the human visual system (or any components that modify the direction(s) in which it travels). It may comprise a physical material through which the light must pass, or some optical arrangement that can modify the direction followed by the light. For example, light emitted from the screens employed in an immersive virtual reality head mounted display (HMD) passes through an optical arrangement before its entry into the eyes (see Section 8.4). Similarly, in the case of the Lenticular display, the re-imaging projection sub-system takes the form of lenslets responsible for ensuring that each eye receives a slightly different view of an image scene (see Sections 6.5.2 and 8.3.1).

The result of the re-imaging projection sub-system is that the observer does not necessarily view the image as depicted within the real image space, but may be presented with an image that appears to reside in some form of apparent image space. This image may have significantly different properties from those of the image depicted in the real image space. This issue is discussed further in Section 6.8, where we also discuss the role of the re-imaging projection sub-system in the generation of so-called free-space images.

1.8 FROM THE LABORATORY TO THE APPLICATION

Three-dimensional display techniques have been the subject of research for many years. Since the pioneering work of Wheatstone and Brewster in the first half of the nineteenth century (see Section 6.3.1), stereoscopes have appeared in many forms. Initially used in conjunction with hand-drawn stereo images, the photographic techniques that were then emerging provided a major boost to their success. Photographs were no longer confined to the world of flatlands and could, by means of the stereoscope, take on a remarkably lifelike appearance thanks to the *relief* made possible by the stereoscope's ability to support binocular disparity.

Since that time, the stereoscope has appeared in many forms, and pioneers working in the 1930s and 1940s were quick to appreciate benefits that could be derived through the inclusion of the binocular parallax depth cue in electronic display systems (see Section 6.3.1, where we briefly discuss the stereoscopic display developed by J.L. Baird for television in the early 1940s, and Section 8.4, where we overview a system developed in the 1940s that perhaps represents the first immersive stereoscopic electronic display). Volumetric displays also possess a long research history; what would appear to be the earliest work in this area dates back nearly 100 years [Blundell and Schwarz 2000]. Interest in displays of this type has been practically continuous since the mid-1950s. However, from published literature we discern that the actual level of activity has been cyclic. Furthermore, there has been considerable repetition of work because each generation of workers frequently reinvent (rather than build upon) the efforts of their predecessors.

Certainly, there can be few areas of research endeavor that have for so long attracted ardent researchers of great inventive spirit and multidisciplinary ability (particularly those with a particular penchant for electromechanical systems). Nonetheless, despite the scale of effort there has been relatively little progress in transferring invention to practical and general usage.

As seen in Section 1.5, in various areas of activity, it is becoming increasingly clear that the conventional computer interface is hampering the human–computer interaction process. However, we continue to tolerate the weaknesses of the conventional interface, and only in a limited number of applications do we see the promotion of creative 3-D techniques. Although over the last 10 years or so there has been progress in producing commercial systems, these continue to be largely targeted at specialist markets and there is little sign that any general-purpose creative 3-D display system is likely to gain widespread acceptance in the immediate future. So, why have so many promising display technologies remained within the confines of the research laboratories in which they were created? Why have commercialization ventures frequently foundered, and why have the relatively few systems that have emerged as commercial products generally only found a home in specialist areas? In the next sub-section, we briefly discuss issues that may have counted against the more general adoption of creative display systems and suggest here and elsewhere in the book some principles that need to be adopted in our approach to the development of systems to facilitate their practical application.

1.8.1   Development Strategies

Here we briefly examine some factors that may have counted against a more widespread adoption of creative 3-D display systems (see also the related discussion in Chapter 9). The points listed below are of a general nature and do not apply without exception to all creative 3-D display techniques. Consequently, they should be viewed as being indicative.

1. The ability of creative 3-D display systems to augment the visualization process has generally been the driving force behind their development. Interaction opportunities have frequently been overlooked or regarded as being of secondary importance. Some creative 3-D systems that could, in principle,

have offered to support new interaction paradigms have simply been equipped with conventional interaction tools. Thus, the synergy existing between the display and interaction processes has tended to be overlooked, with the result that it has frequently proved more difficult to interact with images depicted on creative 3-D display systems than with those depicted on a conventional display.

2. Researchers have often adopted a bottom-up design strategy; 3-D display systems have been developed and subsequently applications sought. In many cases, there has been a lack of communication (and hence understanding) between the display researchers and the end users. At times researchers have promoted display technologies for particular applications without fully understanding the needs of the end users.

3. In the 1990s, some creative display technologies were over-publicized and their capabilities over-claimed, with the result that expectations grew well beyond the bounds of technical possibility. Fact gave way to fantasy. Happily, this situation seems to have improved over the last few years.

4. As we will discuss in later chapters, there are many approaches to the implementation of creative 3-D technologies and these often give rise to markedly different systems. This *embarras de richesse* (see Parker and Wallis [1948, 1949]) has perhaps made it more difficult to identify the most appropriate path to follow, especially as each approach has certain advantages and disadvantages. The problem is exacerbated by the vast number of patents that have been taken out in this field and, of course, the commercial pressures that result from the massive investment made in the manufacture of conventional displays.

5. Weaknesses associated with different creative 3-D display techniques have frequently been ignored by ardent researchers keen to promote their own display architectures. Furthermore, the adoption of bottom-up design strategies has sometimes made it difficult to determine (in advance) the extent of display deficiencies and consequently their impact on a display's suitability for a particular application.

6. Commercial interests have often prevented the proper sharing of information and have led to a failure to adopt consistent terminology. Approaches have been viewed as being directly competitive (rather than complementary), and the comparison of architectures has been clouded by nontechnical issues.

7. Applications software is strongly tied to the traditional flat-screen approach. Without a clear indication that a particular creative 3-D display technique will be beneficial and will gain market acceptance, there is little incentive to make the investment necessary to develop software to support creative display paradigms. This situation is gradually being addressed; see the pioneering work reported by Gregg Favalora and co-workers [Chun et al. 2005].

8. Research into creative 3-D display and interaction paradigms is transdisciplinary, spanning not only key areas of science, but also extending across to the humanities. This makes this type of research activity especially stimulating. On the other hand, the sheer diversity of skills and knowledge that

must be acquired and applied in the development of creative systems can be daunting. The formation of suitably equipped research teams is indeed a challenge.

This list is by no means exhaustive, nor do these comments apply without exception. However, they are presented here to provide the reader with an indication of the types of difficulty that need to be addressed if we are to significantly (and generally) advance the human–computer interface by means of creative 3-D systems. We must also bear in mind that it ultimately rests with researchers working in this area to devise ways of predicting in advance the benefits that may be derived from user investment in these technologies. Currently it is difficult to make such predictions with any degree of certainty.

1.8.2 Generality of Purpose

As will become apparent in subsequent chapters, the characteristics of creative 3-D displays and associated interaction tools are far more diverse than are those of the conventional approach to human–computer interaction. To date it has proved most difficult to develop systems that can be usefully employed across a broad spectrum of applications. For the foreseeable future it seems unlikely that any single creative 3-D display and interaction technology will gain the almost universal acceptance that we associate with the conventional flat-screen display, keyboard, and mouse. On the other hand, the development of specialized systems specifically designed for use in a particular application is likely to result in low-volume sales, and so the purchase of such systems will often denote a significant investment.

One possible solution is to develop common interfaces between the diverse range of hardware and software components that may be used in the implementation of creative 3-D display and interaction systems. In this way it may be possible to implement systems through the use of "off-the-shelf" components. In principle, this approach allows systems to be tailored to specific applications and at the same time makes use of the reduced costs that we associate with high-volume manufacturing. However, this is a solution that is not free from potential problems. For example:

1. In the development of interface standards, great care must be exercised. The standards should be free of any particular commercial interests. Furthermore, as standards evolve, the perceived need for backward compatibility can hamper future development. This has happened (and continues to happen) throughout the computing industry. It is vital that ill-considered standards should not be put in place at too early a stage, neither should the development of such standards be placed in the hands of any one company.

2. Abeyance to standards can often result in reduced system performance or, conversely, make it necessary to increase the computing resources needed to support their incorporation. The introduction of standard software and hardware interfaces should be achieved without the introduction of additional system latencies.

3. The standard software and hardware interface specifications should be fully disclosed, thus ensuring that the products of no single manufacturer are favored and ultimately gain dominance.

1.9   DISCUSSION

In this chapter, we have presented material intended to introduce creative 3-D display systems and place these in context through discussion of the traditional human–computer interface paradigm. We have emphasized areas in which this traditional approach limits and unnecessarily complicates our interaction with the digital world and have identified three general areas in which creative 3-D systems may be beneficial. These are: augmented realism, augmented information content, and creative design. In connection with augmented realism, we have discussed the concept of suspension of disbelief, which has been firmly framed within an historical context and we have sought to highlight the importance of supporting and extending human imagination within the interaction experience.

The basic elements from which visible images are constructed (pixels and image voxels) have been introduced, along with 3-D point form (volumetric) data sets. In this context we have only alluded to the strengths and weaknesses of working with volumetric data. Discussion of display hardware has been limited to the identification of the sub-systems that comprise a display, and in this context, we have introduced the concepts of real and apparent image spaces.

Toward the end of the chapter we considered some problems that may have hampered the application of creative 3-D display and interaction interfaces. Some of these issues (such as the synergy existing between display and interaction devices and the need to develop top-down design strategies) are fundamental to the thrust of this book and will be considered further.

In the following chapters, we continue our voyage of exploration. We begin by discussing the visual perception of our surroundings, and in Chapter 3, we consider the human haptic interface. Clearly, without a sound understanding of our sensory systems, we have little hope of effectively developing new display and interaction interfaces.

1.10   INVESTIGATIONS

1. Research the "evolution" of computer systems from the mid-1970s to the early 1990s. Identify promising hardware and software designs that have fallen by the wayside (especially in the area of the human–computer interface). Suggest possible reasons for their demise.
2. Identify two major advantages and two major disadvantages of working directly with volumetric 3-D data sets, rather than with higher level graphics primitives.

Small tree

Figure 1.11: This stereoscopic pair may be used to demonstrate the "augmented information content" that may be achieved through the inclusion of the binocular parallax depth cue (see Section 2.6.2). Pay particular attention to the small tree in the immediate foreground, and which stands before a larger one. See Investigations Question 5 for details.

3. Gain access to an advanced applications program for 3-D design, such as Alias Maya. Investigate the user interface in terms of the depth of menu hierarchies. Examine the impact of undertaking design work within a 2-D space, and identify tasks that could be simplified and performed more naturally if they were undertaken in a 3-D space.

4. Research the work of the pioneers referred to in Section 1.6.1 in connection with perspective displays. In what way(s) was their work made more difficult (or facilitated) by the use of analog computation?

5. Consider the stereoscopic pair presented in Figure 1.11. Take a copy of the image and attach this to card to enable it to be viewed in a stereoscope. Pay particular attention to the small tree in the foreground. Compare stereoscopic and nonstereoscopic images. The tree has a texture that is similar to the one immediately behind it. Consequently, it is not readily discerned via monocular vision but is readily visible (and stands out) when viewed with the stereoscope, which provides a clear example of the "augmented information content" that may be achieved through the inclusion of the binocular parallax depth cue (see Section 2.6.2).

6. Consider the generation of holographic images (this is introduced in Appendix B). In what ways is this display paradigm described by the set of display subsystems illustrated in Figure 1.10.

2 The Perception of Our Space: Vision

All in a hot and copper sky;
The bloody Sun at noon,
Right up above the mast did stand,
No bigger than a Moon.

2.1 INTRODUCTION

It is unrealistic to imagine that we can effectively design, prototype, and engineer creative three-dimensional (3-D) display and interaction interfaces, without making continual reference to the relevant human mechanisms through which

Creative 3-D Display and Interaction Interfaces: A Trans-Disciplinary Approach, by Barry G. Blundell and Adam J. Schwarz

we perceive and interact with our surroundings. The quest to understand our complex sensory systems (input channels) and the rich forms of human communication (output channels), coupled with the related processing capabilities of the brain, has given rise to an enormous, multidisciplinary field of research that has spanned many centuries. Naturally, this has resulted in a vast wealth of scientific literature, which is impossible to properly review within the confines of a single book, let alone several chapters. Consequently, in producing this chapter and the next, we have not sought to accomplish such a feat but rather to lay various foundations. Our intention is to emphasize issues that are of particular relevance to the general scope of this book and, above all, to give the reader who is new to this area an impression of the fascinating nature of several human sensory systems.

Here, we limit ourselves to the sense of vision, and in Chapter 3, we discuss touch and kinesthesia, which are both especially relevant to our subsequent discussions. We focus in particular on the nature and performance of the biological transducers by means of which physical contact with the outside world is effected, and the pathways via which information is passed to the brain.

In the next section we briefly review various characteristics of light, and in subsequent sections, discuss aspects of the visual system. We begin by examining the eye, which not only forms the transducer by means of which light is converted to electrical signals but also performs some of the most basic processing of the image data. Subsequently, we briefly consider the visual cortex and various visual characteristics. Discussion then moves to our perception of space and form, and here we introduce several depth cues, along with the Gestalt Theory of visual perception. Finally in Section 2.7, we examine aspects of temporal resolution.

As we have mentioned, it is not possible to provide an in-depth discussion in this forum on such diverse and complex subject matter; neither is it possible to present a comprehensive review of published research literature. Consequently, we provide references throughout the chapter that we believe will be especially useful to the interested reader. In terms of sensory systems in general and the human visual system in particular, we recommend the *Handbook of Perception and Human Performance*, which provides a wealth of in-depth discussion [Boff et al. 1986]. Howard and Rogers [2002] provide outstanding and comprehensive discussion on depth perception in their two-volume well-illustrated text. Westheimer [1970] provides a complete, yet succinct, account of the imaging properties of the eye. A series of outstanding publications that appear under the title *Vision and Visual Dysfunction* [Cronly-Dillon and Gregory 1991] also provide excellent coverage of all aspects of the visual system. Those seeking a general overview might find Roberts [2002] especially useful. Many texts deal with cognitive psychology. We would particularly recommend those by Henry Gleitman [1981], Coren et al. [1994], and Schiffman [1990], all of which provide sound and highly readable introductions to this subject. Other publications are referred to throughout the chapter, and additional valuable sources are listed in the General Bibliography at the end of the book.

2.2 SOME FACETS OF LIGHT

> We do not truly see light, we only see slower things lit by it,
> so that for us light is on the edge –
> the last thing we know
> before things become too swift for us.[1]

The eye is a transducer that enables us to perceive a range of wavelengths within the electromagnetic spectrum. We refer to this "visible" portion of the spectrum as "light." Electromagnetic waves might almost be considered to possess mystical properties. Consider the night sky in which a myriad of stars may be seen. The starlight has traversed the hostile void of space, needing no physical medium to support its passage. Oscillatory electric and magnetic fields have traveled at a speed of nearly three hundred million meters per second, but even so the voyage has, from our perspective, been long. Gazing upward, we travel back in time, seeing the stars as they existed perhaps many centuries ago. As we focus on one particular star, the journey of its starlight comes to an end as energy emitted by the star long ago enters our eyes and is focused onto the retina (see Figure 2.1(a)). This energy impinges on photoreceptive elements known as "rods," and is converted into electrical signals that are ultimately passed to the brain. However, the image of the star cast onto the retina does not retain its sharpness but will (even in the case of a perfect (or *emmetropic*) eye) be subjected to various aberrations and be diffracted by the adjustable eye lens. Consequently, like early astronomers, we too may be tricked by the perceived image size[2] [Cameron et al. 1999].

When at last dawn arrives, the level of ambient lighting increases and the less-sensitive photoreceptive cones in the retina begin to respond. The *fovea* (the central region of the eye) contains an amazing 150,000 cones per square millimeter, and can now operate and support super high-resolution imaging. Furthermore (unlike the rods) these cones can distinguish between different wavelengths in the incident light, allowing us to experience the vivid colors of the dawn sky. Of course, *color* as such is not an inherent property of light, but it is a sensation created by our visual system based on the reception of electromagnetic radiation of different wavelengths—a remarkable illusion.[3]

2.2.1 Color

The human observer can perceive light in the range of approximately 400 to 700 nanometers (nm),[4] and under conditions where the light is of sufficient intensity, these wavelengths are perceived as the colors referred to, respectively, as violet

---

[1]C.S. Lewis, *Out of the Silent Planet.*

[2]As discussed later in this section, diffraction may lead to point sources appearing to be magnified.

[3]The remarkable character of light is not confined to its visual sensation. For example, the photons that comprise electromagnetic radiation may, under certain conditions, be observed to possess wave-like properties and on other occasions act as individual "particles." Perhaps even more remarkably, the speed of light in free space is a constant and does not appear to change as we move toward or away from a source.

[4]This is sometimes expressed in units of Angstroms (Å), where $10 \text{ Å} = 1 \text{ nm}$ and $1 \text{ nm} = 10^{-9} \text{ m}$.

(a)

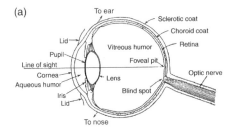

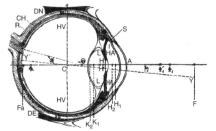

Fɪɢ. 2.—Transverse section of an Ideal or Schematique Eye.

A, Summit of cornea; SC, Sclerotic; S, Schlemm's canal; CH, Choroid; I, Iris;
M, Cillary muscle; R, Retina; N, Optic nerve; HA, Aqueous humour; L,
Crystalline lens, the anterior of the double lines on its face showing its form
during accommodation; HV, Vitreous humour; DN, Internal rectus muscle;
DE, External rectus; YY', Principal optical axis; ΦΦ, Visual axis, making an
angle of 5° with the optical axis; C, Centre of the ocular globe. *The cardinal*
points of Listing — H₁H₂, principal points; K₁K₂, nodal points; F₁F₂, principal
focal points. *The dioptric constants according to Giraud-Teulon:* —H, Principal
points united; φ₁φ₂, principal foci during the repose of accommodation;
φ'₁φ'₂, principal foci during the maximum of accommodation; O, fused nodal
points.

(b)

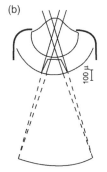

Figure 2.1: The form and major constituents of the human eye (see text for details) are indicated in (a). This structure is contrasted with the eye of the scallop illustrated in (b). In the case of the scallop's eye, light passes through the retina before being reflected at the rear. Subsequently it arrives once more at the retina. [Right-hand image in (a) is reproduced from the 9th edition of the *Encyclopaedia Britannica* 1879 from an excellent entry on the eye by J.G. McKendrick. Left-hand image reproduced by permission from Judd, D.B., *Color in Business, Science and Industry*, John Wiley 1952; © 1952 John Wiley & Sons. Figure (b) kindly provided by Professor Michael F. Land.]

and red. As will be discussed shortly, the eye is not equally sensitive to all colors (hues) within this range and has two peak sensitivities. In daylight conditions when the cones are operating efficiently, this peak is at approximately 555 nm, and in subdued lighting conditions when the rods are dominant, 505 nm. (Both rods and cones are equally sensitive to red light.) The sensitivity of the rods and cones to different levels of illumination is illustrated in Figure 2.2, and their relative sensitivity to different wavelengths is shown in Figure 2.3.

When discussing color, we must consider three key characteristics; these are hue, intensity, and saturation, and their relationship is shown in Figure 2.4 (illustrating the well-known "color spindle"). Moving vertically upward in the diagram

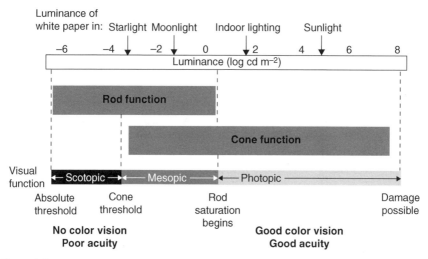

Figure 2.2: The eye is able to operate across a very wide range of lighting conditions. Rods are more much more sensitive than cones, and these two types of photoreceptor essentially provide two separate (and complementary) visual mechanisms. (Diagram kindly provided by Professor Dale Purves.)

corresponds to increasing intensity (and gives rise to a gray scale), whereas moving around the circumference denotes changes to the hue or color of the light. Finally, as we move outward from the central axis, the saturation changes, which corresponds to the purity of color, varying from monochromatic light at the center to vibrant, rich colors at the periphery.[5] The tapering shape of the spindle indicates that the greatest degree of saturation is possible at only moderate degrees of brightness [Osgood 1953].

Artists generally use a subtractive technique for creating colors in their paintings, which involves mixing appropriate pigments in the correct ratios. For example, yellow and blue pigments may be mixed to provide green. The former reflects colors from within the red, yellow, and green portions of the spectrum (absorbing all else), whereas the latter reflects in the green, blue, and violet regions (again absorbing all else). Consequently, when mixed, only wavelengths corresponding to what we perceive as a green coloration will be reflected. This subtractive technique tends to reduce brightness [Osgood 1953]. As further described by Osgood, an additive approach may also be used—paintings by the French Impressionist and Pointillist, Georges Seurat such as *The Port of Gravelines*[6] and A *Sunday on the Grande Jatte*[7] provide good examples. Here, color mixing is achieved by forming the painting from small "dots" of color that, when viewed at a suitable distance, merge and blend to provide

---

[5]Most hues that we encounter in everyday life are desaturated as a consequence of the heterogeneous surface reflectance characteristics [Osgood 1953].

[6]Reproduced in Gleitman [1981].

[7]See http://www.artic.edu/aic/collections/eurptg/28_seurat2.html.

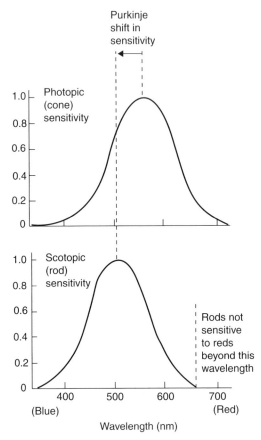

Figure 2.3: Rods and cones have differing peak wavelength sensitivities. The change in apparent brightness with changes in illuminance is referred to as the Purkinje shift, after Johannes Purkinje. He noticed that at dusk, the apparent brightness of different colored objects gradually changes (e.g., reds become darker and blues relatively brighter). [Reproduced by permission from Coren, S., Ward L.M., and Enns, J.T., *Sensation and Perception*, Harcourt Brace & Company (1994); © 2005 John Wiley & Sons.]

overall coloration. The additive technique used by Seurat over 100 years ago is employed today in both conventional and most creative display technologies.

2.2.2   Light Energy

It is useful to introduce some terminology employed in the context of measurements of light energy, and to distinguish such physical measurements from our perception of the level of illumination that we associate with an object or image scene. Physical measurements of light energy may be confusing, because over the years a range of units have been introduced, and when reading older publications, one may be faced with a bewildering variety of units. In this context, Coren et al. [1994] write that,

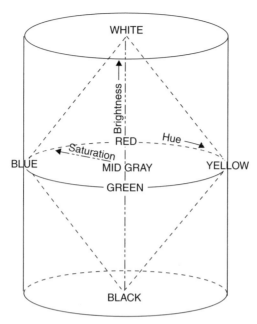

Figure 2.4: The color "spindle." Moving vertically upward corresponds to changes in brightness, moving away from the central axis corresponds to changes in saturation, and moving around the circumference results in changes in the hue. Note that a high degree of saturation can only be achieved at moderate brightness. [Reproduced from Troland, L.T., *The Principles of Psychophysiology*, Van Nostrand (1930).]

"*The result was chaos. Even among the most scholarly scientists, few can tell you how many nits there are in an apostilb or a blondel, or how any of these units related to a candle or a lambert.*" Fortunately, the SI system of units provides us with a rational framework of measures, these being broadly based on the amount of light emitted by a single source. In the discussion that follows, we will loosely follow, that presented by Coren et al. [1994].

The light energy flux emitted by a source (such as an electrical light or candle) is referred to as "radiance" and is measured in units of "lumens," which corresponds to energy emitted per solid angle from a source of one *candela*. When we consider the amount of light energy that falls on a surface, we use the term "illuminance," which has the unit of "lux" (one lux corresponds to one lumen per square meter or ($1 \, \text{lm/m}^2$). The energy of the light reflected by a surface is referred to as the "luminance," and has yet another unit—candelas per square meter (cd/m^2). "Reflectance" is used to relate luminance and illuminance:

$$\text{Reflectance (\%)} = \frac{\text{Luminance}}{\text{Illuminance}} \times 100. \qquad (2.1)$$

Finally, we may refer to the "retinal illuminance"—this provides a measure of the light energy incident on the retina. This quantity is measured in terms of "trolands"

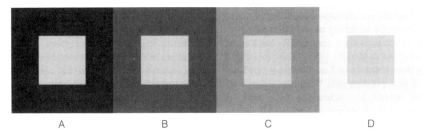

Figure 2.5: Our perception of brightness depends on various factors. For example, consider the four smaller squares illustrated here. Although they are all equally shaded, we perceive them differently as a consequence of the change in background shading. [Reproduced by permission from Coren S., Ward, L.M., and Enns, J.T., *Sensation and Perception*, Harcourt Brace & Company (1994); © 2005 John Wiley & Sons.]

(where one troland corresponds to $1\,\mathrm{cd/m^2}$ viewed through a pupil of area $1\,\mathrm{mm^2}$).[8] These terms relate to the physical measurement of light energy, which of course differs from our visual perception of the surroundings. In this context, we refer to "brightness"—our perception of which is influenced by various factors (for example, see Figure 2.5). To a first approximation, a logarithmic relationship exists between the retinal illuminance and the perceived brightness. Consequently, for example, doubling the number of light sources illuminating an object will not double the brightness.

Often when describing certain spatial characteristics of an image, we are particularly interested in relative differences in the luminance. In this sense, we are concerned with the contrast contained within an image. Consider for a moment the pattern of black lines drawn on a white card as illustrated in Figure 2.6(a). Here, a strong contrast exists as a consequence of the greatly differing reflectance of the black-and-white regions (compare this with the grating illustrated in Figure 2.6(b)). We can define a "contrast ratio" (C) as follows:

$$C = \frac{L_{\mathrm{max}} - L_{\mathrm{min}}}{L_{\mathrm{max}} + L_{\mathrm{min}}}. \tag{2.2}$$

This is a convenient expression since it provides a measure of the difference between the maximum and minimum luminance (denoted as L_{max} and L_{min} respectively) and at the same time C is independent of changes in the illuminance.

The rods and cones within the eye react to incident photons. However, the human visual system can only perceive photons within a particular energy range. Consider incident light that has a wavelength of 530 nm. This wavelength has a frequency (ν)

---

[8]As we will see in Section 2.2.3, the size of the eye's pupil changes with lighting level and thereby influences the amount of light falling on the retina. Retinal illuminance does not take into account the effectiveness of the light impinging on the retina (for example, as we will see, different parts of the retina are more/less sensitive to light).

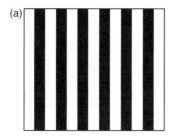 

Figure 2.6: Image (a) exhibits a high contrast ration as a consequence of the differing reflectance of the black-and-white regions. In (b), the contrast ratio has been reduced since a shade of gray has now replaced the white regions used in (a). Note that the contrast ratio is independent of changes in illuminance.

of approximately 5.7×10^{14} Hz, and use of the equation $E = h\nu$ yields a photon energy of approximately 37.8×10^{-20} J (equivalent to ~ 2.4 eV[9]). Reducing the wavelength of the incident light results in an increase in photon energy, and so a figure of 3 eV provides a convenient approximation to the average energy of photons visible to the eye. Photons in the infrared part of the spectrum (i.e., toward lower frequencies) have insufficient energy to stimulate the photoreceptors within the eye, and those in the ultraviolet part of the spectrum (toward higher frequencies) are absorbed during transit (by, for example, the cornea at the front of the eye). Thus, our window of visibility is defined.

2.2.3 Diffraction in Optical Systems

Before arriving at the retina, incident light must pass through the transparent parts of the eye. Indeed, it is these structures that determine the sharpness of the image cast onto the retina. The retinal image is thus subject to optical effects and limited by the physics of optical systems, independently of the nature and distribution of the photo-receptors and subsequent processing of the image by the neural visual system.

A fundamental limit on the sharpness of the image formed by any optical system originates from "diffraction." Consider the simplest form of image—a sharply defined point source of light. Even if all other imperfections and aberrations could be corrected,[10] the point source will not be brought to a perfect focus but will give rise to an "interference pattern"—a direct consequence of the wave nature of light. For a circularly symmetric system (such as the eye), the resulting intensity pattern is known as an "Airy disk"[11] (see Figure 2.7(a)). The intensity

---

[9]The unit eV represents "electronvolts" and 1 eV $\sim 1.6 \times 10^{-19}$ J.

[10]Some major aberrations affecting systems such as the eye are discussed in Section 2.3.1.

[11]The Airy disk and slit interference pattern described here strictly apply in the far-field—or *Fraunhofer*—diffraction regime only. For images formed by apertures only, this requires that the image is relatively distant from the aperture. For systems containing lenses, the position of the image is determined by the focal length of the system, and the Fraunhofer approximation can be applied [Born and Wolf 1959].

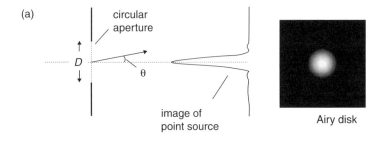

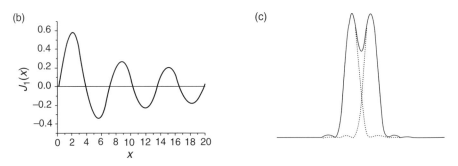

Figure 2.7: When an image is formed using an optical system comprising an aperture or lens(es), the wave nature of light provides a *diffraction limit* on the resolution of the image. (a) The image of a point source is not a point (as would be predicted by geometrical optics) but an interference pattern, which is known as the point-spread function of the system. For a circular aperture, this pattern is known as an Airy disk. (b) The profile of the Airy disk is defined in terms of the Bessel function $J_1(x)$ illustrated here. (c) The angular resolving power of an optical instrument is defined according to the arbitrary criterion laid down by Rayleigh. This criterion is defined as the angle subtended between two stars when the maximum of the diffraction pattern generated by light from one star falls on the first dark ring generated by the light received from the other other. This process results in the intensity falling by a factor of 0.735 in the region between the peaks.

profile of the Airy disk is described by the expression (see, for example, Born and Wolf [1959]):

$$I = I_0 \left(\frac{2J_1(\alpha)}{\alpha} \right)^2, \tag{2.3}$$

where

$$\alpha = \frac{\pi D}{\lambda} \sin \theta. \tag{2.4}$$

Here, D is the diameter of the optical system, λ is the wavelength of the light, and θ is the angle measured from the optical axis (see Figure 2.7(a)). The function $J_1(\alpha)$ is a Bessel function (of the first kind) of order zero. For the purposes of the discussion in this text, it is sufficient to know that $J_1(\alpha)$ has a form comprising decaying oscillations about zero, as shown in Figure 2.7(b).

The Airy disk given by Eq. (2.3) is the point spread function (PSF) associated with an optical system of circular symmetry. All optical systems have an associated PSF, which is observable directly when a point source is imaged, but applying to any image scene observed with the same optical system, because an image may be viewed as comprising a set of discrete point sources (which is indeed a physical reality when we consider images created on electronic displays). As a result, the retinal image comprises a superposition of PSF light distributions from the point sources comprising the scene. The effects of the PSFs are usually most apparent at sharp intensity boundaries.

Consider the image cast by two point sources of light in such a system. Each point will be imaged to an Airy disk. Clearly, if the point sources are too close together, their diffraction patterns will overlap to such an extent that the points will not be resolved (discerned). The traditional criterion used to measure the angular resolving power of an optical instrument (such as a telescope) was defined by Lord Rayleigh as the angle subtended by two point light sources (e.g., stars) when the central peak of the Airy disk from one source coincides with the first minimum (away from the center) of that from a second source (see Figure 2.7(c)). The angle θ_{min} at which this resolution limit occurs is dictated by the position of the first minimum of the Bessel function, $J_1(\alpha)$, which occurs at $\alpha = 3.83$. Rearranging Eq. (2.4) for this value of α, we obtain

$$\theta_{min} = \arcsin\left(1.22\frac{\lambda}{D}\right).$$

For small angles, we can express this in approximate form as

$$\theta_{min} = 1.22\frac{\lambda}{D}, \tag{2.5}$$

where θ_{min} is measured in radians. This calculation is known as Rayleigh's criterion for resolvability. The imaging resolution thus depends on the wavelength of the light and on the diameter of the optical system (the limiting diameter of the lens or aperture).[12] This expression tells us that point sources can be resolved more clearly by larger diameter optical systems, and shorter wavelengths can be imaged more sharply than longer ones. A system in which the limiting factor in formation of the image is from diffraction is referred to as being "diffraction limited."

Consider two stars that subtend an angle α at a convex lens (e.g., the lens within the eye). The image of these two stars will be formed in the focal plane of the lens,

---

[12]Intensity is also a factor.

and they will be seen to be separated by a distance $f\alpha$ (where f denotes the focal length of the lens). Increasing the focal length of the lens employed may clearly increase this separation. "*Unfortunately this increase in linear separation does not help in resolving the two stars, because the scale of their diffraction patterns increases in proportion.... It is important to appreciate clearly the difference between altering the magnification which simply changes the size of the image and increasing the resolution which allows more detail to be seen*" [Smith and Thomson 1975]. In the case of an optical instrument such as a telescope, the angular resolving power may be enhanced by increasing D. For further reading, see, for example, Hecht and Zajac [1974] or Smith and Thomson [1975].

2.3   THE VISUAL SYSTEM

Life forms equipped with visual systems have been traced back to shortly after the Cambrian Explosion (beginning approximately 570 million years ago). In their excellent text, Peter Lindsay and Donald Norman [1972] begin a discussion on the visual system in the following way:

> *Light enters the eye and passes through the various parts – the cornea, the aqueous humor, the iris, the lens, and the vitreous body – until finally it reaches the retina. Each part performs a simple task, but each appears to have flaws. In many respects, the eye is a rather peculiar kind of optical instrument. Certainly, were an optical specialist to try to design an eye, he would avoid some of the flaws found in the human eye: flaws that should make it an unwieldy and imperfect instrument. As is usual with the parts of the body, however, the eye ends up as a beautiful instrument, exquisitely tailored to the function it must perform, more sensitive, more flexible, and more reliable by far than any device made by man.*

The human eye is indeed a remarkable optical instrument—so remarkable that even Charles Darwin [1859] was troubled by its origins. In his work, *The Origin of Species*, he wrote:

> *To suppose that the eye, with its inimitable contrivances for adjusting the focus to different distances, for admitting different amounts of light, and for the correction of spherical and chromatic aberration, could have formed by natural selection, seems, I freely confess, absurd in the highest degree. Yet reason tells me that if numerous gradations from a perfect and complex eye to one very imperfect and simple, each grade being useful to its possessor, can be shown to exist; if further, the eye does vary ever so slightly, and the variations be inherited, which is certainly the case; and if any variation or modification in the organ be ever useful to an animal under changing conditions of life, then the difficulty of believing that a perfect and complex eye could be formed by natural selection, though insuperable by our imagination, can hardly be considered real.* [Cronly-Dillon and Gregory (eds.) 1991].

In the light of current understanding, Darwin need not have been overly concerned by this suggested evolutionary process. It is now considered that the evolution of an eye that can sense and relay spatial information, rather than act as a simple photo-receptor that can detect the presence (or otherwise) of light, occurred over a relatively brief period of a few million years. Land and Nilsson [2002], drawing on the work of Nilsson and Pelger [1994], provide an interesting account to demonstrate that, in principle, based on a selection process favoring improved spatial resolution, evolution (assuming a 0.005% modification from one generation to the next) could have taken place over 400,000 generations.

Today we encounter creatures possessing a rich diversity of optical arrangements within their eyes (see, for example, the scallop eye illustrated in Figure 2.1(b)), and this gives rise to remarkably different visual characteristics. Land and Nilsson [2002] provide an excellent and highly readable account of the optical systems employed by a range of creatures. Certainly, gaining an insight into the great diversity of systems devised by nature can strongly reinforce our understanding of the remarkable form of our own visual system.[13]

The human eye contains approximately 126 million photoreceptors that in the *fovea* (the central region of the eye containing the highest density of receptors) reach a density of 150,000 mm^{-2} (cf. the density of pixels depicted on a conventional computer screen). Information from the receptors is passed to the brain by around one million nerve fibers. As we will discuss, the outputs of some receptors are combined with those of neighboring photoreceptor cells and only a common integrated signal is transmitted further into the brain, whereas those in the *fovea centralis* have individual pathways along which the electrical signals (action potentials) they generate may pass.

The ability of the eye to respond to different levels of lighting is particularly impressive. Consider the range of illumination between a bright sunny day and a sky in which only the stars illuminate the heavens. Between these two extremes the photon flux varies by approximately eight orders of magnitude (10^{20} photons m^{-2}s^{-1} for a sunlit day, and 10^{12} photons m^{-2}s^{-1} for a starlit night [Land and Nilsson 2002]). The eye can operate over this tremendous range (although naturally, within a single image, variations are usually small).

In the next sub-section, we briefly consider some key elements within the eye that work together to create the image on its rear surface (retina). Subsequently, we briefly review the nature and organization of the retina and the impact of eye movements.

2.3.1   The Eye as an Optical Instrument

Key elements of the human eye are illustrated in Figure 2.1(a). The "casing" comprises three layers. The outermost takes the form of a tough protective membrane known as the *scerotic* coat. A darkly pigmented *choroid* layer serves to prevent

---

[13]The article by Richard Gregory (appearing in the text edited by Cronly-Dillon and Richard Gregory [1991]) provides fascinating discussion on the copepod *Copilia quadrate*, which is described by naturalist Selig Exner as "a beautiful, highly transparent pin-head sized creature." Most interestingly she provides us with an example of a scanning eye, which has a single optical nerve for each eye. The eyes each seem to follow a regular horizontal scanning movement, thereby sweeping the light *across* the single receptive element.

the entry of light into the eye other than via the cornea (this is the frontal portion of the *scerotic* coat). Finally, the third and innermost layer (the *retina*) contains elements that react to the incoming light and convert this to electrical nerve impulses [Osgood 1953]. Below, we consider optical components housed within this casing.

(a) The Lens Structure: Light entering the eye is brought to a focus on the retina by two mechanisms. These are as follows:

1. Refraction occurring as the light enters the eye (i.e., at the cornea), which is as a consequence of the difference in the refractive indices between this part of the eye and the air. The focusing action of this interface is nonadjustable and is dependant on curvature. Approximately two thirds of the focusing occurs at this interface. (We will return to this in a moment.)

2. The action of the lens whose focal length is adjusted by changes made to its thickness and hence its curvature. This is achieved by the ciliary muscles that surround the periphery of the lens and can exert tension on it. The lens is pliable and in the absence of any forces is approximately spherical in shape. It comprises many layers of thin crystalline tissue. Of course, all living cells must be supported by a continual supply of nutrient—this is usually derived from the bloodstream. However, the presence of blood vessels in the lens (and cornea) would clearly hamper the passage of light, and so the lens tissue is left to derive its nutrients from the materials with which it is in contact. This would seem to be a nonoptimal solution as it makes it difficult for the inner layers to gain nutrient, and over time dead cells hamper its operation (by, for example, reducing pliability and so increasing the near-point[14] distance with age).

As mentioned above, light entering the eye first passes through the cornea. The largest difference in refractive index of the components through which the light must pass occurs at the interface between the external air and cornea, and so it is here that the maximum refraction occurs. Next, the light passes through an aqueous humor that is in contact with the lens. This maintains the internal pressure of the eye (approximately 12–23 mm Hg), and this supports its shape. On the other side of the lens lies the "jelly-like" vitreous humor filling the eye. The action of the lens in focusing the light is governed not only by its thickness (and hence curvature[15]), but also by the differences in refractive indices of the aqueous and vitreous humors lying on either side of it. The refractive indices of the aqueous and vitreous humors relative to the lens are much less than that at the air–cornea interface,[16] and hence the lens contributes less to the overall focusing action.[17]

[14]The near point is the minimum distance from the unaided eye at which an image component can be brought into focus, i.e., the least distance of distinct vision usually taken to be 25 cm.

[15]The curvature of the two surfaces of the lens is not the same—the curvature is greater on the rear surface.

[16]When, for example, swimming underwater without goggles, much of the focusing action of the cornea is lost (because of the reduced differential in the refractive index).

[17]The refractive indices of the various components are as follows: the cornea 1.34, the aqueous humor 1.33, the lens center 1.41, and the vitreous humor 1.34 [Cameron et al. 1999].

Although it is simple to explain focusing in these terms, issues become much more complex when we try to understand the control of the focusing system. This clearly relies on the presence of a feedback loop in which characteristics of the incoming image are used by the brain to determine the degree of tension to be applied to the lens. Although focusing is achieved unconsciously and automatically, we can deliberately de-focus our vision, and therefore the process must involve higher-level brain function. Focusing is by no means instantaneous; the reaction time to a stimulus is reported as being of the order of 0.3 seconds, with the action being completed within about 0.9 seconds after the onset of the stimulus [Boff et al. 1986]. This response time is influenced by target detail, distance, and level of illumination.

The lens is by no means a perfect optical element and, coupled with the other media in the eye through which light passes, gives rise to various distortions.[18] Major aberrations (defects) inherently associated with a lens system may be summarized as follows:

1. SPHERICAL ABERRATION: Parallel rays of light are generally considered to meet at a common focal point after passing through a convex lens. However, this is an approximation, and in fact the distance of the rays from the optical axis determines the sharpness of focus. Restricting the diameter of the lens can ameliorate this problem, and as indicated below, this is one function of the pupil. Although this is an appropriate solution under brighter lighting conditions, it is less effective when the level of illumination is reduced.

2. CHROMATIC ABERRATION: Different wavelengths of light are bent by different amounts when entering or emerging from the lens. Consequently, the presence of different wavelengths within a parallel beam of light will impact on the sharpness of focus that can be achieved by the lens.

3. ASTIGMATISM: This occurs as a consequence of the lens exhibiting different optical characteristics in different meridians. Thus, for example, a point source object will give rise to an image that is elongated in some direction.[19]

Interestingly, studies directly measuring aberrations in the human eye have found considerable intersubject variation in the severity of each aberration type [Jiang and Williams 1997, Charman and Chateau 2003].

Light passing through the eye will also be subjected to scattering. This is caused by the fluids in the eye and is exacerbated by the need to pass through various retinal layers (see below) before reaching the photoreceptors. Even if aberrations could be completely corrected, and scattering neglected then, as we have seen, diffraction effects ultimately provide a fundamental limit to resolution.

Small differences are likely to exist in the characteristics of the lens in each eye, and these will naturally give rise to slight differences in the two retinal images

---

[18]These are inherently associated with the optical system, and we ignore optical defects giving rise to *myopic* and *hyperopia* conditions, which can be corrected with glasses.

[19]Monochrome Cathode Ray Tube (CRT) based displays frequently provide an astigmatism correction control. This is to correct for asymmetrical characteristics within the electron lensing system that may result in a noncircular beam "spot."

(although Jiang and Williams [1997] found that these were much smaller than differences between individuals). In normal circumstances, such differences cannot be discerned in the binocular image. For example, if there is a 5% difference in size, the two images can still be fused [Cameron et al. 1999].

(b) The Iris: This determines the size of the pupil (the pupil is the hole in the iris) and thereby the extent of the aperture through which light may impinge on the lens. Under bright lighting conditions, the pupil becomes smaller, and it grows in size as the lighting is dimmed. However, the response time to changing lighting conditions is quite slow. It takes approximately 5 seconds to contract fully when going from dim to bright lighting conditions (about 1.5 seconds to reach two thirds of its size). When adjusting to a rapid and strong reduction in lighting level, it takes approximately 10 seconds to dilate to two thirds of the maximum amount, and up to 5 minutes to open fully [Lindsay and Norman 1972], which suggests that the retina must be adaptive to changing levels of lighting conditions. Even neglecting the length of the pupil's adjustment process, another indication of the inability of changes in pupil size to effectively control the level of illumination reaching the retina is provided by considering the range of lighting conditions across which the eye can function, and comparing this with corresponding changes in pupil size. As mentioned previously, the number of photons arriving at the Earth's surface on a bright sunlit day and on a dark starlit night, varies by approximately eight orders of magnitude. In sunlight, a human's pupil is approximately 2 mm in diameter, and in darkness, it is approximately 8 mm [Land and Nilsson 2002]. This provides for a 16-fold increase in pupil area, indicating that the pupil alone may only vary the level of illumination within the eye by a factor of approximately 16 which is very much less than the factor of 10^8 occurring between the sunny and faintly illuminated sky! In fact, it seems that the principle reason for the changing size of the human pupil is not to finely control the amount of light entering the eye, but rather to achieve the best compromise between resolution and sensitivity under different lighting conditions.

2.3.2   The Retina

Here we find the vast array of photoreceptive elements responsible for sampling the incident light, and so, by analogy, the retina is the biological equivalent to the charge-coupled device (CCD) array employed in a digital camera. However, as quickly becomes apparent, any comparison between the two rapidly breaks down when we consider their relative performance characteristics. The retina also contains cell interconnections that are able to perform initial processing of the visual scene.

The human eye employs two types of receptor: "rods" and "cones." The former are far more sensitive than the latter but cannot provide color sensation. Consequently, rods provide the primary mechanism supporting our sense of sight under low lighting conditions and are also more sensitive to rapid changes in the visual stimulus (indeed, rapid changes in the peripheral vision trigger a reflex reaction to turn the head toward the source). Cones are equipped with the photochemical

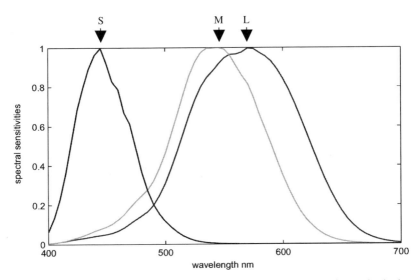

Figure 2.8: The spectral response characteristics of the three classes of cone in the human eye. (Diagram kindly supplied by Professor Steven Westland.)

materials needed for color vision. This is achieved by the presence of three classes of cone, each of which has a different spectral response (see Figure 2.8). In essence, the rods and cones form two separate (independent) visual systems within the eye, and as indicated in Figure 2.9, they are distributed across the retina quite differently. As can be seen in this illustration, the density of rods gradually increases toward the optical axis and then rapidly decreases. This decrease is accompanied by a very large increase in the density of cones, such that the small central region of the eye (the *fovea*), essentially comprises only cones. In this area, the density of cones is extremely high—approximately 150,000 cones per square millimeter. This is the region of the retina where the central part of the image (the region of fixation) is cast and is sampled at the greatest resolution. At any instant, direct color information of the visual scene comes almost exclusively from this area. Naturally, the nonuniform cell distribution gives rise to varying visual acuity across the visual field:

> *So that the image which we receive by the eye is like a picture, minutely and elaborately finished in the centre, but only roughly sketched in at the borders.* [Helmholtz 1873, p. 213]

The human eye contains approximately 120 million rods and 6 million cones [Lindsay and Norman 1972]. Surprisingly, the photosensitive region of these receptors is oriented away from the incoming light; i.e., they point inward (see Figure 2.10). Furthermore, the nerve fibers that form a web of connections and interconnections between photoreceptors lie in the path of the incoming light, and

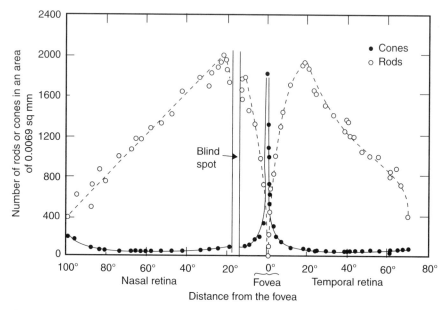

Figure 2.9: Schematic illustration of the variation in the densities of cones and rods across the human retina. Here the distributions are indicated in a horizontal plane. The central region of the retina has a very high density of cones and supports our super high-resolution color imaging (see text for details). [Reproduced by permission from Chapanis, A., Garner, W.R., and Morgan, C.T., *Applied Experimental Psychology*, John Wiley (1949); © 1949 John Wiley & Sons.]

through this the light must pass before being detected.[20] Each eye contains a *blind spot* that is the region via which the connections from the receptor network pass back through the retina and leave the eye. The size of the blind spot is by no means insignificant, and as indicated by Helmholtz [Warren and Warren (eds.) 1968] and mentioned by Cameron et al. [1999], "*it covers an angle equal to 11 full moons placed side by side in the sky!*" It is therefore surprising that the blind spot is not usually visible to us (even when we close one eye), but its presence can be clearly observed when we correctly view Figure 2.11. (See also Investigations Question 8.)

The structure of the retina is illustrated in Figure 2.10. Signals from one or more of the two photoreceptive types are ultimately combined in *ganglion cells*—the output cells of the retina—the axons of which project into the brain and form what is known as the *optic nerve* (see Figure 2.12). In addition to the photoreceptor and ganglion cells, the retina contains other cell types that connect the rods and cones to the ganglion cells. These are the *horizontal cells*, the *bipolar cells*, and the *amacrine cells*. Some bipolar cells are direct intermediaries between the

---

[20]However, in the fovea, the extent of these obstructions is minimized—cones located in this region have direct neural connections.

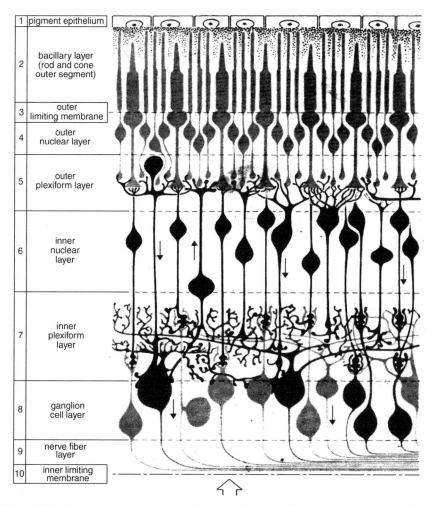

1	pigment epithelium
2	bacillary layer (rod and cone outer segment)
3	outer limiting membrane
4	outer nuclear layer
5	outer plexiform layer
6	inner nuclear layer
7	inner plexiform layer
8	ganglion cell layer
9	nerve fiber layer
10	inner limiting membrane

Figure 2.10: The structure of the retina. Note that incoming light enters this structure from the bottom of the illustration and must pass through various layers before impinging on the rods and cones. Perhaps surprisingly, these point away from the direction in which the light arrives. [Reproduced by permission from Chapanis, A., Garner, W.R., and Morgan, C.T., *Applied Experimental Psychology*, John Wiley (1949); © 1949 John Wiley & Sons.]

photoreceptors and the ganglion cells. However, there is also a lateral network mediated by the horizontal and *amacrine* cells, which allows signals from neighboring photoreceptors to be pooled and gives rise to a "receptive field" structure in the retinal response [Kandel et al. 2000]. The receptive field is an important concept that is repeated in the visual cortex and cortical processing of visual information. It provides a mechanism for combining a number of input signals in such a way as to increase sensitivity to contrast—spatial or temporal changes in light intensity—in

Figure 2.11: The blind spot can be clearly observed when this diagram is viewed correctly. Close your left eye and gaze at the "X" with your right eye. Adjust the distance of the diagram from the eye until the square disappears. It is now being imaged onto your blind spot. Notice that when in this position, although the square cannot be seen (maintain your gaze on the "X"), the horizontal line appears unbroken. The visual system is in some way able to extrapolate the line across the unseen space.

the visual image. The receptive fields of the retinal ganglion cells have the form of concentric "center" and "surround" regions, with the central region typically excitatory and the outer area inhibitory (see Figure 2.13). Thus, small features produce a strong response at the center of the appropriate central region, whereas larger stimuli impinge upon both regions and the response is reduced (since both excitatory and inhibitory signals are generated). We encounter receptive fields again in Section 2.3.4.

Some 90% of the retinal ganglion cells belong to two types: P cells (80%) or M cells (10%).[21] The response profiles of these two cell types are in fact quite distinct—the P cells respond to high spatial frequencies and are wavelength selective but are relatively insensitive to temporal changes, whereas the M cells convey only coarse spatial detail but respond strongly to changes in light intensity[22] [Tovée 1996, Kandel et al. 2000]. The outputs from the M and P channels subsequently feed into processing streams within the brain, which are briefly discussed further in Section 2.4.5.

2.3.3   Eye Movements and Saccades

The eyes are in continual motion. In fact, if this were not so our visual function would be severely impaired, for as Carpenter [1991] writes:

> *A subject whose eyes and head are stationary is to all intents and purposes blind to static objects in the outside world, for their images are stabilized on the retina, and the lack of the element of temporal change they need in order to be perceived.*

He goes on to write:

> *Under natural conditions, the eye is moving all the time, and its velocity radically determines the apparently spatial transfer properties of the visual system. More*

[21]These abbreviations originate from the cell types they subsequently project to in the Lateral Geniculate Nucleus: *parvocellular* or *magnocellular*, respectively. The Lateral Geniculate Nucleus and other details of the visual pathway are summarized in Section 2.4.

[22]The P and M cells are also referred to as X and Y cells [Kingsley 2000] or B and A cells [Livingstone and Hubel 1987], respectively.

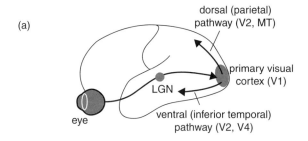

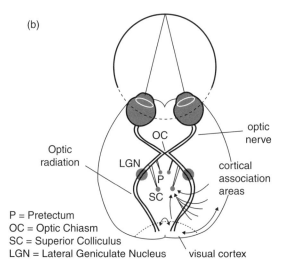

Figure 2.12: Schematic overview of the main signal pathways in the human visual system: (a) side (*sagittal*) depiction and (b) axial depiction. Signals from the *retinae* pass down the optic nerves and cross at the optic chiasm so that the visual hemifields from each eye are combined in the contralateral *Lateral Geniculate Nucleus* and thereafter in the visual cortex toward the back of the contralateral hemisphere of the brain. In addition, retinal input also projects to the *superior colliculus* (controlling saccadic eye movements) and the *pretectum* (controlling pupillary reflexes via feedback to the pupillary muscles). [Diagram (a) reproduced by permission from Kandel E.R., Schwartz, J.H., and Jessell, T.M., *Principles of Neural Science*, McGraw-Hill (2000); © 2000 The McGraw-Hill Companies. Diagram (b) reproduced by permission from Schiffman, H.R., *Sensation and Perception*, John Wiley, (1990); © 1990 John Wiley & Sons.]

precisely, movement of an image across the retina transforms a spatial pattern into a spatiotemporal one, and different velocities favour the perception of different aspects of the spatial character of the image. So when psychophysicists claim to measure the spatial properties of the visual system with their thin lines and sinusoidal gratings they are actually doing nothing of the kind, unless – as is not often the case – they have first taken the precaution of preventing this image motion from generating temporal components from their spatial patterns.

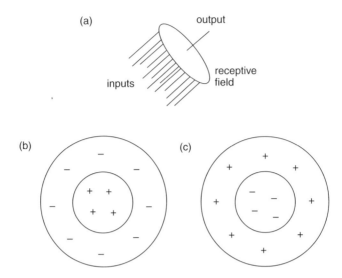

Figure 2.13: (a) A "receptive field" integrates several inputs into a single output. The outputs of many sensory receptors are integrated via subsequent cell layers into summary outputs. In the retina, and in the visual cortex, "center-surround" receptive fields are found: (b) Light on the center of the receptive field generates an increased output, whereas stimulus on the surrounding area has an inhibitory effect ("on-center" fields), or (c) vice versa ("off-center" fields). [Diagrams (b) and (c) reproduced from Kandel, E.R., Schwartz, J.H., and Jessell, T.M., *Principles of Neural Science*, McGraw-Hill (2000); © 2000 The McGraw-Hill Companies.]

The four major types of eye movement are summarized below. Of course, the execution of natural activities involves a mixture of these different eye movements, depending on the nature of the task.

1. *Microsaccades (Tremors)*: Even when vision is fixed constantly on a point of interest, our eyes move several times per second by small, rapid tremors or *micro-saccades* about the average point of fixation. This movement serves to "refresh" the retinal image. This is because the retinal cells are tuned to respond to temporal changes in signal intensity and rapidly saturate in the presence of a constant stimulus [Dember 1960]. The direction of these movements is random, and they are typically ~1–2 minutes of arc in amplitude.[23] As mentioned above, if these motions are artificially compensated for by, for example, an apparatus fixed to the eyeball that provides an unchanged image despite these movements, the retinal image appears to fade and disappear.

2. *Saccades*: When exploring a visual scene, our eyes do not move smoothly. They typically alternate between a short fixation (around 500 ms) and a rapid

---

[23]Angles are measured in the familiar units of radians or degrees, but finer gradations can also be quoted in *arc minutes* (minutes of arc) or *arc seconds* (seconds of arc). By definition, one arc minute (1 arc min., or 1′) is 1/60th of a degree, and one arc second (1 arc sec., or 1″) is 1/60th of an arc minute.

(a) (b)

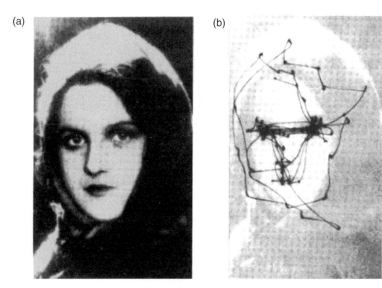

Figure 2.14: The path followed by the eyes of one subject examining the picture in (a) is shown in (b). It can be seen that the path comprises periods of fixation on different parts of the image (seen as dots or kinks in the lines) interspersed with rapid jumps (saccades) from one point to the next (indicated as connecting lines). [Reproduced from Yarbus, A.L., *Eye Movements and Vision*, Plenum Press (1967).]

motion to a new point of fixation, ensuring that the retinal image of the feature of interest falls on the fovea where acuity is maximal. These movements are known as *saccades* (from the French "jerk") and can range from a few arc minutes to $20°$ or more in amplitude but occur rapidly, with maximum velocities on the order of $800°\,\mathrm{s}^{-1}$ [Tovée 1996]. Typically $1-3$ saccades might occur each second, but their total duration is only about 100 ms-actual viewing time is maximized [Schiffman 1990]. Both saccades and microsaccades are "ballistic" motions—the destination is known before the movement is initiated, and the muscles are employed to move the eye to the new orientation as rapidly as possible. The path followed by a sequence of saccades varies according to the content of the scene. Figure 2.14 illustrates an example of the path followed by the point of regard when examining an image. Here, the Saccades are visible as the lines connecting the points of fixation, which appear as dots. As another example, reading results in a regular "staircase" pattern as the eyes scan each line in turn [Schiffman 1990]. Saccades are also used to stabilize the visual image in the presence of head or body motion. Visual signals[24] are suppressed during these eye movements; we never notice "smearing" of our visual environment due to saccade motion.

[24]Specifically, signals from the M cells (most sensitive to temporal changes) but not the P cells (more sensitive to spatial detail) are suppressed during saccades [Tovée 1996]. The M and P cells and their accompanying pathways are discussed in Sections 2.3.4 and 2.4.

3. *Pursuit Eye Movements*: When tracking a moving object, rather than examining a static one, the eye moves by smooth "pursuit movements" in order to maintain the object fixated on the fovea. In contrast to saccades, these are not ballistic movements and are continually updated by feedback to the oculomotor muscles. The maximum target velocity that can be tracked is approximately $30° \, s^{-1}$ [Tovée 1996].

4. *Vergence*: As objects situated at different distances from the viewer are regarded, *vergence* eye movements are employed to ensure that the visual axes of both eyes intersect at the feature of interest and its image is cast onto the fovea of each eye. For distant points of fixation, the visual axes are essentially parallel, whereas for closer objects, the eyes converge (swivel inward) to maintain singleness of vision.

As with so many topics that we refer to in this book, space precludes in-depth discussion. In relation to eye movements, the text edited by R.H.S. Carpenter [1991] provides an excellent starting point for the interested reader.

2.3.4   The Detection of Color

As previously mentioned, the human eye can discriminate differences in the wavelength of the incident light by means of three classes of the cone photoreceptor in the retina (see Figure 2.8). Such a *trichromatic* theory of color vision was, it seems, first proposed by Thomas Young in 1802. In Young's theory, three classes of "nerve fibers" in the retina were sensitive to light of long, middle, or short wavelengths (within the visible range), and these gave a corresponding sensation of red, green, or violet light. Other colors were then perceived by neural combinations of these primary sensations. This theory was extended by Helmholtz, who, later in the nineteenth century, generalized Young's ideas to incorporate response *profiles* of each class of nerve fiber (i.e., the response of the photoreceptor varies smoothly as a function of wavelength). Each class was then understood to be maximally sensitive to a particular wavelength, but also responded to light of other frequencies.

In general, at least two classes of photoreceptor, each with a different response profile, are required in order to discriminate wavelength independently of intensity—the greater the number of classes, the better the wavelength discrimination. Within the animal kingdom, there is some variation in the number of cone classes; for example, non-primate mammals have two, old-world primates (including humans) have three,[25] new-world primates have four, and birds such as the pigeon have five [Tovée 1996]. The spectral response profiles of the three classes of cones in the human eye (indicated in Figure 2.8) are not evenly spaced across

---

[25]Interestingly, the spatial distributions in the retina of the two red–green cone classes seems to vary considerably between individuals (who otherwise report normal color vision) [Roorda and Williams 1999]. Moreover, the human retina seems to have a small ($\sim$100 μm) area in the center of the fovea in which no blue cones are present [Roorda and Williams 1999, Bumsted and Hendrikson 1999]!

the visible region of the spectrum—the two most responsive in the medium/long wavelength range having a high degree of mutual overlap. Although color discrimination might be improved by a more complementary distribution of these response profiles, this overlap in the red–green region improves the spatial resolution of the response to surfaces reflecting in the red–green region (discussed further below), as there is less chromatic dispersion between the profiles—a sharp image is obtained at middle/long wavelengths. In fact, all primates have a single cone class responding maximally at ∼420–440 nm (blue) and two or three additional cone classes with peak responses in the red–green range (∼500–570 nm) [Tovée 1996]. Other *dichromatic* (two color) mammals, such as dogs, have a single response class in the red–green region and another in the blue, effectively providing blue–yellow color discrimination [Neitz et al. 2001].

Although our individual cone photoreceptors respond to the wavelength of incident light according to one of three response profiles, our sensation of colors as such is thought to be mediated by a subsequent "opponent process" combination of cone outputs. First proposed by Ewald Hering in 1920, the outputs from each of the cone classes are combined according to one of the three schemes illustrated in Figure 2.15 [Schiffman 1990, Tovée 1996]. In the *achromatic* channel, signals from each class are combined additively to generate a response dependent on the overall intensity of the incident light. Color discrimination *per se* is accomplished by the red–green channel and the blue–yellow channel. The output of the red–green channel depends on the difference between the responses of the red and green cone classes, whereas that of the blue–yellow channel signals the difference between the blue response and the combination of red and green outputs (i.e., yellow).

The retinal ganglion P cells (see Section 2.3.2) are thought to integrate cone outputs for both red–green and blue–yellow channels. However, it is known that our visual system is more sensitive to sharp intensity changes than sharp color changes, and so it is likely that P cells are also involved in conveying high spatial detail. If both center and surround regions of a P cell receptive field are stimulated, a differential color response will be generated (for example, a "red" center signal minus a "green" surround signal) at a spatial resolution roughly dictated by the size of the entire receptive field. However, if only the center receives input, the response indicates finer spatial detail but color differentiation is lost [Kandel et al. 2000].

2.4 BEYOND THE EYE

The optic nerve proceeding from each eye contains approximately one million projections that carry the output of the retinal ganglion cells into the brain. (This bundle of axons is approximately 3–4 mm in diameter, at least immediately after leaving the eye [Beatty et al. 1998, Karim et al. 2004].) As illustrated in Figure 2.12(b), the two optic nerves initially converge at the *optic chiasm*, where those fibers from the medial half of each retina cross over to the contralateral

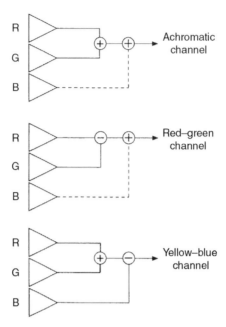

Figure 2.15: It is thought that our color perception, which is mediated initially by the three classes of cone photoreceptor in the retina, proceeds thereafter by "opponent processes," in which each red (R), green (G), or blue (B) signal is combined additively or differentially to give rise to different color perceptions. Three channels are believed to be part of this process—an achromatic channel, in which all signals are combined additively, and two others that give sensations of red versus green and yellow versus blue. [Reproduced by permission from Tovée, M.J., *An Introduction to the Visual System*, Cambridge University Press (1996); © 1996 Cambridge University Press.]

hemisphere to join the fibers originating in the temporal half of the other eye. *In this way, the optical pathway in each hemisphere of the brain thereafter contains information from both eyes, relating to the opposite half of the visual field.* This allows binocular information to be extracted by combining signals from each eye. It is remarkable that although the signals corresponding to each half of the visual field are routed to different hemispheres, no vertical division is apparent in our final perception of the scene. After the intersection at the optic chiasm, the pathways diverge again and project to three main subcortical brain structures (each present in both hemispheres), namely the *Lateral Geniculate Nucleus* (LGN) of the thalamus, which acts as a subterminal for signals subsequently routed into the visual cortex; and the *superior colliculus* and the *pretectal area*, which are involved in reflex actions and oculomuscular responses (see Figure 2.12(a)).

In the following pages, we provide a very brief discussion on the transmission and processing of the retinal image data after leaving the eye. This is intended to give the reader an insight into aspects of our understanding of the complex

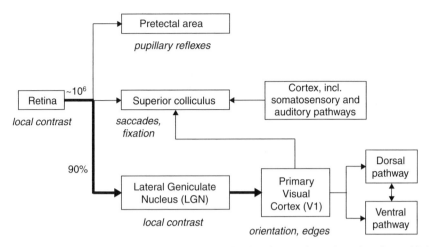

Figure 2.16: Simplified illustration of the main visual pathways from the retina. Some 90% of the approximately one million axons in each optic nerve project to the LGN, and from there into the visual cortex. The arrangements of cells in the retina and LGN are both optimized to respond to local differences in contrast within the visual image. In the visual cortex, the image begins to be reduced into more abstract features, such as object boundaries and motion along specific directions.

mechanisms involved in this highly complex sensory system of which we still understand relatively little.

2.4.1 The Lateral Geniculate Nucleus

The basic pathways of the visual signals that originate in the retina are summarized in Figure 2.16. In the early part of this pathway, through the optic nerves, 90% of the retinal output projects to the LGN. Of this, 50% originates near the fovea, reflecting the high density of ganglion cells in this part of the eye and capturing the fine spatial detail corresponding to maximal spatial acuity (recall Figure 2.9). Each neuron in the LGN receives input from a small number of neighboring ganglion cells in the retina—thus maintaining the *retinotopic*[26] map of the visual image. The LGN operates on the visual signals in a similar way to the retina, responding to differences in local contrast or color via center-surround receptive fields, each covering about 1° of the visual field [Kandel et al. 2000]. The LGN sends its output signals via the *optic radiation* into the *primary visual cortex*[27] (V1), located at the back of the brain (see Figure 2.12).

---

[26]The term "retinotopic" means that the spatial distribution of the signals retains a topographic relationship with those from the retina. That is, neighboring regions of the retina are represented by neighboring regions in the retinotopic map.

[27]The V1 or "visual area 1" is also known as the *striate* cortex. Hence, visual areas 2–5 (V2–V5) are sometimes referred to as *extrastriate* areas.

2.4.2   Reflex Feedback

The iris is a peculiar exception . . . the nerves which make the iris expand come out
from no one knows exactly where, go down into the spinal cord back of the chest,
into the thoracic sections, out of the spinal cord, up through the neck ganglia, and
all the way around and back up into the head in order to run the other end of the
iris. In fact, the signal goes through a completely different nervous system, so it's a
very strange way of making things go.[28]

The majority of the axons in the optic nerve that do not project to the LGN are routed
to the *superior colliculus* and *pretectal* area—regions involved in reflex and *oculo-*
muscular responses to visual stimuli [Tovee 1996, Kandel et al. 2000]. The *superior*
colliculus controls visual fixation (that is, maintaining the gaze on a feature of interest)
and saccades by feedback to the *oculomotor* muscles. In addition to the retinal input
received by way of the optic nerve, it also receives projections from the primary visual
cortex and other cortical areas, including those involved in auditory and somatosensory perception [King 2004]. It is thought that these inputs are involved in the
execution of rapid changes in fixation in response to visual and/or non-visual
stimuli, as well as by conscious direction. The *pretectal area* mediates pupillary
reflexes (changing the pupil size in response to changes in illumination).

2.4.3   The Primary Visual Cortex (V1)

In the primary visual cortex, cells begin to respond to more complex features of the
visual input, and it is thought that this begins a process of reducing the retinal images
into more abstract features. Information delineating the boundaries of objects begins
to be extracted by means of receptive fields sensitive to short line segments of
specific orientations (including color boundaries), as well as to motion of line segments in particular directions. In addition, certain cells are tuned to particular spatial
frequencies, and others respond to differences in binocular disparity. The processing
of the visual signals in the V1 nevertheless remains spatially localized—inputs from
the LGN, covering a small portion of the visual field, are directed to a corresponding
localized region in the V1. These functional units, sometimes known as *hypercol-*
umns as they involve all layers "vertically" through the primary visual cortex, can
process the visual input from both eyes originating in corresponding regions of
the visual field [Kingsley 2000]. Although the retinotopic layout of the V1 functional units retains the topography of the visual field, the spatial distribution of
neurons in the V1 is distorted relative to the retinal image, with greater cortical
volume being occupied by signals originating near the fovea [Howard and Rogers
1995, Kandel et al. 2000]. Perhaps this is because while in the retina the photoreceptor and ganglion cells need to be physically closer together at the fovea to
sample incident light with greater resolution, in the cortex, this requirement can
be relaxed and the cells more evenly spaced. A "magnification factor," typically
defined as the distance along the cortex receiving inputs responding to $1°$ of the

---

[28]Richard Feynman [1963].

visual field, is often used to summarize the relative cortical weight dedicated to different parts of the retinal image. For example, this factor has been estimated at 11.5 mm per degree for the fovea, compared with 4 mm per degree at $2°$ eccentricity [Howard and Rogers 1995].

Although the fundamental organization of the V1 may be considered to be an array of modular functional units, there are also horizontal connections between related cells; for example, between cells in neighboring functional units responding to line segments of the same orientation [Kandel et al. 2000]. These connections may play a role in modulating local responses to more global features in the image, such as object boundaries.

2.4.4   The Dorsal and Ventral Pathways

Most of the output from the V1 is directed into the neighboring V2 region, but with information related to different features of the visual input, such as orientation, color, and binocular disparity, now following different, specialized pathways [Livingstone and Hubel 1987]. Whereas in the V1 the matrix of functional regions reflects the spatial localization of the retinal image, in V2 different parameters derived from the retinal image begin to be processed independently. Moreover, as we proceed along the visual pathways, the receptive fields become larger and respond to more global features of the visual scene.

One current paradigm describing visual perception beyond the V2 area describes two main parallel processing streams, known as the *dorsal* and *ventral* pathways (see Figure 2.17). The dorsal pathway is thought to be primarily responsible for the perception of motion and spatial relationships within the visual scene, whereas the

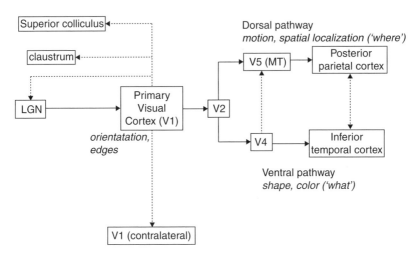

Figure 2.17: The main visual channel proceeds from the LGN into the primary visual cortex, from where derived parameters are extracted from the information. A simplified view of this visual processing is that it occurs via two main parallel pathways—the *dorsal* (responsible for defining where an object is) and the *ventral* (deciding what is the object).

ventral pathway mainly deals with contrast, contours, and color. A simplified view is that the dorsal pathway discerns *where* objects are positioned, while the ventral pathway determines *what* the objects are [Tovée 1996, Kandel et al. 2000].

The dorsal pathway proceeds into the *parietal lobes* through the V2 and MT[29] (or V5) regions. As in the V1, cells in the MT also respond to directional motion but with significantly larger receptive fields. Motion of both luminance boundaries and of edges defined by differences in color or texture are detected. Beyond the MT, visual information is processed in the *posterior parietal cortex* and subsequently interacts with information from other sensory channels and stored memories in "association areas" elsewhere in the brain, which serve to integrate the input from these different sources so as to provide a coherent final perception. The *posterior parietal cortex* is also involved in the planning of movement, in connection with saccadic eye movements, and in the orientation of the eyes and head relative to the scene in the visual field. The dorsal pathway is thus likely to be involved in the processing related to reach and grasp, compensating between shifts in the visual field and those of the body [Sakata et al. 1997].

The ventral pathway proceeds outward via the V2 and the V4 into the inferior temporal lobe of the brain. Visual areas 2 and 4 seem to refine the responses to color and form obtained in the V1. Cells in the V2 respond to contours in the visual scene and to particular orientations, and in the V4 responses to particular textures have been identified [Kandel et al. 2000]. The shading conveyed by variations in intensity and color can provide valuable information as to the form of objects inside identified edges, as light reflected from the surface of an object is rarely uniform. The combination of color and edge information that is processed in the ventral pathway has led to this channel being considered as an important part of our perception of form. As we move from the V2 to the V4, the receptive fields become larger than earlier in the pathway, and so the response to input signals becomes less dependent on the position of the stimulus within the visual field (positional information being primarily handled by the parallel dorsal pathway). Subsequent processing in the inferior temporal cortex has been shown to be related to higher level shape recognition, including anthropomorphic shapes such as the face from different orientations, different facial expressions, hands, and individual fingers [Schiffman 1990, Tovée 1996, Kandel et al. 2000].

2.4.5   The M and P Pathways

In Section 2.3.2, we noted that most retinal ganglion cells providing the signals that proceed into the brain via the optic nerve are of either M type or P type and have quite different sensitivity profiles. These cell types provide input into two important processing channels within the visual system. In fact, the outputs from these two cell types remain distinct in the LGN and into the visual cortex, and there is evidence that they encapsulate from an early stage two complementary channels of information

---

[29]MT is an abbreviation for *mediotemporal* (or middle temporal) area. This region is also referred to as V5.

that feed eventually into the dorsal and ventral pathways [Livingstone and Hubel 1987, Tovée 1996, Kingsley 2000].

The signals originating in the *parvocellular* cells constitute the "P channel" and those from the *magnocellular* cells the "M channel." In the retina, the M cells have relatively large receptive fields and respond best to temporal changes in illumination, whereas the P cells are wavelength (color) selective and report finer spatial detail. In the visual cortex, cells receiving input from the P channel have a relatively high spatial frequency response and respond to color and disparity, whereas those associated with the M channel respond to high temporal frequencies but have relatively low spatial frequency response. This color and orientation information in the P channel continues into V4 along the ventral pathway, while the orientation and motion features in the M channel are predominantly routed into the MT along the dorsal pathway [Tovée 1996].

However, these pathways do not proceed in isolation from each other nor from other visual and cognitive processing areas and attention, for example, can modulate signals between them [Livingstone and Hubel 1987, Vidyasagar 1999, Kandel et al. 2000].

2.4.6 Detection of Binocular Disparity

Binocular disparity (stereopsis) is a powerful depth cue satisfied by various types of a creative 3-D display system. Differences (disparity) in the views obtained by the two eyes as a consequence of their spatial separation provide an indication of the 3-D nature of a scene (see Section 2.6.2). Cells that respond to specific amounts of disparity have been identified in a number of the visual processing areas of the brain, including the V1, V2, V3, and MT, and evidence relating these responses to stereo depth perception is emerging [Howard and Rogers 1995, DeAngelis et al. 1998, DeAngelis 2000]. About half the cells in the V1 are disparity-responsive, and these are mainly tuned to particular local disparities, responding most strongly when corresponding elements of the visual field occur at particular offsets in *retinotopic* location. These responses thus correspond to particular depths behind or in front of the current fixation distance. Subsequent visual processing areas along the dorsal pathway contain increasing proportions of cells that respond to disparity. These cells are typically sensitive to either crossed (features closer than the horopter—see Section 6.4.1), uncrossed (features further away), or zero disparity. Further along this pathway, it has been shown that the MT region contains a map of disparity as a function of location in the visual field [DeAngelis 2000], and this information is combined with signals related to motion. In the MT, many direction-sensitive cells are tuned to stimuli at particular distances. In the medial superior temporal area, which follows the MT in the dorsal pathway, cells have been shown to respond to particular combinations of disparity and motion, such as a stimulus beyond the horopter moving to the left, or one closer than the horopter moving to the right. This corresponds to information related to motion at different depths in the visual field [Kandel et al. 2000], providing an interesting neurobiological connection to the depth cue of motion parallax.

2.5 SOME VISUAL CHARACTERISTICS

In this section, we provide a brief review of various visual characteristics and consider issues that are of particular relevance to those researching creative 3-D display technologies.

2.5.1 The Visual Field

The proportion of the environment in view at any one time is governed by our visual field. The angular limits of visual input are approximately 155° horizontally by 130° vertically for each eye. With both eyes, the total horizontal field of view extends to approximately 180°. The central area of overlap in the visual fields spans about 120° horizontally and is known as the "binocular visual field" (see Figure 2.18). Both eyes receive input from image components lying in this region, and hence, binocular information is available (see Sections 2.6.2 and 6.4). The distance between the eyes is referred to as the *interocular* distance and for adults is on average 6.3 cm [Dodgson 2004].

2.5.2 Spatial Resolution

It is convenient to encapsulate the size of an object and its distance from the eye as a single angular measure (ϕ). As illustrated in Figure 2.19, this is the angle subtended at the eye by an object lying at a distance[30] s and that has a length x perpendicular to the visual axis. Clearly, this is a major determinant of the size of the image cast onto the retina. From the illustration, it is apparent that

$$\tan\left(\frac{\phi}{2}\right) = \frac{x}{2s}. \tag{2.6}$$

From which it follows:

$$\phi = 2\arctan\left(\frac{x}{2s}\right). \tag{2.7}$$

In Table 2.1, we provide values for the visual angle for various objects located at different viewing distances.

From the above and as shown in Figure 2.19, it is apparent that the ratio of the object size (x) to the size of the retinal image (y) may be expressed as

$$\frac{x}{y} = \frac{s}{u}, \tag{2.8}$$

[30]The distance of an object from the eye is often quoted in terms of the reciprocal of the distance (measured in meters). This is assigned the unit of "diopters." For example, an object located at infinity corresponds to zero diopters, and one lying at 5 m corresponds to 0.2 diopters.

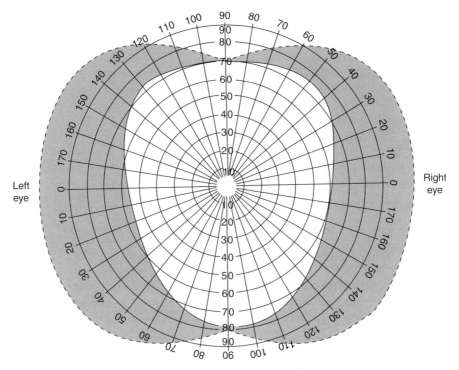

Figure 2.18: Illustrating the visual field. The region of overlap in the visual fields of our two eyes is the area of binocular vision. As is apparent from this illustration, binocular parallax (stereopsis) is not supported across the entire visual field. (Reproduced from Gibson, James J. *The Perception of the Visual World*; © 1950 by Houghton Mifflin Company. Used with permission.)

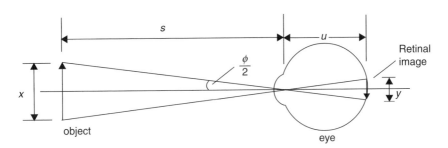

Figure 2.19: An object of length x located at a distance s from the eye casts an inverted image of length y on the retina. See text for details.

TABLE 2.1: Various visual angles.

Object	Visual Angle (ϕ)
Television (40 cm wide) at 4 m	$\sim3°$
Coin (e.g., 1 euro, 1 pound) at arm's length	$\sim1°$
Laptop computer monitor (30 cm wide) at a 60-cm viewing distance	14°
Diameter of the moon	17′
Diameter of fovea	30′
Size of blind spot	7.5° vertical, 5° horizontal

where u indicates the distance between lens and retina (approximately 2 cm). Immediately apparent is that in most situations, the retinal image is extremely small. Take for example the bug crawling on the wall behind my computer. The bug is around 4 mm in length, and the wall is at a distance of approximately 2 m, which gives a retinal image that is only ~0.04 mm in length.

The spatial characteristics of the visual system are determined not only by the nature of the visual stimulus but also by factors such as viewing distance, direction relative to the visual axis, and by the level of illumination. Consequently, when we consider our ability to resolve spatial detail and particularly when we make use of numerical values in this context, we must carefully define the particular viewing conditions under which such values were obtained. Measurements made in the context of resolution are referred to as "acuities." These provide us with information on our capabilities of perceiving high spatial frequencies (fine detail) under high contrast conditions, and their measurement is relatively straightforward. Unfortunately they do not provide us with an insight into the visual system's performance when lower spatial frequencies are viewed under low contrast circumstances [Boff et al. 1986]. However, from the perspective of display system development, acuity measurements can be useful and we summarize some of these below:

1. *Resolution (Grating) Acuity*: This provides a measure of our ability to detect the separation of objects in space and corresponds to resolving discrete elements in a pattern. It may be measured by, for example, varying the distance between two or more black bars drawn on a white background. Such a pattern is referred to as a grating—versions of this are illustrated in Figure 2.20. In the case of the pattern shown in Figure 2.20(a), the reflected light intensity continuously varies across the grating, and this is known as a sinusoidal grating. However, in the case of the grating presented in Figure 2.20(b), the intensity exists in one of two levels—there is no intermediate grayscale. This is referred to as a square-wave grating. The contrast ratio introduced in Section 2.2.2 is determined in terms of the maximum and minimum levels of luminance.

The minimum line spacing in a grating that can be detected is approximately 30″, corresponding to a separation of around 0.15 mm at a distance of 1 m. However, as we will discuss, as with other acuities, resolution acuity depends on a variety of viewing conditions.

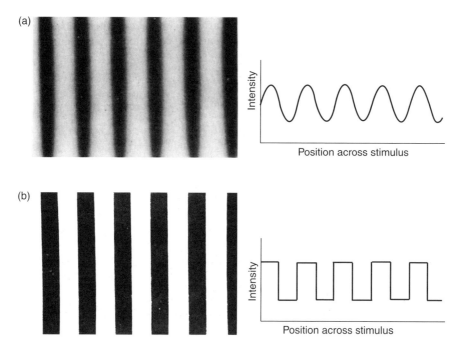

Figure 2.20: Illustrating two gratings. In (a), the grayscale continually (and regularly) varies across the grating, and hence, this is known as a sinusoidal grating. However, in (b), only two grayscale levels exist, and so this is known as a square-wave grating. [Reproduced by permission from Coren, S., Ward L.M., and Enns, J.T., *Sensation and Perception*, 4th edn., Harcourt Brace & Company (1994); © 2005 John Wiley & Sons.]

2. *Detection Acuity*: Consider an isolated object located in the visual field lying normal to the viewing axis. Detection acuity measures the smallest visual angle subtended by the object that we can perceive. As indicated by Coren et al. [1994], an observer with normal vision can easily perceive 1′, which corresponds to 0.3 mm at a distance of 1 m. Based on this visual angle, and assuming a distance along the visual axis between the center of the lens and the retina of 20 mm, then the image size cast onto the retina will be approximately 0.006 mm. Boff et al. [1986], quoting from the work of Hecht and Mintz [1939], consider the detection of a single dark line whose *length* subtends several degrees at the eye and that is superimposed on a bright background (i.e., using optimal conditions). In this experiment, to determine the minimum line thickness that can be detected, and hence the highest acuity, they report a remarkable value of approximately 0.5″. In connection with this, the original publication by Hecht and Mintz is well worth reading. In their experiment, an observer was seated in a dark room. The distance of the chair from an illuminated "window" could be varied and readily measured. Wires of various thicknesses were used and affixed across the window at any chosen orientation. During the trials, the observer would move toward the window until the wire could just

be discerned. Having the observer report on the wire's orientation gave confirmation of the observation. Naturally, before the observations commenced, the observer was given time to adapt to the lighting conditions. Trials were conducted for wires of varying thickness and at different levels of illumination (here the authors stress the importance of uniform illumination). Maximum acuity occurred under the highest level of illumination and gave rise to a detectable retinal image of 0.04 μm—less than the diameter of individual cones. However, this assumes that the retinal image is a perfect rendition of the geometrical image which, as we have discussed, is not the case (see Section 2.2.3). Even in this situation of maximum detection acuity, the retinal image will span more than one row of cones, and Hecht and Mintz calculated the extent of the image as a consequence of diffraction. In this context, they confirm the earlier assertion of Hartridge [1922] that *"the maximum resolving power of the eye is determined by its capacity for intensity discrimination . . . ."*

3. *Localization or Vernier Acuity*: Consider two line segments laid end-to-end. This acuity measures our ability to detect any relative misalignment perpendicular to their common axis. Maximum resolution for this type of task is reported to be in the range $1''$ to $2''$ [Boff et al. 1986]. This is often referred to as "vernier acuity" because of its application to the reading of a vernier scale on, for example, callipers or a micrometer.

4. *Dynamic Acuity*: Another related measure is that of "dynamic acuity," which pertains to detecting and locating moving targets. The human visual limit of dynamic acuity has been reported as being about $1'-2'$ for objects moving at $60° \, s^{-1}$ [Schiffman 1990].

As indicated, visual acuity is a function of the position of the image on the retina. The relative acuity falls off rapidly as the stimulus occurs in more peripheral locations of the retina (see Figure 2.21). This acuity is strongly governed by the distribution of cones in the retina which, as we have seen, are concentrated in the fovea. The rods, of greater density beyond the fovea but having a poorer spatial response, cannot fully compensate.

2.5.3   Sensitivity and the Impact of Spatial Frequency

> It seems profane to be so free with these
> few precious quanta.[31]

On a dark starlit night the flux of photons arriving at the Earth's surface is approximately $10^{12} \, m^{-2} \cdot s^{-1}$. However this does not represent the minimum threshold for human vision as this is approximately two orders of magnitude lower still.

In the early 1940s, Hecht et al. [1942] sought to determine the minimum level of illumination (or rather the smallest number of photons) that could be detected by the

---

[31]Hecht et al. [1942] in the context of the loss of photons traveling through the eye.

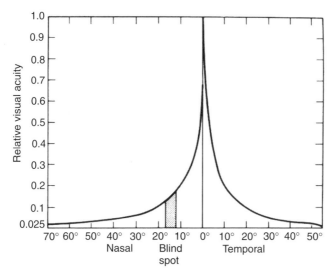

Figure 2.21: The relative visual acuity of the eye, as a function of angular distance from the fovea. (The gap at $\sim 17°$ nasal from the fovea represents the blind spot.) This dependence is governed strongly by the distribution of cones versus that of rods in the retina (see Figure 2.9) and the receptive fields in the ganglion cell layer. [Based on Wertheim, E., *Ueber die Durchführbarkeit und den Werth der mikroskopischen Untersuchung des Eiters entzündlicher Adnexentumoren während der Laparotomie* (1894).]

human eye. Whilst we have previously alluded to various remarkable characteristics of the eye and visual system as a whole (such as the great range of intensity over which the eye can operate, and the high resolution of the fovea), perhaps more amazing still is the eye's sensitivity to very small numbers of photons. Hecht et al. identified optimal conditions for their experiment. They employed a brief flash of light (lasting in the order of 1 ms) impinging on the retina in the region of greatest rod density (about 20° from the visual axis) and of a wavelength optimal to rod sensitivity (510 nm). Participants were first adapted to dark conditions (over a time of 1 hour) before being subjected to the test flashes of light. In this way they identified the minimum number of photons needed in order that the participants could detect flashes. The threshold obtained ranged from 54 to 148 quanta, and it was shown that should a mere 90 photons entered the eye; then the flash was observed 60% of the time (under optimal conditions). However, although remarkable in itself, the result is even more impressive when one takes into account the loss of photons during their transit through the eye. It is estimated that approximately only 50% of the light entering the eye reaches the retina (some being reflected by the cornea, and some lost within the lens and humors). Furthermore, not every photon reaching the retina will impinge upon a rod. Taking into account these factors and the spread of the light flash across the retinal array, it became apparent to Hecht and his colleagues that a rod is able to respond to a single photon. However, as a consequence of noise, a single photon impinging on a rod does not give rise to a visual event. Cameron et al. [1999] briefly discusses "retinal noise" caused by occasional background firing of photoreceptors in the absence of luminous stimuli. Assuming that each rod generates a random action potential every 5 minutes, the total amount of noise emanating from the entire photoreceptor array during the duration of the brief light flashes employed by Hecht et al. is indeed significant. As a consequence, although rods can detect individual photons, a small number of rods must be stimulated simultaneously in order to provide a visual event [Osgood 1953].

Our perception of the intensity contrast within an image is dependent upon its spatial frequency content. In Figure 2.22, we illustrate two gratings, which have the same physical contrast ratio (see Eq. (2.2)) but different spatial frequencies. However, grating (b) appears to have a lower contrast ratio, taking on a gray appearance. This indicates that in the case of this grating, the eye is less able to process this spatial pattern. The "spatial modulation transfer function" is used to provide a measure of a system's ability to capture and decode a spatial pattern. In the case of the human visual system, this transfer function has a maximum when the spatial pattern repeats itself approximately six times for each degree subtended at the eye. Above or below this frequency, the eye is less sensitive, and to maintain spatial acuity, we may need to increase the contrast ratio of an image.

2.6 PERCEPTION OF SPACE AND FORM

When viewing our surroundings we continually gauge the distance of components contained within our visual field—their absolute distance from our location, and their relative distance with respect to each other. This process is supported by various types of information obtained through our visual system. Although the task is greatly facilitated by our binocular vision, this is not an absolute requirement. The forms of information used for this purpose are referred to as "depth cues," and it

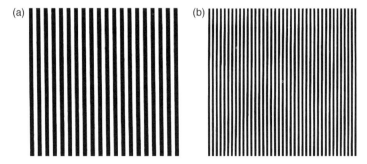

Figure 2.22: Illustrating two square-wave gratings. Despite the use of identical grayscales, (b) is perceived as having a smaller contrast ratio. This is as a result of the increased spacing (increased spatial frequency) of the grating lines in (b). See text for details. [Reproduced by permission from Coren, S., Ward, L.M., and Enns, J.T., *Sensation and Perception*, 4th edn., Harcourt Brace & Company (1994); © 2005 John Wiley & Sons.]

is important to note (from the perspective of creative 3-D display system development) that the relative emphasis placed on these cues varies according to the nature of the scene under observation.

Depth cues are often grouped according to common features, and this may be done in a number of ways. Some cues are based on the properties of the two-dimensional (2-D) retinal image(s) received ("retinal image cues"), whereas others employ feedback from the muscles used to control the relative directions and point of focus of the eyes ("oculomotor cues"). Some require input from both eyes ("binocular cues"), and others work with one eye alone ("monocular cues"). Various cues can be reproduced upon a static image ("pictorial cues"), and some require different viewpoints in either space or time ("parallax cues"). A number of depth cues are summarized in Table 2.2, along with these grouping properties, and Figure 2.23 indicates the distances over which each is most effective. In the sub-sections that follow, we outline various major depth cues, which are grouped for convenience into pictorial and oculomotor/parallax categories.

2.6.1 Pictorial Depth Cues

Pictorial depth cues are those indications of depth that may be used in depicting a 3-D scene on a static 2-D surface. As discussed further in Chapter 4, a mastery of these cues has enabled artists to enhance the visual realism of their works and create, for example, photo-realistic images upon a 2-D tableau. Some of the pictorial depth cues are briefly summarized as follows:

(1) Occlusion (Interposition): The form of this cue is illustrated in Figure 2.24. Here we assume that one opaque rectangle is partially occluding the view of a

TABLE 2.2: Subclassifications of depth cues.

	Classification Scheme		
Depth Cue	Retinal Image/ Oculomotor	Parallax/Pictorial	Binocular/ Monocular
Binocular parallax (stereopsis)	Retinal image	Parallax	Binocular
Motion parallax	Retinal image (+ Oculomotor)	Parallax	Monocular
Linear perspective	Retinal image	Pictorial	Monocular
Occlusion (interposition)	Retinal image	Pictorial	Monocular
Familiar size	Retinal image	Pictorial	Monocular
Shading and shadows	Retinal image	Pictorial	Monocular
Aerial perspective	Retinal image	Pictorial	Monocular
Texture gradient	Retinal image	Pictorial	Monocular
Height in the visual field	Retinal image	Pictorial	Monocular
Accommodation	Oculomotor	—	Monocular
Convergence	Oculomotor	—	Binocular

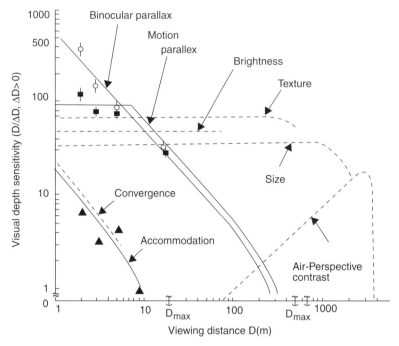

Figure 2.23: Here we provide an indication of the relative depth sensitivity of various depth cues as a function of distance from an observer. [Reproduced by permission from Ellis, S., (ed.), *Pictorial Communication in Virtual and Real Environments*, 2nd edn., p. 533, fig. 3., Taylor & Francis Ltd (1993); © 2005 Thomson Learning.]

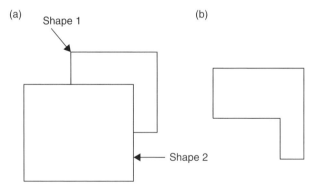

Figure 2.24: In (a) we provide a simple illustration that demonstrates the occlusion depth cue. We assume that Shape 1 is in fact rectangular and not as illustrated in (b). Consequently, Shape 2 is assumed to be occluding our view of Shape 1, and the latter is therefore judged to be further away. If we presume that both rectangles are physically of the same size, then the fact that Shape 1 generates a smaller retinal image will re-enforce our perspective of the scene. The illusion of three-dimensionality is further augmented by a third depth cue. The reader is left to identify this cue.

second rectangle, and so is closer to the viewpoint. If we believe that the rectangles are physically the same size, then our supposition will be reinforced should the partially occluded rectangle appear to be smaller—as indeed it does in the illustration. In this respect, we are making use of the "linear perspective" cue.

(2) Linear Perspective: This cue arises as a consequence of the optical arrangement of the eye as illustrated in Figure 2.25. As may be seen from this diagram, when the object is repositioned so as to be further away, then it casts a smaller retinal image. The convergence of railway lines in the distance (to a vanishing point) and the gradual apparent shortening of the distance between the "sleepers" lying between them provide an illustration of this cue (see also the illustrations provided in Chapter 4).

(3) Shading: The distribution of smooth or abrupt changes in intensity within an image can provide a powerful indication of the shape of the surface of an object. This often involves an implicit assumption about the direction of the light causing the shading—the brightness variations are usually interpreted by the brain as if the light was incident from above [Ramachandran 1988].

(4) Height in the Visual Field: When, for example, we look out to sea, the sky and water merge at the horizon. It is in fact as if the water ascends and the sky descends until they eventually meet. Consequently we assume that objects which are further away and that are located below the horizon (for example, boats in the water) will appear higher in the image scene (i.e., closer to the horizon). Similarly, objects located above the horizon (for example, clouds) will be perceived as being

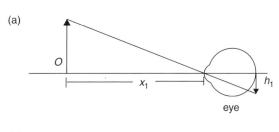

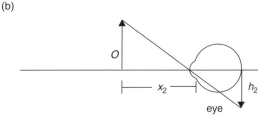

Figure 2.25: In (a) an object O located at a distance x_1 from the eye gives rise to a retinal image of height h_1. However, as indicated in (b), when the object is brought closer to the eye, a larger retinal image is formed. The dependence of the size of the retinal image on the distance of an object from the eye gives rise to linear perspective. The use of this cue in painting is discussed in some detail in Chapter 4.

further away should they be seen as lying lower in the visual field (i.e., closer to the horizon).

(5) Aerial Perspective: Consider looking toward distant mountains on a fine sunny morning. It is likely that they will have a slightly bluish hue. This is caused by the scattering of light from small particles in the atmosphere (such as water vapor) whose size is smaller than (or approximates) the wavelength of light. When a beam of light impinges on such particles, they radiate the beam in all directions and it is because of this phenomenon that the sky is blue. The process is referred to as Rayleigh scattering (being researched by Lord Rayleigh in around 1870). The degree (intensity) of scattering (I) is dependent on wavelength (λ) and is given by

$$I \propto \frac{1}{\lambda^4}. \tag{2.9}$$

This relation indicates that, as the wavelength decreases, the extent of scattering increases rapidly. Thus, blue light is scattered strongly and is therefore defused throughout the atmosphere. Additionally, larger dust particles within the atmosphere will tend to impede the passage of light, which makes more distant objects less distinct. Consequently, when objects take on a blue hue and appear less distinct, we judge them to lie at a greater distance.[32]

(6) Texture Gradient: A textured surface, be it a repeating pattern or, more generally, variations in intensity or color with a certain dominant length scale, provide another cue to depth. The regular elements in the texture appear largest in the retinal image for parts of the surface closest to the observer and decrease gradually in size for parts of the surface further away. Thus, the texture provides a continuous indication of the relative depth (and hence slant or orientation) of the surface on which it lies [Dember 1960].

(7) Familiar Size: Our familiarity with objects in a scene can be used to help interpret its contents. In particular, the known size of familiar objects can provide a strong indication of the object's distance [Schiffman 1990]. Indeed, as discussed further below, the known size of objects can provide an absolute indication of their distance and hence "calibrate" the depths of features within a scene.

2.6.2   Oculomotor and Parallax Cues

Information related to the physiological control of our eyes—maintenance of a focused retinal image and the alignment of the optical axis of each eye on the point of fixation—is also available to assist in the determination of depth and distance. Moreover, differences between the retinal images seen separated in space

---

[32]It is said that during the lunar expeditions, astronauts had difficulty judging the distance of landscape features. This was as a result of the lack of atmosphere and so the absence of the aerial perspective depth cue.

(i.e., from each of our two eyes) or in time (successive images of a changing scene) provide "parallax" information.

(1) Accommodation: In order to focus on the current fixation point, exertions of the ciliary muscle alter the shape of the lens of the eye and so modify its focal length. The magnitude of the tension applied to these muscles can be used by the brain to provide a cue to the depth in the field of view of the object under scrutiny. Moreover, when an object of interest is in focus on the retina, other features of the scene, closer or further away, will be out of focus. (The depth range that is in-focus is known in optical terms as the "depth of field.") Accommodation effects are likely to be most useful as depth cues for nearby objects (closer than a couple of meters); at greater distances, the lens is effectively fully relaxed. However, it is not clear how accurate accommodation is as a cue to depth. For example, Künnapas [1968] found that distance estimates from accommodation alone were inaccurate, even for stimuli at 1–2 m from the observer.

(2) Convergence (or Simply Vergence): In order that both eyes center their gaze on the same feature of interest, the eyes are swiveled inward so that corresponding points are aligned in the retinal images [Howard and Rogers 1995]. The brain makes use of the muscular forces exerted on the eyes to obtain depth information. Convergence is most effective as a cue to depth for nearby objects.

(3) Binocular Parallax (or Stereopsis): Each of our eyes sees a slightly different view on a 3-D scene. This is because they are situated at different spatial positions, and is clearly demonstrated by alternately closing one eye and then the other while looking straight ahead. By the processes of vergence and accommodation, when looking at an object of interest, this point of fixation is cast in focus onto the fovea in each eye. However, the positions of other more or less distant features of the scene in the retinal images are offset by different amounts in each eye [Howard and Rogers 1995]. This disparity between corresponding points in the two images provides a powerful sensation of depth. Interestingly, the brain is capable of deriving such *stereoscopic* depth information completely independently of monocular cues (i.e., in the absence of any retinal image cues to depth). This phenomenon has been popularized in recent years by random dot stereograms, which are commonly available as posters, postcards etc. Such processing, where features are extracted centrally (within the brain) from the two images, is referred to as "cyclopean."[33] Binocular parallax is discussed further in Section 6.4.

(4) Motion Parallax, Motion Perspective, and the Kinetic Depth Effect: Although stereopsis makes use of disparities in the retinal images originating from the different spatial viewpoints of the two eyes, parallax information is

---

[33]As discussed by Howard and Rogers [1995, chap. 1], the term "cyclopean" has in fact been used in different ways by different authors. Current usage, and our definition in the text, tends to follow that of Julesz [1971]. In fact, Julesz further considered cyclopean perception in the "strong sense" (where binocular features extracted centrally are not evident in the individual retinal images) and in the "weak sense" (where the binocular feature is also present in the individual images).

also available from temporal changes in either the scene or the viewer's position. Coherent changes in the relative motion of different features in a 3-D scene can provide a strong sensation of depth even within a monocular image. Motion parallax arises due to relative motion between the observer and the image scene. The related effect of "motion perspective" refers to gradients in depth conveyed by continuous changes in motion of a large number of features distributed in space (for example, raindrops near the viewer appearing to fall quicker than those further away [Drascic and Milgram 1996]); motion perspective is in some ways the temporal analog of the texture gradient depth cue discussed above. Coherent relative motion of features within the scene (rather than the viewer) gives rise to the "kinetic depth effect" [Dember 1960]; this is often used to enhance the visualization of 3-D data sets on computer graphics monitors in which stereo display is not available, by rotating or oscillating the data set about a vertical axis. As with stereopsis, the kinetic depth effect can provide a sensation of depth and shape in the absence of monocular image cues by, for example, the coherent motion of particular dots in a seemingly random pattern, which in any individual time frame contains no pictorial depth information.

2.6.3 Absolute and Relative Depth Perception

Although most cues, considered in isolation, provide only relative or ordinal depth information, prior knowledge or familiarity on the part of the observer can resolve ambiguities and provide a good approximation to absolute distance.[34] For example, binocular parallax provides information solely on depth relative to the current fixation point. Occlusion also only provides information about relative (ordinal) differences in depth—whether one object is closer to or further away from the viewer than another. However, when combined with the viewer's experience and familiarity with the qualities of the objects in view (size being an important attribute in this regard [Künnapas 1968]), the depth cues available to us can nevertheless provide a good indication of distance in most situations. In fact, it has been shown that assumptions about the size of a familiar object based upon the viewer's experience can dictate the perceived distance of the object [Schiffman 1990].

The different depth cues operate most effectively at different viewing distances (see Figure 2.23). The oculomotor cues of accommodation and convergence are most effective for nearby objects, where greater physical changes are required to maintain convergence and focus. However, their value decreases as viewing distance is increased. Binocular parallax also becomes less sensitive with increasing viewing distance; greater relative distances between objects are required before they are discerned by the viewer.

---

[34]Oculomotor cues can potentially yield absolute distance directly for very near objects (see, for example, Viguier et al. [2001]), but the precise nature of the depth information provided by these cues has yet to be unequivocally determined [Cutting 1997].

2.6.4 Consistency and Conflict Between Depth Cues

Although often considered individually, in natural vision, depth cues rarely operate in isolation and our perception of a 3-D scene is augmented by a combination of information from several sensory sources and by means of both our prior experience and expectation. The relative importance of the different depth cues and the emphasis we place on them depends on the nature of the scene under observation. Display systems up to the present satisfy only a subset of all available depth cues. Accordingly, the consequences and impact of the missing cues depend on the nature of the visualization task for which the system is designed, and consideration of this is important in obtaining a good match between the visual system, the display device, and the application. Thus, the presence or absence of a particular depth cue is not of itself an indication of a "good" or "bad" display.

Nevertheless, as a general rule, it is useful to consider the consistency between the depth information imparted via the different depth cues in a visualization system. In some cases, this can involve depth cues that are not explicitly controlled by the system, but arise as a consequence of the way in which the display device is implemented. An example of this arises in some stereoscopic display systems, where the images are depicted on one or two flat screens relatively close (<1 m) to the viewer. In such situations, the eyes accommodate (focus on) the depth of the screen but converge at different depths according to the binocular parallax information conveyed. (This situation is discussed further in Chapter 6.) Such rivalry between different depth cues can have a range of consequences. For example, it can result in the suppression of the information from the "weaker" cue, cause unstable alternation between the different interpretations of the inconsistent depth information, and even lead to a situation, in which an intermediate depth is perceived [Drascic and Milgram 1996]. In interactive applications, the accuracy with which a task can be performed may be adversely affected in conflict situations. The decoupling of accommodation and convergence mentioned above has been suggested to be a factor in eye fatigue or headaches that have been reported with viewing immersive virtual environments [Mon-Williams et al. 1993, Wann et al. 1995]. However, both the symptoms and the likely causes of so-called "simulator sickness" are varied, and may be due to a number of sensory conflicts (such as an image update lag after user motion) and comfort issues beyond depth cue conflict *per se* [Costello 1997, Peli 1998, Cobb et al. 1999]. The impact of any side effects on the utility of a display device depends upon its intended use. For example, if a system is only used for short periods of time, slight or moderate side effects might be considered tolerable when traded off against the visualization and potential interaction benefits.

Although it is useful to be aware of possible sources of conflict, the utility of a particular 3-D display technique and the gravity of any drawbacks arising from absent depth cues (be they physiological side effects or difficulties in perception) may well, in practice, be best determined through implementing and actually using the system.

In immersive virtual reality (IVR) applications, where a synthetic world—visually, haptically, and perhaps aurally—is presented to participants, it is important to recognize the above situation. Deviations from natural or expected appearances, relationships, and context of objects can impair understanding and perception. However, some applications may involve a synthetic world in which natural behaviors or relationships are altered. The human brain can, with time, adapt to such situations. Clearly, the more severe the disruption of natural behaviors, the longer the time required to adapt. The experiments performed by George Stratton [1896, 1897] provide a classic example. The subject (Stratton) immersed himself in an inverted world by wearing a tube containing lenses that provided an image of his visual environment rotated through 180° (hence the retinal image was in fact vertically "noninverted"). The apparatus provided a visual field of 45° in extent to his right eye only (to avoid difficulties in obtaining corresponding images with two such tubes [Stratton 1896]), with the left eye blindfolded. Stratton performed two such experiments: In the first, he wore the apparatus for a total of $21\frac{1}{2}$ hours over a period of 3 days [Stratton 1896], and in the second (5 months later) for a total of 87 hours over 8 days [Stratton 1897]. In each experiment, the apparatus was worn throughout the day with the eyes being blindfolded at night, thus providing effectively a continual period of inverted vision. Naturally, he was disoriented at the beginning of the experiments as the visual scene (especially as regards to its relationship with his body) seemed incongruous. Stratton reports that early in the second experiment, individual objects began to take on an appearance of normality, but the perception of the spatial relationships between them was still inaccurate[35]:

> *I sat for some time watching a blazing open fire, without seeing that one of the logs had rolled far out on the hearth and was filling the room with smoke. Not until I caught the odor of the smoke, and cast about for the cause, did I notice what had occurred.* [Stratton 1897, p. 345]

However, in time, he gradually adapted to the new visual input and was able to interact more naturally with his environment. The "new" visual input gradually took precedence over the "old" (remembered) visual characteristics, as experience with the combination of the new visual and other sensory inputs accumulated:[36]

> *Movements of the head or of the body, which shifted the field of view, seemed now to be in keeping with the visual changes thus produced; the motion seemed to be toward that side on which objects entered the visual field, and not toward the opposite side, as the pre-experimental representation of the movement would have required.* [Stratton 1897, p. 358]

Schiffman [1990] discusses further experiments by Ivo Kohler in the 1950s and 1960s, in which similar optical headwear was used to provide subjects with left–right reversal only. Subjects could adapt almost completely, given long enough

---

[35]Stratton's comments here are from the first day of his second experiment.
[36]Stratton's comments here are from the sixth day of his second experiment.

exposure to the altered stimuli (sometimes several weeks). Although these experiments are rather extreme examples, they serve to emphasize the key principle of being consistent in the rules followed by objects in the synthetic world and allowing time for adaptation, especially at first exposure. As exposures become more frequent and experience of the new situation is accumulated, adaptation on reexposure becomes easier. Adaptation to video games and the different set of rules and possibilities therein provides a good analogy. However, carryover effects after transition from the real world to the synthetic, and vice versa, may persist.

2.6.5 The Perception of Form

A key theme in the complexity of form perception is that known in the psychology of perception as "figure–ground differentiation." Based on the complex collection of colors, shapes, and shadows that comprise the retinal images of most scenes we see, how are certain parts of this pattern distinguished and considered distinct from the remainder? That is to say, how are individual objects ("figures") perceived as well defined and separate from the rest ("ground")? The figure is normally the object of current attention, both physiologically and mentally. One might suppose that figure–ground differentiation involves the experience of the user—recognition of familiar objects—however, it has also been reported that those whose first visual experience occurs as adults (following cataract removal), display figure–ground differentiation prior to discrimination and identification of figures [von Senden 1960]. This is consistent with emerging evidence suggesting object boundary identification in the visual cortex (see Section 2.4).

Ambiguity in figure–ground relationships is at the heart of many well-known visual illusions, in which the figure and the ground can be alternated. Such illusions are specially constructed and much simpler than the 3-D scenes of typical everyday experience. Nevertheless they illustrate certain principles underlying the perception of figure versus ground. That which is perceived as figure, or foreground, is more easily able to be perceived as a "thing" *per se*, than the background. Of course, in natural situations, we rarely need to interpret a single visual "snapshot." Moreover, other senses such as touch, smell, or hearing can augment the visual information.

2.6.6 The Gestalt Theory of Visual Perception

As discussed above, how and why we perceive certain groups of features in the visual scene as a unified whole, distinct from the remainder of the image, represents a fundamental aspect of our visual perception. For example, a coffee cup, chair, table, or person is each perceived as such, whatever their distance and orientation, in the presence of partial occlusion by other objects and over considerable differences in ambient illumination. A key requirement of a theory of vision is therefore to explain how the 2-D retinal projections received by the eyes are transformed into a stable object-based perception of the contents of the visual scene.

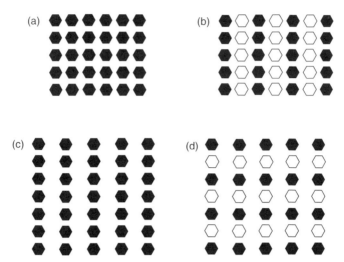

Figure 2.26: Variations in the layout of a 2-D array of dots can serve to illustrate the Gestalt grouping principles of proximity and similarity. When an equally spaced grid of black dots is viewed, no particular organization into rows or columns is perceived—see (a). However, if the color of alternate rows is changed (without changing the horizontal spacing) the dominant perceived organization is one of columns (b) or rows (d), explicable by the principle of similarity. If the horizontal spacing is increased without changing colors, a collection of columns, is perceived (c).

An important step forward in understanding the way in which our visual system distinguishes figure from ground is the *Gestalt* psychological theory of visual perception, originating with the work of Wertheimer, Koffka, and Kohler in Germany in the 1920s [Schiffman 1990, Kandel et al. 2000]. (The German word *Gestalt* translates approximately as "form" or "shape.") A main idea of Gestalt theory was that the final perception could not be explained by a simple cumulative buildup of "atomic" local phenomena, such as edges or direction. Rather, the fundamental units of perception were themselves held to be precepts comprising "non-local" features in the retinal images. This approach was somewhat counter to the prevailing scientific tendency of those times, which was one of reductionism. Just as chemistry and physics were being successfully explained in terms of basic atomic building blocks, so in the psychology of perception, it was anticipated that the final result, or percept, was arrived at by a simple hierarchical progression from local visual features [Schiffman 1990]. The Gestalt school identified a number of "holistic" principles explaining the basis on which different parts of the visual scene were perceived as belonging together [Dember 1960, Schiffman 1990, Tovee 1996]. Some of the Gestalt rules are very briefly summarized below:

- *Similarity.* The brain tends to associate features in the scene whose visual characteristics are similar to one another. This is illustrated in Figure 2.26(b,d), where a uniform grid of dots is perceived as comprising several columns, if the dots are able to be grouped by their color.

- *Physical Proximity.* Those features perceived as being physically close together tend to be associated with one another in the final perception. In Figure 2.26(c), the array of black dots tends to be perceived as a set of vertical columns, as the vertical spacing is smaller than that horizontally.

- *Common Fate.* The brain tends to group together features of the visual scene that are moving in a similar way, especially in the same direction. This reflects the situation of the motion of a solid body.

- *Good Continuation.* Features that seem to follow a straight line or simple curve are perceived as defining a boundary. The identification of object boundaries is an important aspect of figure/ground separation. Figure 2.27 illustrates several examples of contour perception consistent with the principle of good continuation.

- *Closure.* Contours or boundaries that are almost closed tend to be mentally completed by the observer. This is also a useful feature in separating figure from ground, particularly in the presence of partial occlusion or a cluttered visual scene.

A further, overarching Gestalt principle that is often cited is known as "the Law of Praganz." This can be summarized as a general tendency to perceive the simplest interpretation of the retinal images received. It can be seen that the above principles embody this idea. Although illusory contours and contrast had also been described in the late nineteenth century by Mach and Hering [Spillman and Dresp 1995], the Gestalt principles provided a coherent framework in which perceived features in

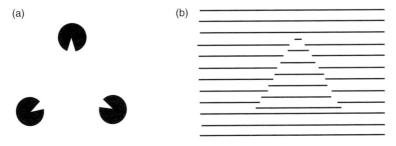

Figure 2.27: In (a) a central triangular figure is clearly visible, despite only a small fraction of its boundary being suggested by the cutouts in the black circles. Interestingly, the white triangle is usually perceived as brighter than the white background, although there is no contrast or color difference between the two. In (b) the discrete discontinuities are interpolated to provide a perception of a triangle (in accordance with the principle of good continuation). [Reproduced by permission from Schiffman, H.R., *Sensation and Perception*, John Wiley (1976); © 1976 John Wiley & Sons.]

visual illusions or diagrams, such as those shown in Figures 2.26 and 2.27, could be explained.

The speed and content of visual perception can also be affected by the viewer's attention, by practice, and by familiarity with scene content. As we noted in Section 2.4, there appear to be at least two major visual "processing streams" within the brain (with interaction and exchange of information occuring between them). The current paradigm of visual processing is that it is performed in a distributed fashion, yet also involving modulatory input from many brain areas beyond the basic visual pathways [Kandel et al. 2000, Kapadia et al. 2000]. The role of "familiarity" of features in the observed scene is sometimes cited as another Gestalt principle [Tovée 1996]: As discussed earlier in this section, familiar objects or patterns (or a collection of features that suggest one) are recognized and perceived as a single entity. This illustrates the role of other brain structures, involving memory and association, in visual perception.

As previously discussed in Section 2.4, the brain areas involved in the basic visual pathways contain increasingly large receptive fields as the pathways progress from the V1 along the dorsal and ventral pathways, responding to larger areas of the visual field. However, evidence is also emerging that global features of the retinal image are extracted at a very early stage in visual processing—in the primary visual cortex. For example, the V1 neurons respond to scene content over regions much larger than that covered by individual receptive fields in a manner consistent with the Gestalt principles of closure and good continuation [Kovacs 1996, Kapadia et al. 2000]. Kovacs and Julesz [1993] also showed that contours were more easily perceived from discrete features if they followed smooth paths, such as lines or circles as opposed to curves containing acute corners or sharp kinks. The perception of such closed contours also enables an early separation of figure from ground [Kovacs 1996] and can improve the visual detectability of features enclosed within the figure area [Kovacs and Julesz 1993, 1994].

2.6.7 The Pulfrich Effect

Several interesting visual effects can be experienced by placing a dark filter (neutral density filter) over one eye. Probably the most well known of these illusions is the "Pulfrich effect," which can be observed with a pendulum swinging from side to side in front of the observer. When viewed with a filter over one eye, the pendulum is perceived as swinging in a horizontal ellipse rather than in a plane. Carl Pulfrich[37] described this effect in 1922. His explanation was based upon the fact that the visual system responds more rapidly to brighter input [Walker 1978]. *"Thus the signals about the object's position are relayed to the visual cortex with a temporal offset"* [Howard and Rogers 2002]. Attenuating the brightness of the input to one eye means that this eye provides a slightly delayed

---

[37]Pulfrich became blind in one eye in 1905—some 17 years before his publication on the effect that is named after him and which he could no longer observe. He gave credit to F. Fertsch for the discovery of its cause and died in a boating accident in the Baltic in 1927 [Howard and Rogers 2002].

view of, for example, the pendulum in comparison to the other (also see [MacDonald 1978]). The corresponding disparity in the views in each eye is interpreted as indicating depth, and the pendulum appears closer when swinging in one direction and further away when moving in the other.

Using a single filter can provide enhanced sensations of depth in more complex scenarios, such as when watching television. Here a strong sensation of depth is readily associated with moving objects (see Investigations Question 7 at the end of this chapter).

As discussed by Howard and Rogers [2002] (who provide an excellent discussion on the Pulfrich effect), several other explanations of this effect have been proposed. One of these is built on saccadic suppression; the duration of this suppression (which accompanies eye movements) relates to the level of illumination. Consequently, when a filter is worn, the suppression periods of the two eyes may be asymmetrical [Howard and Rogers 2002]. A second hypothesis is founded on the possibility that "... *the visual system monitors the temporal difference in the stimulation of corresponding points on the two retinas*" [Howard and Rogers 2002].

2.7 TEMPORAL RESOLUTION: FUSION AND MOTION

Virtually all electronic display devices repeatedly activate their image elements many times per second. The physical process underlying the luminous display is usually transient, and so the activation must be repeated or "refreshed" sufficiently quickly so that the viewer perceives the image as being continually present or "fused." Common appliances such as television sets, computer monitors, and fluorescent lights present a rapidly modulating visual stimulus that is perceived as being a steady source. However, if the image or stimulus is not refreshed quickly enough, flicker is perceived. This perceptible, regular modulation in image intensity can lead to discomfort, particularly when a display is viewed for extended periods of time.

The temporal refresh frequency at which flicker disappears is known as the "flicker fusion frequency," or "critical flicker frequency" (CFF) and represents an important parameter of electronic display systems. However, the CFF varies from individual to individual and depends on many factors, including aspects of both the visual stimulus and the visual system. In general, the CFF increases with increasing source luminance; more intense stimuli require higher refresh frequencies so as to be fused. Conversely, flicker tends to be less noticeable in displays viewed at low intensities under dim ambient lighting. The functional form of this relation has been empirically determined to follow the Ferry–Porter Law:

$$CFF = a + b \log(L), \tag{2.10}$$

where L is the source luminance and a and b are constants. This relationship has been shown to hold over a wide range of image intensities.

Many variations in the CFF arise due to the different temporal response characteristics of the rod and cone photoreceptors, the associated M and P systems, and their dependence on the nature of the visual environment. One important aspect is that, due to the respective distributions of the rods and cones over the retina, the visual system is more sensitive to temporal changes in the peripheral vision. Thus, flicker can be more easily perceived in a larger retinal image. In addition, as discussed by Dember [1960], the duty cycle of the time-varying stimulus can affect the CFF; at low intensities, the visual system is most sensitive to variations with equal light and dark periods (a duty cycle of 50%), whereas at high intensities, the CFF tends to decrease with increasing duty cycles.

In practical terms, an electronically displayed image can often be perceived as being continually present at refresh frequencies above approximately 15 Hz, but with noticeable flicker. Such images are difficult to look at for extended periods of time. As the refresh frequency is increased, perceptible flicker is reduced. Values of 25–30 Hz are sometimes quoted as sufficient,[38] and indeed the perceived flicker is considerably less than at 15 Hz. However, residual (or even subliminal) flicker can still cause viewing discomfort or headaches, and so for this reason commercial computer monitors currently use refresh frequencies in the range 60–120 Hz.

The "update frequency" required for a dynamic image sequence to appear to change smoothly is approximately 10 Hz. In an electronic display depicting a moving scene, it is therefore not necessary to alter the displayed image frame at each refresh. For example, if a display system operates with a refresh frequency of 30 Hz, the image space only needs to be changed (at least in principle) every third refresh cycle.

2.8   DISCUSSION

As we indicated at the outset of this chapter, our purpose in preparing it was not to provide a comprehensive review of our sense of sight, but rather to provide a brief overview and framework upon which readers new to this subject matter can build. We have especially sought to emphasize concepts that will be important to our subsequent discussions. The eye has been introduced as a transducer possessing some astonishing properties, and the visual system when considered as a whole operates in a remarkable way, especially as the image created on the retina is by no means a perfect rendition of the scene under observation. Light is converted into neuronal impulses by photoreceptor cells, and preliminary retinal processing of these signals to detect local changes in contrast helps the eye to function over a very

---

[38]These considerations are particularly relevant to developmental 3-D display systems, in which a high number of image elements often need to be addressed during each refresh cycle (to convey visual information relating to the third dimension). This process often leads to the use of refresh frequencies lower than those employed in standard 2-D display devices. A number of 3-D display techniques and associated bandwidth issues are discussed in Chapter 8.

considerable range in ambient light conditions. High spatial acuity and color information (in "daylight" conditions) is sensed almost exclusively from the small fovea
region on which the incoming light is most sharply focused. Continual eye motion
serves to explore the visual scene and maintain photoreceptor signaling.

Our remarkable sense of sight cannot be understood by consideration of the eye in
isolation, for the eye is simply a component (albeit a highly complex component)
within a highly integrated imaging system. It is for this reason that we have provided
a brief description of some aspects of the far less well-understood processing of the
image data after it passes from the eye. The human brain is extremely adept at
processing and interpreting complex visual environments. Although our knowledge
of how the brain processes the inverted images formed on each retina to obtain
consciously recognized objects at specific locations in an external coordinate
space remains very much incomplete, evidence to date suggests that the central
processing of the retinal images can be considered to have both hierarchical and parallel aspects. Different processing streams within the visual channel have been identified; each is specialized in extracting certain information from the retinal input. In
general, as the signals are propagated further along these pathways, more complex
information is extracted and processed to determine key features such as depth,
shape, and form. There is also substantial cross-talk between these pathways at
various points in the hierarchy, and this "bottom-up" processing is combined with
"top-down" input including memory, context, and attention, to determine the final
perception. Certainly, our understanding of the complex interplay between depth
cues—at what point in the perceptual pathway their information is combined and
interpreted—remains incomplete (for discussion, see, for example, Landy et al.
[1995], Hillis et al. [2002], and Volbracht et al. [1998]).

The nature and limitations of our perception of form and depth should be pivotal
considerations in the development of creative 3-D display systems. Much work has
been performed to attempt to quantify these mechanisms—often in isolation from
each other to minimize confounding effects. However, in most day-to-day situations,
the various depth cues are available concurrently and the prior experience of the
observer is continually brought to bear. In general, distances are estimated more
accurately as more cues to depth are available. Our remarkable ability to ascertain
absolute and relative distances and discern objects has evolved in this situation
of redundancy or duplication of information, with different cues most effective at
different distances. This ability has implications for creative display systems in
which only a subset of the depth cues are satisfied consistently.

2.9 INVESTIGATIONS

1. Estimate the density of pixels on a conventional high-resolution computer
   display. Compare this to the density of photoreceptors in the *fovea*.
2. Estimate the size of the retinal image cast by a single pixel depicted on a
   conventional computer display situated at a typical viewing distance.

3. Consider the retinal images cast by the screen of your computer monitor and your television when each is viewed at a typical distance. Do these images extend beyond the dimensions of the *fovea*?

4. As we have seen, scattering gives rise to the blue color of the sky. However, clouds remain white (or gray). Why is this the case?

5. By means of observation, estimate the maximum distance at which overhead power or phone cables may be discerned against (a) a blue skyline and (b) a cloudy background. In each case, estimate the size of the retinal image. How does the size of this image compare with the dimensions of the eye's photo-receptors?

6. Pointillists such as Georges Seurat employed paint daubs (which, when viewed at a distance, blend to form an overall coloration), rather than the more conventional mixing of pigments. Identify one advantage of the Pointillist technique.

7. Try watching television holding a dark filter over one eye. Do you get a greater impression of depth? Which cues seem to be particularly strong? How does the impression depend on the displayed scene content?

8. Helmholtz, writing in connection with the blind-spot indicates: "*The blind spot is so large that it might prevent our seeing eleven full moons if placed side by side, or a man's face at a distance of only six or seven feet. Mariotte, who discovered the phenomenon, amused Charles II and his courtiers by showing them how they might see each other with their heads cut off.*" [Warren and Warren (eds.) 1968]. With reference to the position of the retinal image relative to the physical image, experiment with this technique (practice is usually required).

3 The Perception of Our Space: Haptics

Alone, alone, all all alone,
Alone on a wide wide sea!
And never a saint took pity on
My soul in agony.

3.1 INTRODUCTION

Aristotle is generally recognized as being the first to classify our five senses, and these are commonly referred to as touch, taste, sight, smell, and hearing. However, as K.M. Dallenbach writes, *"This classification is a heritage from the past, impressed upon us by the doctrine of the five senses which has come down to us from antiquity. It has long*

Creative 3-D Display and Interaction Interfaces: A Trans-Disciplinary Approach, by Barry G. Blundell and Adam J. Schwarz

been known, however, that 'touch,' the so-called fifth sense, is a congeries of unrelated sensory qualities . . ." [Boring et al. 1935]. He goes on to add:

> *The sensory qualities popularly ascribed to touch derive, as we shall see, from a variety of organs and tissues: skin, muscles, tendons, ligaments, bones, joints and other internal organs. Since the structures they involve are so widely spread throughout the body (soma), they are fittingly called somesthetic sensations.*

As indicated, somesthetic (or somatosensory) perception relates to sensations "of the body,"—being derived from a multitude of internal sensory receptors and from the great network lying within the structure comprising the skin. In this latter case, the receptors can operate across a broad spectrum of conditions, detecting stimuli ranging from those perceived as being excruciatingly painful to those that generate a sense of exquisite pleasure. Unlike the senses of sight, smell, and hearing, we cannot readily "turn off" the somatosensory channels, and therefore, it is rather difficult to instinctively appreciate the important roles they play as we occupy, and interact with, our spatial surroundings.

The importance of incorporating various types of somatosensory feedback has long been recognized in those areas where the human operator forms an integral part of an electromechanical control loop (for example, in avionics and telerobotics). Consider an operator manipulating a physically remote robotic arm to perform actions upon a delicate object. Without appropriate feedback, the operator could easily cause damage through the application of needlessly large forces, and similarly an aircraft pilot could readily overstrain vital control surfaces. In fact, in systems where there is no mechanical linkage via which "real" forces may be relayed to the operator, the sense of force is often created artificially by electromechanical systems.

There is growing interest in the development of interaction devices that can provide various types of somatosensory information within the context of the human–computer interaction process. Despite the difficulties associated with the implementation of such tools, various systems are commercially available (see Chapter 7 and also Burdea [1996]). These interaction paradigms generally support, to a limited extent, the sensations of force and/or of touch, which are commonly referred to as sources of "haptic feedback." The word "haptics" is derived from the Greek *haptesthai*, which means "to come into contact with," but it is often used more broadly in the field of interactive visualization to include "motor" actions in reaching for and grasping objects, as well as in sensing their inertia, weight, and rigidity.

Unlike our other senses, the haptic channel is bidirectional and permits output to our surroundings, as well as the converse. In the case of conventional human–computer interaction, however, it is used almost exclusively for output as our motor systems interact with mouse, keyboard, or touch screen. In these examples, haptic sensation to the user is obtained via the passive physical properties of the devices themselves, and is not actively controlled by the system. As creative display systems become more widely used, it is likely that the benefits that may ultimately be derived from properly supporting an active, bidirectional haptic channel across a variety of applications will be properly understood, and so better exploited.

Making use of the bidirectional capabilities of the haptic channel within the context of the computer interface is especially demanding since the hardware (such as special forms of glove or exoskeleton) must be in physical contact with the user. Naturally, this can restrict freedom of movement and potentially cause discomfort and strain during prolonged periods of usage. Furthermore, when the computer system is empowered to provide force feedback to skeletal joints, great caution has to be exercised to prevent incorrect operation (and unforeseen bugs!) causing physical damage to the user.

To imagine that some form of body suit could provide a fully immersive haptic experience mimicking real-world sensation is without scientific basis; our haptic systems are far too complex. However, some of the real benefits that may be derived from more limited and technically achievable interfaces are becoming increasingly evident.

In order to lay the foundations for our subsequent discussions, we present in this chapter preliminary information concerning the multifaceted nature of the complex human somatosensory processes, although we will generally restrict this discussion to those aspects that fall within the haptic classification. In the next section, we briefly consider the general facets of somatosensory perception, and in the following two sections we discuss our senses of touch (or more precisely cutaneous sensitivity) and proprioception. As with the previous chapter, we seek to provide the reader with an overview of aspects of this area of research activity, together with references that will be particularly useful in further study. Additionally, we recommend chapters of the extensive text edited by Boff et al. [1986] and the book edited by David Roberts [2002]. Also, Burdea [1996] provides a wealth of highly interesting discussion on haptics in general and haptic interaction devices in particular.

We hope that this brief chapter will at least begin to convey to those new to this fascinating subject a sense of the considerable challenges to be met if we are to effectively interface our haptic channels with the digital world.

3.2 SOMATOSENSORY RECEPTORS

We can assign to somatosensory sensation five general modalities. These may be summarized as follows:

- The sense of touch (cutaneous sensitivity)
- The sense of posture (position) and of the motion of the limbs (prioperception)
- The sense of the force experienced by the body and limbs—either created externally and/or internally (prioperception)
- The sense of pain (nocioception)
- The sense of temperature relative to the skin

As with the other sensory systems, somatosensory sensation begins with a range of specialized transducers located within, or close to, the surface of the body. These sensory receptors, whose overall purpose is to provide information to the central nervous system (CNS), may loosely be classified according to the type of energy to which they are sensitive. When viewed in this way, we can identify four categories: "mechanoreceptors," "thermoreceptors," "chemoreceptors," and "nocioceptors." Although grouping these receptors according to functionality offers a tidy solution, in practice, a receptor may respond to more than one type of stimuli—"some mechanoreceptive nerve fibres exhibit a modulation of firing rate with temperature change" [Sherrick and Cholewiak in Boff et al. 1986]. Consequently, it should be noted that grouping receptors according to their functionality must be viewed with caution. In their excellent chapter on cutaneous sensitivity, Carl Sherrick and Roger Cholewiak (cited above) describe the "Weber Illusion" (originating from the early nineteenth century) in which a coin (warm or cold) is placed on the forehead of the participant, when lying down. Oddly, the colder but otherwise identical coins are perceived as being heavier, which could be taken as an indication of the presence of a receptor sensitive to both temperature and pressure. However, the authors also review more recent similar trials, as reported in 1978/79 by J.C. Stevens, in which the experiment was repeated on various parts of the body. The earlier findings of Weber were confirmed, and moreover, it was found that in case of the forearm, cold and warm objects appeared to be heavier than neutral ones (i.e., those at local body temperature).

From the perspective of the human–computer interface, it is the mecanoreceptor and thermoreceptor types that are of particular importance, and so we will confine our discussion to these, and set to one side the chemoreceptor and nocioceptor.

1. *Mechanoreceptors:* These play an important role in both cutaneous sensitivity and proprioception. As their name implies, they respond to mechanical stimuli such as force, tension, and pressure. Different regions of the body are more sensitive to pressure than others, and Schiffman [1976], drawing on the work of Verillo, indicates that under certain circumstances, a skin displacement of less than 0.001 mm can be sensed. The face (and particularly the lips) is noted as being the most pressure-sensitive part of the body, and the tip of the tongue has the highest acuity. However, although one part of the body may be especially sensitive to one particular form of stimulus, it may be less sensitive to another. For example, although the lips exhibit great sensitivity to pressure, they are considerably less responsive than the fingers to vibrotactile stimulation [Boff et al. 1986, chap. 12].

2. *Thermoreceptors:* These respond to differences between the temperature of the air or objects touched and the skin temperature.[1] As with our sensitivity to mechanical stimuli, so our sensitivity to thermal stimuli varies for different parts of the body. The "Specific Receptor Theory," attributed to Max von Frey (1852–1932) suggests the presence of two receptor types: warm and cool. Each has a different

---

[1]This is not uniform across the body; clothed areas are around 35°C, the hand 33°C, and the ear lobe where blood flow is sluggish can be significantly lower (20°C) [Schiffman 1976].

temperature sensitivity profile, and the combination of the inputs from these two receptor populations provides the CNS with an indication of temperature relative to the local body temperature. An alternative theory (the "Vascular Theory") suggests the use of a single mechanism in which "... *thermal sensations occur from the constriction and dilation of the smooth muscle walls of the blood vessels of the skin ... The direct responses of smooth muscle tissue producing size changes of the vessels initiate activity in the sensory nerve endings*" [Schiffman 1976].

In the next two subsections, we briefly discuss some issues relating to the modalities of touch and proprioception.

3.3 CUTANEOUS SENSITIVITY

> *In science, by a fiction as remarkable as any to be found in law,*
> *What has once been published, even though it be in the Russian*
> *Language, is spoken of as* known, *and it is too often forgotten*
> *That the rediscovery in the library may be a more difficult*
> *And uncertain process than the first discovery in the laboratory.*[2]

Skin, that complex covering for both external and internal surfaces of the body, enables us to sense physical stimuli. This communication function is made possible because of the multitude of sensory receptors located within the structure of the skin. The area of the skin of an average adult is $1.8\ m^2$ (it is our largest organ), and as indicated by Carl Sherrick and Roger Cholewiak in Boff et al. [1986], this is more than three orders of magnitude greater than the combined area of the retinas. Each eye provides output to the CNS via some 10^6 axons, whereas (despite the far greater surface area) the sensory receptors converge on the CNS via some 1.1×10^6 axons. Although these figures do not directly relate to the number of sensory receptors, they are indicative and provide a suggestion that the density of sensory receptors within the skin is not as great as we first may think, based on experience derived from our bodies. The receptors are not uniformly distributed, and their density varies with location and factors such as age.

Each receptor type is sensitive to input over a certain area, known as its "receptive field." The "two-point threshold" measurement provides an indication of spatial resolution and corresponds, for example, to the minimum distance by which two physical points generating a pressure on the skin must be separated so that they are perceived as two distinct entities (see Figure 3.1). This measurement varies greatly with location; on the arms and legs, it is around 40 mm, whereas the index finger provides a far greater spatial resolution of approximately 3 mm [Gleitman 1981].

The firing of different receptors can depend on how long the stimulus has been active; some receptors rapidly adapt to the presence of the stimulus and so fire only for a short time. These more sensitively convey information on changes in the stimulus. The receptors are classified as fast adapting (FA) and slowly adapting (SA), where the

---

[2]Attributed to Lord Rayleigh, 1884. Quoted from Boff et al. [1986, preface].

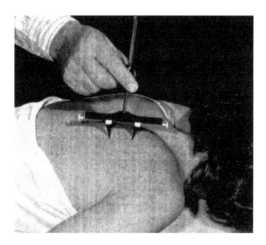

Figure 3.1: Determination of the two-point threshold by means of an Aesthesiometer. Consider two-points lightly in contact with the skin. The two-point threshold corresponds to the minimum separation required in order that they be resolved as two (rather than as one) different stimuli. This varies with location on the body. [Reproduced from Munn *Psychology: The Fundamentals of Human Adjustment*, 5th edn., Houghton Mifflin Company (1996).]

adaptation rate denotes the decrease in the rate of firing following a sustained stimulus. Both of these classifications have subclasses I and II (see Stanley Bolanowski writing in Roberts [2002] for an extremely lucid and interesting discussion).

Sherrick and Cholewiak writing in Boff et al. [1986], draw on the work of Hill [1967] to describe research indicating that when the sensory system experiences a mechanical impulse stimulus, it performs temporal summation (i.e., integration over time). Trials are reported as being carried out on the finger and involved the application of a series of short duration pulses (at a rate of 2 pulses per second). The pulse amplitude was gradually increased until the pulse sequence could be perceived. The duration (t) of the impulses (measured in milliseconds) was varied (whilst retaining their temporal separation), and in each case, the minimum signal amplitude (A) required for stimulus perception was measured. The results obtained satisfied the relation:

$$A = \frac{2}{\left[1 - \exp\left[\frac{-t}{1.5}\right]\right]}. \qquad (3.1)$$

This equation represents an integrator with a time constant of 1.5 ms. For pulse durations greater than 10 ms, the threshold amplitude remained constant ($2\ \mu m$). However, for pulses of shorter duration (the researchers used pulses as short as $350\ \mu s$), larger amplitude stimuli were required. Such basic research concerning the characteristics of the sensory systems is clearly of fundamental importance to the exploitation of the haptic channel within the context of the human–computer interface.

Most of the exterior body is covered by "hairy skin" (this does not mean that the skin is necessarily obviously hairy, nor that it has associated with it a single form of hair). A second, simpler skin type is the *mucous membrane*, which is found internally. *Mucocutaneous* skin lies at the interface between the "hairy" and *mucous membrane* forms of skin (e.g., the lips). *Glabrous* skin is found on the palms, soles of the feet, and parts of the fingers. This skin is "*thick, richly innervated, and deeply furrowed, thus providing protection, high sensitivity, and good gripping qualities to the manipulative surfaces of the body*" [Scharf 1975]. Glabrous and hairy skin (which are of interest to us) comprise various structures. These are generally divided as lying within the *epidermis* (outer layers) or *dermis* (inner layers).

The sense of touch is mediated by various types of mechanoreceptors lying within the skin's structure—specifically within the *dermis* (see Figure 3.2). There are four main types of mecanoreceptor: *Meissner's corpuscles, Merkel's disks, Pacinian corpuscles*, and *Ruffini endings*. In hairy skin, an additional receptor located at the hair root is present and responds to hair displacement. Free nerve endings respond to heat and painful stimuli. (See Burdea [1996], Coren et al. [1994], and Roberts [2002] who provide interesting and important detail.)

Several properties of the four primary touch mechanoreceptors are summarized in Table 3.1. The superficial Meissner's corpuscle and Merkel disc receptors both

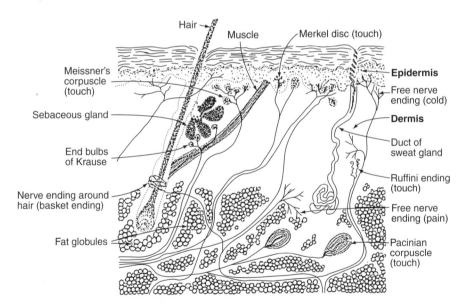

Figure 3.2: Illustration of a cross section of hairy skin showing various types of mechanoreceptors lying within the skin's structure. Here we find *Meissner's corpuscles, Merkel's disc, Pacinian corpuscles*, and *Ruffini endings*. An additional receptor is found in hairy skin and is located in the region of the hair root. This responds to hair displacement. Free nerve endings respond to heat and painful stimuli. [Reproduced by permission from Coren, S., Ward, L.M., and Enns, J.T., *Sensation and Perception*, 4th edn., Harcourt Brace & Company (1994); © 1994 John Wiley & Sons.]

have small receptive fields and are thus able to distinguish between sensations with a high spatial resolution—in contrast to the Ruffini endings and Pacinian corpuscles. Reviewing a number of sources on the physiology of touch, Kaczmarek et al. [1991] report a median receptive field area of approximately 13 mm^2 and 11 mm^2, respectively, for the former two receptor types, in contrast to 59 mm^2 and 101 mm^2 for the latter two. Moreover, the temporal properties of these receptors also differ. The Meissner's corpuscles are "rapidly adapting"; they signal changes, and their firing rapidly dies away at sustained input. Conversely, the Merkel disc receptors are SA and signal sustained pressure. The Pacinian corpuscle is physiologically similar to the Meissner's corpuscle and likewise is rapidly adapting, responding to rapid indentation but not sustained pressure [Kaczmarek et al. 1991, Kandel et al. 2000]. This corpuscle is responsible for the detection of vibration and "*is a large ovoid corpuscle, having onion-skin coverings, which projects to the spinal cord and possibly the brain, via a single, direct fiber*" [Katz 1989]. Ruffini endings are slowly adapting, and, in particular, sense any stretching of the skin. Blake et al. [1997], in experiments designed to distinguish the contributions of slowly and rapidly adapting signal pathways, report that Merkel disks appear to convey most of the information relating to the perceived roughness of a surface.

Peter Cahusac writing in Roberts [2002] provides an excellent discussion on the perception of touch and distinguishes between "active" and "passive." He illustrates his description by a well-known example that draws on our everyday experience of testing fruit for ripeness, which is one of numerous situations where we place greater reliance on touch than on sight. Through the application of gentle pressure (much to the vendor's dismay), we can quickly assess ripeness—a process that is made easier by holding the fruit in the hand. As he writes, "*Our hands are most suitably adapted to perform active touch as they work together to grasp, palpate, prod, press rub and heft the tested object.*" When next testing for ripeness, try the less accurate passive touch approach, and simply prod the fruit without picking it up. For additional reading, see, for example, Gibson [1962] and Gordon [1977].

TABLE 3.1: Some properties of touch mechanoreceptors.

Receptor Type	Stimulus Frequency in Hz	Adaptation Rate Code[a]	Receptive Field
Merkel disks	0–10	SA-I	Small Well defined
Ruffini endings	0–10	SA-II	Large Indistinct
Meissner corpuscles	20–50	RA-I	Small Well defined
Pacinian corpuscles	100–300	RA-II	Large Indistinct

[a]SA = slowly adapting, RA = rapidly adapting.
Source: Adapted by permission from Burdea, G. C., *Force and Touch Feedback for Virtual Reality*, John Wiley (1966); © 1966 John Wiley & Sons.

3.4 PROPRIOCEPTION

> The centipede was happy quite,
> Until a toad in fun,
> Said, 'Pray, which leg goes after which
> When you begin to run?'
> That worked her mind to such a pitch,
> She lay distracted in a ditch,
> Considering how to run.[3]

Let us pause for a moment and consider three simple examples that involve movement in, and interaction with, the three-dimensional (3-D) space within which we live. Firstly, consider the pleasurable occupation of drinking a chilled and crisp New Zealand Chardonnay at dinner. How often do we find ourselves, as a consequence of being distracted by delightful conversation, inadvertently pouring this sacred liquid into our ear, or shattering the glass between our fingers because of the unsensed application of a mighty and therefore inappropriate force to the fine vessel? Alternatively, consider navigating a staircase while immersed in a textbook. Given the complexity of this process (and here we refer to the movement rather than the reading) in terms of the number of joints that we must accurately move, as well as our constant change of posture, it is impressive that stairwells are not littered with those who have failed miserably in this challenging task. Finally, consider the seemingly straightforward task of maintaining balance when standing or walking? Under analysis, this process is itself a remarkable feat (when considered in the context of navigating a staircase while reading a book and sipping wine, it becomes almost miraculous). Given the small contact area that our feet make with the ground, and the location of our center of gravity (which is rather high), it is surprising that we can even stand, let alone balance on one foot if necessary, without apparent effort. Although the inner ears provide the source of information that is pivotal to the balancing process (more specifically, the *vestibular sacs* and *semicircular canals*), this information is based on the orientation (i.e., coordinate system) of the ear, and hence the head, with respect to the physical environment. This is different from the coordinate system that we could assign to the body. In order to achieve balance, the CNS must be able to map between the two (and the parameters used in this mapping will continually change as we shift in our posture). Consequently, the CNS must carefully measure flexing of the neck—a background task that is carried out without conscious thought. No doubt if safety officials fully appreciated the mental complexity of such a task we would be denied the right to use mobile phones while standing!

To enable us to interact effectively with our surroundings, and undertake the types of task mentioned above, it is necessary for the CNS to have an accurate knowledge of the position and orientation of our limbs within 3-D space, together with relevant information concerning their motion and the forces that we exert (or that are exerted on us) during any interaction process. In this context, the terms

---

[3]Author unknown. From Munn [1966].

"Proprioception" (*proprius* from the Latin "own") and "Kinesthesis" (*kine* from the Greek "movement") are both commonly employed. For our discussions, we will adopt the former term, within the context employed by Osgood [1953], who writes:

> *The term 'kinesthesis' which refers quite literally to sensations of movement introspectively determined, has been largely replaced by the term 'proprioception,' which emphasizes receptor and sensory nerve action neuro-physiologically determined – this is part of a general shift in psychological orientation during the past half century.*

In an excellent introduction to this subject, Ian Lyon [Roberts 2002, chap. 20] refers to the work of Charles Sherrington who in a publication that appeared in 1900 defined *proprioceptors* as "*receptors sensitive to stimuli that are 'traceable to the actions of the organism itself'*" [Sherrington 1900]. As Lyon indicates, our receptors may be considered as proprioceptors because when we move a limb, we may (for example) observe the movement visually, it may be audible, and we may sense the stretching of our skin. However, it is usual to limit proprioceptors to those receptors in our joints, muscles, and tendons that provide information to the CNS concerning the position and movement of our joints. Also included within this classification are sensors within the skin that contribute to our ability to correctly sense our spatial position [Roberts 2002].

We can, of course, sense the position of our limbs without any visual cues: close your eyes and attempt to bring together a finger from each hand. Now repeat the process under more difficult circumstances; start with your hands behind your back. Such tasks are easily accomplished, and under normal circumstances, we are entirely unaware of the considerable processing necessary to determine and maintain posture and, furthermore, to effect controlled changes to it. However, although visual sense is generally not considered as a form of proprioceptor, sight does generally augment aspects of the proprioception process.

Proprioception is multifaceted and an intriguing area of multidisciplinary study (see Figure 3.3). Nonetheless, despite an extensive period of major research activity, many core issues remain unanswered. Francis Clark and Kenneth Horch [Boff et al. 1986] begin an interesting and extensive discussion on kinesthesia in the following way:

> *Our current understanding of the mechanisms underlying the kinesthetic sense differs remarkably little from the views that prevailed at the turn of the century, although the intervening years saw these early ideas systematically challenged, discarded, re-explored and finally reinstated.*

Although this may be an oversimplification, it does loosely indicate the way that ideas have evolved. During the nineteenth century, the concept of a "sense of innervation" was popular. In brief, this hypothesis supposed that control was achieved not by sensory receptors monitoring position and movement, but by "*a sensory experience resulting from some internal monitoring of the impulses originating in the brain and destined for the muscles*" (Clark and Horch writing in Boff et al. [1986]). Hermann Helmholtz appears to have favored this concept and

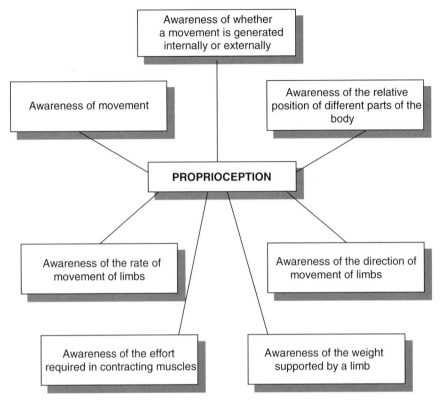

Figure 3.3: Proprioception is multifaceted. Some aspects of proprioception are indicated here, although this is certainly not exhaustive. The reader is left to consider other facets that may be included in this illustration. (Diagram © 2005 Q.S. Blundell.)

made an extremely plausible case in connection with conscious eye movement, in which he saw no requirement for sensors able to monitor such movement. In connection with the concept of a "sense of innervation," Charles Sherrington [1900] quotes from, and comments on, Helmholtz's work[4] as follows:[5]

> *A phenomenon cited by Helmholtz is the following: "When the right external rictus is paralysed, the right eye can no longer rotate to the right. So long as it turns only to the nasal side it makes regular movements, and the correct position of objects is perceived. When it should be rotated outwardly, however, it stays still in the primary position, and*

[4]Helmholtz's work is well worth perusal, generally, and especially in the context of his discussion on vision and "innervation." Richard and Roslyn Warren [1968] provide an English translation of some of his writings (other English translations are accessible via the Internet).

[5]Sherrington adds the following footnote: "*I quote from W. James' translation in 'Principles of Psychology', vol, ii, p. 507, which is from the 1st edition of the 'Physiol.Optik.' The passage remains unaltered in the 2nd edition, p. 744 (1896), which is a part of the volume lying beyond that revised by Helmholtz before his last illness.*"

the objects appear flying to the right, although the position of eye and retinal image are unaltered." The left sound eye is covered. "In such a case," Helmholtz goes on to say, "the exertion of the will is followed neither by actual movement of the eye, nor by contraction of the muscle in question, nor even by increased tension in it. The act of will produced absolutely no effect beyond the nervous system, and yet we judge of the direction of the line of vision, as if the will had exercised its normal effects. We believe it to have moved to the right, and, since the retinal image is unchanged, we attribute to the object the same movement we have erroneously ascribed to the eye. . . These phenomena leave no room for doubt that we only judge the direction of the line of sight by the effort of will with which we strive to change the position of our eyes . . . We feel, then what impulse of the will, and how strong a one, we apply to turn the eye into a given position."

Despite the plausibility of Helmholtz's case, enthusiasm for the innervation approach declined after the discovery of the abundance of sensory receptors in joints, muscles, and beneath the skin, together with a growing awareness of the importance of sensory information for effective motor control. Sherrington (building on the earlier work of Charles Bell in the first half of the nineteenth century) seems to have been instrumental in the move away from the concept of a sense of innervation, and in the work which we quote above, he includes two comments that are of particular relevance to us:

1. *In Connection with the Views of Helmholtz*: *"But the interpretation neglects . . . the movement of the covered eyeball as a source of peripheral sensation."*
2. *As a General Comment*: *"Our conclusion is therefore that "sensation of innervation" – provided that memory revivals of muscular sensations of peripheral origin be not included under that term – remains unproven."*

In this excellent publication, he proposed that:

We may treat of the muscular sense as of other senses. The parts of its apparatus may be distinguished as peripheral, internuncial, and central; among its phenomena may be distinguished centripetal impulses, sense impressions sense perceptions, judgements and ideas.

This question of the relative contribution made by the various forms of proprioceptors to the range of proprioception activities has given rise to a great deal of research activity, and as is often the case in nature, the answers are seldom simple. Some decades after Sherrington's original hypothesis, research results seemed to indicate that sensory receptors located in joints played the dominant role. Researchers Rose and Mountcastle writing in the 1959 *Handbook of Physiology* are quoted in Boff et al. [1986] as follows:

It is now apparent that the sense of position or of movements of the joints depends solely on the appropriate receptors in the joints themselves. There is no need to involve a mysterious muscle sense to explain kinesthetic sensations and to do so runs contrary to all the known facts concerning the muscle stretch receptors.

However, it was eventually found that although joints are equipped with ample receptors, they do not always seem to be spatially tuned to provide feedback on joint position across the entire range of movement. Experimentation with a cat's knee joint showed that most receptors responded only at extreme flexion of the joint and did not encode movement across the entire range of joint position [Burgess and Clark 1969]. Furthermore, after being equipped with artificial joints, patients often found no major loss in proprioception, thus demonstrating that sensory receptors in the joints are not a requirement for sensory feedback. Today, we have returned to the remarkably astute views of Sherrington since muscle receptors have (in some experiments) been shown to provide considerable information needed for prioperception,[6] although the relative importance of feedback from different receptor types is likely to vary between joints (see Ian Lyon writing in [Roberts 2002, chap. 20]). The degree to which feedback from sensory receptors is augmented with any sense of innervation is still not known.

It may seem odd that this debate has continued for so long, but the issues involved and the tasks facing researchers in this area have been by no means easily overcome. It is recommended that the interested reader consult either Boff et al. [1986, chap. 13] and references cited therein or [Roberts 2002, chap. 20] for a more detailed account of this fascinating history.

Muscles contain two types of receptor: "muscle spindles" and "Golgi organs." The former are situated in parallel with the main muscle fibers, and signal changes in length and the rate of change of length[7] (they in fact have both sensory and motor function, and this duality of purpose has complicated research efforts). Golgi organs are arranged in series with the main muscle fibers, and so signal tension in the muscle. (See Clark and Horch in Boff et al. [1986 chap. 13] for a comprehensive discussion on these types of receptor; also see Howard and Templeton [1966] who provide an interesting discussion on receptor composition together with overviews of trials conducted in connection with aspects of human proprioception.)

3.5 SOMATOSENSORY AND MOTOR PATHWAYS

There appear to be two major somatosensory pathways carrying sensory information from the receptors in peripheral parts of the body into the brain, where the responses of the different receptors are combined and the sensation is perceived. As indicated (Figure 3.4(a)), one of these is thought to be responsible for tactile sensation and limb proprioception (the *dorsal column pathway*), while the other transmits painful and thermal stimuli (the *anterolateral pathway*) [Kandel et al. 2000]. Having reached the brain, each of these pathways has a juncture in the thalamus, with subsequent projections into the *somatosensory cortex*.

---

[6]Australian Ian McCloskey was driven to having a tendon in his foot cut. When this was pulled, he experienced a sensation of the movement of the relevant toe, despite this being immobilized. Other similar experiments have yielded less conclusive results as to the importance of the muscle sensory receptors [Roberts 2002].

[7]These are more able to signal stretching than decreases in length.

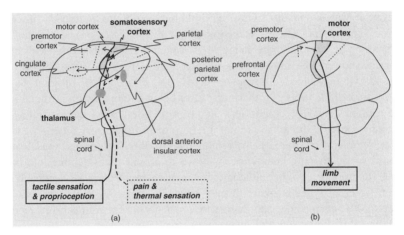

Figure 3.4: Schematic diagrams of somatosensory and motor pathways into and out of the brain. (a) Two main pathways convey somatosensory stimuli from receptors under the skin and in muscles and joints from extremities into the brain. One is responsible for tactile sensation and proprioception, whereas the other transmits pain and thermal stimuli. Each projects into the thalamus and then to the primary somatosensory cortex. Perception is completed by subsequent communication with other parts of the brain. (b) The motor pathway has its main originating node in the motor cortex. However, this output is conditioned by communication with other brain areas, including the premotor cortex, sensory input, and association areas. [Reproduced from Kandel, E.R., Schwartz, J.H., and Jessell, T.M., *Principles of Neural Science*, McGraw-Hill (2000); © 2000 The McGraw-Hill Companies.]

The axons comprising these ascending pathways retain an organization that reflects the different body parts from where the sensory signals originate. This spatial "map" of the projections within the pathways is continued into the *somatosensory cortex*, which forms a strip down the cortex on each brain hemisphere (see Figure 3.4(a)) and is divided spatially into areas responsible for input from different parts of the body (see, for example, Ramachandran and Hirstein [1998] who present a fascinating discussion of "phantom limbs"). The sensations from different areas of the body are thus routed to the appropriate part of the *somatosensory cortex*. In this way, the brain not only registers the sensation but can also localize it. The size of the portion dedicated to each area of the body relates to the degree of density of receptors of the respective body part. Sensitive areas, such as the face and fingers, thus have a greater portion of the *somatosensory cortex* dedicated to them than relatively insensitive areas such as the elbow (see Figure 3.5). This cortical representation of the human body is known as the *homunculus* and is sometimes represented as a human figure distorted so that the size of each body part is proportional to its corresponding cortical sensory area.[8]

---

[8]The homunculus concept dates back to the work of neurosurgeons including Wilder Penfield in the 1950s, who mapped the somatosensory cortex using electrical stimulation during brain operations (see, for example, Ramachandran and Hirstein [1998] and Saper [2002]).

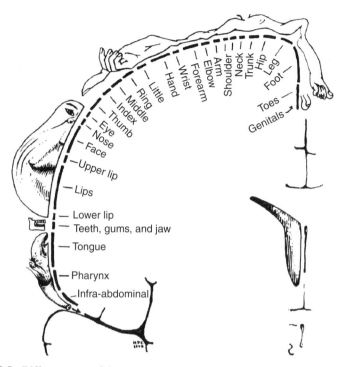

Figure 3.5: Different parts of the somatosensory cortex receive input from different parts of the body. The area of cortex dedicated to each body part relates to the density of somatosensory receptors in that part. Sensitive areas such as the fingers and lips have a greater dedicated portion of the somatosensory cortex than relatively insensitive areas such as the elbow. A similar distribution is present in the motor cortex. This cortical representation of the body is known as the *homunculus*. [Reproduced by permission from McClintic, J.R., *Physiology of the Human Body*, 2nd edn., John Wiley (1975); © 1975 John Wiley & Sons.]

After initial receipt of the stimulus in the primary somatosensory cortex, subsequent processing involves other brain regions where information from different sensory inputs is integrated with memory and other cognitive functions and can be used to drive subsequent actions [Kandel et al. 2000, Faw 2003, King and Calvert 2001, Wallace 2004]. The motor pathway for voluntary actions approximately follows the reverse route from that of somatosensory perception (described above). The main pathway is indicated in Figure 3.4(b), from the primary motor cortex, down the spinal cord, to the target extremity. It seems, however, that the primary motor cortex is not as strictly organized in a "map" of destination extremities as is the somatosensory cortex; there is some overlap in the regions that affect different body parts or muscles, and these are not necessarily arranged in a sequential manner [Schieber 2001]. Moreover, the motor cortex receives input from other cortical areas, such as the *prefrontal* and *premotor cortex* (thought to be involved in planning actions) and other sensory cortices

[Jeannerod et al. 1995, Freund 2003]. These descending pathways also project to deeper brain areas such as the *thalamus, basal ganglia, midbrain*, and *cerebellum*, which in turn send feedback projections back to the motor and *premotor cortices* via the *thalamus* [Kandel et al. 2000].

3.6 DISCUSSION

It is clearly not possible in so limited a space to provide more than a glimpse of this fascinating area. As indicated in the introduction to this chapter, our primary consideration is to provide the reader new to this area with some basic concepts, to give appropriate references to facilitate further study and, above all, to emphasize both the intricacy and complexity of a remarkable sensory modality. It is clear that the proper development of interaction tools that can provide us with sound haptic sensation requires that we first study this sensory channel—such a voyage enables us to learn from what is already known, and to appreciate the extent of the void where certainty does not flourish. Indeed, despite the remarkable efforts to date in the area of somatosensory perception, this void is still extensive.

In terms of the human–computer interface, our ultimate goal is to effectively support (and so derive synergy from) multisensory communication. In this respect it is natural to ask: What are the relative sensitivities of our sensory systems? Naturally, any response must be based on many suppositions because in comparing senses, we are not comparing like with like. Furthermore, the responsiveness of senses when viewed in isolation is likely to be rather different from when they are viewed in combination as a whole, integrated system. In short (and as with the individual components that comprise our sensory systems), the senses (or sensory components) complement each other, and the whole is greater than its constituent parts.

TABLE 3.2: The use of the Weber fraction as an indicator of relative sensory sensitivity. Trials employed mid-range sensory conditions.

Sensory Modality	Weber Fraction $\Delta I/I$
Vision (brightness, white light)	1/60
Proprioception (lifting weights)	1/50
Pain (thermally aroused on the skin)	1/30
Audition (tone of middle pitch, moderate loudness)	1/10
Cutaneous pressure	1/7
Smell (of India rubber)	1/4
Taste (table salt)	1/3

Source: Reproduced by permission from Geldard F.A., *Fundamentals of Psychology*, John Wiley (1962); © 1962 John Wiley & Sons.

Despite this, it is still instructive to make a rough comparison of sensitivity. This has often been done by use of the *Weber fraction* that may be expressed as

$$\frac{\Delta I}{I} = C, \tag{3.2}$$

where, for a particular sensory modality, I represents a particular level of physical stimulus and ΔI the least perceptible change in the stimulus that can be detected by an observer. C represents a "constant" for the particular sense under investigation. Gleitman [1981] illustrates this approach by means of a simple example in which he supposes that a person can just detect the difference in illumination derived from 100 or 102 candles (i.e., the addition of two candles represents the "just noticeable difference" for a background illumination of 100 candles). Assuming the validity of the above expression, if we double the number of candles, we will then need to add four more in order to produce the smallest change in illumination that is detectable by the observer. Although there are various approximations and assumptions in this approach, it is useful, particularly as the Weber fraction is dimensionless and consequently we are able to compare values for the various sensory systems (see Table 3.2). From our current perspective, it is interesting to see that one aspect of proprioception appears so highly in the list. It is important to note, however, that this approach produces the best results only for mid-range intensities, breaking down as the sensory systems are driven by stronger or weaker stimuli.

And so our all-too-brief discussion of the human visual and somatosensory systems comes to an end. In Chapter 4, we will consider aspects of a history in which those with great creative skill endeavored to devise techniques that would enable them to create an accurate rendition of the 3-D world on 2-D media. As we shall see, the difficulties that they experienced so long ago parallel, in a number of ways, the uncertainties that we face today in developing creative display and interaction interfaces.

4 A Backward Glance

Like one that on a lonesome road
Doth walk in fear and dread,
And having once turned round walks on,
And turns no more his head;
Because he knows a frightful fiend
Doth close behind him tread.

4.1 INTRODUCTION

Many of the techniques and ideas that we now use to represent a three-dimensional
(3-D) space within the confines of two-dimensional (2-D) media are derived directly
from methods developed in Italy during the fourteenth and fifteenth centuries. It was
at this time that the systematic techniques needed to represent geometrical effects

Creative 3-D Display and Interaction Interfaces: A Trans-Disciplinary Approach, by Barry G. Blundell
and Adam J. Schwarz

such as linear perspective were derived, disseminated, and put to use in painting and other forms of pictorial art. Indeed, it was during this period that, among others, Giotto di Bondone, Filippo Brunelleschi, and Leon Battista Alberti significantly contributed to the development of techniques widely used today in computer graphics.

In this chapter, we take a brief glance into this past and discuss the development of selected ideas and techniques that now underpin our understanding of the perception and depiction of 3-D environments within a 2-D space. We also allude to some similarities between current challenges and those faced 600 or more years ago. After all, the consideration of creative display and interaction techniques intended to significantly advance the human–computer interaction interface denotes a major paradigm shift; we must think in new ways and not be bound in any way by established approaches. In this respect it is perhaps appropriate to quote (by way of analogy) from the notes of Leonardo da Vinci (1452–1519):

> *Hence the painter will produce pictures of small merit if he takes for his standard the pictures of others, but if he will study from natural objects he will bear good fruit. . . . After these came Giotto, the Florentine, who was not content with imitating the works of Cimabue his master . . . after much study he excelled not only the masters of his time but all those of many bygone ages. Afterwards this art declined again, because everyone imitated the pictures that were already done. . . Oh how great is the folly of those who blame those who study from nature, leaving uncensored the authorities who were themselves the disciples of this same nature.* [Richter 1998]

In Sections 4.2–4.4, we focus on the development of techniques enabling the accurate mapping of 3-D space onto a 2-D surface. Section 4.5 revisits the human visual system within the context of an historical perspective. The *Cameras Obscura* and *Lucida*, both of which offered (at least in principle) to assist in the creation of images on 2-D media, are briefly outlined in Section 4.6. We hope that the interested reader will be encouraged to pursue these fascinating topics further and that the references cited in the chapter will offer a useful starting point.

4.2   THE DEVELOPMENT OF PERSPECTIVE TECHNIQUES

After a certain high level of technical skill is achieved,
science and art tend to coalesce
in aesthetics, plasticity and form.
The greatest scientists are always artists as well.[1]

The European Dark Ages are, as the name implies, often viewed as representing an intellectual and cultural winter. Whether this is an accurate portrayal of Europe at those times or rather a gross simplification and generalization is an interesting debate, and certainly when, for example, we regard at first hand the great churches

---

[1]Attributed to Albert Einstein.

and sculptures that were created during this period, we are indeed left with a sense of great respect. However, this is not a debate that need concern us for the moment. Of immediate relevance is the contrast between our perception of this period and the Renaissance (rebirth) that followed. The Renaissance flourished in Italy from the fourteenth to the sixteenth centuries and is justly renowned for exceptional architectural and artistic works. In fact, developments made at that time were to dramatically influence Western society—and continue to do so. If the Dark Ages were in fact an intellectual and cultural winter, then the period that followed may be viewed as denoting springtime—a time in which art, science, and mathematics seem to have coalesced. This coalescence was perhaps the essential ingredient required for the progress made during that period and strongly parallels our current need to promote wide-ranging trans-disciplinary research so as to make major advances in the development of creative computer interface techniques and visualization paradigms.

Prior to the Renaissance, we see artistic works in which perspectives are distorted, angles are awkward, and objects within a scene are twisted in odd ways. Indeed, as can be seen from the two examples shown in Figure 4.1, there is an overall lack of realism, and to us, accustomed to the accurate rendition of perspective and the framework that this imposes, such works may be considered to possess a child-like quality. In fact when I (BGB) first began to examine such images, I found them filled with distraction; they inspired a sense of irritation. Indeed, I found that unless I made an effort to do otherwise, I was continually drawn to (and dwelt on) perspective inaccuracies rather than upon the work as a whole. With time, my outlook has changed, and so too has my focus; perhaps I have overcome my conditioned need for accurate perspective order. I can now view such images for what they are and for their often very remarkable content (for example, the facial expressions in Figure 4.1(a)—the absence of [or inaccuracy in] perspective adding to, rather than detracting from, the work as a whole).

In his interesting text, Samuel Edgerton [1976] discusses the remarkable nature of the transition brought about by the application of geometric techniques to image depiction on the 2-D surface. He writes:

Today we are the tired children of their discovery; the magic of perspective illusion is gone, and the "innate" geometry in our eyes and in our paintings is taken for granted. Linear perspective has been part and parcel of psyche and civilization for too many centuries . . .

And so we often take the presence of perspective for granted, assured by our knowledge that it is an inherent part of the physical world—simply a matter of optics and elementary geometry. However, it is in fact an illusion—as much so as the transparency of the glass in the window before me, the opacity of the surrounding wall, and the color of the winter sky. It is perhaps only when we see imagery in which real-world perspective is in some way distorted (or absent) that we can fully appreciate the important role that it plays in our everyday visualization process.

Figure 4.1: In (a) we reproduce a painting said to have originated in the fifteenth century. This depicts the execution of Sainte Valérie. Note the lack of perspective, shadows, and shading (*chiaroscuro*). It does not, however, detract from the information content; see in particular the facial expressions. Image (b) is called "The Man of Sorrows" and was painted *circa* 1260 (using egg *tempera* on wooden panel). [Figure (a) is reproduced by kind permission of the Mayor of Chambon-sur-Voueize, La Creuse, France and is located in the Abbatiale Ste-Valérie. Figure (b) is reproduced by kind permission of The National Gallery, London.]

It seems that pre-Renaissance artists had much less difficulty in performing accurate 3-D renditions when working directly in a 3-D space (for example, creating sculptures or buildings). The ability of pre-Renaissance workers to envisage and create remarkable 3-D structures is demonstrated by the magnificent architecture of the many churches constructed during that era. The ancient Abbatiale Ste-Valérie here in La Creuse and also Durham Cathedral provide us with convenient and typical examples of such work (see Figure 4.2). The latter forms a sound basis, as in the early 1990s it was the subject of an engineering analysis, described in a brief but most interesting book by the Rev. Michael Jackson [1993]. Work is reported to have commenced on this mighty edifice in 1093—a project that, in the first instance, was to last nearly 150 years. One can only speculate on the form

(a)   (b)

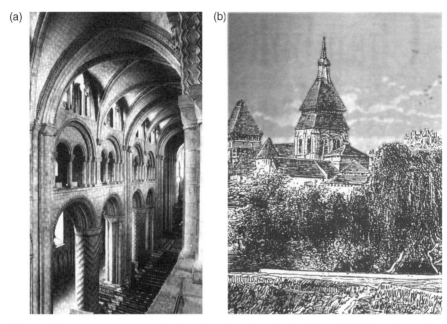

Figure 4.2: In (a) we present an interior view of Durham Cathedral and (b) depicts the exterior of the Abbatiale Sainte-Valérie at Chambon-sur-Voueize. Both of these remarkable buildings have their origins in the European Dark Ages, and their immense size emphasizes the linear perspective depth cue. See text for discussion. [Image (a) reproduced by kind permission from Jackson, M.J., (ed.), *Engineering a Catherdral*, Thomas Telford (1993); © 1993 Thomas Telford Ltd, London. Image (b) attributed to "Almanach du département de la Creuse," Guéret, Betoulle, 1806–1825.]

and detail of the plans and drawings that may have been prepared in order that all concerned with the project could have envisaged such an immense 3-D structure. To what degree were details such as arches and the fine ceiling structures (see, for example, Figure 4.3) sketched, were physical models used, or did detail simply evolve over time as structures grew?

Leonardo da Vinci writes of the contrast between sculpting and painting [Richter 1998]—a matter that we will return to in Section 8.7 within the context of volumetric displays. For the present, it is appropriate to simply say that sculpture (see, for example, Figure 4.4) assumes no viewing perspective and various depth cues are inherently associated with the final image. By contrast, the painter must encode depth cue information within the painted scene and of course assumes a certain viewing position, as is the case with various creative 3-D display systems.

The artistic skills and craftsmanship of pre-Renaissance artists cannot be questioned—one has only to view their works at first hand. Ancient churches gain much of their magnificent and awe-inspiring effect from their physical scale and hence the remarkable perspective views that they provide. It is as if their architecture is intended to exaggerate (or at least emphasize) this cue. Furthermore, the realism

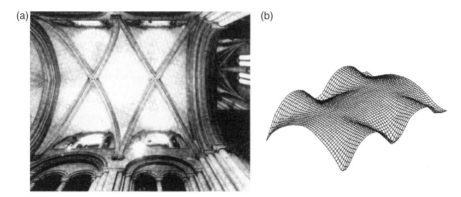

Figure 4.3: In (a) we show a view of the fine structure of a vaulted roof of Durham Cathedral. Its delicately curved form is shown in the computer-generated profile illustrated in (b). The data for (b) are reported as being obtained by means of photogrammetry. Here two separate photographs are taken from different locations (and so create a stereopair; see Chapter 6). This technique is widely used in aerial surveying. [Reproduced by kind permission from Jackson, M.J., (ed.), *Engineering a Cathedral*, Thomas Telford (1993); © 1993 Thomas Telford Ltd, London.]

exhibited in sculptures (created with materials such as granite and wood) shows that our ancestors could achieve almost flawless excellence when working within a 3-D space. However, when we view their paintings, we see that the mapping between 3-D and 2-D space was problematic (assuming that their intention was in fact to mimic real world perspective). This implies that this mapping is by no means intuitive and is, for the majority at least, a skill that must be learned. Interestingly today when performing, for example, creative computer-aided design we generally work within the confines of a 2-D design space and assume that the mental processes needed to map (and so envisage) a 2-D design in its ultimate 3-D form are part of a natural process. Perhaps the difficulties experienced by our ancestors in undertaking the converse mapping provides us with an indication that it is by no means intuitive and requires considerable cognitive skill.

As part of our voyage of discovery, let us for a moment go back in time, as far back as the thirteenth century. Here, in around 1260, we may encounter an English monk, Roger Bacon (~1220–1292) writing an immense treatise, *Opus majus*. Of course, the relevance of this ancient text[2] to a book written more than 700 years later in connection with creative display systems may not be immediately apparent, and certainly one has to look carefully before finding the relevant content. However, in the passage reproduced in Footnote 3 we see that Bacon was in essence making a case for depiction techniques that can support "augmented realism" as discussed in Section 1.5.1. Consider those living at that time within the influential religious community—frustrated by the difficulty of conveying the scriptures to an audience, largely by the spoken word alone. Pictorial representations would naturally assist in

---

[2]This included a part devoted to light, color, and vision. See Lindberg [1996].

Figure 4.4: An early sculpture of the *Pietà* from the Abbatiale St-Valérie at Chambon-Sur-Voueize. Despite being damaged, the attention to fine detail and realism of form are readily apparent. Unlike paintings depicted on the 2-D canvas, the artist need assume no particular viewing position, and moreover, various depth cues (including binocular parallax, linear perspective, and shading) are automatically associated with the final work (cf. Volumetric images—see Sections 6.5.3 and 8.5). (Reproduced by kind permission of the Mayor of Chambon-sur-Voueize, La Creuse, France.)

this process, but these failed in their attempts to provide realism; they failed to set their narrative within a natural space, and therefore, a gulf existed between their content and the literal message it was hoped that they would convey. Clearly, Bacon attributed importance to adopting a proper geometrical structure within artistic religious works[3] and, furthermore, understood the vital importance of the visual image both in augmenting realism and that all-important "suspension of disbelief."

---

[3]*Now I wish to present the ... [purpose]. ... which concerns geometrical forms as regular lines, angles and figures both of solids and surfaces. For it is impossible for the spiritual sense to be known without a knowledge of the literal sense. But the literal sense cannot be known, unless a man knows the significance of the terms and the properties of the thing signified. For in them there is the profundity of the literal sense, and from them is drawn the depth of spiritual meanings by of fitting adaptations and similarities, just as the sacred writers teach, and as is evident from the nature of Scripture, and thus have all sages of antiquity handled the Scripture. Since therefore, artificial works, like the ark of Noah and the temple of*

Giotto di Bondone ($\sim$1267–1337) is one of the pre-Renaissance artists who is regarded as having made an important contribution to the pictorial depiction of geometrical perspective and photorealism. As discussed in some depth by Edgerton [1991], Giotto's work highlights an important transition from the European painting style of the Dark Ages to a visually realistic depiction of pictorial space. The Frescoes in the upper church of San Francesco, Assisi of the "Life of St. Francis" provide one example and as indicated by Edgerton [1976], *"epitomize, it may be said, the end of the middle ages and the dawn of the Renaissance."*[4] A further and less contested example of Giotto's work is the "Lives of the Virgin and Jesus" in the Scrovegni Chapel in Padua, Italy. Within the chapel, Giotto painted 53 panels as well as other details covering all walls. Pictorial depth cues such as height in the visual field, shading, and linear perspective are used convincingly in these images.[5] An example of one painting attributed to Giotto is presented in Figure 4.5.

The realism conveyed in Giotto's work is likely to have influenced subsequent artists. However, the degree to which Giotto understood the theory of linear perspective may never be known for sure. Clearly, he was a remarkably gifted practitioner, and simply as a consequence of his instinctive talent and understanding of human emotion, he may have been able to enhance realism without recourse to theory.

It is generally accepted that the first known demonstration of an accurate, mathematically based perspective was performed by Filippo Brunelleschi (1377–1446). This demonstration probably took place some time between 1410 and 1425. Brunelleschi was an architect and therefore had a mathematical background (particularly a familiarity with geometrical construction). His demonstration of the accurate application of mathematical techniques to the translation of 3-D space to the 2-D tableau centers on two paintings. One of these was of a Florentine Baptistery and is better documented because, although lost, it was described in some detail by

---

Solomon . . . it is not possible for the literal sense to be known, unless a man have these works depicted in his sense, but more so when they are pictured in their physical forms; and thus have the sacred writers and sages of old employed pictures and various figures, that the literal truth might be evident to the eye, and as a consequence the spiritual truth also. For in Aaron's vestments were described the world and the great deeds of the fathers. I have seen Aaron thus drawn with his vestments. But no one would be able to plan and arrange a representation of bodies of this kind unless he were well acquainted with the books of the Elements of Euclid and Theodosius and Milleius and of other geometricians. For owing to the ignorance of these authors on the part of theologians they are deceived in matters of greatest importance . . . Oh, how the ineffable beauty of the divine wisdom would shine and infinite benefit would flow, if these matters relating to geometry, which are contained in Scripture, should be placed before our eyes in their physical forms . . . . And for the sake of all things in general let us recall to mind that nothing can be known concerning the things of this world without the power of geometry, as has already been proved. Also a knowledge of thins is necessary in Scripture on account of the literal and spiritual sense as has been set fourth above. For without doubt the whole truth of things in the world lies in the literal sense, as has been said, and especially of things relating to geometry, because we can understand nothing fully unless its form is presented before our eyes, and therefore in the Scripture of God the whole knowledge of things to be defined by geometrical forms is contained and far better than mere philosophy could express it . . .
From the translation of *Opus Majus* [Burke 1962] quoted in Edgerton [1976].

[4]There has in fact been considerable debate as to whether these are the work of Giotto.

[5]Details and pictures of the Scrovegni chapel can be found at http://www.cappelladegliscrovegni.it/.

Figure 4.5: A painting ("Pentecost") attributed to Giotto di Bondone (*circa* 1306–1312). Note the presence of perspective, but the lack of consistency and the apparent absence of a vanishing point. In fact, the top "frieze" can be seen to "switch" so as to appear to lie either above the figures (presumably the intended location) or in front of them. This effect is brought about by the lack of depth cue consistency. (Reproduced by kind permission of The National Gallery, London.)

Brunelleschi's biographer Antonio di Tuccio Manetti (apparently from first-hand knowledge).

Interestingly, the panel painted by Brunelleschi was not intended to be viewed directly but in the manner illustrated in Figure 4.6. Parts of Manetti's description concerning this remarkable feat are outlined by Martin Kemp [1978]:

> *The necessary conditions for viewing were that the spectator should peep from the back of the panel through a small hole at a mirror, in such a way that the painted surface was visible in reflection ... The peep-show system was used because the painter needs to presuppose a single place from which the painting must be viewed ...*

One of the most important aspects of this viewing approach is the explicit acceptance of the fact that an accurate construction of linear perspective assumes a single specific viewpoint. However, this does not necessitate the use of a mirror, and perhaps the inclusion of this optical arrangement was for other reasons. Edgerton [1976] discusses the possibility that the painting may have been created, not by the artist

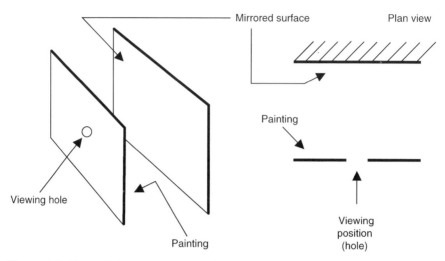

Figure 4.6: The technique reported as being used for viewing the two images created by Filippo Brunelleschi (1377–1446) and which are commonly believed to have provided the first known demonstration of an accurate, mathematically based perspective. The painting was not viewed directly, but rather via a hole cut through its center. The observer then viewed the reflection of the painting. Various suggestions have been made concerning possible reasons for the adoption of this technique (see text for details). Also note that this approach precludes stereoscopic viewing and provides an "immersive" experience.

facing the Baptistery, but rather from its image reflected in a mirror. If this was the case (and Kemp [1978] highlights the difficulty of painting from the reflected image), then the painted image would have been laterally inverted. The correction of this inversion could, of course, have been the reason for viewing the painting via its reflection. Various other suggestions have been made, and in considering these, it is important to remember that mirrors in use at that time differ greatly from those we take for granted today. Edgerton [1976] makes various speculations including:

> *The shrewd master may have realised something which has received attention from perceptual psychologists in recent times: that perspective illusion is strong only when the observer's awareness of the painted picture surface is dispelled. When the viewer loses his "subsidiary awareness" as the phenomenon is now called, he tends to believe the picture surface does not exist and that the illusionary space depicted is actually three-dimensional.*

Whatever the reason (we comment on this further in the next section), Brunelleschi's use of a "peep-show" system mimics today's immersive display paradigm and

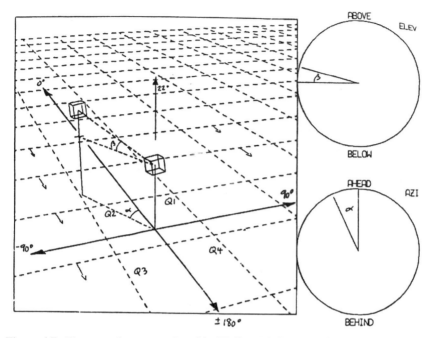

Figure 4.7: The type of scene employed by Wallace McGreevy and Stephen Ellis for trials concerning our ability to judge and extract information from a 3-D scene depicted upon a conventional 2-D display. The cube at the image center represents the viewers' "own" aircraft and the other (in this case, the cube to the upper left) the target. The participant judges the azimuth and elevation angles. A response is indicated on the two "dials" shown on the right-hand side. (Reproduced by permission from McGreevy, M.W., and Ellis, S.R., "Direction Judgement Errors in Perspective Displays," *Twentieth Ann. Conf. on Manual Control*, NASA Ames Research Center 1984; © 1984 NASA.)

precluded binocular viewing of his images.[6] Perhaps this was intentional, or perhaps as an illusionist he simply enjoyed a little showmanship—optical arrangements adding to the viewing sensation (and blurring image defects)!

The difficulties of accurately reconstructing 3-D spatial relationships from images rendered on a 2-D medium are exacerbated when the image is not viewed from the correct position. In a study, Michael McGreevy and Stephen Ellis [1984] created a display environment intended to evaluate aspects of the reconstruction process. A conventional display screen was used to depict the type of image illustrated in Figure 4.7. Here, the two cubes represent aircraft located above a grid, and in trials, participants were asked to judge the azimuth and elevation angles

---

[6]When allowing others to judge his painting by comparing it with the physical Baptistery, he may have encouraged them to view each through the hole in the painting (i.e., mirror present and mirror absent). In this case, both would have been observed without stereopsis. Naturally, this would have enhanced the perceived realism of his painting.

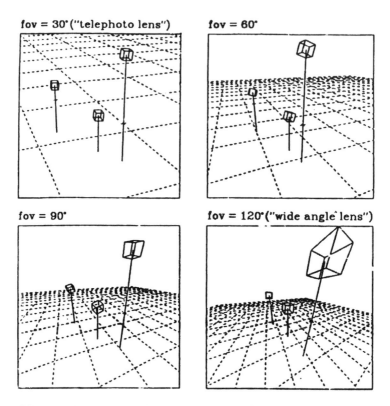

Figure 4.8: As indicated by Wallace McGreevy and Stephen Ellis in relation to trials concerning our ability to judge and extract information from a 3-D scene depicted on a conventional 2-D display, an image scene appears to change dramatically as the field of view in varied. This impacts on our ability to accurately extract information from the scene. Here the same scene is shown for four different values of field of view. Viewing distance and location remain fixed. (Reproduced by permission from McGreevy, M.W., and Ellis, S.R., "Direction Judgement Errors in Perspective Displays," *Twentieth Ann. Conf. on Manual Control*, NASA Ames Research Center 1984; © 1984 NASA.)

between the reference cube (their own plane—appearing at the center of the display screen) and the target (the cube positioned to one side). As discussed by McGreevy and Ellis, the 2-D projection varies dramatically in appearance as the field of view is changed (see Figure 4.8). Not only did McGreevy and Ellis conduct trials in which this parameter was varied, but they also considered the effect of the participant not viewing the image from the intended center of projection. (Here we can see the wisdom (intended or otherwise) of Brunelleschi's image depiction technique, which constrained both the viewing distance and the orientation.) The results reported by McGreevy and Ellis are well worth examining (see also McGreevy et al. [1986]),

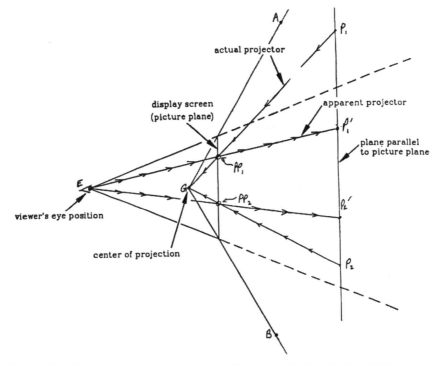

Figure 4.9: Illustration of the "virtual space effect" described by Wallace McGreevy and Stephen Ellis. The geometry depicted here indicates the impact of viewing the display screen from a location that differs from the designated center of projection (see text for details). (Reproduced by permission from McGreevy, M.W., and Ellis, S.R., "Direction Judgement Errors in Perspective Displays," *Twentieth Ann. Conf. on Manual Control*, NASA Ames Research Center 1984; © 1984 NASA.)

and in connection with the importance of viewing a 2-D rendition from the correct location, they write (for context see Figure 4.9):

> *When the eye is not at the geometrically correct station point the projectors are effectively bent at the point where they pierce the viewing screen. We call this the "virtual space effect". If the subject assumes that all projectors are straight, just as they are when looking through a window, then the apparent 3D scene will differ from the true 3d scene. We call the subject's assumption the "window assumption".*

4.3 THE TRANSITION TO PERSPECTIVE IN PAINTING

It is both interesting and instructive to briefly consider the factors that led to the incorporation of a geometrically accurate linear perspective and which ultimately enabled artists to surpass photorealism. In relation to this history, there are those who focus their arguments on the importance of texts that apparently resurfaced. For example, it is understood that Greek writings were essentially lost to Europe during the Dark Ages after the collapse of the Roman Empire, and from about the twelfth century, they were rediscovered via Arabic translations. In the intervening centuries, copies of many Greek texts had been maintained in the Islamic world, where Arabic scholars made additional contributions.[7] Both the climate of scientific enquiry as well as the writings may have helped fuel approaches to the more accurate representation of 3-D space [Edgerton 1991]. Certainly, sooner or later, the geometric rigor present in some Greek texts is likely to have been influential in the development of accurate perspective. The firm understanding of planar and solid geometry present in classical Greece is perhaps exemplified by the longevity of Euclid's *Elements*. From about 300 BC, Euclidean geometry was also applied to the study of vision in Euclid's *Optics* [Burton 1945, Howard and Rogers 1995]. This included a number of theorems that essentially encapsulate accurate descriptions of how we see the world around us, including concepts that we would now describe in terms of motion parallax, the horopter (see Section 6.4.1), and perspective effects related to the visual cone. The work of Claudius Prolemaeus Ptolemy ($\sim$85–165 AD) in the second century AD contained applications of mathematics (as well as experimental observations) in many fields, including astronomy, cartography, and optics [Toomer 1970]. Unfortunately, many of his works survive only as (partial) translations of translations. Nevertheless, Ptolemy appears to have considered several aspects of vision, including the size and positions of objects reflected in mirrors, and applied single-point perspective projection to map the surface of the Earth onto a 2-D plane. Edgerton [1976] argues that this was a crucial influence in the discovery of perspective mapping schemes in fifteenth-century Florence.

The extent to which such texts influenced the development of geometric techniques in the fourteenth and fifteenth centuries is a matter of considerable debate. Martin Kemp [1978] writes "...*even in their own terms, both medieval optics and classical cartography possess severe limitations as potential sources for Brunelleschi.*" Setting this question to one side, we can certainly envisage those with inquiring and creative minds studying existing works of art, such as those attributed to Giotto and in which perspective was not incorporated in a consistent manner. Surely they would have wondered why certain objects appeared more or less realistically rendered than did others. Equally they would have considered the degree of realism achieved through the positioning of objects within a scene. Filippo Brunelleschi is credited as having made the major step forward in his two lost paintings. However, we cannot know for sure how this feat was achieved— perhaps as an architect, his insight was acquired as he drew plans of classical structures, or perhaps available texts played a part. Certainly he would have been assisted by the general cultural climate of the time; the quest for the visually realistic portrayal of space in the medieval and Renaissance periods was a part of a broader shift in thinking—it was an age of enlightenment (see Edgerton [1976, 1991] and Lindberg [1976]). We cannot be absolutely certain as to the role played by his mirror during the painting process. It is *possible* that his images were painted directly on the mirror's surface (this would have been equivalent to employing

---

[7]Some of these contributions are mentioned further in Section 4.5.

the *camera obscura*—see Section 4.6). Clearly, had this been the case, then the degree to which he understood the relevant geometrical constructions would be thrown into question. John Lynes [1980] provides a most interesting discussion on this subject and provides a *"conjectural reconstruction of the first perspective."* In his article he suggests the possibility that the perspective was painted directly onto a mirrored surface in which a reflection of the Baptistery was visible. Naturally this would have resulted in a lateral reversal of the painted image. Lynes suggests that Brunelleschi may have envisaged this and therefore selected a subject (the Baptistery) that demonstrated a high degree of symmetry. However, perhaps, as mooted by Lynes, during the painting process Brunelleschi realized that by ensuring that an observer should see only the reflection of his painting (rather than the direct view), the image reversal problem would be corrected. If this was indeed the case, Brunelleschi guarded his secret well. Toward the end of his article, Lynes references Prager and Scaglia [1970] who quote from text attributed to Brunelleschi:

> *Do not share your inventions with many, share them only with the few who understand and love the sciences. To disclose too much of one's inventions and achievements is one and the same thing as to give up the fruit of one's ingenuity. Many are ready, when listening to the inventor to belittle and deny his achievements, so that he will no longer be heard in honourable places, but after some months or a year they use the inventor's words, in speech or writing or design.*

Certainly if Brunelleschi employed the mirror painting technique, he acted on these thoughts. We cannot even be sure of the influence of Roger Bacon in his plea for pictorial realism to better support the teaching of the Scriptures. After all, Bacon's work was produced in approximately 1260—approximately 160 years before Brunelleschi's demonstration, and nearly 200 years before Leon Battista Alberti wrote his treatise on painting (see the next section), which is acknowledged as the first record of the linear perspective technique. Would his comments on image depiction still have been considered to be applicable or current after such a passage of time? Of course we cannot necessarily apply our concept of time (or other notions) to those living so long ago. Today we seek instant results in practically every area of endeavor, and we could not conceive of a modern building project spanning generations. However, it would appear that our ancestors' participation in the construction of vast churches was driven by faith, sufficient in itself, and compared to which issues such as time, cost, and effort, were overshadowed.

4.4 MATHEMATICAL SCHEMES FOR LINEAR PERSPECTIVE

Leonardo da Vinci is well known as one who perfected perspective and photorealism (see, for example, Figure 4.10). In one of his notebooks, we find the following reference to perspective:

> *There are three branches of perspective; the first deals with the reasons of the (apparent) diminution of objects as they recede from the eye, and is known as Perspective of*

(a)

(b)

(c)

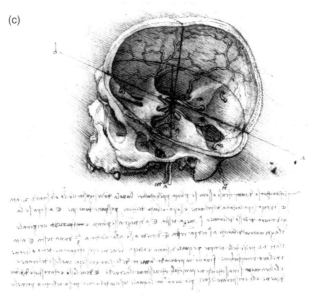

Figure 4.10: Sketches by Leonardo da Vinci. Reproduced in (a) is the "Study of Drapery" (*circa* 1480), in (b) the "The infant and womb" (*circa* 1509–1514), and in (c) "The skull sectioned." [Reproduced by kind permission: (a) Musée du Louvre, Paris and (b) and (c) The Royal Collection; © 2005, Her Majesty Queen Elizabeth II.]

*Diminution; the second contains the way in which colours vary as they recede from the
eye; the third and last explains how objects should appear less distinct in proportion as
they are more remote. And the names are as follows: Linear Perspective, the perspective of colour, the perspective of disappearance.* [Richter 1953]

Whether such an understanding of pictorial cues (see Section 2.6.1) required for the depiction of accurate linear perspective in pictorial representations was known and used in earlier ages is, unfortunately, not known for certain. Ptolemy's cartographic methods perhaps come closest [Edgerton 1976].

Giotto's work, discussed in the previous section, provides a good example of (literally) the "state of the art" in the early fourteenth century. Just over 100 years later, the first known set of rules for depicting linear perspective accurately were set down in fifteenth-century Florence. As discussed by Edgerton [1976], whether or not this was a discovery, a rediscovery, or an invention remains the subject of debate. However, as described above, it is generally accepted that the first known unequivocal demonstration of an accurate, mathematically based perspective was performed by Filippo Brunelleschi in about 1415 [Edgerton 1976, Lindberg 1976]. The earliest surviving pictures that make use of Brunelleschi's method are by fellow Florentines Masaccio and Donatello and date from about 1425 [Edgerton 1976].

The use of an accurate perspective became more widely known through Leon Battista Alberti's book *Della Pittura* ("On Painting" ∼1435).[8] Here, a methodology that a painter could follow to obtain the correct perspective 2-D rendering on the canvas was set out [Ivins 1973, Edgerton 1976]. This methodology was proceeded by a system of constructing lines and marks on the canvas that served to guide the placement of elements within the composition. In brief, Alberti's system includes:

- A central vanishing point at which converging guidelines meet.
- A horizontal horizon line through the vanishing point.
- Setting the horizon and vanishing point at the same vertical position as that of the heads of human figures in the picture (and thus at approximately the eye level of the standing viewer). All people were then depicted with their heads at approximately the same level, their feet higher, and overall size smaller in accordance with increasing distances from the viewer. This reflects the horizon line at eye level in the typical everyday viewing experience.
- Vertical divisions along the lines of convergence corresponding to steps of equal distance away from the observer. These were obtained by setting the effective viewing distance such that the depth depicted appeared as shallow or as deep as desired.

This approach would now be considered as a form of one-point perspective, i.e., constructed with respect to a single vanishing point. As this perspective approach

---

[8]*Della Pittura* is the title of the Italian version of Alberti's book. In fact, he also produced a Latin version, *De Pictura*. There are some slight differences between the two versions [Edgerton 1976].

Figure 4.11: A woodcut by Albrecht Dürer (1525) showing Leon Battista Alberti's velo method, which subdivides the overall image scene into a set of simpler image components. In the limiting case, each image element (mesh hole) would correspond to the pixel employed in today's electronic displays. Naturally, for this approach to work correctly, the artist must maintain a single viewing position, and it is for this reason that Dürer shows the artist employing a pointer by which the viewpoint is defined. (Reproduced by kind permission of the Albertina, Vienna.)

became more widespread, variants on this system, including two- and three-point perspective, were developed.

Alberti also described what he called the method of the "velo" (veil) to capture a visually exact representation of a scene on a 2-D canvas by using a matrix of grid lines (such as might be provided by a grill or loosely woven veil) positioned in front of the subject [Lindberg 1976, Edgerton 1991]. Mapping the visual content of each square (from a given viewing location) onto a corresponding area of the canvas in this way was extremely useful in depicting a realistic visual copy of the subject. Effectively, it provided a mapping of the 3-D scene onto a 2-D coordinate grid on the canvas. An illustration by Dürer showing Alberti's velo method is provided in Figure 4.11.

The works of artists such as Leonardo da Vinci and Albrecht Dürer from the late fifteenth and early sixteenth centuries (within 100 years of Alberti's treatise) demonstrate an outstanding mastery of both perspective and other pictorial depth cues. It is, however, interesting to speculate on the speed with which these ideas spread across Europe and on the rapidity of their acceptance.

Ultimately, artists learned the skills needed to create on the 2-D tableau photorealistic reproductions of the physical 3-D world. With these skills came the opportunity to portray their own interpretations of physical, mental, and emotional imagery. As with the virtual worlds which we now seek to create, the artist who possesses the necessary skills and talents can create images the form and content of which are bound only by that most precious possession—human imagination (see, for example, the images reproduced in Figures 4.12 and 4.13).

4.5   EVOLVING IDEAS OF VISION AND PERCEPTION

At the time in which Brunelleschi and others initiated the use of linear perspective schemes to accurately map a 3-D scene onto a 2-D surface, the image-forming

Figure 4.12: Four altar panels by J.B. Amaranthes located in the Abbatiale Sainte-Valérie of Chambon-sur-Voueize and said to have been painted in the early seventeenth century. [Reproduced by kind permission of the Mayor of Chambon-sur-Voueize, La Creuse, France.]

(a)

Figure 4.13: (a) Peter Paul Rubens, *The Judgement of Paris* (*circa* 1632–1635). Here, Rubens depicts the mythological tale in which Paris, son of King Priam of Troy, awards the golden apple to Venus. The jealous goddesses Juno and Minerva, the Fury, Alecto, and the god Mercury look on. (b) Raphael, *The School of Athens* (*circa* 1508–1511). In this fresco, Raphael brings together some of the most renowned philosophers and scholars in ancient history, including Plato, Aristotle, Ptolemy, Pythagoras, and Euclid. Raphael incorporates pictures of the faces of some of his contemporaries, e.g., Leonardo da Vinci as Plato and Michelangelo as Heracleitus, along with a self-portrait. (c) A rendition of the Last Supper (artist unknown, *circa* eighteenth century), located in the Abbatiale Sainte-Valérie of Chambon-sur-Voueize. (d) A rendition of the Annunciation (artist unknown, *circa* eighteenth century), located in the Abbatiale Sainte-Valérie of Chambon-sur-Voueize). Artists who have learned the skills needed to achieve photorealism can create superlative works. They are able to express a narrative and render imagery in a natural manner and are bounded only by the limits of their individual imaginations. [Image (a) reproduced by kind permission of the National Gallery, London. Image (b) reproduced by kind permission of the Vatican Museums. Images (c) and (d) reproduced by kind permission of the Mayor of Chambon-sur-Voueize, La Creuse, France.]

properties of the human eye were not yet understood. The precise manner in which the eyes receive images of the world, and theories of vision generally, remained the subject of much debate. One of the main issues in the philosophy of visual perception at this time concerned whether vision was an *intromissive* (rays or other information entering the eye) or an *extromissive* (involving ocular beams or rays emitted from the eye) process, or, indeed, to what extent an intermediate medium was

(b)

Figure 4.13: *Continued.*

necessary. When classical and Arabic texts became more available (from about the twelfth century), they provided a wealth of different theories and ideas on how the visual process took place [Edgerton 1976, Lindberg 1967, 1976].

Manuscripts from classical Greece alone provided a variety of philosophies of vision, and it is instructive to briefly consider some of these ideas.[9] One school of thought held that all objects continually emit thin images of themselves (known as *simulacra* or *eidola*), and it is these that give rise to visual sensation when they enter the eye. Some philosophers in this tradition thought that the intervening air must participate as an active medium—the visual image consisting of "consolidated air" between the object and the observer. Plato proposed that a "visual fire" is emitted from the eyes and combines with light to form an active visual medium that serves to transmit the visual characteristics of an object to the observer. Aristotle, however, rejected the idea of the emitted *simulacra* by arguing that these would also be physical bodies of some kind, thus emitting their own *simulacra*, and so on! He also disagreed with the suggestion that ocular beams are emitted from the eye, on the basis that these would need to reach extremely distant objects (such as stars). On the other hand, Aristotle did, it seems, think that vision proceeded by objects affecting the state of a pervasive transparent medium by means of which the observer "senses" the visual state of the object. Aristotle's writings on vision

---

[9]Texts such as Lindberg [1976] provide a thorough discussion of these and later theories of vision.

(c)

(d)

Figure 4.13: *Continued.*

comprise one of the earliest surviving in-depth studies on the subject and, as with
many of his other philosophies, were extremely influential in medieval Europe. It
was not until the work of Kepler in the sixteenth century that the *intromissive/extro-
missive* argument concerning the process of vision was finally laid to rest.

   One of the most influential texts on optics in medieval Europe was that of the
Arabic scholar Alhazen, who lived and worked in the eleventh century [Lindberg
1967]. Alhazen built on earlier approaches by Islamic philosophers such as
Al-Kindi, Avicenna, and Averroes, as well as on Greek theories from writings
that had been translated into Arabic [Lindberg 1976]. Previously, geometrical
descriptions of vision, such as those of Euclid and Ptolemy, were associated with

extromissionist theories of vision—the eye emitting rays through a visual cone. However, *intromissionist* theories tended to center on the receipt of physical bodies such as the *simulacra* introduced above. As discussed in some detail by Lindberg [1967], Alhazen constructed the first *intromissionist* theory of vision that built on the geometrical rigor of Euclid and Ptolemy and presented the first scheme describing how a representation of a visible object is produced in the eye by considering the paths of light rays proceeding from points on the object's surface. To avoid the problem of visual confusion caused by rays reflected in different directions from the same point being registered in the eye, Alhazen hypothesized that only rays entering the eye perpendicular to the surface were effective in forming the visual impression. He thus made the important conceptual steps of postulating a one-to-one mapping between points in the visual scene and a "retinal image" within the eye and of considering the eye as an optical system. Moreover, he seems to have appreciated a distinction between the optical (light entering the eye) and the non-optical (inference on the resulting sensations by the brain) aspects to visual perception [Lindberg 1976].

Faced with this varied input of ideas, many medieval European scholars, such as Roger Bacon and John Pecham in the thirteenth century, endeavored to synthesize these various theories that had come to light:

> *I have determined not to imitate any one author; rather, I have selected the most excellent opinions from each.*[10]

As the study of natural laws became more widespread, a methodical approach to explaining and characterizing the physical world began to take shape.[11] However, most visual theories were still based on a belief that the eye's lens was spherical in form, was located in the center of the eye, and represented the seat of visual perception. Advances in ocular anatomy in the sixteenth century gradually established the structure of the eye more accurately [Lindberg 1976]. At the university of Padua, Italy, Matteo Colombo asserted that the lens was in fact biconvex and situated toward the front of the eye, whereas in Basle, Switzerland, Felix Platter not only produced accurate physiological drawings of the structure of the eye, but also considered the retina (see Section 2.3.2), as an extension of the optic nerve over the back of the eye, to be the organ responsible for visual sensation. Another notable figure at this time was Giovanni Battista Della Porta, who made the important (in hindsight) analogy that the eye functions in a manner similar to the *camera obscura* (see Section 4.6). However, it appears that he did not connect this idea any more formally with the process of visual perception, and along with many of his

---

[10]Roger Bacon, *Opus Tertium*, quoted in Lindberg [1976].

[11]John Pecham's *Perspectiva Communis*, Bacon's *Perspectiva*, and Witelo's *Perspectiva* were among the texts known and studied as optics references in several universities in the fourteenth and fifteenth centuries, including those in Paris (the Sorbonne), Vienna, Prague, Leipzig, Cracow, Oxford, and Cambridge.

contemporaries believed instead that the eye's lens was the seat of visual perception [Lindberg 1976]:

> ... *The image is let in by the pupil, as by the hole in the window; and that part of the Sphere, that is set in the middle of the eye, stands instead of a Crystal Table.*[12]

The modern picture of (inverted) image formation on the retina was finally formulated by Johannes Kepler in the early years of the seventeenth century, while he was working with the astronomer Tycho Brahe in Prague. According to Lindberg [1976], Kepler helped to picture optical properties by stretching pieces of thread to trace out the paths of light rays and produced an accurate analysis of image formation in the *camera obscura.* Although lenses have been in use since at least 2500 BC (Enoch and Lakshminarayanan [2000] discuss an interesting application in the eyes of Egyptian statues) prior to Kepler's time, analyses of refraction had not been extensively developed,[13] and he was apparently unaware of the contemporary work of Maurolico and Della Porta. Familiar with the anatomical work of Felix Platter, he extended his work on image formation by apertures (such as the *camera obscura*) to consider the human eye. Kepler assigned the primary refracting properties in the eye to the combination of vitreous humor and lens (see Section 2.3). The formation of an inverted image on the retina then followed as a natural consequence of these considerations and the anatomical layout. The fact that the image was inverted was to a great extent contrary to intuition; previous theories often went to some lengths to maintain an upright projection beyond the lens of the eye [Howard and Rogers 1995]. However, Kepler could not find a satisfactory alternative to this result and finally concluded that the inverted image was the unavoidable consequence of optical laws and the structure of the eye—how the brain dealt with this to yield an upright perceived world was a separate problem. No diagram by Kepler himself appears to have survived, but within a few decades, his theory had been adopted by philosophers such as Rene Descartes.

The fact that each eye perceives a slightly different view of a 3-D scene had been recognized at least since classical times. However, philosophers were generally more concerned with explaining how the mind perceives only a single image, rather than with "seeing double." The increased near-field depth perception obtained by binocular vision was noted by philosophers from Aristotle, Euclid, and Galen to Leonardo da Vinci, but it was assumed to be due to the cue of convergence alone. Descartes acknowledged both accommodation and convergence as important depth cues, and that by means of an "innate" knowledge of the interocular distance

---

[12]Porta [1669], quoted in Wade [1987, p. 794]. In this extract, Porta sketches an analogy between his understanding of the eye and a *camera obscura* setup with a lens in the aperture. The crystal table referred to was used as the screen on which the image was cast in the *camera obscura* experiment; Porta considered the back surface of the lens (which he explicitly states here to be positioned in the center of the eye) to be the ocular equivalent.

[13]The focusing properties of glass spheres filled with water (sometimes referred to as "burning spheres," "burning glasses," or "burning lenses") were known qualitatively from classical times. In the eleventh century, the Arabic scholar Alhazen devoted one of his books to the subject (*On the Burning Sphere*).

and the convergence angles corresponding to different distances the visual system was "*a natural geometer*" [Sedgewick 1986]. As quoted in Wade [1987], Molyneux in his text entitled *Treatise of Dioptricks* [1692] discusses the following experiment:

> *Experiment that Demonstrates we see with both Eyes at once: and 'tis, that which is commonly known and practised in all Tennis-Courts, that the best Player in the World Hoddwinking one Eye shall be beaten by the greatest Bungler that ever handled a Racket; unless he be used to the Trick, and then by Custom get a Habit of using one Eye only.*[14]

4.6 THE CAMERAS OBSCURA AND LUCIDA

> When we remember we all are mad,
> the mysteries disappear and life stands explained.[15]

In this section, we briefly consider the *cameras obscura* and *lucida*, both of which can assist in the accurate depiction of physical objects within the confines of a 2-D surface.

1. *The Camera Obscura:* This enables a visible image to be cast onto a surface and in its most elementary form employs a small hole through which light may pass from well-illuminated surroundings into a darkened chamber such as a room or viewing box (the classic pin-hole camera). Providing that the size of the hole is not too great, such an implementation gives rise to a well-defined and inverted image on a screen. The use of a lens is not a requirement and a hole suffices, although as the dimension of this hole is increased (to increase image brightness), image clarity suffers.

John Hammond [1981] provides an excellent account of the history of this device and traces its origins back to the Chinese and Greek civilizations in the fourth and fifth centuries BC (incorrectly, the *camera obscura* is often attributed to the Renaissance artist Giovanni Battista della Porta). However, it appears that it was not until the fifteenth century that a biconvex lens was first used instead of the small hole and corrective elements were employed to produce an erect image (see Figure 4.14). This figure shows various forms of *camera obscura*, and as may be seen, images may be created within a chamber (the immersive form of camera)[16] or cast onto a screen to be visible to an externally located observer.

In its various forms the device was frequently used by astronomers and, for example, provided a safe method by which eclipses could be viewed. Hammond [1981] quotes Freidrich Rissner who in the fifteenth century suggested the use of the *camera obscura* for copying drawings, particularly as it would support their enlargement or

---

[14]Wade [1987, p. 789].

[15]Attributed to Mark Twain.

[16]The classic 1940s film "A Matter of Life and Death" provides a vivid demonstration of a *camera obscura* in operation.

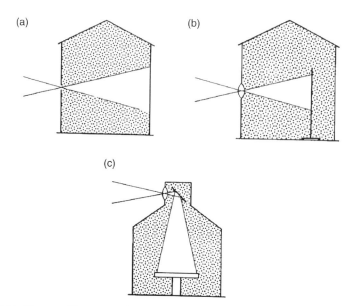

Figure 4.14: Here we illustrate various forms of room-based *camera obscura.* In (a) a small hole is used to permit the creation of an inverted image, and in (b) the use of a lens permits the creation of a brighter image and a movable screen enables the image to be properly focused. In (c) the incorporation of a mirror enables the image to be cast onto a horizontal table. [Reproduced by permission from Hammond, J.H. and Austin, J., *The Camera Lucida in Art and Science*, Adam Hilger (1984); © 1984 IOP Publishing Ltd.]

reduction. He also provides an interesting discussion on the use of the *camera obscura* by artists as a convenient method of generating perspective images.

2. *The Camera Lucida:* The *camera lucida* has a much briefer history than does the *camera obscura*. It was invented by Dr William Hyde Wollaston at the beginning of the nineteenth century and supports the creation of accurate perspective views. Simple forms of *camera lucida:* are shown in Figure 4.15. The basic principle of operation of the device may best be understood by reference to the first of these illustrations and is as follows:

> *If a piece of glass be fixed at an angle of 45° with the horizon, and if at some distance beneath, a sheet of paper be laid horizontally on a table, a person looking downwards through the glass will see an image of the objects situated before him; and as the glass which reflects the image is also transparent, the paper and pencil can be seen at the same time with the image so that the outline of the image may be traced on the paper.* [Encyclopaedia Britannica 1876]

The use of an inclined glass plate for image generation is one that is of interest to us. In Section 6.8.1, we see this same technique used for the creation of theatrical illusions (Pepper's Ghost), and in Section 8.4.4, we discuss its usage for the

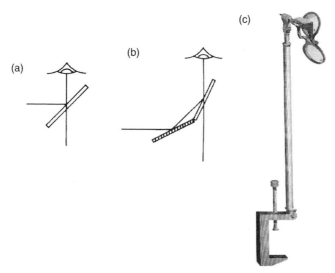

Figure 4.15: Two basic forms of *Camera Lucida*. In (a) the simplest implementation is shown—the device consisting of a single glass plate (cf. Pepper's Ghost) in which both the reflected image and the image being created are both visible. The image is, of course laterally reversed. This reversal problem may be overcome by means of a double reflection as shown in (b)—(cf. the technique used by Filippo Brunelleschi—see Section 4.2). Image (c) illustrates an implementation of (b). [Figures (a) and (b) reproduced by permission from Hammond, J.H. and Austin, J., *The Camera Lucida in Art and Science*, Adam Hilger (1984); © 1984 IOP Publishing Ltd). Image (c) reproduced from the *Encyclopaedia Britannica*, 9th edn, Vol. IV, Adam and Charles Black, Edinburgh (1876).]

production of a 3-D image space within which a user can interact with computer-generated images via physical interaction tools (the "direct interaction" paradigm discussed in Section 6.6.2).

The approach described above has several weaknesses. These are as follows:

1. The image is laterally inverted. This was remedied by employing a double reflection as shown in Figure 4.15(b).

2. The user must maintain a fixed viewing position, this was achieved by viewing both the image reflected in the glass and the pen and paper through a hole located in a card positioned above the apparatus.

3. The reflected image and the image being sketched on the paper are located at two different focal depths (this problem is similar to the one we experience when using a direct interaction tool in combination with stereoscopic images—see Chapter 6). In the case of this version of the *camera lucida*, the problem was remedied by introducing a lens through which reflected light emanating from the paper passes before reaching the glass plate.

The approach described above is referred to by John Hammond and Jill Austin [1984] in their comprehensive book on this subject as the "see through" technique. An alternative embodiment employs a four-sided prism and is referred to as a "spit pupil" technique. Both the *camera lucida* and *camera obscura* (together with other optical drawing devices such as the *optigraph*, see *Encyclopaedia Britannica* [1876]) offered to assist artists in the accurate portrayal of perspective, and the *camera lucida* has certainly been widely used for sketching and as an aid to scientific drawing. To what extent such devices were in fact used by "professional" artists is a subject for debate.

4.7 DISCUSSION

The application of precise geometrical constructions has provided a means whereby a natural sense of perspective may be incorporated within the 2-D rendition of a 3-D space. Although this supports "augmented realism" (see Section 1.5.1), it does not automatically enhance information content that, for example, in the case of a painting may be derived from detail such as facial expression, posture, and so on. For example, although the images reproduced in Figure 4.1 do not include accurate perspective, this does not detract from the "story"—see the expression of resignation on the face of the person about to be executed and the look of macabre joy on the face of the executioner. Certainly as we have already discussed, in the quest for realism, we should not seek to replace the need for human imagination, and indeed many artists have used perspective as a technique through which scenes could be framed so as to stimulate both imagination and human emotion. Others have broken away from (or manipulated) the bonds of perspective, creating visual images that often impact more on our mental processes rather than upon our visual systems. The drawing by Leonardo da Vinci reproduced in Figure 4.16 provides an example of powerful imagery in which, although there is no sense of any photorealistic quality, our imagination is captivated.

In this chapter, we have drawn parallels between the goals of those seeking to capture a natural perspective on canvas some hundreds of years ago and today's quest for the development and application of new 3-D display paradigms. There is, of course, one vital difference concerning the nature of the image. From the traditional artist's perspective the image content is fixed; there is certainly no support for an interaction process. However, a major impetus in the development of creative 3-D display systems concerns (or should concern) their ability to support new synergistic interaction paradigms. By setting an image within a real or apparent 3-D space and through the support of pictorial, oculomotor, and parallax cues, we can create an environment in which natural interaction can potentially be achieved. In this way it may be possible to support more intuitive image construction and manipulation techniques, and so advance the interaction process. In parallel, creative 3-D display systems offer to provide opportunities for the advancement of the visual arts, providing tableaux that offer to support new forms of imagery. As Edgerton [1976] writes

Figure 4.16: Reproduction of a sketch made by Leonardo da Vinci in his later years—"Cataclysm." This powerful image captivates the imagination without recourse to photorealism or the constraints of accurate perspective. (Reproduced by kind permission. The Royal Collection; © 2005, Her Majesty Queen Elizabeth II.)

when considering a future traveler able to journey beyond the bounds of our solar system:

> It, too, [perspective] *will become "naïve," as they discover new dimensions of visual perception in the eternal, never ultimate, quest to show truth through the art of making pictures.*

4.8 INVESTIGATIONS

1. Consider that the human eye was of a different form—namely that the retina and optical components forming the focusing system were not separated. For example, you may consider the retina to be the front surface of the eye and ignore the issue of image focusing. What impact would this have on our perception of perspective?

2. Continuing with the imaginary eye structure referred to in 1 (and disregarding the issue of focusing), consider a person accustomed to viewing the physical

world with this ocular system. How would such a person perceive a Renaissance painting conveying conventional linear perspective?

3. View a painting or photograph in the manner prescribed by Filippo Brunelleschi. What are your observations?

4. The following is quoted from earlier in the chapter: "*However, it is in fact an illusion—as much so as the transparency of the glass in the window before me, the opacity of the surrounding wall . . .*" In what way(s) are these illusionary?

5. The following is quoted from earlier in the chapter: "*Giotto di Bondone, Filippo Brunelleschi and Leon Battista Alberti significantly contributed to the development of techniques widely used today in computer graphics.*" From your study of the chapter and other literature, discuss the accuracy of this statement. Was their contribution limited to linear perspective?

6. Examine samples of pictorial art created prior to the fourteenth century in which linear perspective is lacking or inconsistently applied. Do you feel that the application of accurate perspective to these images would have enhanced, detracted from, or had no impact upon their overall information content?

5 Traditional Interaction Mechanisms

In mist or cloud on mast or shroud,
It perched for vespers nine;
While all the night through fog-smoke white,
Glimmered the white Moon-shine.

5.1 INTRODUCTION

From the 1950s through until the mid-1970s, average end users of computer technology seldom interacted in real time with the systems on which their programs executed. Generally programs were submitted on media such as a set of punched cards or magnetic tape and, when loaded by a computer operator, would run until

Creative 3-D Display and Interaction Interfaces: A Trans-Disciplinary Approach, by Barry G. Blundell and Adam J. Schwarz
Copyright © 2006 John Wiley & Sons, Inc.

completion (or failure!). This situation gradually changed with the growing avail-ability of desktop terminals connected to both mainframe and minicomputers that could support multitasking operating systems. Even then, however, interaction opportunities were limited as reliance on a centralized processor within a time-sharing environment made it impossible for users to have a guaranteed real-time response to their input stimuli. Furthermore, as mentioned in Chapter 1, terminals (VDUs) usually lacked graphics capabilities and so the computer interface was command (rather than event) driven. All this changed with the decentralization of computing resources and the introduction of bitmapped graphics able to support the event-driven user interface (see Section 1.3). In short, the introduction of the workstation and personal computer gave each user guaranteed performance and pro-vided interaction opportunities that offered an alternative to the traditional command line input. The mouse, which was first conceived in the mid-1960s, provided an intuitive interaction tool ideally suited for use with the event-driven interface. Con-sequently, over a relatively short period of time, the typical human–computer inter-face evolved to better support bidirectional activity and was no longer entirely reliant on the keyboard for input. Indeed today it is difficult to imagine the frustra-tions experienced by those computer users who, not so very long ago, could not interact with their programs during execution.

In this chapter, we focus on the interaction process as supported by the conven-tional monocular computer display. We will give particular attention to three key issues: the form of the interaction tools, the ways these tools are used (interaction modalities), and interaction efficiency (considered from the viewpoint of both the computer and the user). In subsequent chapters, we build on and extend this discus-sion and in Section 9.2 briefly consider bi-manual interaction.

Initially we briefly examine interaction tools that permit both the navigation of a cursor on a 2-D screen and the selection or acquisition of displayed objects. In Section 5.2, we confine this discussion to devices that were evaluated in a widely cited study conducted in the mid-1960s [English et al. 1967]. In this publication, familiar tools such as the mouse and joystick are evaluated alongside others that have not gained widespread acceptance, such as the Grafacon and knee control. The evaluation criteria centred on measurement of speed and accuracy in making selections of displayed objects. Similar studies have been conducted since that time, and interaction device performance models have been continually refined. Paul Fitts formulated one such model in the early 1950s in connection with the human motor system [Fitts 1954] and this continues to be widely used (Fitts' Law). However, the use of the term "law" is perhaps unfortunate because the excel-lent work undertaken by Fitts led to a mathematical model that is by no means a precise, rigorous, and fundamental rule governing a phenomenon. Although not wishing to be pedantic in our choice of terminology (and immediately perhaps being so!), we consequently prefer to refer to this relationship more accurately as Fitts' Model rather than as Fitts' Law. This is in keeping with the nature of our "trans-disciplinary" approach; for within some disciplines a "law" is regarded as a fundamental rule rather than an approximate behavioral model. To avoid con-fusion, we therefore prefer to use the term "law" judiciously.

In Section 5.3 we introduce this model and place it within the context of the pioneering work undertaken in the 1940s by Shannon and co-workers in connection with information theory. On this work Fitts constructed his model. We also briefly review some of the work that has been undertaken in connection with this model's application to interaction device evaluation.

The evaluation and modeling of interaction devices for use with the conventional display should, in principle, be a straightforward undertaking. However, this has not proved to be the case. Trials have often led to dissimilar results and have frequently focused on quantifying issues relating to the computer system (such as speed and accuracy of selection), rather than on more subjective usability issues that become increasingly important when interaction tools are used for extensive periods of time. Clearly, if the relatively straightforward task of modeling interaction devices for use with conventional display systems has proved problematic (and here at least the display itself is now of a standard and well characterized form), then the evaluation of emerging interaction devices (including those supporting bi-manual interaction) for use with a whole range of creative 3-D display systems is likely to prove much more complex.

In Section 5.4, we introduce three interaction paradigms: "transferred interaction," "direct interaction," and "pointer-based interaction." However, for the present, we confine our discussion to interaction modalities involving the traditional computer display. In the next chapter (see Section 6.6) we will build on this introduction by placing the interaction models within the context of a 3-D workspace.

5.2 AN EARLY EVALUATION OF SOME INTERACTION TOOLS

> Most of today's books
> have an air of having been written in one day
> from books read the night before.[1]

Traditionally, our senses are grouped into have five general categories (see Section 3.1), and these provide the channels through which we can accept input from our surroundings. However, we have only two (although extensive) controlled output channels: speech and motor functions (movement). Although the former provides a mechanism for issuing commands and inputting text into a computer system, it does not readily lend itself to use with a graphically based interface, and therefore, for our purposes, this form of interaction may be overlooked. We are left to focus on interaction based on the complex human motor system.

The purpose of an interaction tool is to convert stimuli (in this case, movement) provided by an operator who wishes to effect some change(s) within a host computer system, into a form that can be passed to, processed by, and acted on by the computer. For even the most trivial interaction operations, feedback is essential. This not only assures us that a specified action has been properly implemented, but also provides pivotal assistance with the interaction task. For example, when using an

---

[1]Sebastien-Roch Nicolas de Chamfort 1741–1794. *Plus ça change ...*

event-driven user interface, visual feedback provides essential navigation information to enable us to move across and through menu systems. Consequently, the creation of a feedback loop, such as that illustrated in Figure 5.1, is fundamental to the human–computer interaction process. This highlights the synergy that must exist between the display and interaction paradigms—both of which are key elements within the loop.

Although the devices most frequently used for interaction are the keyboard and mouse, there are many other modalities. The earliest comparative (and quantitative) study into the effectiveness of some interaction devices for use in conjunction with a computer display was, it appears, made by English et al. [1967] working at Stanford University. As a convenient means of introducing various conventional interaction tools and placing them within an historical context, we will briefly discuss, in the next sub-section, those used in this study. The work carried out by English and his co-workers forms the basis for a considerable amount of research that has since been carried out. In Section 5.2.2 we therefore review this study, and in Section 5.2.3, we bring together some of the issues that originate from this discussion.

5.2.1 Interaction Space and a Tool Set

Although the mouse is the tool most widely used to augment the keyboard, a variety of other interaction devices have been developed. Most of these "continuous"[2]

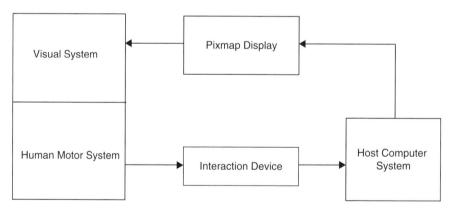

Human Operator

Figure 5.1: The interaction process generally requires that a feedback loop be created. Interactive operations are initiated by the human motor system. The visual system usually provides the stimulus needed by the operator to accurately navigate the interaction device(s) and also provides confirmation that the operation has been successfully implemented.

---

[2]We use the word "continuous" to distinguish between stepped input devices (e.g., those requiring the repeated depressing of a button or key such as the step (arrow) keys on the keyboard) and devices such as the mouse, which *for the moment* may be considered to be nondiscrete in their response to motion. Later we will refer to the discrete nature of the mouse's ability to position a cursor.

interaction tools react to spatial repositioning, and therefore, we can associate with them an interaction space. This corresponds to the region in which motion can be applied to, and sensed by, the interaction device. Hence an interaction device such as the mouse has associated with it a region in which it can detect and measure some form of operator movement. Motion within the confines of this space is mapped in some way (which as users we expect will be intuitive) into the image space of the display system and causes the movement of a reference cursor.

It would be most pleasing if the concept of an interaction space could be applied universally to all interaction tools without *any* exceptions. However, as with many aspects of creative 3-D display and interaction techniques, the great diversity of approaches that may be adopted in their design and implementation creates exceptions to almost every rule. In this particular case, we can identify various continuous interaction techniques that do not have an associated interaction space. For example, although a joystick is usually implemented as a device that responds to movement, this need not be the case. Card et al. [1978], whose work is discussed in Section 5.3.1, employed a joystick utilizing strain gauges to measure force, rather than the more commonly encountered potentiometers and optical encoders that measure movement. Such a joystick has no associated movement, and therefore, we cannot consider there to be an associated interaction space. A similar difficulty is experienced when we consider interaction tools that respond to pressure, and does it really make sense to associate an interaction space to a system using eye-tracking as the means of effecting cursor movement? However, we will put such exceptions to one side, as the concept of an interaction space is useful in discussing most continuous interaction tools.

In the case of the conventional monocular computer display, interaction tools tend to have a 2-D interaction space associated with them. However, when we consider interaction supported by creative 3-D display systems, we expect to be provided with interaction tools that can operate within a 3-D interaction space.

In this subsection we briefly review the interaction devices used by English et al. [1967]. Our purpose is not, however, to provide extensive discussion on these devices as they feature in many other works. Furthermore, over time some tools developed for navigating a cursor on a computer screen, such as the knee control and Grafacon, have faded into obscurity, whilst others such as the touch screen have been developed. The devices referred to below are therefore simply indicative of conventional interaction opportunities.[3] A more detailed discussion of interaction tools may be found in many computer graphics texts (for example, Salmon and Slater [1987], Newman and Sproull [1979], and Demel and Miller [1984]).

(1) *The Mouse*: This interaction tool was apparently first prototyped in about 1964 for use in the study conducted by English et al., which was mentioned above. In its original form, the mouse was constructed in a wooden case as illustrated in Figure 5.2(a). This device employed two orthogonally positioned wheels, each connected to potentiometers. As with the modern mouse, the motion of these

---

[3]For related reading, see also Goodwin [1975].

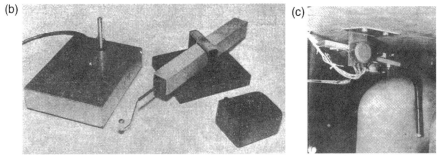

Figure 5.2: Interaction devices used in the evaluation carried out by English et al. [1967]. In (a) the mouse developed for this trial in its wooden housing (viewed from below), in (b) the Grafacon (central item), and in (c) the knee-controlled input device (this operated on sideways and vertical motion of the knee). [Reproduced by permission from English, W.K., Engelbart, D.C., and Berman, M.L., "Display-Selection Techniques for Text Manipulation," *IEEE Transactions on Human Factors in Electronics*, (1967); © 1967 IEEE.]

wheels (both absolute and relative) enables a movement velocity vector to be determined. However, the essential differences between this prototype and current mice (apart from the wooden case!) are that in the case of the mechanical mouse, we now drive the wheels indirectly via a ball and the analogue potentiometers have been replaced by hardware able to directly encode movement digitally. Alternatively a modern mouse may use no mechanical components—movement information being obtained from the reflection of optical signals by a rectangular grid of lines marked out on the mouse mat.

(2) *The Lightpen*: Current lightpens employ a phototransistor that reacts to the level of light to which it is exposed. Pixels depicted on a Cathode Ray Tube (CRT) are sequentially addressed, and the light output from each gradually fades following the excitation process. Consequently, when the phototransistor contained in the light pen is placed over a single pixel, it is possible to detect the instant at which it is addressed by the electron beam (which corresponds to its maximum light output). By simply looking up the current pixel being output from the frame buffer, the pixel (and hence the lightpen's position on the screen) may be determined by the host computer. The lightpen employed by English et al. in their trial did not

employ a phototransistor, but rather a much more bulky photomultiplier vacuum tube. As a consequence of its size, this could not be housed within a lightpen. Interestingly, constructing a pen that consisted of a fiber-optic bundle solved this problem. This carried light from the front of the light pen to the photomultiplier tube (which was located elsewhere).

(3) *Joystick*: As with the mouse, the deflection of a joystick is traditionally measured by two potentiometers. These are mounted orthogonally so as to be able to measure the combined vertical and horizontal deflection. In their trials, English et al. employed two modes of operation: "absolute" and "rate" mode.

In the case of absolute mode, the distance moved by the cursor (d) is directly proportional to the deflection of the joystick from its rest position (x). That is, $d = k\,x$, where both d and x are vector quantities. The constant of proportionality (k) represents the factor scaling the interaction space into the image space. The maximum deflection of a joystick is often quite small, and therefore, when this interaction space is scaled to accommodate the size of a typical computer screen, a relatively large value of k is required. Here we note that increasing the scaling factor can impact on the accuracy of navigation, and interaction tools that support an adjustable scaling factor are helpful in this context.

The rate mode referred to above operates on a somewhat different basis. Deflection of the joystick from its rest or neutral position causes the cursor to move in the corresponding direction. However, in this case, the speed of motion is proportional to $|x|$. Consequently, the greater the joystick deflection, the greater is the cursor speed, and movement stops only when the joystick is returned to its rest position. Therefore, the cursor velocity (v) is given by $v = k\,x$ and hence the deflection of the cursor may be expressed as $d = k\,x\,t$, where t denotes the duration of joystick deflection (at position x). Unlike the absolute mode of operation, and as with the mouse, this modality does not require that k be determined by the ratio of screen dimensions to maximum permissible movement of the interaction tool (interaction space).

The relationship between x and v need not of course be linear, and in fact English et al. used a square law such that; for example,

$$d = t\sqrt{kx}. \tag{5.1}$$

(4) *Grafacon*: In their trials, English et al. evaluated this device [illustrated in Figure 5.2(b)]. It consisted of an extensible (telescopic) arm located on a pivot. Changes in the length of the arm or rotation of the arm about the pivot were used to provide cursor motion in a 2-D space. In addition to the paper by English et al. [1967], see also the RAND Tablet discussed by Davis and Ellis [1964]. Interestingly, they open their discussion in the following way: *"Present-day user-computer interface mechanisms provide far from optimum communication, considerably reducing the probability that full advantage is being taken of the capabilities of either the machine or of the user."*

(5) *Knee Control*: The keyboard plays a pivotal role in the conventional computer interface, and when augmented with an interaction tool such as those mentioned

above, it is necessary to continually move between two forms of input device. Positioning a hand on a mouse, or lifting a light pen and moving it to the screen occupies a finite time, and so it can be claimed that this reduces the efficiency of the interaction process.[4] The knee control implemented for their study by English et al. alleviated the need for the hand to switch between interaction tools and ensured that the tool was always immediately available (see Figure 5.2(c)). Sideways movement of the knee produced horizontal motion of the cursor, vertical movement being achieved by raising or lowering the knee. Clearly, it is most unlikely that the knee can (even with practice) match the hand in terms of dexterity. However, as we shall see, this form of input device seemed to produce good results in the trial.

Interaction tools that are intended for use with a graphical computer interface provide two essential functions: navigation and selection. To accommodate the latter, the tools evaluated by English et al. included some form of button whereby once a cursor had been properly positioned, a selection/acquisition operation could be effected. Naturally, if physically located on the interaction device and unless carefully implemented, the depressing of a button could result in the cursor (or "bug" as they then called it) being jolted from its proper position so causing an acquisition error. In fact, the authors acknowledge that this was a problem in the case of both the Grafacon and the joystick.

5.2.2 Interaction Tool Evaluation

For their study, English et al. employed a 2-D image array comprising (for example) three-by-three elements (each element being a character "X"). These arrays were generated at random positions on the screen, and at any time after their appearance, the operator could press the space bar to initiate timing. The objective was then to use the interaction device to navigate the "bug" and select either the centrally located "X" (in the three-by-three array) or a central group of "X's" (in larger arrays).[5] Correct selection was acknowledged, and a new array was generated. Alternatively, in the case of an incorrect selection, the user was given another chance. Trials were conducted with both experienced and inexperienced operators.

In the case of experienced users, the mouse demonstrated the lowest acquisition time and lowest error rate. For the trials conducted with inexperienced users, there was little difference between the acquisition time of the knee control, light pen, and mouse (although the mouse exhibited the lowest error rate). English et al. also recorded (every 10 ms) the position of the "bug" as it was navigated toward its target. In analyzing the data, they could discern target overshoot when the Grafacon and joystick (in rate mode) were employed, and the erratic motion of the "bug" when navigated by the knee control. The analysis of the difficulties encountered by

---

[4]Although from an analysis of the interaction paradigm alone this may be accurate, human factors must also be considered. Switching between tasks and thereby breaking up repetitive operations is likely to reduce operator fatigue.

[5]Selection of individual characters could be interpreted as representing a 2-D (rather than a one-dimensional (1-D)) navigational exercise.

English et al. in effectively developing what is a relatively straightforward evaluation are well worth reading, as many of their comments maintain their relevance.[6] Perhaps it is appropriate to complete this subsection by quoting from the closing remarks that the authors make in their 1967 publication:

> *Thus it seems unrealistic to expect a flat statement that one device is better than another. The details of the usage system in which the device is to be embedded make too much difference. Irrespective of the speeds with which one can make successive display selections with a given device, the tradeoffs for the characteristics of fatigue, quick transfer to and from the keyboard, etc., will heavily weight the choice amongst the devices. And these tradeoffs, and the possibilities for designing around them, are not apparent until after a good deal of design and analysis has been done for the rest of the system.*

5.2.3 Interaction Issues

In order that an interaction tool may be used in the most efficient manner, a user must develop skills that take advantage of the tool's strengths and compensate for any weaknesses. Below, we highlight some of the issues that need to be considered when we attempt to assess the strengths and weaknesses of an interaction device. For convenience, we limit our discussion to some devices employed by English and his colleagues, as these in themselves are sufficient to highlight some important issues.

(1) *The Extent of an Interaction Space*: The mouse, the joystick in both rate and absolute mode, and the lightpen demonstrate different characteristics when considered from the perspective of the extent of the interaction space and the mapping that exists between this space and the image space.[7] These characteristics are summarized below for each of the four devices:

a. THE MOUSE: This device imposes no fundamental restriction on the extent of the interaction space. In practice, limitations are imposed by practicalities such as convenience/comfort (in terms of wrist and arm movement) and space availability.[8] However, even when lateral motion of the mouse is restricted, the scrolling action supported by the device as it is lifted off the desk and moved back to a closer position does not make it necessary to change the scaling factor (k) between the interaction space and the image space. It may be instructive to spend a moment varying the "mouse speed" (i.e., k) on your computer. Under Windows, this may be done by selecting the mouse icon from within the control panel.

b. THE JOYSTICK (ABSOLUTE MODE): The joystick limits the physical extent of the interaction space to the extent of its motion. The value of the scaling factor (k) is therefore defined by $|d|/|x|$.[9] The dimensions of the image space and range of movement offered by the joystick impact upon cursor positioning accuracy.

---

[6] It is likely that the results obtained in these trials were significantly affected by the lack of refinement in the design of the prototype interaction tools used.

[7] As elsewhere in this chapter we refer to joysticks that respond to motion rather than, for example, force.

[8] As I (BGB) write, I notice that because my desk is covered in vast amounts of paperwork, my mouse is currently confined to a working space measuring approximately 12 cm in width!

[9] Although different scaling factors may, in principle, be adopted in the vertical and horizontal directions.

c. THE JOYSTICK (RATE MODE): As in the case of absolute mode, the physical design of the joystick limits the extent of the interaction space. However, this does not necessarily impact on the value of k as the amplitude of motion of the cursor is also determined by t, and in turn this is dependent on the chosen form of the relationship between x and v. In this mode, cursor placement accuracy can therefore (at least in principle) be achieved by a reduction in cursor speed, and irrespective of the value of k there is no limit to the distance over which the cursor may be moved. Of course, this approach may impact negatively in any trial in which speed of placement is measured.

d. THE LIGHTPEN: In the case of the lightpen, the extent of the interaction space equals that of the image space.

(2) *Selecting or Acquiring an Object*: Objects are generally selected by means of one or more buttons located on the interaction device. As indicated previously, if the depressing of a button causes the interaction tool to move even momentarily, this can cause a selection error. It is likely that this would have been a significant problem in the original trials conducted by English et al., particularly in view of the lack of design refinement in the prototype interaction tools that were used.

(3) *Reaching for the Interaction Tool*: Unless we are prepared to employ an interaction tool such as the knee control used by English et al., which is continuously in contact with the body, or an imaging system that can visually detect motion, then it is necessary to continuously move between keyboard and interaction tool. For inexperienced users this process is likely to be nonautomatic, and therefore, they will have to use visual cues. Including this time in the speed measurements made by English et al. may well have masked interesting results concerning the actual efficiency of a device for navigating and making selections in an image space. In the trials conducted by Card et al. [1978] (see Section 5.3.1), provision is made for the separate measurement of device acquisition and navigational times.

5.3 FITTS' MODEL AND ITS APPLICATION

> Then proudly smiled that old man
> To see the eager lad
> Rush madly for his pen and ink
> And for his blotting pad –
> But, when he thought of *publishing*
> His face grew stern and sad.[10]

In the early 1950s the application of information theory to areas outside traditional communications became vogue. There was (for example) great interest in applying the major advances that had been made in the area of information theory to the modeling of various human sensory, perceptual, and motor functions. In

---

[10]Carroll, L., Poeta *Fit, Non Nascitur*, Phantasmagoria. (*The Complete Works of Lewis Carroll*) Wordsworth Editions (1996).

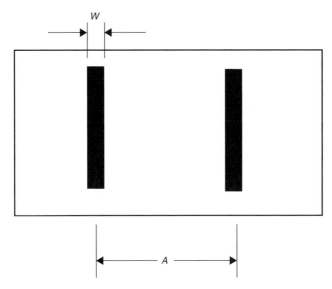

Figure 5.3: In one of the trials conducted by Fitts [1954] a pointer is moved as quickly as possible between two rectangles of width W separated by a distance A. In the trial, both A and W were varied. Different combinations of A and W result in the same index of difficulty (see text for details).

connection with this, Paul Fitts [1954] published a paper that described trials he had conducted in connection with the human motor system. One set of trials, for example, related to the movement of a pointer between two rectangular targets of width W and separated by a distance A (see Figure 5.3). The participants were asked to move the pointer repeatedly and as quickly as possible between the targets. This process was repeated for targets of different size and separated by various distances. Movement times were recorded. Fitts believed that human movement could be modeled by analogy to the transmission of information [MacKenzie 1992], and specifically to a theorem given by Claude Shannon in the seminal work first published in 1948 [Shannon 1948, 1949]. This theorem (Number 17) concerns the transmission of "continuous"[11] information through a communications channel and is as follows:

The capacity of a channel of band W perturbed by white thermal noise[12] *of power N where the average transmitted power is limited to P is given by:*

$$C = W \log_2 \frac{P+N}{N}. \tag{5.2}$$

---

[11]In this context, "continuous information" refers to, for example, the transmission of speech in contrast to discrete symbols.

Although simple in form, this equation is fundamental to communications systems and is rich in meaning. Essentially it tells us that given a transmission channel such as a cable connection, wireless link, etc. which is subjected to white noise, then whatever ingenuity is employed in the development of coding schemes, the transmission of data at a rate greater than C will simply result in increased error.

To gain an insight into the work of Claude Shannon and Paul Fitts, it is instructive to consider for a moment the meaning assigned to the term "information." In its common form, we assume that information is, in some way, derived from the processing of data. For example, data may be obtained by conducting some type of survey, but in itself it has little (if any) meaning. By processing this data in an appropriate fashion we can derive or extract information and hence gain knowledge. However, in terms of information theory, the term "information" has a far more specific and interesting meaning. As explained by Warren Weaver in Shannon [1949]:

> ... two messages, one of which is heavily loaded with meaning and the other of which is pure nonsense, can be exactly equivalent from the present viewpoint, as regards information.

In this context, information relates to freedom of choice in setting out a message—here again quoting Warren Weaver:

> ... information in communication theory relates not so much to what you do say, as to what you could say.

More specifically, given two messages one of which must be chosen for transmission (and we assume that the selection process is not biased to make it more likely that one will be selected rather than the other), then this situation is defined as corresponding to the transmission of one unit of information. Similarly, selecting one message from four corresponds to two units of information, and one from eight, three units of information, and so on. The relationship between choice[13] and information is therefore given by:

$$Amount \ of \ information = log_2(the \ number \ of \ choices).$$

In short, taking the logarithm of x (where x denotes the number of items in a series) gives the number of digits needed to represent the number in the base of the logarithm.

---

[12]White noise is an idealized form of noise—the power spectral density of which is independent of frequency. The term "white" is used in analogy to white light, which contains approximately equal amounts of all frequencies within the visible electromagnetic spectrum [Haykin 2001].

[13]Shannon [1949] and Weaver (writing in the same text) describe stochastic processes in which sequences of symbols are selected according to certain probabilities, consider the Markoff process (in which probabilities depend on previous events), and place choice within the framework of entropy. The latter may be illustrated as follows. Considering n independent symbols whose probability of choice is given by $p_1, p_2, p_3 \cdots p_i$ leads to an expression for information (H) given by $H = -\Sigma p_i log p_i$. By analogy this expresses information within the context of entropy.

For example, if $x = 16$, $\log_2 16 = 4$. This indicates that to represent 16 values (0–15) we require four binary digits (bits).[14] Returning now to Eq. (5.2), because both P and N have the same units, their ratio is dimensionless. When we use the $\log_2$ function, this supplies us with an amount of information (given in bits[15]).

Turning to the model created by Fitts, which, as we have said, was obtained by analogy to Shannon's theorem, Fitts [1954] defined an index of task difficulty (I_d) such that:

$$I_d = -\log_2 \frac{W}{2A}, \qquad (5.3)$$

where I_d is indicated in bits and, as previously mentioned, W corresponds to the width of two target rectangles separated by a distance A. The inclusion of a some-what arbitrary factor of 2 in the denominator of the term within the logarithm pro-vides an offset adding 1 bit ($-\log 1/2$) to the index of task difficulty. Consequently, for all practical situations, the index will always be greater than zero [Fitts 1954]. An index of performance (I_p) may also be defined:

$$I_p = \frac{I_d}{t}, \qquad (5.4)$$

where t is the average time (in seconds) per movement. The negative sign appearing in Eq. (5.3) arises because it is assumed that $W < A$, and hence, the value obtained from the logarithm is negative and a positive value of I_d is required. Substituting Eq. (5.3) into Eq. (5.4) and rearranging to remove the need for the negative sign, we obtain:

$$I_p = \frac{1}{t}\log_2 \frac{2A}{W}. \qquad (5.5)$$

Here we see that combinations of A and W will give the same value of I_p. For example, if we double both A and W, I_p remains unchanged.[16]

In the next sub-section we will consider the application of Fitts' original hypoth-esis, and in Section 5.3.2, we review other aspects of this model.[17]

5.3.1 An Application of Fitts' Model

Since the pioneering work of English et al. [1967], a number of studies have been conducted into the evaluation of interaction devices, and the development of

---

[14]The logarithms of the values of x given here have integer results. The situation becomes less intuitive in the case of noninteger results. For example, in the case of six choices, we would claim to have 2.585 bits of information.

[15]This is often quoted in publications as being measured in *units* of bits—this can cause confusion!

[16]Note that doubling the distance of movement (A) or halving the target width (W) will both result in increasing I_p by 1 bit.

[17]For related reading, see for example, Fitts [1964, 1966].

models from which their performance may be predicted. Work reported by Card et al. [1978] built on and extended the previous work of English et al. For example:

1. The time to access the interaction tool was measured separately from the time taken to undertake the screen navigation task.
2. Trials were conducted to investigate the effect of varying the distance to target.
3. A more rigorous analysis of the data was performed; the results of which were shown to be generally in agreement with those predicted by Fitts' Model.

The devices used in the trials were the mouse, joystick (rate mode), step keys (arrow keys), and text keys. Participants were inexperienced in computer usage, and therefore, one aspect of the trial focused on studying their rate of improvement as they used the interaction tools. Such a learning process can be approximated [De Jong 1957] by

$$T_N = T_1 N^{-\alpha}, \tag{5.6}$$

where T_N represents the positioning time of the Nth trial, T_1 is that of the first trial, N is the trial number, and α is an empirically determined constant. Taking the log of this expression gives

$$\log T_N = -\alpha \log N + \log T_1,$$

which indicates that a graph should demonstrate a linear relationship between $\log T_N$ and $\log N$ with the gradient yielding a value for α. Results obtained showed good agreement with this prediction. Card et al. then proceeded to consider navigation results in the context of Fitts' Model. For this they used the version of Fitts' Model given by Welford [1968]:

$$T = K_o + K \log_2 \left(\frac{A}{W} + 0.5 \right), \tag{5.7}$$

where as previously indicated A is the distance to target, W is the target width, and T is the positioning time. The value of K_o includes the time for the hand to grasp the interaction tool and to make the selection of the target (and so excludes the navigation time). K is a measure of the information processing capacity of the eye–hand coordinate system and is the reciprocal of the index of performance (I_p) referred to in the previous sub-section. (I_p is usually measured in bit s^{-1}.) For the mouse and joystick, the values obtained for K and K_o by regression analysis[18] were:

1. Mouse: $K_o = 1.03$ s, $K = 0.096$ sbit^{-1}. Hence $I_P = 10.4$ bits s^{-1}
2. Joystick: $K_o = 0.99$ s, $K = 0.220$ sbit^{-1}. Hence $I_p = 4.6$ bit s^{-1}.

---

[18]As we have not included information on the error analysis undertaken by Card et al., these values should be seen as being simply indicative. The interested reader is referred to the original publication.

This indicates a time of approximately one second for acquiring the interaction device. The value of K for the mouse was found to be in line with eye–hand tracking trials that had been previously reported, of which the best performance ($K = 0.08 \text{ sbit}^{-1}$) was obtained in a pointing trial conducted by Pierce and Karlin [1957]. Card et al. therefore suggested that the *optimum* performance of an interaction tool when considered from the perspective of the time to select an object may be modelled as:

$$T = 1 + 0.08 \log_2\left(\frac{D}{S} + 0.5\right) \tag{5.8}$$

If so, the mouse would appear to offer near-optimal performance. Whilst it may be possible to reduce K_o—i.e., the time to reach for the interaction tool—the value of K cannot be significantly reduced as it is close to the limit of the central information processing system's capacities for the eye–hand guidance.

It would seem appropriate that this brief history should end with these apparently clearcut findings. However, this is certainly not the case and research concerning the application of Fitts' Model and the evaluation and modeling of interaction devices continues to increase (see Footnote 21 in the next sub-section). There is not, however, complete agreement concerning the results obtained!

5.3.2   Further Aspects of Fitts' Model

Drawing upon Information Theory, Fitts proposed that tasks involving movement require the transmission of information via a "channel." This information is coded in a way that is analogous to, but much more complex than, an electronic communications system, and in carrying out a task, the motor system may be described as transmitting so many bits of information. Subsequent to its appearance, researchers have sought to derive a formal basis for Fitts' Model. However, with any model that does not necessarily provide an absolute representation of a natural system (and where the bounds of its validity are not fully understood), great caution must be exercised. Without due care, we can, for example, end up fitting the person to the new clothes rather than the more acceptable converse. In short, in fulfilling our natural desire to derive a certain mathematical result, we may be forced to make basic assumptions that are not necessarily accurate and that color our perception of the basic system. With this in mind, we present a simple derivation of Fitts' Model (drawn from material presented by Card et al. [1983] and MacKenzie [1992]). We leave the reader to consider aspects of this analysis that may contain potential flaws (see also Investigations Question 2).

Consider a target of width W lying at a distance A from the hand. We begin by assuming that in moving toward a target, the hand follows a series of discrete micro-movements, with each movement being carried out to a certain level of accuracy. Drawing on the Human Model Processor, we can define the time for each of these corrective movements as being the sum of three events. These are the time for the Perceptual Processor to observe the hand (τ_p), the time for the Cognitive Processor to decide on a corrective movement (τ_c), and the time for the Motor

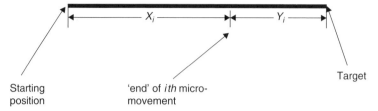

Figure 5.4: Motion toward a target is assumed to consist of a series of micromovements. For each of these movements, the distance moved toward the target is $(1 - P)$ times the distance remaining. See text for details.

Processor to make this correction (τ_m). Given that to reach the target n such corrective moves are required, then the total positioning time (T) may be expressed as:[19]

$$T = n(\tau_p + \tau_c + \tau_m) = nt. \tag{5.9}$$

We assume that for each micromovement, the distance covered is $(1 - p)$ times the remaining distance (where p represents a constant of proportionality). Thus, as shown in Figure 5.4, in the ith movement, we move a distance x_i and the distance remaining to the target is denoted by y_i. Hence:

$$x_1 = (1 - p)A \qquad y_1 = A - (1 - p)A = Ap,$$

$$x_2 = (1 - p)Ap \qquad y_2 = Ap - (1 - p)Ap = Ap^2, \text{etc.}$$

After n such micromovements, the distance remaining is given by Ap^n, and of course when this is less than or equal to one half of the target width, the overall movement is completed. Thus we can say

$$Ap^n = \frac{w}{2},$$

and so rearranging and taking the logarithm (base p), we obtain

$$n = \log_p \frac{w}{2A}.$$

Changing from the base p logarithm to base 2, we obtain

$$n = \log_2 \frac{w}{2A} = \frac{\log_p \dfrac{w}{2A}}{\log_p 2} = c \log_2 \frac{2A}{w},$$

where $c = -1/\log_p 2$. Substituting the expression for n into Eq. (5.9) gives

$$T = ct \log_2 \frac{2A}{w}.$$

[19]Card et al. [1983] suggest a value of 200–500 ms for the action/perception feedback loop.

This is in the same form as that given by Fitts. There are in fact various modified forms of Fitts' Model, such as the Welford [1968] version used in the previous sub-section. Researchers have also proposed various other distinctly different models. In terms of Fitts' Model, it has been observed that there is a disparity between experimental results and predicted behavior for small values of I_d, and that the error rate increases for smaller values of target width (which is to be expected) but not as the movement amplitude gets larger (which is definitely not as expected).

In a most informative and comprehensive publication, MacKenzie [1992] examines the results obtained by six different sets of researchers who have conducted trials with a number of interaction tools.[20] The results of these trials are summarized by MacKenzie and are surprising in their lack of numerical consistency. For example, in the case of the mouse, Card ct al. [1978] obtained a value for I_p of 10.4 bit s^{-1}, whereas Epps [1986] reports a value for I_p of 2.6 bit s^{-1}. MacKenzie provides considerable discussion describing possible reasons for the inconsistency of results.[21]

The lack of consistency in results obtained from more recent trials is particularly surprising, as researchers have at their disposal standardized forms of display hardware and fairly standardized forms of interaction devices upon which to base their work. Furthermore, in the main, trials conducted to date have focused on 1-D and 2-D tasks. In future trials aimed at evaluating new interaction paradigms (possibly bimanual) that are to be used in conjunction with creative 3-D display technologies and in which neither the display hardware nor the interaction tools have been standardized, result consistency is likely to be even more problematic. Certainly, the inclusions of interaction involving a third dimension is likely to considerably complicate the situation. In short modeling the interaction opportunities offered by creative display technologies within the context of 3-D applications is likely to be far more fraught with difficulty than the majority of trials conducted to date in connection with monocular displays.

5.4 INTERACTION PARADIGMS

> The Reverend Charles Lutwidge Dodson was
> a mediocre mathematician who taught at
> Oxford for twenty-seven years without
> brightening the hour of a single student or
> producing anything of lasting value to his subject.[22]

As discussed previously, the conventional flat-screen display plays a vital role in the human–computer interaction process. Not only does it provide some form of

---

[20]For related reading, see also [MacKenzie et al. 2001].

[21]Interest in Fitts' Model appears to be by no means on the decline and certainly this is an interesting area of study. An on-line search conducted earlier today (mid-2004) using the 'Web of Knowledge' (which supports searches as far back as 1981) revealed the following number of citations in connection with Fitts' original 1954 publication: 1981–84: 85 citations, 1984–94: 321 citations, 1994–present: 492 citations.

[22]Newman, J. R., *Commentary on Lewis Carroll*, in "The World of Mathematics," Vol 4, George Allen and Unwin (1956), opening sentence.

indication of the results of computational processes, but it is also pivotal in the interaction feedback loop. Without doubt, whether we are using keyboard, mouse, or some other kind of input device, they are all supported by visual cues supplied by the display, and without the display, all but the most trivial task would become impossible. In this section, we introduce three general interaction paradigms within the context of the conventional display and interaction model (we exclude gesture-based interaction). In subsequent chapters, these will form the basis for discussion in connection with user interaction within a 3-D image space.

5.4.1 Transferred Interaction

In the case of transferred interaction, the operator uses some type of interaction tool to navigate a virtual cursor to any location on the 2-D screen, and once correctly positioned, some kind of button(s) may be used to trigger the required operation(s) (for example, an object selection) or in some way acquire an object. The cursor therefore provides a visual cue on which we focus our attention when moving the interaction tool. This interaction modality is almost universally used for our interaction via the mouse with the event-driven user interface. Essential to the transferred interaction model is the generation of a virtual cursor and the mapping that exists between the interaction device and the cursor location on the planar screen. Because the cursor is created in software, it may take on different forms so as to indicate current functionality (for example, scissors denoting a "cut" operation) or may indicate computer activity (for example, the Windows hour glass). Although navigating a cursor on a 2-D screen is intuitive and requires minimal skill, it is not quite so easily effected when we migrate from a 2-D to a 3-D image space.

5.4.2 Direct Interaction

Although transferred interaction requires some form of cursor to provide a visual cue of the current location on the screen pointed to by the interaction device, the direct interaction model brings together the image and interaction tool and therefore no cursor is required. Although less commonly employed in the conventional human–computer interface than the transferred interaction approach, the lightpen and touch screen closely resemble this model. Of the two, the touch screen perhaps offers the most natural form of direct interaction, since in order to form a selection we simply "touch" image components. In the next chapter, we consider the use of the direct interaction technique in some depth as it raises some interesting possibilities (and creates some significant problems) when applied to a 3-D image space.

5.4.3 Pointer-Based Interaction

The conventional computer interface employing the monocular display does not employ this interaction model, and pointer-based interaction is in fact feasible for use in conjunction with only a very small number of creative 3-D display systems. Therefore, although this approach is not supported by existing conventional interaction tools, it is introduced at this point for reasons of completeness.

In the case of transferred interaction, the interaction tool and screen are physically separated and a cursor associates the interaction and image spaces. Conversely, in the case of direct interaction, the interaction and image spaces are effectively brought into contact. Pointer-based interaction represents an interaction modality that lies somewhere between these other two. Although the interaction and image spaces are physically separate, a computer-generated cursor is not employed for mapping between them, but rather a beam emanating from the interaction tool provides the visual cue. This beam provides the reference indicating the orientation of the pointer with respect to the image space.

5.5 DISCUSSION

In preparing this chapter we have sought to highlight some basic concepts relating to the conventional computer display-interaction interface. The modeling and evaluation of interaction tools has featured in this discussion; not as a consequence of our interest in exporting traditional modalities of interaction to systems incorporating creative 3-D display system techniques, but rather because of the general issues highlighted by such a discussion. It is certainly doubtful that when in the early 1950s Paul Fitts undertook his original trials he had any idea as to the extent of the research effort his model would generate. The fact that the model he proposed was created by analogy to information theory, which at that time was highly topical, shows considerable insight on his part. However, in such cases, there is always the risk of reading too much into the parallels that appear to exist between two somewhat different areas of research activity. Furthermore, although Fitts' Model provides us with a framework from which we can develop an excellent understanding of macroscopic aspects of the interaction process and of the efficiency of interaction tools, it must be applied judiciously, and results obtained viewed alongside other equally important interface metrics.

Despite so much effort, the modeling and evaluation of conventional computer interaction tools has proved not to be a trivial undertaking. It is likely that the extension of this type of activity to encompass creative display and interaction techniques will be even more difficult. For example, can we assume that when we extend Fitts' Model from the 1-D to the 3-D situation, the time required to select or acquire an image element can simply be represented as the linear combination of three terms, each of the form given in Fitts' original equation?

Interaction tools such as the mouse are not continuous in terms of their repositioning of a cursor. Although they have a finite precision in their ability to measure movement, this precision is sufficiently accurate for our needs. More importantly, the sampling rate determines how frequently the mouse is sampled and the cursor location is updated. This may be readily observed by rapidly moving the mouse from side to side. In trials involving high-speed target acquisition, this may be a source of some small inaccuracy.

5.6 INVESTIGATIONS

1. Identify as many interaction devices as possible that are used (or have been used) for interaction with the conventional monocular display, e.g., the tracker ball, lightgun, and so on. In each case, determine the appropriateness of assigning an interaction space to the device.

2. In Section 5.3.2, we presented an elementary derivation of Fitts' Model. This is based on certain ideas and makes various assumptions. Identify strengths and weaknesses of this derivation, and especially question the assumptions that are made.

3. In connection with the conventional monocular display, determine the typical rate at which a mouse is sampled, estimate the time required to compute an updated cursor position, and factor in a typical screen update rate. What (if any) impact could the resulting lag have on target acquisition trials?

6 Depiction and Interaction Opportunities

Her lips were red, her looks were free,
Her locks were yellow as gold:
Her skin was as white as leprosy,
The Nightmare Life-in Death was she,
Who thicks men's blood with cold.

6.1 INTRODUCTION

In the first part of this chapter, we consider some of the underlying techniques that
may be used for the development of creative three-dimensional (3-D) display system

Creative 3-D Display and Interaction Interfaces: A Trans-Disciplinary Approach, by Barry G. Blundell
and Adam J. Schwarz
Copyright © 2006 John Wiley & Sons, Inc.

architectures. For now, we will not be particularly concerned with issues relating to their implementation, but will focus on general characteristics and introduce some classes of display that will be discussed in more depth in later chapters. Consequently, the concepts described here will be considered mainly without reference to specific system implementation details. However, we will occasionally mention particular embodiments to either reinforce the discussion by providing concrete examples of techniques or where we feel the need to augment current literature.

As indicated in Chapter 1, a range of approaches may be adopted in the implementation of creative 3-D display hardware. In order to avoid confusion, we therefore need to adopt a framework within which we can structure our discussion. To this end, we begin by providing a simple classification scheme. Within this context, we describe how the conventional flat-screen display may be augmented by additional hardware (specifically the re-imaging/projection sub-system introduced in Section 1.7) to exhibit stereoscopic characteristics. We will then extend this display paradigm to realize systems that exhibit autostereoscopic properties.

After the introduction of various classes of display and discussion of aspects of the geometry associated with stereopsis, we turn our attention to fundamental issues relating to the interaction process. The three general interaction paradigms introduced in Section 5.4 are extended and considered within the context of the image space offered by creative 3-D display technologies. We particularly emphasize interaction from the perspectives of the image space supported by the display, the types of tool that may be employed in the interaction process, and usability issues. As with the discussion concerning display systems, we will not, focus on matters relating to the physical implementation of the interaction environment.

Direct interaction by means of a physical tool that may be inserted into a physical or apparent image space is particularly challenging and raises a number of interesting issues. Some classes of display do not directly permit this type of activity (e.g., volumetric systems). However, it may be possible to augment displays with additional hardware (specifically optical components within the re-imaging/projection sub-system (see Figure 1.10)) so that they can do so. Discussion on this topic leads on to the issue of free-space image creation as described in Section 6.8.

The traditional approach to display system classification employing the monocular, stereoscopic, and autostereoscopic, categories provides a useful way to generally distinguish between classes of display. Toward the end of the chapter (Section 6.9), we discuss some of the weaknesses of this structuring technique and emphasize the complexities associated with the development of classification schemes that are general enough to account for the breadth and diversity of display characteristics.

In summary, this chapter lays down key concepts in relation to creative displays and associated interaction techniques. Many of the issues introduced here are fundamental to research in this area. Where appropriate we emphasize multidisciplinary issues and frame discussion within an historical context.

6.2 A TRADITIONAL CLASSIFICATION OF CREATIVE 3-D DISPLAYS

As discussed in Chapter 4, methodologies developed by artists from the earliest times form the foundations of computer graphics and enable the creation of images on the conventional flat-screen display. The result is that we have at our disposal an electronic tableau, which from the standpoint of its ability to provide depth cue information is equivalent to the traditional canvas medium. However, although accommodation, convergence, and stereopsis are cues that are of great importance in everyday life, neither the artist's canvas nor its basic electronic equivalent provide this information to our visual system.

A traditional classification of creative 3-D display systems is indicated in Table 6.1. This provides three categories within which various classes of display are listed. The conventional flat-screen approach is placed in the "monocular" category indicating that, when an image is viewed, each eye receives identical information; there is no retinal disparity. Consequently, the impression of *relief* that we associate with, for example, a stereoscopic image is absent. Through the use of computer graphics techniques, 3-D image scenes may be rendered for depiction on the two-dimensional (2-D) surface of the screen (the "real image space creation sub-system" introduced in Section 1.7). This rendering process assumes a certain viewpoint as defined by the surface of the screen which acts as a virtual window

TABLE 6.1: A traditional classification scheme in which display paradigms are classified under the headings "Monocular," "Stereoscopic," and "Autostereoscopic."

Class of Display	Monocular	Stereoscopic	Autostereoscopic
Example(s)	Conventional flat-screen	Anaglyph (chromatic coding) Temporal coding Spatial coding	Virtual reality (VR and IVR) Augmented reality AutoQ (volumetric, varifocal, electro-holography) Multi-view (e.g., lenticular, parallax barrier)
Visual characteristics	2-D rendition of a 3-D object	Addition of the binocular parallax depth cue	Stereoscopic perspective maintained over a wide range of viewing positions
Viewing characteristics	Direct viewing	Indirect viewing Single viewing direction	Direct viewing Viewing freedom

Although this simple approach is often convenient it does, as discussed in Section 6.9, exhibit various limitations. Note that electroholographic systems (see Section 8.3.3) may be considered as representing an AutoQ or multiview technique.

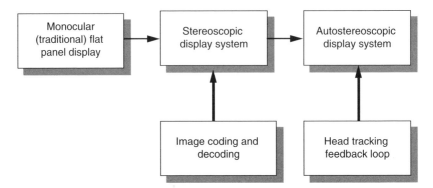

Figure 6.1: Through the addition of additional hardware and software systems, the basic flat panel display can transcend the three basic categories of display appearing in the traditional classification scheme (see Table 6.1). Although this diagram is useful, it does not embrace all approaches (for example, multi-view displays). (Diagram © 2005 A.R. Blundell.)

into a 3-D world. However, unlike a physical window, perspective does not change with viewing direction, and without additional hardware and software systems we cannot move our viewing position in order to more clearly discern the form and spatial separation of image components.

Although the binocular and motion parallax cues are not present in the image depicted on a conventional flat-screen display, this display paradigm may be extended to support these cues. Figure 6.1 shows schematically the conventional flat-screen display being augmented with additional components, thereby enabling it to transcend the three categories of display indicated in Table 6.1. Referring back to Figure 1.10, it will be apparent that the monocular display comprises only the lower three sub-systems and viewing is achieved directly from position A. The additional hardware needed to permit the monocular display to exhibit stereoscopic and autostereoscopic characteristics forms the re-imaging/projection sub-system shown in the illustration, and viewing is then achieved from position B. However, although this permits the inclusion of the binocular and motion parallax cues, as discussed in Section 6.4.3, decoupling of the accommodation and convergence cues is an inherent limitation of the flat-screen approach.[1]

Although the traditional classification scheme provides a useful framework for our current discussion, it fails to account for the breadth of characteristics and diverse nature of creative 3-D displays. Consequently, in Section 6.9, we revisit this scheme and discuss the difficulties of developing simple approaches to display classification that do not overemphasize certain aspects of a display's attributes and underemphasize (or even overlook) other important characteristics.

---

[1]When discussing creative 3-D display systems, it is inadvisable to make absolute statements concerning inherent limitations. For example, one approach involves the rapid reciprocating mechanical motion of a flat-screen display (see Blundell and Schwarz [2000, p. 100]). Multiple frames are output to the screen during each cycle of movement. This approach indeed supports the accommodation and convergence depth cues! However, we will set such exceptions to one side.

6.3 ENHANCING THE MONOCULAR DISPLAY

In this section, we discuss the advancement of the conventional monocular display so as to enable it to exhibit stereoscopic and autostereoscopic characteristics. This discussion will be used to describe some general properties of the different categories of display referred to in Table 6.1.

6.3.1 Creating a Stereoscopic Display

> A painting, although conducted with the greatest Art
> and finished to the last perfection,
> both with regard to its Contours,
> its Lights, its Shadows and its colours,
> can never show a *Relief* equal to that of Natural Objects,
> unless these be viewed at a distance and with a single Eye[2]

The conventional flat-screen display can be made to satisfy the binocular parallax depth cue (see Section 2.6.2) through the use of additional hardware, which thereby forms a stereoscopic system. The underlying principle is by no means new and finds its origins in the first half of the nineteenth century. The stereoscope provides the left and right eye with two slightly different perspectives of a scene. Just as when we view our surroundings, differences in the two views are interpreted as providing a sense of *relief*. Scenes no longer appear to lie within the confines of Flatlands (see Section 1.4) but possess a remarkable three-dimensionality.

In its early days, there was considerable controversy over the original inventor of the stereoscopic technique. Charles Wheatstone claimed to be the first to properly investigate the phenomena but did not widely publish his findings [Wade 1983], nor did he demonstrate his instruments until 1838, some 6 years after his original research and prototyping of stereoscopes[3] (one using mirrors and the other prisms). Some years later (1849), David Brewster[4] developed a lenticular (refracting) stereoscope. Although this device was deemed superior to Wheatstone's approach (and particularly suited for use with photographic images that were then gaining acceptance), Brewster was unable to put his instrument into production in the United Kingdom. Consequently, it was subsequently patented and produced in Paris by Duboscq. The Wheatstone and Brewster stereoscopes are illustrated in Figure 6.2, together with a simple "slit" stereoscope and the "Kaiser Panorama."

---

[2]Leonardo da Vinci (1452–1519), *A Treatise on Painting* translated from Italian, London: Sener and Taylor (1721).

[3]The name "stereoscope" appears to have been assigned by Wheatstone: "... The frequent reference I shall have occasion to make to this instrument will render it convenient to give it a specific name. I therefore propose that it be called a stereoscope, to indicate its property of representing solid images." (Wheatstone (1838) in Wade [1983]). In this context, Wheatstone uses the term "solid images" to distinguish between physical objects and their rendition on a 2-D surface.

[4]This was a period of great scientific advancement. In fact, David Brewster together with Charles Babbage (mentioned in Section 1.3) were instrumental in the establishment of the British Association for the Advancement of Science in 1831.

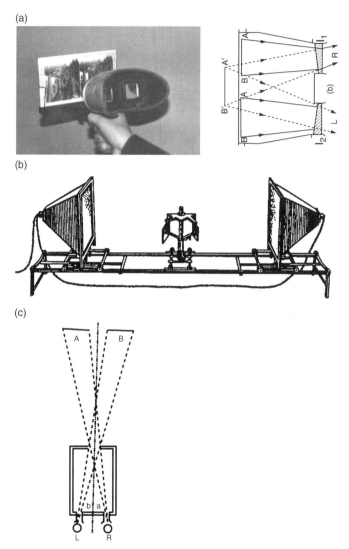

Figure 6.2: Four stereoscope configurations. Figure (a) shows the form attributed to Brewster. Two wedge-shaped lens elements are used so that both halves of the stereopair appear to emanate from the same location. In this way, fusion can take place readily. In (b), the Wheatstone form of stereoscope is illustrated. Here two mirrors (or prisms) are used to direct the two images of the stereopair to the eyes. The mirrors may be inclined so that the two virtual images formed are superimposed, so facilitating stereoscopic fusion. In (c), a simple "slit" stereoscope is illustrated. The construction of the chamber ensures that only one of the two images in the stereopair (physically located at A and B) may be seen by either eye. (d) The Kaiser Panorama enabling up to twenty-five people to view fifty stereoscopic images which change position every few minutes. [Figure (a), (right illustration only), together with (b) and (c) reproduced from Valyus, N., *Steroscopy*, Focal Press, London (1962). Image (d) kindly created by Professor Rüdiger Hartwig; © 2005 R.R. Hartwig.]

(d)

Figure 6.2: *Continued.*

In approximately 1856, Brewster, who was by then in his mid-seventies, appears to have set his mind on going to practically any length to deny Wheatstone the credit for the invention. Correspondence appeared in the *Times* newspaper as these two giants of the Natural Sciences waged battle. Brewster was, it seems, keen that practically anybody other than Wheatstone should receive credit, and among others, he promoted James Elliot (a teacher of mathematics) and Jacopo Chimenti (an artist) as alternative originators of the technique. Elliot, it seems, had conceived the idea of the stereoscope in 1834 but did not construct an actual device until 1839. A pair of drawings attributed to Chimenti who had lived more than 200 years before the controversy broke were (and still are by some) said to represent a stereopair. These drawings are reproduced in Appendix A, where we give a short account of this interesting episode.

The lengthy correspondence appearing in the *Times* between Wheatstone and Brewster is reproduced by Wade [1983] who provides an excellent account of this odd history. At times the level of ill feeling between the two scientists is surprising, especially as it was expressed in a public forum:

David Brewster to the *Times*:

> *... and I think your readers will share with me in the surprise that so remarkable invention as the stereoscope, if actually constructed and exhibited in 1832, should have remained six years in Mr Wheatstone's desk, and make its appearance before the public only in 1838! ...*

Charles Wheatstone to the *Times*:

> *... I deny Sir David's right to challenge me to a combative discussion; but since nothing else will satisfy him, I accept his defiance ...*

And so the debate continued, and it is indeed interesting to think of the long hours spent by these two great figures as they ruminated on and wrote their missives. In fact, their disagreements extended beyond the subject of invention and involved the underlying science behind the stereoscopic technique. Brewster believed that the effect of three-dimensionality occurred as a result of convergence alone, whereas Wheatstone recognized that the disparity between the two retinal images provides a cue of distance. However, some features of stereoscopic depth perception are not easily explained by attributing the operation of the device to stereopsis alone. For example, Wheatstone produced an instrument that he called a "pseudoscope." This device employs two prisms by means of which the two monocular views are reversed. This is equivalent to reversing the images of a stereopair within a conventional stereoscope. In principle (and if retinal disparity is the only determinant of stereo-scopic depth perception), then this should reverse our perception of binocular depth, making closer objects appear further away and vice versa [Purves and Lotto 2003]. In fact, this generally does not occur as other cues, such as occlusion, play a vital role.

The stereoscope has continued to find usage over the years as a fashionable enter-tainment in the Victorian era ("*a piece of domestic apparatus without which no drawing-room is complete*" Wade [1983] quoting Pepper (1869)) and as a technique for enhancing the information content in areas such as, for example, military recon-naissance and scientific visualization. In the form of the "View-Master" stereoscopic images continue to entertain.

Two electronic display screens, one viewed by the left eye and the other by the right eye, may replace the drawings or static photographic images associated with the traditional stereoscope. Such a parallel imaging system requires that a host com-puter outputs frames simultaneously to the two displays. Ideally these screens are located very close to the eyes, ensuring that they fill most, if not all, of the visual field. This is the approach adopted in the implementation of immersive virtual reality (IVR) headsets, and it is interesting to note that this technique is directly derived from the work carried out by pioneers more than 150 years ago.[5] We examine this technique in more depth in Sections 6.5.1 and 8.4 (and in Section 8.4.1, we discuss an implementation dating back to the 1940s which perhaps rep-resents the first stereoscope employing electronic displays).

Any stereoscopic system employing two separate screens, each of which is directed to a particular eye, may, from the perspective of the "image element activation sub-system" (see Figure 1.10), be said to represent a non-coded image production tech-nique, and we will adopt this name in our discussion. Other approaches employ image coding, in which case, both the left and the right views of the stereopair are created on a single display. Various techniques can then be used to direct the relevant image to the appropriate eye. Images may be spatially, temporally, or chromatically coded. In literature, temporally and spatially coded techniques are often referred to as "temporal multiplexing" and "spatial multiplexing," respectively. However, referring to the latter as a multiplexing technique can lead to confusion. We therefore

---

[5]Possibly had Wheatstone and Brewster fully appreciated the longevity of the stereoscopic display principle, their discourse may have been even more acrimonious!

prefer to consider these approaches as simply representing different ways in which image data may be coded to provide binocular disparity and motion parallax to the human visual system. Below, we briefly distinguish among the three techniques:

(1) *Spatial Coding*: In this case, the left and right views of the stereopair are created and cast simultaneously onto the flat panel display. Displays of this type are generally referred to as multi-view systems of which the parallax barrier and lenticular approaches are perhaps the best well known. The lenticular principle is introduced in Section 6.5.2, and discussion on various multi-view techniques is presented in Section 8.3.

(2) *Temporal Coding*: As with spatial coding, the left and right views of the stereopair are depicted on a single flat screen. However, in this case, the two views are not drawn simultaneously but are portrayed as sequential frames. Consequently, for example, frames 1,3,5, etc. may correspond to the left view of the stereopair; in which case, frames 2,4,6, etc. form the right view. Additional hardware is then used to ensure that only odd-numbered frames are seen by the left eye, and that even-numbered frames can only be observed by the right eye. This hardware forms the re-imaging/projection sub-system introduced in Section 1.7. Early approaches to temporal coding required the user to don viewing headgear comprising mechanical shutters. The opening and closing of the shutters over each eye was synchronized to the frame rate of the display. This is certainly no easy task given the need to ensure that each eye receives frames at a rate in excess of the flicker fusion frequency (see Section 2.7). Fortunately, lightweight, vibration-free headgear based, for example, on liquid crystal shutters has now superseded its mechanically driven predecessor.

(3) *Chromatic Coding*: In the case of this approach, the two stereo views are each depicted in a particular color[6] and the observer dons filtered glasses such that each eye may see only one of the two views. This technique is generally referred to as the anaglyph method. Naturally, to work effectively, this approach requires that the filters employed have a sufficiently sharp spectral response to eliminate image cross-talk (in this context, cross-talk indicates that each eye receives not only the designated image but is able to discern, to some degree, the image intended for the other eye) [MacDonald and Lowe 1997].

In Figure 6.3, an unusual stereoscopic image capture and display system is illustrated. This was pioneered by J.L. Baird in the early 1940s [Wireless World 1942] and offered to provide color stereoscopic television (for further reading in connection with Baird's TV focused research, see McLean [2000]). Furthermore, his technique did not require the user to don any viewing apparatus. It is instructive to briefly examine the operation of this system:

1. The Cathode Ray Tube (CRT) shown on the left side of the illustration provides the source of light that is to be scanned across the image scene. The electron beam in the CRT rapidly scans out 100 line frames.

---

[6]The left and right views are depicted in complementary colors. See Section 8.2.2 concerning the use of this technique for color image generation.

2. A spinning disk placed in front of the CRT filters the white light generated by the CRT and enables the image scene to be scanned sequentially in red, green, and blue. An identical synchronized disk at the receiving end allows the user to perceive the color contained within the image scene. Interlacing techniques are reported as having been used to provide an image comprising 500 lines.

3. The mirror arrangement and shutter at the transmission end are responsible for the creation of the stereo image. The mirrors create two parallel beams approximately separated by the interocular distance. The shutter ensures that only one of these beams may scan the image scene at any one time. Thus, the image scene is scanned from the perspective of one eye by red, green, and blue light in sequence. This process is then repeated from the perspective of the other eye.

4. At the receiving end, an identical synchronized spinning shutter ensures that the results of each sequential red, green, and blue scan are seen by the appropriate eye and cannot be seen by the other.

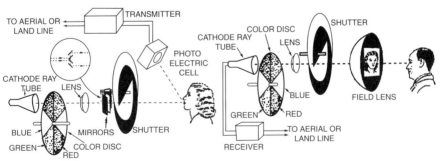

Figure 6.3: The system developed by J.L. Baird in the early 1940s for recording and displaying stereoscopic, color television images. Note that the observer (right) does not need to don special viewing glasses. See text for details on the operation of this system (Reproduced from *Wireless World*, "Stereoscopic Colour Television," February 1942.)

Maintaining an appropriate viewing position is said to have been critical, but it is reported [Wireless World 1942] that:

> *If the colour production lacked the ability in this early experiment to differentiate the subtler shades, it dealt faithfully with the bolder colours. The stereoscopic effects were an unqualified success, and when the person being televised reached towards the "camera," his arm at the receiving end seemed to project out of the lens towards the viewer.*

Irrespective of whether a stereoscopic implementation employs temporal, spatial, or chromatic coding, the image scene must be rendered from two slightly different viewpoints corresponding to the natural viewing position of the two eyes. In principle, this doubles the computational cost as compared with the monocular display technique; although as discussed in Section 8.2.4, techniques may be employed to reduce the computational overhead. The increase in computation is needed to support the binocular parallax depth cue, which in turn will often provide the observer with a greater sense of the 3-D nature of an image scene (augmented realism (see Section 1.5.1)) and may enhance the observer's ability to understand and extract information from complex spatial data sets (augmented information content (see Section 1.5.2)). Only through the careful assessment of a particular application can the interface designer determine to what extent the additional complexities associated with the use of stereoscopic displays will enhance the human–computer interface. Critical to this assessment is the support that a depiction technique will offer for synergistic interaction, and this is often overlooked. For example, computer monitors offering temporal coding of stereoscopic images have been available for some time. These are equipped with a transmitter able to drive special viewing glasses so as to synchronize the switching of the eyepieces with the frames appearing on the display in such a way that each eye is only able to view alternate frames. Typically, the monitors have a very high refresh rate in order to overcome image flicker and can operate in both monocular and stereo mode (see Section 8.2). Unfortunately, these displays and the associated graphics cards have often been procured without proper consideration of the interaction process, and in some circumstances, the use of the stereo mode actually hampers interaction.

Figure 6.4 summarizes viewing opportunities offered by the general forms of stereoscopic display: non-coded, spatially coded, temporally coded, and chromatically coded.

6.3.2 Creating an Autostereoscopic Display

> However rude the age, or uncultivated the people
> from whose hands they came, the products of human ingenuity
> are ever invested with a peculiar and even solemn interest.[7]

In Table 6.1, various classes of display are listed in the autostereoscopic category. The conventional distinction between stereoscopic and autostereoscopic displays

---

[7]From *League of the Ho-de-no-sau-nee or Iroquois*, Volume II, Burt Franklin (pub.) (1901).

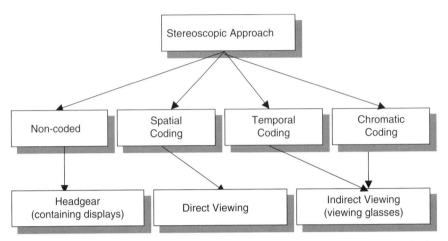

Figure 6.4: Summary of stereoscopic display configurations. Display techniques employing spatial coding permit direct (natural) viewing. Temporally and chromatically coded systems require the viewer to don special glasses. This diagram does not include autostereoscopic systems (e.g., various multi-view techniques). (Diagram © 2005 Q.S. Blundell.)

lies in the latter being able to support direct viewing (i.e., no special viewing glasses are required). Considerable freedom in viewing direction may also be attributed to autostereoscopic systems [Blundell and Schwarz 2000]. In Figure 6.1, the capabilities of the conventional monocular display are shown as being extended, so enabling it to offer stereoscopic functionality. This is achieved through the provision of additional software and through the addition of a re-imaging/projection subsystem (see Section 1.7). This allows support for the binocular parallax depth cue, although viewing remains restricted to a single orientation. However, as indicated in Figure 6.5, with the introduction of a feedback loop enabling the host computer to monitor changes in the observer's orientation relative to the display, it is possible to update the image in such a way as to take into account changes in viewing direction. For this approach to work realistically (i.e., for it to reinforce rather than detract from the "suspension of disbelief"), three essential conditions must be met:

(1) Changes in the observer's angular viewing position relative to the display must be measured with sufficient resolution to ensure that images are seen to move smoothly and do not appear to step through views (motion quantization). Generally, systems of this type only monitor and react to horizontal movement by the operator. Vertical components of motion, rotation of the two eyes from the horizontal, and changes in viewing distance are often not measured and therefore do not cause the image scene to change. Furthermore, this approach only works optimally for a single viewer.

(2) Changes in the observer's angular viewing position relative to the display must be measured with sufficient precision.

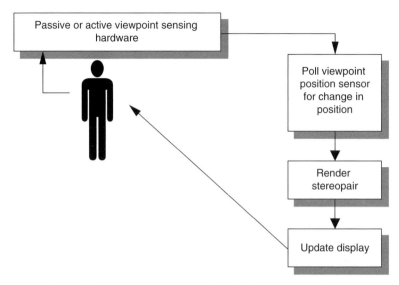

Figure 6.5: The addition of a viewing orientation feedback loop enables the stereoscopic display to exhibit the autostereoscopic characteristic of viewing freedom. Position sensing may be achieved in various ways (see Section 8.4).

(3) The host computer must be able to render each stereopair sufficiently quickly to ensure that the observer does not perceive any latency between head motion and image update (image lag).

Major elements of the feedback loop are indicated in Figure 6.5. Clearly, this approach requires that both the peripheral hardware and the host computer offer appropriate performance. Although motion quantization and image lag may not be physically apparent, they may be problematic in the case of systems that are to be viewed continuously over extended periods, as a consequence of subliminal perception.

6.4 THE GEOMETRY OF STEREOPSIS

When we view our surroundings, the two eyes rotate so that their optical axes meet at the point of fixation (convergence). This fixation point appears at the same location in the retinal image of each eye, and so by definition has zero binocular disparity. However, points in front of or behind the fixation point project to different positions on the left and right retinas. Provided that the resulting disparity is not too great, this does not lead to "double vision" (whereby we perceive two separate images) but provides the cue of stereopsis (binocular parallax). We can easily disrupt this process by lightly pressing on the side of one eye—thereby seeing two separate images—one being more distinct than the other. In turn, we can merge these two views by applying appropriate pressure to the other eye.

Stereopsis is a complex and fascinating subject, and our knowledge of the mechanisms employed beyond the eye to support this powerful visual cue is very much incomplete. For the sake of brevity, in the following sub-sections, we make various simplifications. However, the texts by Boff et al. [1986], Howard [2002], and Howard and Rogers [2002] (and references cited therein) provide an excellent starting point for the reader wishing to pursue this topic in greater depth. (See also books such as Bruce et al. [2003], Purves and Lotto [2003], and McAllister [1993] for a wealth of highly useful additional information.)

6.4.1 Stereoscopic Fixation and the Horopter

> When one comes into contact with a man of first rank,
> the entire scale of his [ones] intellectual conception is modified for life;
> contact with such a man is perhaps
> the most interesting thing which life may have to offer.[8]

When our two eyes fixate at a certain point in space, their optical axes are oriented so that in each retinal image, this point is cast onto the fovea. For any given point of fixation, there are other points in space that also project onto the same *relative* positions in each retina (these are referred to as "corresponding points"). Within this context, we use the term *horopter* as "... *the locus of points in space that project images onto corresponding points in the two retinas*" [Howard and Rogers 2002]. The means of determining the form of this set of points for a given point of fixation has received attention since the time of Father Franciscus Aguilonius (1567–1617) [Boff et al. 1986], and in fact fascination with binocular vision goes back further (see, for example, the work of Alhazen in the eleventh century, and writings of Aristotle—a history that is briefly discussed by [Howard 2002]). In fact, it was Franciscus Aguilonius, who in 1613 introduced the term "horopter" to describe the locus of points in space that have no binocular disparity (Tyler writing in [Regan (ed.) 1991]. However, as Tyler indicates:

> *There has been some considerable confusion in literature due to laxity in the definition of the horopter.... The definition may be based upon zero binocular disparity, zero horizontal disparity, equally perceived distance from the observer, etc.*

In this subsection, we do not consider the various types of horopter but focus on one theoretical form known as the Vieth–Müller[9] circle. This is defined by Aries Arditi writing in Boff et al. [1986] in the following way:

> *Assuming that the eyes are perfect spheres, and the optics perfectly spherical, and that the eyes rotate about axes passing only through their optical nodes, the horopter through the horizontal plane through the eyes, which contains the foveas, is a circle known as the Vieth-Müller circle.*

---

[8]Written by Helmholtz in connection with Johannes Peter Müller (1801–1858), under whom he studied in around 1840 [Warren and Warren 1968].
[9]Gerhard Vieth (1763–1836).

This is illustrated in Figure 6.6(a) for a horizontal plane. The thicker line depicted in this diagram connects the nodes of the two eyes and forms a cord on the circle. Basic geometry indicates that "angles at the circumference of a circle and which are erected on the same cord are equal." Hence, for the two arbitrary points lying on the circle, angles α and β are equal, from which we can deduce that angle x and y are also equal. Thus, the rays of light emanating from the two points lying on the circle subtend the same angle at each eye and illuminate geometrically corresponding points. In fact, all points located within the binocular visual field and lying on the Vieth–Müller circle will (at face value) give rise to corresponding points in the two eyes. As indicated in Figure 6.6(b), the diameter of the Vieth–Müller circle changes with the distance of fixation.

Unfortunately, the Veith–Müller circle provides only an approximate representation of correspondence (zero disparity). Various additional factors must also be taken into account. For example, it is assumed that the eyes rotate about axes that pass through the optical nodes, and this is not the case (the optical nodes and the center of rotation are separated by approximately 5.7 mm [Howard and Rogers 2002]). Furthermore, we must consider with care the very nature of corresponding points. As indicated by Helmholtz, Johannes Müller was somewhat vague in his definition, "*For each point of one retina, there is on the other a 'corresponding point.'*" [Warren and Warren 1968]. The nature of corresponding points is discussed by Howard and Rogers [2002]. They describe the concept of "physiological corresponding points" projecting to the same binocular cell in the visual cortex,

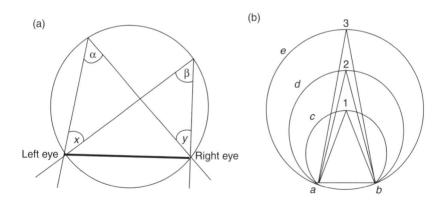

Figure 6.6: In (a) we illustrate the Vieth–Müller circle. The thicker line is drawn between the optical nodes of each eye and forms a cord on the circle. Consequently, angles α and β are equal in size (see text). From this it follows that the angles x and y subtended at the eyes are equal, which results in corresponding points. Figure (b) illustrates a series of Vieth–Müller circles corresponding to different fixation distances. In each case, the circle passes through the optical nodes of the two eyes. Unfortunately, the basic Vieth–Müller circle provides only an approximate representation of points in the horizontal plane giving rise to corresponding points. [Figure (b) is reproduced from the *Encyclopaedia Britannica*, Adam and Charles Black, Edinburgh (1879).]

"geometrically corresponding points," which are defined in terms of their congruent geometrical location in the two eyes, and "empirical corresponding points," which relate to the position at which points comprising an identical image cast onto the two retinas must lie in order to provide, for example, "singleness of vision." In short, horopters measured by experiment deviate from the theoretical ideal, and their precise form depends on the criteria used to define them [Patterson and Martin 1992, Howard and Rogers 1995, 2002].

Although only points on the horopter are strictly corresponding, there is in fact a region slightly away from the horopter within which objects are successfully fused, thus appearing as single images. This region is known as "Panum's fusional area" after Peter Ludvigh Panum who carried out basic experimentation in connection with this effect in 1858 [Howard 2002]. Its size depends on a number of parameters, and it is larger horizontally than vertically—see, for example, Howard and Rogers [1995] or Ware [2000] for details. Nevertheless, an approximate estimate of the maximum angular disparity with which images can be successfully fused at the fovea is around one tenth of a degree (6 arc minutes) [Patterson and Martin 1992]. Panum's fusional area thus defines, for a given point of fixation, the effective region of space in which binocular parallax can be used as a cue to depth. If the disparity between the two retinal images becomes too great, then *diplopia* (a double image) occurs.

6.4.2 Horizontal Disparity

Horizontal disparities are directly related to the location of objects relative to the horopter and have been demonstrated to be a sufficient cue for stereopsis [Julesz 1971]. That is, other monocular or pictorial information is not required; the cue can operate in the absence of any other structure or monocular information in the image. This is the basis for the "random dot stereograms" that have been very popular in recent years (see Figure 6.7). Bela Julesz in the 1960s was perhaps the first to realize the significance of the cyclopean stereo effect and developed the use of such images as a research tool. However, earlier examples also exist, such as those by Boris Kompaneysky in 1939 and Claus Aschenbrenner in 1954.

Consider two arbitrary points denoted by A and B lying within Panum's fusional area. We assume that point A lies beyond the point of fixation (P), and that point B is located closer than P (see Figure 6.8). Assuming that the convergence angle of the eyes is denoted by θ, then in the horizontal plane, the angle subtended at one eye (χ) by A, relative to the optical axis, may be expressed as

$$\chi = \frac{\theta}{2} - \frac{\phi}{2}.$$

From which we express a binocular disparity for A as

$$\delta_A = \theta - \phi. \tag{6.1}$$

Figure 6.7: A simple example of a single-image random dot stereogram. If this image is correctly viewed, a circular region can easily be observed at the center, offset in depth from its surroundings. Such images demonstrate that the cue of stereopsis operates independently of other depth cues.

The disparity of points closer than the Veith–Müller circle, such as B, have a disparity which may be expressed as

$$\delta_B = \varphi - \theta. \tag{6.2}$$

The depth resolution of binocular parallax is determined by the smallest perceptible difference in visual angle. This is known as the "stereo acuity," and its value is influenced by a number of factors.[10] In the context of stereoscopic acuity, Poole [1966] writes:

> *The minimum value of this angle varies rather widely among individuals, being about 2 arc seconds in the best observers, and as high as 100 arc seconds in others. A figure of 10 arc seconds however, is typical for most observers. Converting this to depth perception at an 18-inch viewing distance for two spots 0.25 inch apart indicates that observers can ordinarily tell relative depth to better than 1/16 inch.*

[10]See Aries Arditi writing in Boff et al. [1986] for details.

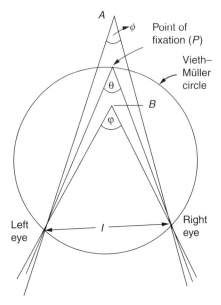

Figure 6.8: The Vieth–Müller circle is the locus in the horizontal plane on which points have (in principle) zero disparity for a given fixation point *P*. Panum's fusion area is the volume about the horopter in which the disparate views of each eye can be successfully fused without giving rise to a double image. Here we illustrate two points (*A* and *B*) lying on either side of the point of fixation. Note that the distance of these points from the Vieth–Müller circle has been exaggerated for clarity.

The relationship between the basic parameters of stereoscopic resolution can be determined based on the construction presented in Figure 6.9. Here we see that:

$$\tan\frac{\theta}{2} = \frac{I}{2D}$$

and

$$\tan\frac{\varphi}{2} = \frac{I}{2(D-d)}.$$

In this simplified treatment, the disparity is then given by

$$\delta = \left[\arctan\left(\frac{I}{2(D-d)}\right) - \arctan\left(\frac{I}{2D}\right) \right]. \tag{6.3}$$

Here, *I* is the interocular distance, *D* is the absolute distance to the point of fixation, and *d* is the relative depth to be resolved. Using the small angle approximation[11]

[11]Where *x* is measured in radians.

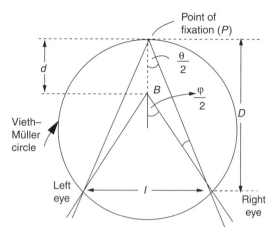

Figure 6.9: Here we illustrate the angular disparity for a point lying within the Vieth–Müller circle. The eyes are fixated at point P. Since the stereoscopic acuity of the eye is an angular measure, this geometrical construction can be used to determine the distance dependence of relative stereoscopic depth perception (see text for details).

$\arctan(x) \approx x$, we may express Eq. (6.3) as

$$\delta \approx \frac{Id}{2(D^2 - dD)}.$$

(6.4)

We may also assume that in a typical case, $D^2 \gg dD$ and so

$$\delta \approx \frac{Id}{2D^2}.$$

(6.5)

The angular horizontal disparity is thus approximately proportional to the relative depth d and inversely proportional to the square of the viewing distance. Inverting this relationship, for a given stereo acuity δ_s, the minimum depth that can be resolved is given by

$$d_s \approx \frac{2\delta_s D^2}{I}.$$

(6.6)

As previously discussed, the fovea is the central region of the retina where vision is most acute. In the center of the fovea, the maximum disparity before fusion breaks down is only $0.1°$ in the worst case, whereas at six degrees eccentricity (from the fovea), the limit is $0.3°$. As a result, stereoscopic displays provide anisotropic resolution (i.e., the *depth* resolution is significantly less than that supported in the plane of the screen). This issue is discussed in some detail by Ware [2000].

6.4.3   Accommodation and Convergence

Consider for a moment a stereoscopic display employing either a temporal or spatial coding technique. Since the images (which constitute the "stereo window") are presented on a plane perpendicular to the line of sight, the eyes focus on this plane; i.e., the distance of the stereo pair from the eyes determines the focal depth. On the other hand, in regarding the 3-D image, convergence changes according to the perceived distance of image components within the scene. In short, accommodation and convergence cues become decoupled, and this is not consistent with our real-world experience. This matter is briefly discussed in Lipton [2001], where he refers to it as the "*A/C breakdown.*" Although when we are accustomed to viewing stereo images we may be able to decouple these cues without difficulty, this is a factor that can cause discomfort in viewing some images. (Note: This adverse effect may be ameliorated by employing optical components via which the stereoscopic image is viewed; however, this may impact on direct interaction opportunities—see Section 6.6.2.)

Clearly, the degree of relief attributed to a stereo image determines the amount by which the A/C cues are decoupled (i.e., provide conflicting information). The degree of relief is defined by the rendering process where we specify the separation of the two different views (although it is important to note that in the case of the conventional non-coded stereoscope, since each eye can only observe a single image, the separation of the images by the *interocular* distance plays no part in determining the degree of disparity). We may ameliorate the extent of the decoupling between the A/C cues by positioning central image components (i.e., central in terms of depth) in the plane of the stereo window so that parts of the image scene may lie on either side of this plane. In this way, the degree to which the A/C cues are decoupled is reduced. However, as discussed in Section 6.7.1, this is not an option if we wish to employ a direct interaction technique.

6.4.4   Vertical Disparity

The differential binocular views of objects in space generally also give rise to "vertical disparities." This is due to features presenting different vertical visual angles to each eye and can be appreciated by considering an example, such as the checkerboard illustrated in Figure 6.10. Held vertically in front of the observer, squares on one side will be closer to the corresponding eye and thus present greater angles, both horizontally and vertically[12]—an object closer to one eye than the other will cast a correspondingly larger retinal image. The vertical horopter, where points present the same vertical angle to each eye, is a line passing through the point of fixation [Howard and Rogers 1995]. Only features lying on either the vertical meridian or the horizontal plane of regard do not give rise to vertical disparity.

---

[12]In stereoscopic video applications, this vertical disparity effect is known as "keystone distortion," and can be avoided by having the cameras aligned with their optical axes parallel (rather than converged) [Woods et al. 1993, Jones et al. 2001].

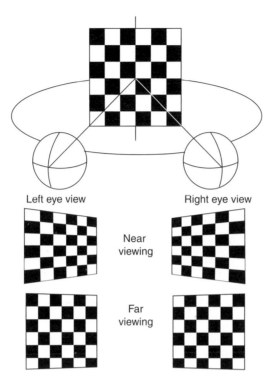

Figure 6.10: Binocular vision also supplies *vertical* disparity gradients (in particular for large visual angles). This arises due to the convergence of the two eyes on the fixation point. [Reproduced from DeAngelis, G.C., "Seeing in Three Dimensions: the Neurobiology of Stereopsis," *Trends Cogn. Sci.*, **4** (3) pp. 80–90 (2000); © 2000 with permission of Elsevier.]

The approximate expression provided in Eq. (6.5) enables the depth of an object to be calculated relative to the point of fixation. Naturally, it leads us to consider how absolute or egocentric depth information may be obtained. DeAngelis [2000] briefly summarizes the research of Mayhew [1982] and Bishop [1989], and provides an approximate value for the vertical disparity (δv) which is of the form:

$$\delta v \approx \frac{I\theta_h\theta_v}{D}. \tag{6.10}$$

Where I represents the interocular distance and D is the viewing distance (see Figure 6.11). θ_h and θ_v are the horizontal and vertical angles subtended at the eye by a point in space. Here we note that, in principle, the absolute distance of the point could be computed from this information.

The role and relative importance of vertical disparity in the perception of depth remains unclear. The *relative* vertical disparity between two points gives rise to a vertical size ratio between their perceived spacing as seen by each eye [Howard and Rogers 1995]. More generally, there is some evidence that horizontal gradients

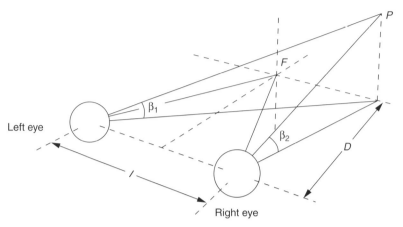

Figure 6.11: The geometry governing vertical disparity originating from binocular vision. A point P offset from the current fixation point will be seen at different vertical visual angles (β_1 and β_2 in the left and right eyes). [Reproduced from Bishop, P.O., "Vertical Disparity Egocentric Distance and Stereoscopic Depth Constancy: A New Interpretation," *Proc. R. Soc. London Ser. B.* **237**, (1989); © The Royal Society.]

in the vertical size ratio could provide distance information, particularly for large fields of view ($>25-30°$) [DeAngelis 2000, Brenner et al. 2001]. The publications by both Bishop and Mayhew, together with Howard and Rogers [2002], are especially recommended to the reader wishing to persue further the nature and consequences of vertical disparity.

6.5 SOME CLASSES OF AUTOSTEREOSCOPIC DISPLAY

> We had a friend, Hopworth, and he got a book from Denys
> and he didn't return it.
> Denys was furious, and I said to Denys you wouldn't
> lose a friend for the sake of a silly book
> would you? And he said, no, but he has, hasn't he?[13]

In this section we will briefly introduce various classes of creative autostereoscopic display system. These are generally considered from a functional perspective. More detailed discussion on display theory, computational requirements, and implementation issues is deferred until Chapter 8.

6.5.1 Virtual Reality Systems

Although virtual reality (VR) is commonly associated with immersive environments, the title has been used ever more widely to describe systems that have a

---

[13]From "Out of Africa," Universal Studios (1985).

3-D graphics capability and are perhaps (although not necessarily) able to provide the user with a multisensory computer-generated experience (generally audio and/or limited haptic). The seemingly ad hoc application of the vogue VR title has caused confusion and does not assist in the classification of creative display and interaction technologies (most, if not all, of which could now be said to fall loosely under the broad VR heading). However, these problems have been caused because the VR title is open to wide ranging interpretation. In fact, the current tendency to apply the fashionable term "holographic" (either in full or in an abbreviated form) to various display technologies which in no way operate on holographic principles has much less justification and appears to be driven only by market forces.

Current literature defines VR in many ways, and rather than formulating yet another definition of the VR approach, we prefer to present two definitions taken from the literature, and briefly discuss general aspects of this title:

Virtual Reality is the use of computers and human-computer interfaces to create the effect of a three-dimensional world containing interactive objects with a strong sense of three-dimensional presence. [Bryson 1996]

Or alternatively:

Virtual reality is a high-end user-computer interface that involves real-time simulation and interactions through multiple sensory channels. These sensorial modalities are visual, auditory, tactile, smell and taste. [Burdea and Coiffet 2003]

Burdea and Coiffet then go on to identify three pivotal characteristics of VR, namely interaction, immersion, and imagination (see Figure 6.12). Consider for a moment interaction and immersion. Although these are fundamental tenets of the VR approach, they are not easily quantified, and as more spectacular and often unrealistic visions of VR have been put to one side and we have learned to focus on what is feasible, the VR title has become increasingly applicable to many technologies and system architectures. Clearly the degree of immersion varies between display paradigms. However, this is not the only factor that must be considered, and other issues such as the interaction opportunities, multisensory feedback opportunities, and the very nature of the application play a dominant role. It is, for example, possible that for certain applications, a conventional monocular display may offer a highly immersive environment.

In an excellent publication by the inventors of the CAVE (an immersive VR technology which will be introduced shortly) [Cruz-Neira et al. 1992], the authors begin by describing their approach in terms of the "suspension of disbelief" (see Section 1.5.1) and the "viewer-centered perspective" that it offers to support. When coupled with interaction opportunities, these terms offer a highly descriptive (although perhaps subjective) insight into the very nature of many creative display and interaction technologies. As a consequence, we find that the VR title can quite appropriately embrace systems that purists have traditionally considered to reside outside

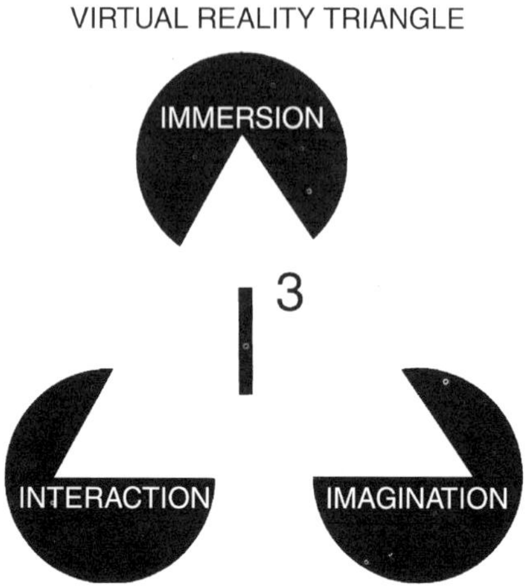

VIRTUAL REALITY TRIANGLE

Figure 6.12: The three key aspects of the virtual reality approach: Immersion, Interaction, and Imagination. [Reproduced from Burdea, G.C., and Coiffet, P., *Virtual Reality Technology*, 2nd edn., John Wiley (2003); © 2003 John Wiley & Sons.]

this classification. However, in this book, we employ the term "virtual reality" in a conventional manner.

In summary, it is important to bear in mind that the VR title has such breadth, that it is not easily restricted to a limited number of high-end techniques. However, as this area of research matures, it is likely that the name "virtual reality" will be augmented or superceded by more meaningful and precise terms.

For the remainder of this subsection, our discussions will be limited to Immersive Virtual Reality (IVR) systems. Pioneering work in connection with this approach dates back to the 1960s. In 1962, a patent issued to Morton Heilig described the Sensorama [Heilig 1962]. This placed a single user within an immersive environment in which the imaging system occupied the user's entire visual field. Stereo sound was incorporated within this "virtual theater," and realism is said to have been further enhanced via mechanical systems providing airflow, vibration, etc. Heilig also worked on a head-mounted display (HMD) system, and later in the 1960s, Sutherland developed an IVR HMD employing two small CRTs that could project images into each eye and so satisfy the binocular parallax depth cue [Sutherland 1968]. (See Section 8.4.1.)

Below we briefly discuss issues relating to this conventional approach to the implementation of IVR and an alternative technique known as the CAVE. Later, in Section 8.4, we reexamine both of these approaches in more depth.

1. *Entering Cyberspace by Means of a Non-coded Stereoscopic Display*: The CRT-based IVR headsets that were pioneered by Heilig and Sutherland now generally make use of LCD-based technologies for image production. Optical components are used to provide image magnification (so as to fill the user's field of view) and at the same time permit the user to focus on the image source (given its close proximity to the eye). This optical

arrangement constitutes the re-imaging/projection sub-system. Magnetic or ultrasound signal transmission provides a convenient means by which head tracking may be achieved.

This approach enables a user to enter an image space in which all visual objects are synthesized, including depth cues. As a consequence, although high-performance IVR systems are computationally demanding, they are very flexible. However, because of the image being located at a fixed distance from the eyes, the convergence and accommodation depth cues are decoupled as with all other stereoscopic methods. Further details on this type of display paradigm may be found in Section 8.4.

2. *Entering Cyberspace via the CAVE*: Another approach to the implementation of IVR systems enables one or more viewers to enter an artificial world contained within the confines of a room and necessitates only the wearing of stereoscopic glasses rather than a more cumbersome projection headset. An example of this technique (known as the CAVE) employs stereoscopic images that are cast onto the walls and floor from outside the room by means of red, green, and blue (RGB) projection systems. The position of one observer is monitored, and the stereo images are computed for this viewing position. Other observers therefore view an inferior (although generally acceptable) image. Despite the computational overheads, the difficulty of accurately aligning the projection systems, aliasing, and the interference of the visible edges and corners of the room, the results are impressive. Images appear to occupy the room, and the degree of realism is such that sensations such as vertigo and of collision with virtual objects are readily apparent. (For further discussion, see Section 8.4.2 where the Cybersphere is also introduced.)

6.5.2 Multi-view Systems: The Lenticular Sheet

Multi-view displays can be implemented in a variety of ways, employ spatial coding, and allow an observer to view images directly without the need for any viewing glasses. In the simplest case, these systems assume a particular viewing position, and this can restrict operator mobility. Much ongoing research centers on reducing viewing position restrictions and so, enabling freedom in viewer location. The lenticular display (based on the work of F. E. and H. E. Ives in the first half of the twentieth century) provides a simple example of the multi-view technique. In one form, a "lenticular" faceplate comprising a set of cylindrical lenslets is located on the outer surface of a conventional display. A stereopair is then interleaved in such a way that, the lenslets are able to direct portions of the appropriate image to each eye, as illustrated in Figure 6.13. Multi-view displays are discussed in more detail in Section 8.3.

6.5.3 AutoQ Systems

For the purposes of this book, we will use the title "AutoQ" to refer to displays in which various depth cues (particularly binocular and motion parallax and usually

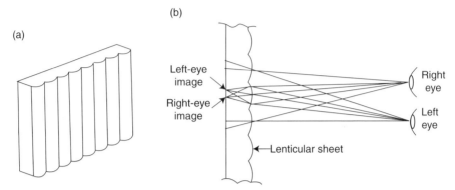

Figure 6.13: Showing the general principle of operation of a "lenticular"-based display. A lenticular faceplate comprising a set of cylindrical lenslets (shown in (a)) is fitted to the outer surface of a conventional display. A stereopair is then interleaved in such a way that, the lenslets are able to direct the appropriate image to each eye, as illustrated in (b). [Reproduced from Okoshi, T., "Three-Dimensional Displays" *Proc. IEEE*, **68** (1980); © 1980 IEEE.]

accommodation and convergence) are *inherently* associated with the depicted image. Consequently, when considered from this perspective, AutoQ systems and IVR displays lie at opposite ends of the spectrum. In the case of the IVR approach, all depth cue information associated with an image scene is artificially generated, and as a result, the IVR approach offers great flexibility (since depth cue information is computed, we are free to make adjustments to it[14]). On the other hand, this flexibility increases the computational cost associated with the IVR technique and this impacts on applications in which high-quality images must be rendered in real time in order to permit interactive operations.

In the case of AutoQ techniques, various depth cues are implicitly associated with the image. Although this reduces computational cost, it results in a reduction of flexibility. For example, linear perspective is generally controlled by the spatial extent of the image data set, when scaled to fit within the bounds of the image space. Consequently, for volumetric displays that permit all-around viewing, the depth of field cannot be greater than the depth of the image space.

Volumetric display systems represent the most common form of display falling into the AutoQ category [Blundell and Schwarz 2000, Blundell 2006]. Displays of this type permit point form voluminous data sets to be displayed within a physical transparent volume (see, for example, Figure 6.14 and Section 8.5). Since the displayed image may be drawn within a physical 3-D image space, various depth cues (including accommodation, convergence, binocular parallax, and motion parallax) are inherently associated with it. This natural inclusion of depth cue information can be advantageous as it minimizes the adjustment that must be

---

[14]Remembering the inherent decoupling of the accommodation and convergence (A/C) cues.

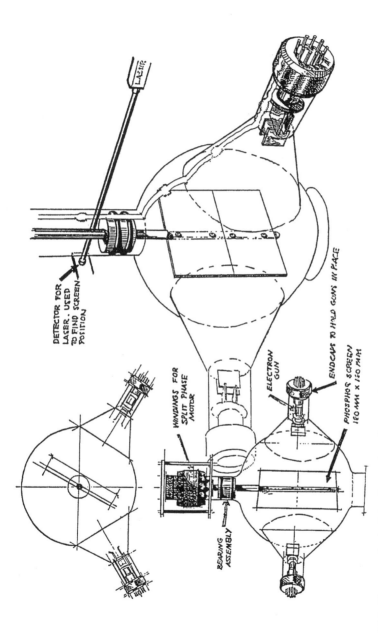

Figure 6.14: The general principle of operation of one particular approach to the implementation of a volumetric display. This display is classified as a swept-volume architecture. A rotating (phosphor-coated) planar target screen rotates at a rate in excess of the flicker fusion frequency. As it rotates, it sweeps out a cylindrical volume. Two electron beams are used to address the screen as it rotates. This gives rise to visible voxels within a 3-D image space. Under suitable computer control, 3-D images may be formed. This system is known as the Cathode Ray Sphere and is discussed further in Section 8.5. (Original drawing by Warren King.)

made by the human visual system when switching between the physical world and the displayed image.

In principle, various volumetric display system architectures impose very little viewing angle restriction, enabling a number of observers to simultaneously observe an image scene from practically any orientation. However, in reality, many approaches suffer from various weaknesses, and as a consequence, image quality is often determined by image positioning and observer location. Although this is discussed in greater detail later, it is appropriate to list three of the major weaknesses here:

(1) A lack of isotropy and homogeneity within the physical volume in relation to voxel[15] placement.

(2) A lack of optical uniformity. This impacts on the rectilinear passage of light as it propagates from the image scene to the volume boundary (image distortion) and may also cause image brightness to vary with viewing location.

(3) Refraction of light as it emerges from the physical volume in which the image is depicted (image distortion)

In short, even if (1) above can be overcome, the creation of a "perfect" image provides no guarantee that it will be perceived as such. Unfortunately, in the case of many volumetric embodiments, images often look most pleasing when positioned in a certain place and viewed from a certain direction.

A volumetric display creates a real image within a physical volume, and although to date volumetric systems give rise to images that emit light, it may ultimately prove possible to implement a system in which images are nonemissive and therefore can only be seen when externally illuminated [Blundell and Schwarz 2000, p. 178, Blundell 2006]. The benefit to be derived from this approach is that images can be "solid" and thereby satisfy the occlusion depth cue. Furthermore, shadows can be easily cast using external light sources.

The "varifocal mirror" technique denotes another approach to the implementation of the AutoQ class of display, and although in principle images may be either real or virtual, the latter is the most common. The basic principle of operation of this type of display is illustrated in Figure 6.15. Since images are created by transient luminescent phenomena, image opacity cannot be achieved and so the occlusion depth cue cannot be satisfied (techniques such as hidden line removal must be used to provide a sense of occlusion). The varifocal technique is discussed further in Section 8.5.3.

Images created using the "electro-holographic" technique discussed in Section 8.3.3 may also fall into the AutoQ classification. Alternatively, as indicated in Chapter 8, current embodiments can be considered to represent instances of the multiview approach.

From the user's perspective, the volumetric, varifocal mirror, and holographic approaches permit the direct viewing of an image scene without the need to employ

---

[15]Volumetric images are constructed from voxels—these being a generalization of the pixel which is the fundamental element used by other display techniques for image construction. See Section 1.6.3.

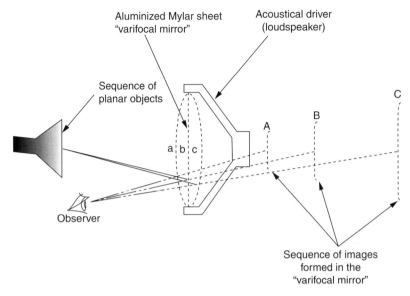

Figure 6.15: The general principle of operation of a varifocal mirror display. A flexible mirrored membrane is driven (most commonly by air pressure created by a loudspeaker located behind the membrane) so as to oscillate between concave and convex states. Consequently, a curved mirror is created which has a continuously varying focal length. Image slices are cast onto the mirror and reflected from it. The observer looks into the mirror, and volumetric images occupying an apparent image space may be observed without the need for any special viewing glasses to be worn. [Reproduced from Rawson, E.G., "Vibrating Varifocal Mirrors for 3D Imaging," *IEEE Spectrum*, (1969); © 1969 IEEE.]

any form of viewing glasses, but they differ in their provision of viewing freedom. The practically unrestricted freedom offered (in principle) by volumetric systems is more limited in the case of the varifocal mirror technique, and high computational cost generally determines the viewing freedom associated with electro-holographic systems.

6.6 INTERACTION PARADIGMS IN 3-D SPACE

As previously discussed, although creative display technologies offer to augment the visualization process, this represents only one of the reasons for their development. Of equal importance is their potential to provide new synergistic interaction opportunities. We particularly refer to the ability of creative systems to enable tasks that are inherently 3-D in nature to be carried out within a 3-D space. In this section, we bring together some of the concepts introduced so far, and frame our discussion within the context of the three general interaction paradigms introduced in Section 5.4. These interaction techniques were previously discussed in the context of the conventional flat-screen display, and in the sub-sections that follow we will examine each from the perspective of their use within a 3-D image space.

We will confine our current discussions to the transferred, direct, and pointer-based interaction paradigms that in principle allow an operator to navigate naturally within a 3-D space (either physical or apparent in nature) without recourse to command input via, for example the keyboard or speech recognition systems. Furthermore, we postpone for now the two-handed (bi-manual) interaction paradigm; this is briefly considered in Chapter 9.

6.6.1 Transferred Interaction

In Section 5.4.1, we considered transferred interaction from the perspective of the conventional display. In the case of this modality, the cursor is navigated via a physical interaction tool such as a joystick or mouse to any location on a screen's surface. When extended to the 3-D situation, the physical interaction tool (located outside the image space) is used to move some kind of virtual object(s) *within* 3-D space. As with the 2-D case, a correspondence exists (which we anticipate is intuitive) between the motion of the physical tool (within the interaction space) and that of the virtual object(s) (within the image space).

Accurate and rapid interaction with objects lying either in a physical or an apparent 3-D space may be significantly more difficult than in the 2-D case. Consider for a moment two pens, held vertically in each hand—one held upward and the other downward. The pens are at arm's length, and we attempt to align them (without their touching) so that one is directly above the other. Although positioning them so that they are aligned in the horizontal plane is trivial, their accurate alignment in terms of depth is more problematic.[16] Should the pens not be coincident, they will appear to move relative to each other when the head or body are moved to provide a different perspective. This relative motion is referred to as "parallax," and the expression "no parallax" is used to describe the situation in which objects are aligned and there is no relative motion between them when the viewpoint is changed. Here it is important to note that accurate placement may often only be achieved by our movement relative to such objects. Should the objects be located at a greater distance, then head movement may be insufficient and we may need to move to a different viewing location.

The ability of our visual system to discriminate between the depths of two or more objects relies on our interpretation of a plurality of information. Stereoscopic acuity was previously discussed in Section 6.4.2. We may enhance our ability to discriminate between the spatial separation of objects by changing our orientation (or by reorientating the image). In the case of some display architectures, head movement alone may provide sufficient information for us to clearly discern spatial separation. Other approaches may require that we make major changes in viewing location (e.g., some volumetric implementations; see Section 8.5). User mobility issues are briefly discussed in Section 6.7.3.

---

[16]In this scenario, positioning the two pens is facilitated by our inherent knowledge of the spatial location of our limbs; see Chapter 3. Consequently, a more realistic trial involves fixing one pen in some sort of clamp so that only one is held in the hand.

6.6.2 Direct Interaction

In this scenario, we consider that the physical interaction tool may be moved *within* the region appearing to contain the image scene, i.e., the physical or apparent image space. The freedom of movement of the device within 3-D space is constrained by either the boundaries of the volume or as a consequence of the tool making contact with "solid" image components. Naturally, image components will only appear as having substance if the interaction tool is coupled to hardware able to provide the operator with a sense of force feedback and if the software systems can perform collision detection in real time (see Chapter 7). As with the transferred interaction techniques, accurate positioning relative to image components will often rely on changes in viewing position so as to detect that there is no parallax between the interaction tool and the relevant image component. However, in the case of systems supporting force feedback, the sensation of collision provides other sensory input that makes it unnecessary for accurate visual alignment.

The introduction of a physical interaction tool within an image space can cause additional problems. By way of example, consider for a moment a stereoscopic system employing temporal coding and in which the image appears to lie between the image generation hardware and the observer (see Figure 6.16). A physical opaque object (interaction tool) is now inserted into the image space. As can be seen from this figure (in which the scale is exaggerated for clarity), the presence of the physical object may occlude not only that part of the image that appears to lie behind it (which is appropriate), but it may also prevent image formation in front of the object (which is certainly not appropriate). Consequently, the object may create a region of image space that is void; we will refer to this as the "stereoscopic *umbra*" so as to distinguish between this region and another small area that may be visible to only one eye. This we will appropriately refer to as the "stereoscopic *penumbra*." Thus, the *umbra* contains no image, the *penumbra* provides only a monocular view, and the remainder of the image space is undisturbed by the presence of the physical object and so provides the normal stereoscopic view.

Depth cue conflict is a further problem that may occur when a direct interaction tool is placed within an image space (see Section 6.7.1).

6.6.3 Pointer-Based Interaction

In this case, interaction is achieved by means of a pointer that casts into the image space a visible collimated beam generated, by, for example, a laser diode contained in the pointing device. The passage of the beam through the volume acts as a positioning locator for the observer. This technique is only appropriate for use with a very small number of classes of display as the purpose of the beam is to provide positioning information to the observer, and therefore, its passage through the volume must be clearly visible. This restricts the technique to certain systems employing a physical image space. Finally, it is worth noting that the beam cast by the pointer

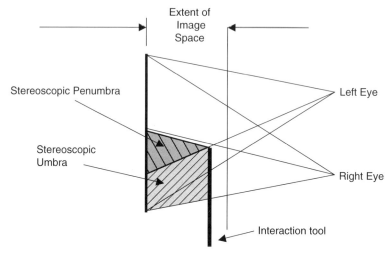

Figure 6.16: Here we illustrate the types of problem that may occur when a physical (opaque) interaction tool is used in conjunction with, for example, a temporally coded stereoscopic display. The apparent image space is assumed to lie in front of the stereo window. The interaction tool is inserted into an image space and not only occludes a part of the image that lies behind the tool (this is appropriate) but also a portion of the image in front of the tool (which is clearly undesirable). We may consider the tool as giving rise to a stereoscopic *umbra*, in which no image is visible, and a stereoscopic *penumbra*, in which only a monocular image is seen. The diagram simplifies the image space disruption and, for clarity, exaggerates the scale. (Diagram © 2005 A.R. Blundell.)

may do no more than provide a visual feedback cue to the user; in which case, additional hardware located both within and external to the pointer determine the position and orientation of the pointer. Alternatively, it is possible that the beam itself may be used by the host computer as a source of directional information.

6.7 WORKING IN A 3-D SPACE

When we examine the suitability of a particular display paradigm for use in a specific application, many factors should be considered. However, it is perhaps only natural that we intuitively focus on visual characteristics such as augmented realism, information content, and ease of image interpretation. Unfortunately, should we unduly concentrate on visual issues, we may overlook other equally important facets of a display's essential character, not the least of which relate to the interaction process.

In the first part of this section, we consider some of the interesting issues that may arise when we choose to employ a direct interaction tool in conjunction with a particular display technique. We then briefly discuss ways in which we may enhance the interaction process by reducing the need for precise positioning of the interaction device. Finally, in Section 6.7.3, we turn our attention to user mobility.

6.7.1 The Application of the Direct Interaction Technique

Direct interaction requires that four essential conditions be fulfilled:

(1) It must be possible to insert the interaction tool into the region occupied by the image or into the region from which the image appears to emanate, i.e., the physical or apparent image space. The user must be free to move the tool to any location within this space (unless, of course, inhibited from entering some regions by some type of force feedback system).

(2) The user should be able to change the orientation of the interaction tool so as to, for example, drag objects.

(3) The presence of the interaction tool must not interfere with the image production process; in particular, the interaction tool should not obstruct portions of the image located between the interaction tool and the observer. The need to have the freedom to change the interaction tool's orientation alluded to in (2) should not exacerbate this problem. This could, for example, occur if, in order to achieve certain orientations, the user's hand has to enter the image space.

(4) The presence of the physical interaction tool within the physical or apparent image space must not cause depth cue conflict as the user's gaze switches between image components and the interaction tool.

We are, of course, taking other requirements for granted. For example, we are assuming that hardware is available to track the position and orientation of the interaction tool, and that once positioned at the required location, buttons are available to enable the user to carry out specific functions such as select, drag, etc. Furthermore, we are assuming that any haptic feedback system can be disabled to allow the interaction tool to pass through "solid objects" to reach other parts of the image space. However, the four requirements listed above are perhaps the most challenging and are the ones that particularly impact on display design. In fact, these requirements are not frequently met by display architectures, and although the use of the direct interaction method may seem to be particularly intuitive, proper implementation can be problematic. In Table 6.2, we consider the use of the direct interaction approach in connection with several display paradigms and illustrate the ability of each to meet each of the above requirements.[17]

As the reader will note, the stereoscopic display is referred to twice within the table, and the difference between these two entries concerns the position of the perceived image relative to the stereoscopic window. Previously we considered the way in which it is possible to define the image location relative to this window and indicated that so as to reduce the level of decoupling between the accommodation and convergence (A/C) cues, the image is often made to lie on either side of the window

---

[17]It is important to remember that classes of display may generally be implemented in many ways and may therefore take on various forms. Consequently, Table 6.2 is only intended to be indicative, providing a general indication that does not take into account possible exceptions.

TABLE 6.2: **Although the use of a direct interaction tool is of interest in offering an intuitive means of interacting with a 3-D image scene, implementation issues must be considered carefully. The display must permit the insertion of the interaction tool into the image space (be this physical or apparent), and the tool should not prevent image formation in the region of image space lying between the tool and the observer.**

Display Class	Image Space Accessibility	Visual Obstruction	Depth Cue Conflict
Stereoscopic display (image appearing to lie behind the stereo window)	Not accessible	N/A	N/A
Stereoscopic display (image appearing in front of the stereo window)	Accessible	Yes	Possible
Volumetric display	Not accessible	N/A	N/A
Volumetric display + re-imaging sub-system	Accessible	Yes	Possible

(this is in fact not an option should we wish to use direct interaction techniques). Consequently the two entries made for the stereoscopic implementation in Table 6.2 simply differ in the parallax value assigned to image components within a scene. Should the image be perceived as lying behind the stereo window, then this clearly precludes the insertion of a physical interaction tool into the image space (and so contravenes condition (1), above). In fact, "no parallax" between image components and the interaction tool can only be achieved when the image lies between the stereo window and the observer. However, in such a case, the size of the interaction tool should be kept to a minimum (for example, a probe that is needle-like in form) to minimize the obstruction caused to parts of the image by the presence of the tool. This may also help in reducing depth cue conflict (when the tool is viewed, the accommodation and convergence cues will be coupled in a natural manner, but as the gaze returns to the stereoscopic image, these two cues will become decoupled).[18]

Volumetric systems are also listed in Table 6.2. Although volumetric images occupy three physical dimensions, the user is prevented (by the mechanisms used for the generation of the volume) from gaining direct access to them. Image space creation mechanisms are discussed further in Section 8.5, and for our present purposes, it is sufficient to say that the volume may, for example, be formed by rapidly moving components (e.g., Figure 6.14), be comprised of a solid medium, or be defined by a transparent display vessel wall containing a gas at low pressure. Whatever the case, a physical interaction tool cannot enter the image space. However, in Section 6.8, we revisit both the volumetric approach and the stereoscopic display in which the image appears to be located behind the stereo window. As we will see, the insertion

---

[18]The use of a physical interaction tool in connection with a traditional stereoscope (non-coded system) provides an interesting exercise and is raised in the Investigations Section at the end of this chapter.

of an interaction tool into the image space is not an intrinsic limitation of either approach but may be accomplished with additional hardware.

In assessing the direct interaction method, we must also consider usability issues. For example:

(1) If the interaction process is to take place frequently, or over long periods of time, then discomfort may be caused as a consequence of holding the interaction tool in space without being able to rest the hand on a surface.

(2) From (1), the absence of a rest surface which can act a static point of reference may increase the difficulty of achieving precise operations.

(3) Should this approach necessitate large movements (as compared with, for example, the joystick and mouse), then this is likely to impact on movement time and increase operator strain.

The concept of providing one or a range of direct interaction tools to enable a designer to sculpt within 3-D space denotes an interesting application. Although, for example, this approach offers many opportunities for freehand sketching, accuracy is likely to be problematic when compared with the equivalent pen-and-paper approach unless supported by appropriate software facilities (see the following subsection). When writing in the conventional way, the motion of the fingers achieves fine movement (as they are more precisely controlled than the joints in the arm). Furthermore, friction between a pen and the paper is intuitively adjusted and maintained for long periods of time as a consequence of the reference point supplied by the wrist. This enhances dexterity, and moreover, minor tremors of the fingers and hand may be damped out by the automatic adjustment of pressure between the writing implement and the texture of the medium. However, in the case of a 3-D space in which interaction is achieved via a direct interaction tool, the most likely static reference point will be provided at the elbow rather than at the wrist and this, coupled with the absence of frictional contact between sculpting tool and the medium, is likely to reduce drawing accuracy and introduce error should any hand tremor occur.

On the other hand, we are highly adaptive, and although the above comments need to be considered with care, they should not deter research into this approach as the benefits that may be derived from this type of creative technique are likely to be significant.[19] Furthermore, when faced with any new medium, we adapt our ways of working and generally it is very difficult to fully anticipate the ultimate result of this adaptation process.

6.7.2 Assisted Interaction Within a 3-D Space

A fundamental *raison d'être* of creative 3-D displays is to facilitate the interaction process. Should the interaction with data sets depicted in a 3-D image space prove

---

[19]See the "painterly" technique referenced in Section 9.4.

more complex than when these same data are displayed by conventional means, then the system is doomed to failure. For our present purposes, it is instructive to briefly mention three techniques that may be used to facilitate the interaction process. Here, conventional techniques used on a standard display can generally be extended to the 3-D image space. For example:

1. Employing a snap-to-grid technique may advance the speed and accuracy with which components may be placed. However, although in the 2-D case, grid lines may be made visible to assist in the placement process, this is more problematic when extended to a 3-D image space. (As indicated in Section 7.2.1, such lines may be haptically (rather than visually) sensed.)

2. Artificial feedback may be supplied to an operator navigating an interaction tool within a physical or apparent image space. For example, an image scene may be defined as comprising a set of discrete objects. An indication can then be provided when an interaction tool passes through the space physically occupied by an object (or its apparent space). This feedback may, for example, follow the approach taken by a conventional web browser, where hypertext changes color as a cursor passes over it. Thus, a simple color change can provide a clear indication of coincidence between object and cursor.[20]

3. The interaction tool may be equipped with mechanical or electromechanical devices providing the sensation that the interaction tool is being moved through a viscous medium. Thus, tremors of the hand may be damped and the rate at which the interaction tool may be moved can be controlled. This approach may be extended so that when the user lets go of the tool, it remains fixed in its location within the image space.

6.7.3   User Mobility Issues

The nature of an application will often impact on the freedom that we wish to exercise in terms of physical mobility. When, for example, undertaking text-based interaction activities, we are essentially static in terms of our reference position relative to the computer display. On the other hand, we may wish to have freedom of movement and so may be willing to regularly change our position relative to the image space (as in the case of some volumetric display systems, the stereoscopic workbench, and the CAVE) in order to best interact with images. In short, we must consider the extent of the space not only in which we perceive the image to lie but also of the space in which we wish to exercise freedom of movement.

---

[20]At least one early windowing system (Apollo Aegis—referred to in Chapter 9) reduced the need for precision in cursor positioning when, for example, selecting a window for resizing. When triggered, the selection process was assumed to apply to the window edge closest to the cursor. This type of technique permitting approximate positioning may be extended for use with certain forms of 3-D data sets (particularly sparse data—for example, the depiction of airborne objects).

Freedom of motion must be supported by both the display and the interaction tools. For example, although the IVR technique employing a head-mounted display appears to support user mobility, this may not in fact be the case as an operator is disconnected with their physical surroundings. Consequently, maintaining a sense of balance may be problematic. Any system providing haptic (especially force) feedback is likely to impose constraints on operator mobility and would, for example, be generally unsuited for use with large-volume, volumetric systems (supporting considerable freedom in viewing angle) and in which an operator may wish to regularly move to new viewing locations. The viewing freedom offered by certain types of volumetric display may impose additional problems in relation to user disorientation. Consider by way of example the application of such a display to air traffic control. Although, in principle, the display is suited to the task as it is able to provide clarity in terms of the spatial separation of airborne objects, there is a danger that an operator may make incorrect decisions as a consequence of their ability to view the scene from any compass direction.

Large-screen stereoscopic displays support freedom of movement and also (through the use of appropriate hardware) may support gesture-based interaction. This is a fascinating area of research, although it is unclear if this paradigm will ultimately support fine and detailed interactive operations.

6.8   THE "FREE-SPACE" IMAGE

From the perspectives of realism, viewing freedom, and image manipulation, the ability to create images that appear to be suspended in free-space appears (at least in principle) to be particularly attractive. Creative display systems, such as those introduced previously in this chapter, delude the visual system by creating an illusion concerning the presence of tangible 3-D image components. The illusion is further reinforced when we extend display systems to include haptic feedback, by means of which a user can experience contact forces or feel the texture of virtual objects. Workers in this field are indeed the illusionists referred to by Frederick Brookes in the quotation provided in Section 6.9, and it is likely that our greatest illusion concerns the generation of free-space images! In an excellent review article, Michael Halle [1997] succinctly clarifies the nature of free-space images by defining what he refers to as the "Projection Constraint." He defines this as follows:

> *A display medium or element must always lie along a line of sight between the viewer and all parts of a spatial image.*

He goes on to add:

> *Photons must originate in, or be redirected by, some material. The material can be behind, in front of, or within the space of the image, but it must be present. All claims to the contrary violate what we understand of the world . . . Technologies lavished with claims of mid-air projection should always be scrutinized with regard to the fundamental laws of physics.*

In short, and disregarding relativistic phenomena, light travels in a rectilinear manner unless influenced to do otherwise as a consequence of the presence of some material. Therefore, when we observe an image that appears to be suspended in space, we must either be looking directly toward the source of the visible light, i.e., the image generation sub-system, or be looking directly at some media which lies between the eyes and the image generation sub-system. However, the presence of this media may not be readily apparent. In this section, we briefly consider several image projection techniques.

6.8.1   A Theatrical Illusion

> Do not bother to sell your Gas shares. The electric light has no future.[21]

In the 1860s, Pepper's Ghost made a sensational appearance on the London stage. This theatrical "special effect" provides not only an excellent illustration of the illusionary nature of the "free-space" image, but moreover the principle is employed today in creative 3-D display and interaction system (see, for example, Section 8.4). The basic principle of the technique (which in fact seems not to have been invented by John Pepper but rather by a little known engineer called Henry Dircks), uses an angled glass plate as illustrated in Figure 6.17. Light emanating from region A can pass straight through the plate, but light from region B is reflected by the glass (due to total internal reflection). From the perspective of a theater audience, the actors who are located on the far side of the glass plate (region A) appear as normal. However, the brightly illuminated phantom that is located below the stage (region B) can also be seen as the plate reflects its image. In accord with a basic law of reflection, the phantom's virtual image lies as far behind the glass plate as the physical phantom is below it. Consequently, to the audience, the phantom appears within the real space occupied by the actors and there can indeed be no parallax between actors and ghost.

There were many variations on this basic illusion, and in fact Dirck and Pepper were not the first to have created such special effects. The Phantasmagoria was an earlier projection device that cast ghostly images into, for example, smoke. It is said that this device was used during the French Revolution to terrify and hence demoralize combatants. A refinement of Pepper's Ghost and the Phantasmagoria involved the use of fine barium oxide powder. An ultraviolet image cast into this fine dust causes it to glow and shimmer. However, under normal lighting conditions, the presence of the powder is less noticeable.

Whatever the particular embodiment, some physical medium is needed into which the specter's image may be cast, or by means of which the image may be reflected. This is in accord with Michael Halle's "projection constraint" and in terms of the terminology adopted in this book represents the "re-imaging projection sub-system."

Pepper's Ghost (or perhaps more appropriately Dirck's Ghost) places the real objects (the actors) behind the glass plate, and although the specter's image also appears to lie behind the glass, this is an illusion. Consequently, the approach ensures that the presence of the actors in region A (Figure 6.17) cannot interfere

---

[21]Attributed to Professor John Henry Pepper in connection with Thomas Edison's electric light.

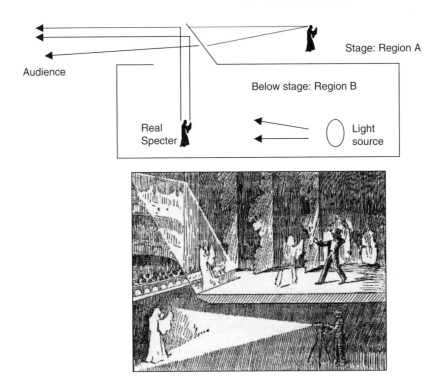

Figure 6.17: Pepper's Ghost. The presence of the angled glass plate does not hamper the audience's view of the actors located in region A. However, the brightly illuminated phantom located in region B is superimposed and appears to be located in region A. In another embodiment, the glass plate may be angled so as to allow the physical phantom to be located at the side of the stage. At least one stereoscopic display with integrated force feedback system employs this technique (see Section 8.4). (Lower image reproduced from Low, A.M., *Popular Scientific Recreations*, Ward, Lock and Co. (1933).)

with the formation of the image, as would be the case should the specter's image be transmitted through region A. In Section 8.4, we briefly consider a creative display system that employs this same principle, and in Figure 6.18, we summarize image space accessibility issues.

6.8.2 Volumetric Image Projection

The confinement of volumetric images within a physical volume (comprising either rapidly moving components or a physical medium located in some sort of containing vessel) causes images to appear to be just as remote as do tropical fish within a tank. When using displays of this type, one rapidly becomes frustrated by the impossibility of reaching out and entering the image space. Direct interaction by means of, for example, a haptic glove is precluded and the presence of the media generally detracts from the visualization and interaction experience offered by this type of technology.

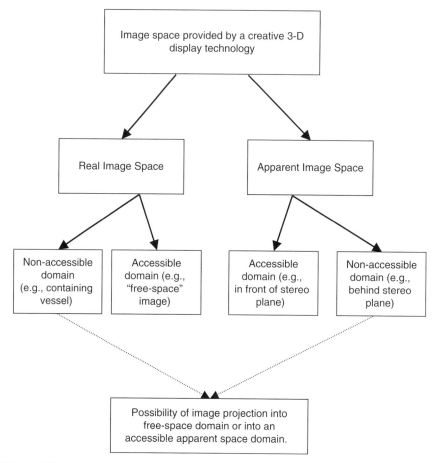

Figure 6.18: We consider that an image space may occupy three physical dimensions or that it may be a region from which the image appears to emanate (an apparent space). In either case, there is the possibility that access to this region via a physical interaction tool may be possible or may be physically precluded. Should the space prove inaccessible, the possibility exists of using additional optical components so as to change the image domain. (Diagram © 2005 Q.S. Blundell.)

One possible solution is to create a "re-imaging projection sub-system" that can cast the volumetric image into free space. This approach may, in principle, offer additional opportunities by, for example, supporting image magnification. This could enable a reduction of the volume of the real image space and thereby facilitate the development of more portable volumetric systems.

Kameyama and co-workers demonstrated in the early 1990s two systems that could support the generation of "free-space" volumetric images. The original volumetric images were created by the translational motion of an active matrix display (see Section 8.5.1). The optical apparatus illustrated in Figure 6.19 was then used to

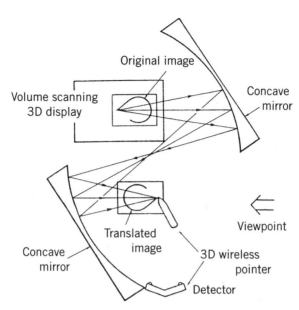

Figure 6.19: A volumetric display system described by Kameyama et al. employing a re-imaging/projection system by means of which an image is projected out of the enclosed volume. (Reproduced from Kameyama, K., Ohtomi, K., and Fukui, Y., "Interactive Volume Scanning 3-D Display with an Optical Relay System and Multidimensional Input Devices," *Stereoscopic Displays and Applications IV: SPIE Proceedings*, (1993); © 1993 SPIE.)

project a real image into "free space" [Kameyama et al. 1993, Kameyama and Ohtomi 1993, Blundell and Schwarz 2000, Blundell 2006]. The authors combined this with a haptic device enabling the user to interactively shape a displayed volumetric surface. The pioneering work undertaken by Kameyama et al. is fascinating, and their publications are strongly recommended to the interested reader.

Another possible approach is to use a biconvex mirror arrangement. As illustrated in Figure 6.20, the two identical parabolic mirrors cast a real image of an object placed inside the optical system into free space.[22] Replacing the object by a volumetric display (and scaling the size of the mirrors appropriately) would allow a free-space copy of an image to be viewed. Unfortunately, the geometry of this mirror arrangement is such that its physical extent is much larger than the size of the projected image. Also, the image is visible from a restricted range of viewing angles. Despite these problems, this offers (at least in principle) a simple technique for the generation of "free-space" volumetric images.

However, direct interaction with such a projected image space is compromised by the fact that any real object moving across the optical path will occlude part of the image.

---

[22]A desktop gadget using this principle is available: http://www.optigone.com. This does not operate on holographic principles!

Figure 6.20: A simple approach to the projection of a real image residing within a physical image space into an apparent image space. This consists of two concave mirrors. The small pig that can be seen in (a) is actually resting on the lower concave mirror arrangement. These mirrors project an image of the pig so that it appears to be located just above the hole in the upper mirror. The viewing angle is limited; in (b), the pig is no longer visible. If used for the creation of, for example, a free-space volumetric image, this arrangement would necessitate the use of large mirrors residing, for example, beneath a viewing platform. (Image © 2005 A.R. Blundell.)

6.9 REVISITING THE TRADITIONAL CLASSIFICATION SCHEME

We now return to the display classification scheme previously illustrated in Table 6.1. This categorizes displays in terms of their ability to satisfy the binocular parallax depth cue, provide viewing freedom, and permit viewing with or without special glasses.

It is instructive to pause for a moment and consider which attributes we believe to be especially relevant in the classification of display techniques. For example, should particular emphasis be placed on issues relating to a system's ability to match the human visual requirements or on the visual content offered by the display paradigm (e.g., augmented realism or augmented information content)? Perhaps we need to distinguish between display architectures according to physical attributes, such as the extent of the image space (its form, dimensions, etc.) or according to issues such as display portability, user mobility, and the ability of the display to support viewing by a plurality of observers?

In reality, as soon as we consider a display from a single viewpoint, we are likely to overemphasize certain characteristics, and underemphasize other issues that will most probably, once the system is in use, turn out to be of equal importance. Without a doubt, this discussion, together with the related issue concerning the development of metrics able to permit display architectures to be compared quantitatively in a meaningful manner, is fraught with difficulty.

In Table 6.3, we revise the previous classification table to indicate some of the diverse characteristics that may be exhibited by displays within the stereoscopic and autostereoscopic categories. In order to highlight the difficulty of providing a simple and meaningful classification scheme, we will briefly consider some of the issues that develop with the traditional approach.

First, when developing a classification scheme, we must decide whether we are attempting to classify particular instances of a technique or inherent strengths and limitations of the overall display class. These are two quite different undertakings and so need to be carried out separately. The traditional approach tries to achieve both objectives, and this is unsatisfactory. For example, consider the stereoscopic display. As we have seen, the original nineteenth-century stereoscope provided a non-coded imaging technique satisfying the binocular parallax depth cue and permitting images to appear either in front of or behind the stereo plane. The photographic images have given way to electronic displays, and imaging systems are available that may be non-coded or coded (either temporally or spatially). These advances do not, however, change the underlying operation of the approach—nor do they define an upper boundary to its operational characteristics for, as we have seen, additional hardware and software can support viewing freedom. However, particular instances of this general approach vary widely and range from the conventional flat-screen stereoscopic display equipped with head tracking facilities, to the CAVE and the IVR headset. In fact, since in order to enter the image space this latter approach requires the user to don special headgear, should it be classed as autostereoscopic or as something else?

Any classification dealing with specific embodiments of general techniques must be sufficiently flexible to account for a wide range of characteristics. Equally, in classifying general methodologies, we must assess limitations with great care and ensure that those identified are in fact inherent and not limitations associated with a particular embodiment. For example, the stereoscopic technique does not intrinsically limit the user to a single viewing orientation; this is not an inherent limitation and although stereoscopic systems generally require the user to don special glasses, this is not *always* the case. Here again, we encounter another difficulty; when determining general characteristics that may be associated with a class of display, should we be willing to tolerate the occasional exception to the rule? If we seek to identify

TABLE 6.3: A return to the traditional classification scheme previously illustrated in Table 6.1. Here we highlight the diversity of characteristics that may be demonstrated by classes of display falling into the three categories.

	Monocular	Stereoscopic	Autostereoscopic
General techniques	Traditional flat-screen 2-D rendition of a 3-D scene	Anaglyph Frame sequential	Holographic systems Immersive virtual reality Augmented reality AutoQ displays Lenticular Sheet
Comments on depth cues	Lacking accommodation, convergence and binocular parallax	Addition of the binocular parallax depth cue. Decoupling of accommodation and convergence cues.	Binocular parallax cue is present. Accommodation and convergence cues may be satisfied or may be decoupled. Occlusion cue may, or may not, be satisfied.
	Direct viewing Single viewing direction	Use of viewing glasses Single viewing direction	Direct viewing, but it may be necessary to don viewing equipment. Freedom in viewing orientation, although the degree of freedom varies widely.

truly inherent characteristics, then we run the risk of being overrestrictive, and in view of the diversity of approaches that may be taken when implementing a class of display, we may find it difficult to identify strengths and weaknesses that apply without any exception.

There are of course some inherent characteristics that we may confidently associate with various classes of display. For example, the decoupling of the accommodation and convergence cues is implicitly associated with the stereoscopic approach. On the other hand, in the case of volumetric systems, it appears that all embodiments developed to date have failed to support the occlusion depth cue. However, unlike the decoupling of the accommodation and convergence cues in the case of the stereoscopic approach, it is possible to foresee volumetric techniques that may alleviate this potential weakness [Blundell and Schwarz 2000]. Here again, we have to exercise caution in defining an inherent limitation—should we allow for possible future developments?

Although the stereoscopic and autostereoscopic categories have, for some time, been generally used by researchers to loosely categorize techniques, it is possible that the growing diversity of implementations have made this classification framework less meaningful. Consequently, alternative approaches should be sought and perhaps the time has come to reexamine and possibly rationalize some of the display classes that we commonly use. For example, when referring to a stereoscopic display, should we limit ourselves to systems providing only a single viewpoint, or should we include all systems that find their roots in the original ideas of Wheatstone and Brewster (not to forget Elliot!)? In this case, the IVR headset and CAVE would fall into the stereoscopic class of display. On the other hand, although this approach to classification may in some respects be useful, it would serve little purpose should we be wishing to focus on the interaction opportunities offered by different classes of display.

In his excellent book, Poole [1966] suggests the classification of displays in three categories: illusory, volumetric, and representative. In this chapter, we have made the distinction between approaches giving rise to apparent and physical image spaces, and this is approximately equivalent to Poole's "illusory" and "volumetric" categories. The "representative" category is perhaps of less relevance because it refers to systems which do not have the ability to provide binocular cues, and in which information content concerning the third dimension is provided through the use of symbolic entities. As we are confining our discussion to systems able to support stereopsis, the third category can be ignored.

This broad classification approach has some merit, because it provides an abstraction that is removed from any hardware considerations. However, the choice of classification names and their focus is less helpful when viewed with hindsight some 40 years after the publication appeared. As discussed in Section 6.5.3, the AutoQ approach represents a particular class of display whose essential characteristic is the automatic association of various depth cues with the displayed image. The volumetric technique represents a particular instance of this class, in which inherent depth cue information is associated with the image scene through the provision of a physical 3-D image space. Alternatively, the varifocal approach achieves essentially the same objective without the use of a physical 3-D image space. It is as a consequence of their common objectives that we have sought to group them under the AutoQ title. The fact that the image is created within a physical volume (or otherwise) is not a requirement but rather a means of achieving a particular end. Poole's use of the category title "volumetric" is therefore somewhat misleading. Similarly, the choice of the term "illusory" is perhaps ill-advised. All processes associated with our visual perception are, to a greater or lesser extent, illusory and this applies particularly to 3-D display technologies. As Frederick Brookes writes in the foreward to the Burdea [1996] text:

We often dream of achieving such technological virtuosity that our travellers in virtual worlds will no longer need imagination. That dream is, I think, the illusionist's own illusion: we shall never achieve it, and if we did, we should be immeasurably impoverished by our loss.

Those working on the development of creative displays are of course the illusionists referred to, and all display systems irrespective of the technologies employed are illusory. This includes volumetric systems, and to imply that they are not illusory would be incorrect; they are no less illusory than, say, the stereoscopic or holographic approaches.

Perhaps we can simply adapt Poole's original approach of providing a broad and generally useful high-level classification. Why not initially categorize systems according to the nature of depth cues associated with the depicted image? This is approximately equivalent to his original scheme, and we can adopt the titles "AutoQ" and "syntheticQ" as category names. This focus is entirely hardware-independent and identifies a pivotal characteristic that leads naturally to a subclassification dealing with the nature of the image space. By adopting this scheme, we have accounted for two major display facets:

(1) When important depth cues are naturally associated with an image scene rather than synthesized, there is less chance of conflict with the human visual system.

(2) As we have seen, the nature of the image space impacts on various display characteristics, especially interaction opportunities.

Conversely, this approach also has various inherent weaknesses. For example:

(1) The initial AutoQ and syntheticQ categories provide a highly asymmetric classification. Specifically, the AutoQ category contains volumetric, varifocal, and holographic systems, whereas the syntheticQ contains all of the other approaches.

(2) As discussed previously, in the case of some display techniques, a physical image space may be recast so as to give rise to an apparent image space. Consequently, we cannot view a physical image space as necessarily representing a "limitation" to a particular approach.

(3) There are many other display characteristics that we have not considered, and our approach is already biased to particular display characteristics—can we really be sure that for a given application these will be the most critical?

6.9.1   A Multifaceted Approach

As we have seen, the characteristics of the display cannot generally be simply defined by reference to the visual domain. In fact as illustrated in Figure 6.21, there are four general aspects that must be taken into account when considering the essential character of a display: visual opportunities, interaction opportunities, usability issues, and networking potential. These facets of a display are interlocked in such a way that one cannot normally be considered in isolation.

The classification of creative 3-D display systems is made particularly difficult because the four different sets of characteristics (each of which when considered

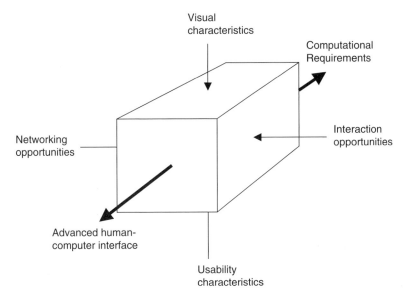

Figure 6.21: A Characterization Cube. Four of the faces represent aspects of a display's character. Each of these is defined by a set of parameters. Complex issues arise as a consequence of the parameters being interrelated. The remaining two faces of the cube represent the display's interface to the computer system and to the end user(s). Consequently, four sets of characteristics embedded into the display architecture determine its interfaces to both computer and operator. (Diagram © 2005 A.R. Blundell.)

individually is in itself quite complex) cannot be considered in isolation; they are somewhat interdependent. For example, some usability issues define the required visual characteristics and in turn impact on interaction opportunities. In Figure 6.22, we neglect networking issues and position the remaining three facets of a display's character on a set of rectangular axes. Perhaps it may ultimately be possible to develop such a characterization space and so provide a mechanism for visualizing the strengths and weakness of various types of creative 3-D display. In this way, we may perhaps best match display and interaction techniques to particular applications. However, much remains to be done in this area.

6.10 DISCUSSION

In this chapter, a number of important concepts have been introduced in relation to the creative display and interaction paradigms. Traditional monocular, stereoscopic, and autostereoscopic display classifications have been introduced, together with several classes of display (specifically stereoscopic, immersive virtual reality, lenticular sheet, volumetric, and varifocal systems). Knowledge of these techniques has allowed us to highlight issues relating to the nature of an image

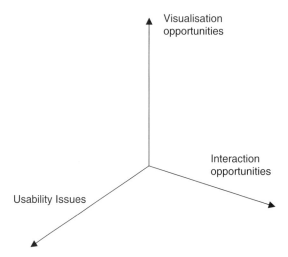

Figure 6.22: Neglecting networking issues, various interface characteristics and application needs may be described within a 3-D space. Although various difficulties are associated with this approach, it does potentially offer to provide a means of visually characterizing the interface and matching this to the requirements of end users. (Diagram © 2005 Q.S. Blundell.)

space and to discuss general interaction techniques. Three broad approaches to inter-action have been introduced, and these are as follows:

1. *Direct Interaction:* Involving the insertion of a physical interaction tool into the actual space occupied by the image scene (real image space) or into the space from which the image scene appears to emanate (apparent image space).

2. *Transferred Interaction:* Involving the navigation of a virtual cursor through the image space.

3. *Pointer-Based Interaction:* Here, directional cues may be obtained from, for example, a laser beam emanating from a pointing device. This is cast into an image space.

The problems associated with the implementation of the direct interaction technique have been discussed in some detail, particularly the impact that the presence of a physical interaction tool may have in terms of interfering with an operator's view of an image. Naturally, this discussion led us to consider the concept of the so-called "free-space" image. Finally, we returned to the traditional classification scheme introduced at the beginning of the chapter. Weaknesses in this approach have been indicated, and various other strategies have been discussed in a general way. Unfortunately, the diversity of display characteristics makes it especially difficult to come up with schemes that are both accurate and useful. However, coherent classification techniques are vital if top-down design strategies are to be properly adopted to enable end-user needs to drive the design and configuration of creative display and interaction systems.

6.11   INVESTIGATIONS

1. Determine the degree of 3-D relief contained in the Chimenti drawings that are reproduced in Appendix A. Stereoscopic viewing may be achieved by photocopying the drawings and viewing them via a conventional stereoscope. Alternatively, they can be scanned and then two images may be attributed a different color and merged, to form an anaglyph image. In this latter case, a little experimentation will be required in aligning the images with respect to each other.

2. Consider the image capture and display technique illustrated in Figure 6.3, which was pioneered by J. L. Baird. Determine if this uses temporal or spatial coding.

3. Consider the varifocal mirror technique introduced in Section 6.5.3. Do you consider that this approach supports the accommodation and convergence depth cues? Give reasons. What advantages or disadvantages would be associated with using the mirror across its entire range of motion? Determine the impact of noise associated with mirror movement; could a noise cancellation system be successfully employed?

4. Obtain a conventional stereoscope and stereoscopic image pair. Investigate the introduction of a pointing device (such as a pen) into the space lying between the image plane and one of the eyepieces. Do you notice that you can switch between two modes: "pointer-opaque" and "pointer-transparent." What is the reason for this? In the case of the "pointer-transparent" mode, is the image that lies beneath the pointer stereoscopic?

7 The Haptic Channel

He went like one that hath been stunned,
And is of sense forlorn:
A sadder and a wiser man,
He rose the morrow morn.

7.1 INTRODUCTION

Interaction with objects in the world around us implicitly involves our haptic channel. Almost by definition, any two-way relations involve feeling, touching, and moving objects, with the accompanying feedback providing sensations of resistance, weight, texture, and so on, in accordance with physical laws and the material properties of the environment. As discussed in Chapter 3, the unconscious dexterity with which the various somatosensory and kinaesthetic inputs into the brain are continually used in a feedback loop, supplying motor output and allowing us to operate smoothly and freely, is remarkable. However, as well as allowing us to pick up, push, pull, or squeeze objects in the environment, our hands relay to our brains a rich stream of information about the immediate environment via the sense of touch. We sense whether an object is hard or soft, hot or cold, or heavy or light; we sense resistance to the motion of our fingers or between two objects because of friction. Our hands in particular, and to a lesser extent other parts of the body, are thus amenable to both input and output in an interactive visualization scenario.

To date, however, most conventional human–computer interaction mechanisms have not fully capitalized on this impressive capability. In a typical scenario at the present time, interaction with a virtual scene involves an interaction device such as a mouse, with which the user can move a cursor, which can be thought of as a virtual representation of the mouse (the "transferred interaction" paradigm (see Section 5.4.1)). With the aid of the mouse buttons, and an appropriate graphical user interface, objects can be selected and moved, dragged, and dropped. It has a certain degree of similarity to some "real-world" operations. However, this paradigm (and conventional interaction tools in general) are limited in two major respects. First, the scene is usually restricted to two spatial dimensions, and second, the only haptic feedback received by the user is that from the physical construction of the mouse and friction between the mouse and the mouse pad, resistance to finger pressure on the buttons, and so forth. That is, the contents and configuration of the image scene have no bearing on the haptic sensations of the user. Kim et al. make the comment:

> *Imagine trying to tell Michel Angelo to sculpt David within the confines of the computer interface. This would be equivalent to restricting him to the use of only one eye since the monitor only provides 2D images and to the use of only one arm since he works through the mouse. It would be necessary to disengage his nerve endings because the mouse provides no force feedback and his arm must be confined so that so that it can only move in one plane at a time.* [Kim et al. 2003a, p.217]

Nevertheless, in recent years, researchers have begun to investigate more extensive haptic interaction with virtual objects and environments by means of specialized devices and control software, particularly since interactive three-dimensional (3-D) workspaces have become more widely used. As discussed in Chapter 3 in the context of the perceptual aspects of touch and proprioception, haptic interaction implies a bidirectional channel, with the device supplying haptic feedback in addition to enabling user input into the system [Hayward and Astley 1996]. This represents a key difference from the visual channel, for which perhaps only the use of eye tracking allows a limited degree of user input. Consequently, in practically all situations, the visual channel can be considered as output only, transmitting information from the visualization system to the user. By analogy with computer graphics where a virtual scene is rendered for visual display, the term "computer haptics" refers to synthesizing computer-generated forces, textures, and other tactile sensations that can be "displayed" to the user by means of specialized devices [Srinivasan and Basdogan 1997]. More specifically, we can refer to "haptic rendering" as the computational procedures for calculating this haptic output [Salisbury et al. 1995]. As both research efforts and commercial ventures involving haptic interaction with 3-D environments have multiplied in recent years, a great many different areas of application have been explored, from a number of medical uses to scientific visualization, entertainment, and mechanical design.

Our hope is that this chapter will provide the reader with an appreciation of some areas in which haptic interaction has begun to find application and some different types of devices that can be used, along with an understanding of some issues concerned with rendering force feedback and how these requirements impact on multichannel interaction with 3-D data sets. In Section 7.2, we begin with a brief introduction to several selected applications for which haptic feedback has shown some promise. Although far from exhaustive, this will give a flavor for the potential utility of a haptic channel and provide some "real-world" context as we then move on to illustrate some different types of interaction devices that have been developed to date. In Sections 7.3 and 7.4, we explore various issues associated with haptic rendering in a little more depth. We concentrate primarily on the single-point haptic interaction paradigm, providing three components of force feedback to the user. This simple approach to providing haptic feedback has seen a great deal of research effort. Moreover, an understanding of the basic interaction and computational requirements in this scenario provides a platform for consideration of more complex interaction paradigms (see Section 7.5). In Section 7.6, we consider haptic interaction with volumetric data, in which the 3-D scene is represented as a collection of image voxels, rather than as surface primitives. Finally, we examine in Section 7.7 the implications of the haptic channel for the software architecture for multisensory visualization systems.

References cited throughout the chapter provide further details for the interested reader. In addition, we recommend the text by Burdea [1996] for an excellent discussion of haptic feedback systems. Hayward et al. [2004] also provide a very useful summary of hardware devices. The recent review articles of Salisbury [1999] and Salisbury et al. [2004] also serve as excellent overviews of haptic interaction issues.

7.2 PHYSICAL CONTACT WITH VIRTUAL OBJECTS

It is useful to begin by considering some scenarios in which the incorporation of a haptic channel is likely to provide tangible benefits to the user, and to illustrate this discussion by reference to various example systems. In this text, we are primarily concerned with applications that inherently involve a virtual representation of a 3-D workspace and the interaction with objects therein. When dealing with the intrinsically interactive scenarios that accompany many 3-D scenes of this kind, the incorporation of a haptic feedback channel is perhaps likely to provide operational benefits. Indeed, a number of applications developed (particularly over the past 15 years or so) have served to illustrate both immediate and potential advantages of incorporating a haptic channel.

7.2.1 Some Example Applications of Haptic Interaction

In this subsection, we briefly consider various indicative areas of application for systems incorporating some form of haptic feedback system.

1. *Medical Training*: One application for which haptic feedback appears particularly well suited is in simulation-based training for surgical or other medical procedures [Gibson et al. 1998, Satava 2001b, Cosman et al. 2002, Champion and Gallagher 2003]. Typically, replicas of the surgical instruments are coupled to immersive virtual reality (IVR). displays. Operations can range from simple wound closure, intravenous or epidural injections, and needle biopsies to full surgical procedures [Satava 2001a]. The ability for trainees to practice on a virtual patient brings advantages such as the ability to repeat the procedure (perhaps concentrating on a particular part of the operation that is proving troublesome) and recording of the user's movements for later evaluation [Satava 2001a]. One area that has received particular attention is that of minimally invasive surgery, in which the operation is performed by manipulating tools located at the end of a thin tube (laparoscope) [Ota et al. 1995, Schijven and Jakamowicz 2003, Dayal et al. 2004, Tholey et al. 2005]. The laparoscope itself is inserted through a small "keyhole" incision in the patient, and so the surgeon views the operation by means of images on a video monitor, which is transmitted from a tiny camera at the end of the instrument via a cable. As this new approach has become rapidly established in recent years, it has brought with it a need for new approaches to training. Traditional mentor-based teaching methods for open surgery are less well suited to such remote tool-based procedures where mimicking the mentor's actions is more difficult [Schijven and Jakamowicz 2003]. In a controlled study directly assessing the benefits of VR-based training on subsequent performance in gall bladder removal, Seymour et al. [2002] found that VR-trained surgical residents performed the operation 29% faster and were significantly less likely to commit operative errors. The ability for the user to feel realistic resistance and other physical properties of the virtual tissue while performing the operation is clearly advantageous if the real-world situation is to be accurately simulated [Dayal et al. 2004, Tholey et al. 2005]. This applies even to seemingly straightforward procedures; for example, the administration of an epidural anesthetic into the spine involves the needle encountering a succession of different resistance forces as it penetrates the different tissues *en route* to the spinal cord [Bostrom et al. 1993, Kyung et al. 2001]. Haptic feedback is becoming a key part of commercial surgical simulators and VR-based training suites; of the 12 simulators reviewed by Schijven and Jakamowicz [2003], 6 incorporated force feedback and it was an optional extra on a further 3.

2. *Virtual Sculpture, Prototyping, and Design*: Another potentially rich field of application is the creation or modification of virtual objects, in scenarios ranging from the artistic (see, for example, Foskey et al. [2002]) to the industrial (see, for

example, Sener et al. [2003]). This latter area can include, for example, virtual prototyping and Computer-Aided Design (CAD). This is an area in which advances in 3-D representation (both on 2-D media and creative 3-D visualization) have often found ready application (see, for example, Morrill [1964] or Clark [1976]). With the advent of graphics displays and computers capable of supporting real-time interaction with relatively complex 3-D virtual spaces, several research groups in both industry and academia have actively explored the direct creation and manipulation of virtual objects within a 3-D workspace (with or without haptic feedback); see, for example, Avila and Sobierajski [1996a], Young et al. [1997], Snibbe et al. [1998], Wesche and Seidel [2001], and Sener et al. [2003] for a range of different approaches and applications (we discuss some of these shortly). The capability to create and modify objects within a 3-D workspace in a direct fashion, with the addition of haptic feedback conveying a tangible touch response, will hopefully provide a more natural and intuitive interaction experience [Sener et al. 2002]. In virtual prototyping, the emphasis is on a rapid and intuitive creation and alteration of virtual models at an early, conceptual stage of the design process—analogous to pencil sketching [Wesche and Droske 2000]. The inherently digital nature of the prototype allows possibilities such as cloning a draft design to facilitate rapid exploration of alternatives without having to start again from scratch. Interestingly, in a workshop evaluating virtual prototyping within IVR environments with practicing designers from a range of disciplines reported on by Deisinger et al. [2000], the need for the software environment to also be able to support greater quantitative precision and constraints for design refinement was identified. That is, the ability to move rapidly and transparently into a more CAD-like environment seemed like a natural extension of the virtual prototyping environment. In this type of scenario, haptic interfaces are likely to find a natural role in increasing the realism of the virtual models depicted. Indeed, applications have been developed in which a user can model or construct objects with haptic feedback within a virtual 3-D image space (see, for example, Avila and Sobierajski [1996a], Young et al. [1997], Snibbe et al. [1998], McDonnell et al. [2001], Sener et al. [2002], Chen and Sun [2002], and Plesniak et al. [2002]). These provide the user with a sensation of operations such as modeling with "virtual clay," building with blocks of virtual LEGO or sculpting virtual wood, analogous to the real world. However, although realistic responses and interaction metaphors can be extremely helpful, we can also make use of new possibilities that arise when dealing with purely virtual objects. The article by Snibbe et al. [1998] is interesting in this respect as they discuss some issues regarding constraints on the direct creation of digital models in a 3-D workspace. One feature they implemented was a haptic 3-D grid of force "grooves" within the workspace to guide the positioning of the interface device and aid in the creation of straight lines. That is, they assigned haptic properties to the *space itself* rather than to objects within it. They also found that with this haptic grid users were more likely to move *into* the interaction space.

3. *Molecular Simulation and Docking*: One of the longest running research programs in haptic feedback with computer-generated images is that at the University

of North Carolina (UNC), dating back to the late 1960s[1] [Brooks et al. 1990, Taylor 1999]. One of the projects carried out involved the simulation of interactions between a molecule and its protein receptor site. In the development of new drugs, computational chemists model the interactions of the molecule with its target receptor(s), and possibly other receptors to which the molecule may have an affinity. The goal of these simulations is to guide further refinements in its molecular structure by identifying which functional groups in the molecule might be critical to retain or change as the molecular structure is refined to optimize the binding profile of the drug. Although computational techniques are improving [Gilson 1995, Gilson et al. 1997, Taylor et al. 2002], an exact calculation of the binding energy for all different conformations remains difficult [Meyer et al. 2000, Nagata et al. 2002]. A complementary approach is to allow the chemist to "dock" the molecule themselves in a more interactive scenario. The use of a haptic channel in this context allows chemists to "feel" directly the attractive and repulsive forces on the molecule as they attempt to maneuver it into a binding position. The "Docker" application developed at UNC [Ouh-Young et al. 1988, Taylor 1999, Salisbury 1999] allowed chemists to do just this by providing six-degrees-of-freedom (6-DOF) feedback (i.e., forces and torques). Other groups are continuing to develop similar applications[2] [Wanger 1998, Nagata et al. 2002, Birmanns and Wriggers 2003].

4. *Incorporating Alternative 3-D Displays and Haptic Widgets*: Most of these haptic applications have been developed in concert with some form of 3-D display as the visual channel. These have typically been a stereoscopic display (including immersive virtual reality scenarios) or surface/volume rendering on a conventional 2-D display monitor. However, several groups have also begun to explore the combination of haptic feedback with other types of creative 3-D display systems (see, for example, Kameyama and Ohtomi [1993], Chen et al. [1998], Grant et al. [1998], Arsenault and Ware [2000], Basdogan et al. [2002]). Plesniak et al. [2002] used a force feedback stylus in combination with an electro-holographic 3-D display (see Section 8.3.3) to allow the user to carve a cylindrically symmetrical digital form—analogous to a virtual lathe. This project is interesting not only because it employs a novel autostereoscopic display approach to "*feel and sculpt three-dimensional shapes made only of light,*" (Plesniak et al. [2002]) but also because they explicitly discuss some key issues that develop in combining haptic and visual channels in a direct interaction scenario.[3] In particular, they mention spatial misregistration between the visual image and the force feedback, discrepancies between the visual and tactile appearance of the virtual

---

[1]Many of these came under the umbrella of the long-running GROPE project and related activities (see, for example, Brooks et al. [1990]). In addition to the "Docker" project discussed here, the nanoManipulator project provides force feedback coupled to real-time atomic force microscopy scanning, allowing the user not only to sense individual molecules on a sample surface, but to move them about [Taylor 1999, Guthold et al. 1999].

[2]The inclusion of haptic feedback in molecular interaction simulations is also likely to be advantageous in teaching applications; see, for example, Sankaranarayanan et al. [2003].

[3]*Direct, transferred*, and *pointer-based* interaction scenarios are introduced in Section 5.4.

objects, inconsistent depth cues, and undetected collisions with parts of the inter-action device that are not modeled.

In addition to the manipulation and/or creation of virtual objects as emphasized in the discussions above, it might be beneficial to include more abstract elements similar to those employed in conventional Windows, Icons, Menus & Popups (WIMP) interfaces, such as buttons, widgets, and menus, into the 3-D workspace. The inclusion of haptic properties associated with these objects might also be helpful, selection and navigation of a drop-down menu may well feel more natural if some resistance force is associated with its face. Indeed, research into haptic properties of buttons and widgets has been undertaken (see, for example, Miller and Zeleznik [1999], Oakley et al. [2002], Doerrer and Werthschuetzky [2002], De Boeck et al. [2003], Komerska and Ware [2003, 2004]). Human factors studies have also begun to address the advantages (or otherwise) of incorpor-ating a haptic feedback channel when interacting with virtual data. These have ranged from assessments of a complete system targeted at a particular application, such as a study of the benefits of minimally invasive surgery simulators discussed in (1) above, to more focused studies of particular "atomic" tasks. For example, Wagner et al. [2002] reported that force feedback was beneficial in reducing tissue-damaging errors in surgical dissection training, and Feggin et al. [2002] reported the benefits of using haptic feedback to guide trainees through the motor actions of a surgical procedure. Arsenault and Ware [2000] showed that force feedback corresponding to object contact improved the speed with which subjects made contact with virtual targets, and Wall et al. [2002] found that associating attractive forces with targets within a 3-D workspace improved the accuracy with which these were selected. Interestingly, the latter study showed no improvement in the time required to select the targets. In short, the utility and optimal choice of interface is likely to depend on many factors, including the nature of the user's interaction and the application to which the visualization system is targeted. This is an ongoing and important aspect of haptics research.

The above overview has covered only a few application areas in which haptic interaction has shown promise, but it will serve as a background for a closer exam-ination of some exemplar haptic interaction devices, to which we now turn.

7.2.2 Some Examples of Haptic Interaction Devices

Interest in haptic feedback coupled to virtual data sets dates back to the 1960s when innovative visions of complete sensory interaction with computer graphics first attracted widespread attention in research circles [Brooks et al. 1990, Salisbury et al. 2004]. Then, as now, devices developed to provide haptic feedback to the user drew much from advances in telerobotics, where an operator maneuvers a replica ("master") of a mechanical device ("slave") operating in a remote or hazar-dous environment—the slave following the movements of the master [Salisbury et al. 1995, Burdea 1996]. In more recent years, as research into and applications of advanced graphics and human–computer interaction has become a thriving field in its own right, the interaction with virtual data itself has become a major driver in the development of haptic interaction.

A wide range of devices providing force and touch feedback, ranging from full-body or arm exoskeletons, tension-based devices controlled by a web of cables, arms suspended from ceilings or mounted on the floor, to glove devices, desktop-mounted 3-D force-feedback systems, and modified mice or joysticks have been developed for multisensory visualization applications. In approaching the vast array of haptic interface devices, it is natural to attempt to classify them in some way. There are numerous ways in which this can be approached. For example, Burdea [1996] mentions possible classifications in terms of the nature of the transducer used to transmit the haptic sensation to the user's body part: *"We can thus distinguish between hydraulic, electric or pneumatic force-feedback systems."* He also discusses device portability and the key feature of how the feedback forces are grounded (for example, devices can be mounted on a desk, on the ceiling, or on the user's back (in exoskeleton-based approaches)). Another important parameter is the number of degrees of freedom in the feedback provided [Salisbury et al. 2004]. Here, a device providing three spatial components of force feedback (a 3-D force vector) is a three-degree of freedom device (3-DOF) whereas if three components of torque are also available, the device now displays haptic properties with 6-DOF.

Below, we briefly discuss various feedback devices.

1. *Force Reflecting Desktop Devices*: Figure 7.1 illustrates two desktop force feedback devices that are commercially available. Each of these is used to manipulate a point in the image space—in this respect similar to a joystick, trackball, or other 3-D *input* device. However, the force feedback devices also *output* resistance forces to the user, depending on the spatial interaction between the contents of the

(a)

(b)

Figure 7.1: Two examples of force feedback desktop interaction devices. (a) The PHANTOM Omni haptic device, providing 6-DOF positional sensing within a 160 W × 120H × 70D-mm workspace. (b) The OMEGA 3-DOF haptic device, providing a cylindrical 16-cm (diameter) × 12-cm workspace. [Image (a) reproduced with kind permission of SensAble Technologies, Inc.® Image (b) reproduced with kind permission of Force Dimension.]

virtual scene and the point that is being piloted within it. Force (and possibly torque) reflecting versions of "standard" interface devices such as joysticks, trackballs, or mice have also been developed (see, for example, Balakrishnan et al. [1994], Kerstner et al. [1994], Münch and Stangenberg [1996]).

The PHANTOM device,[4] illustrated in Figure 7.1(a), has been one of the most popular force feedback devices to date. With this device, the user manipulates a pen-like attachment to move a virtual point around within a 3-D workspace [Massie and Salisbury 1994]. This point is mapped to the end of the "pen," and the user feels resistance forces (and, in some models, torques) at this point corresponding to the interaction between the virtual point and the virtual scene. Interaction with digital data with such devices can be considered a "tool-based" paradigm of haptic interaction [Srinivasan and Basdogan 1997]. That is, the user holds and controls a physical device of which typically only the end is "in contact" with the virtual scene (direct interaction—see Section 5.4.2). The user can thus probe the 3-D image space in a similar way to which one might probe a real space with a pen or the end of a screwdriver. (A further variant on this approach, implemented in early versions of the PHANTOM, provides a thimble-type device with which the user probes the virtual space. Here, an analogy would be to feeling the surroundings with one's finger in a sewing thimble.)

Although they do not capitalize fully on the capabilities of our haptic sensory systems such as the fine sense of touch in the fingertips, with simple tools such as a pen or a finger probe, the system only needs to track interactions between the virtual representation of the relevant parts of the tool (for example, the tip of the device) and the virtual environment. This approach thus represents a dramatic simplification of the actual situation; the full motion of the tool is reduced to three components of position at its tip—i.e., the motion of a point in space. This simplification has allowed numerous issues pertaining to haptic rendering to be explored and practical algorithms and usable systems to be implemented [Basdogan and Srinivasan 2002]. We discuss haptic rendering within a point-based paradigm in more detail shortly.

2. *Glove and Tension-Based Devices*: Although the single-point interaction paradigm has proved exceedingly useful, the range of interaction can be extended to enable virtual objects to be picked up, grasped, or manipulated (in ways similar to the physical world) if at least one other independent point of interaction is incorporated (for example, corresponding to thumb and forefinger) [Wall and Harwin 2001]. One approach to enable grasping of virtual objects with several points of contact is that of glove-based haptic interaction devices. Here, the thumb and one or more of the fingers feels an independent force depending on its individual contact with the virtual scene. By appropriately modeling object deformations and resistance, the feeling of squeezing a virtual object can be conveyed [Popescu et al. 1999]. Glove devices typically provide forces on the fingertips relative to the palm [Bouzit et al. 2002] or the back of the hand or forearm [Springer and

---

[4]The name "PHANTOM" derives from "Personal HAptic iNTerface Mechanism" [Massie and Salisbury 1994]. See also http://www.sensable.com.

Ferrier 2002, Turner et al. 1998]. The Rutgers Master II (New Design) restricts finger closure by pneumatic pistons between rings around the tips of three fingers plus the thumb and the palm [Bouzit et al. 2002]. An embedded PC in the device maintains local stable forces and communicates with the host computer maintaining the overall visual scene. By contrast, the CyberGrasp glove[5] restrains the fingers via tensioned cables from the back of the arm to the fingertips [Turner et al. 1998].

Glove devices have the advantage of portability and hence provide fewer restrictions in the movements of the user than do some other approaches. However, although grasping forces can be displayed, the weight of an object (corresponding to a global downward force caused by gravity) cannot. To achieve this, the devices would need to be "grounded" on the fixed surrounding environment (for example, the desk or floor), but this often comes at the expense of the size of the interaction space. A pragmatic approach to this was taken by Wall and Harwin [2001], who combined three PHANTOM single-point devices to provide absolute force feedback to two fingers and the thumb within an interaction space of $20 \times 30 \times 15$ cm^3.

A further class of haptic interaction devices comprises those in which one or more interaction fingertip holders, handles, or knobs is suspended within a workspace by tensioned cables attached to the corners (see, for example, Lindemann and Tesar [1989], Ishii and Sato [1994], Williams [1998], Kim et al. [2003a], and Tarrin et al. [2003]). By tracking the current extended length of each cable, the position of the handle can be determined. If at least six cables are attached appropriately to a manipulable handle, torques in addition to forces can be conveyed [Williams 1998, Kim et al. 2003a]. Configurations offering three independent 3-DOF force feedback points (for thumb and two fingers, as with the approach described above) have also been developed [Tarrin *et al.* 2003]. These devices tend to offer a larger interaction space compared with desk-based approaches. However, the physical presence of the cables can provide physical restriction or interference for large motions or twists of the hand.

3. *Tactile Feedback*: So far we have only discussed devices that provide force, and possibly torque, feedback to the user. As discussed in Chapter 3, receptors in and under our skin, particularly in sensitive regions such as the fingertips, also provide a rich set of tactile input as we touch and hold objects in our everyday activities. Devices providing vibration feedback, for example, can convey signals at the high temporal resolution supported by the Pacinian corpuscles in the fingertips. Spatial discrimination can be added by the use of an array of small elements in contact with the fingertip. A wide range of methods have been investigated to deliver such tactile sensations, including arrays of movable or vibratory elements [Cohn et al. 1993, Ikei et al. 1997], controlling the air pressure in miniature cavities [Asamura et al. 1998], electrical stimulation [Kaczmarek et al. 1994, Kajimoto et al. 2001], and piezoelectric bristles providing a local strain along the surface of the fingertip [Pasquero and Hayward 2003]. Tactile displays are in fact of current interest for interaction with electronic devices generally, for example, van Erp [2002] provides an interesting discussion of the use of conveying information (in a range

----

[5]See also http://www.immersion.com.

of scenarios, and considering applications to parts of the body beyond the fingers) by vibro-tactile stimuli. Devices of this kind are likely to play an increasing role in future interaction with virtual 3-D image spaces.

7.3   THE HAPTIC CHANNEL IN MULTISENSORY VISUALIZATION

Having discussed a few of the applications to which haptic interaction between humans and computers is likely to be beneficial, and having briefly encountered some different types of interaction device, we can now consider the nature of the haptic channel within the visualization system in a little more detail. We start by considering the key steps in the haptic interaction loop, before discussing requirements on the force update rate and system stability.

7.3.1   The Haptic Interaction Loop

The haptic interaction loop is the part of the control algorithm that tracks the position of a virtual representation of the haptic interaction device within the digital scene and calculates and transmits appropriate haptic feedback signals to the physical device for display to the user. (Note that even if the visualization system is such that the visual display volume is directly accessible to the interaction device such that the real and virtual objects are superimposed, a virtual representation of the interaction device is still required to compute the interactions and update the virtual scene appropriately.) This virtual representation is a simplified or abstract representation that captures the essential elements pertaining to the interaction—similar to the cursor in conventional GUI environments. It is sometimes referred to as an "avatar," in parallel with terminology applied to virtual representations of faces or the whole person in a virtual reality context [Salisbury et al. 2004]. The form of the virtual representation depends on the capabilities of the interaction device and the complexity of the interaction with the virtual scene that is being modeled. In the simplest case of single-point interaction, the virtual representation of the interaction device is itself a single point. This is sometimes referred to as the "Haptic Interaction Point" (HIP) [Srinivasan and Basdogan 1997, Ho et al. 1999], and we use this terminology here.

As the user manipulates a probe through a virtual scene, the control software must rapidly perform a number of tasks that ensure realistic feedback and timely reaction to interaction events [Huang et al. 1998, Basdogan and Srinivasan 2002, Salisbury et al. 2004]. The main algorithmic requirements of a haptic channel can be summarized as follows:

1. *Device Location*: The coordinates of the interaction device(s) are sampled[6] and used to update the virtual representation of the device within the virtual scene. In a simple 3-DOF situation, the device coordinates comprise the x, y, and z spatial

---

[6]Strictly speaking, this applies to "impedance devices," which read the position of the user-controlled part of the device and display forces. Less common "admittance devices" do the opposite—they sense the force applied by the user and control the position of the device interaction interface [Salisbury et al. 2004].

positions of the haptic device. If the device can also display torques to the user, the orientation of the device might also be sampled. Furthermore, the device might have additional transducers (analogous to mouse buttons) that enable input of actions beyond spatial position and orientation. In this case, the state of these additional inputs would also need to be determined.

2. *Collision Detection*: Tests are performed to determine whether, and to what extent, the virtual device is interacting with any objects in the virtual scene. In the case of single-point interaction, this involves checking for spatial collisions between the device point and the scene contents. That is, has the virtual device "hit" or "penetrated" any objects within the scene? In dynamic scenes, collisions between two or more objects within the scene are also checked.

3. *Haptic Feedback*: In this step, the appropriate haptic feedback is calculated and sent to the haptic interface device for display to the user. Continuing our example of 3-DOF single-point interaction, this involves calculating the magnitude and direction of the force vector appropriate to the latest device position. More generally, torques and texture output would also be calculated at this haptic rendering step. (Of course, if no collision was detected in step 2, no forces are usually displayed, as the user has not encountered any of the objects within the scene.)

4. *Image Update*: The objects within the virtual scene are altered or updated according to the interaction with the input device. (In dynamic scenes, this can include computation of modified object trajectories or shapes—generally referred to in computer graphics as "collision response.") This step occurs if the virtual scene can be altered by interaction with the user; a simpler scenario is a static scene, in which the user can "feel" the contents using haptic feedback, but the scene contents do not change in response to this interaction.

Step 1 can be considered as the input portion of the loop. Collision detection, in step 2, is a critical part of most interaction or graphics animation algorithms and is discussed in greater depth in Section 7.4. In animated computer simulations, the collisions sought are those between different objects within the virtual scene. Here, we concentrate primarily on collisions between the virtual input device and objects within the scene. The results of these collisions on the objects within the scene are calculated and the virtual objects updated in step 4. In fact, in general terms, each of steps 1, 2, and 4 also applies in the absence of haptic feedback; for example, the position of an input device relative to components of a virtual scene is used for input in WIMP-based event-driven interfaces [Jones 1989, Flanagan 1999]. Step 3, involving the calculation and display of a force vector (and possibly more sophisticated qualities) to the user, is specific to haptic feedback. In Sections 7.4–7.6, we consider collision detection and haptic rendering, concentrating on the widely used case of a 3-DOF single-point interaction.

7.3.2   Force Feedback Refresh Requirements

A fundamental issue with multisensory visualization systems involving haptic feedback is that the required refresh rates of the haptic and visual channels are very different. Here, it is important to distinguish the "refresh rate" required for a particular channel from the "update rate." We define the refresh rate as the rate at which the information in the channel need be repeatedly output to the user. In contrast, the update rate is the rate at which the virtual scene must be altered to provide the illusion of motion or a perceptibly immediate response.

Recall from Section 2.7 that for visual display, the refresh rate is determined by the flicker fusion frequency of the human visual system. It is usually considered to be at least 25–30 Hz, and higher refresh rates of 100 Hz (or greater) are used in high-end computer monitors to minimize adverse effects caused by residual flicker that might be subliminally perceptible. However, the update rate required to provide the illusion of motion to the visual system is only 10 Hz. In contrast, the mechanoreceptors under our skin respond to temporal frequencies in tactile stimuli that are somewhat higher than the limits of the visual system. These receptors are maximally sensitive to vibrations of 200–300 Hz, but they can also detect a wide range—for example, the responsive frequency extends to approximately 1000 Hz even for modest skin indentations on the order of 20–50 μm [Kaczmarek et al. 1991, Kandel et al. 2000].[7]

In haptic interaction systems, a range of force response refresh rates have been used, for example, from 500 Hz [Taylor 1999] to 5 kHz [Avila and Sobierajski 1996a]. As a general rule, a refresh rate of at least 1 kHz has been found to ensure both stability (which we discuss shortly) and a subjective firmness of rigid surfaces. Higher frequencies provide a crisper force response but limit the computations that can be performed between each force refresh. With lower refresh frequencies, hard surfaces are not rendered well and tend to feel soft or vibrating rather than rigid [Rosenberg and Adelstein 1993, Mark et al. 1996]. In haptics research and development to date, the value of 1 kHz has represented an acceptable compromise between the complexity of the virtual scene that is sensed haptically and the crispness of the contact in the case of rigid objects [Basdogan and Srinivasan 2002]. As computing power increases, and depending on the requirements of particular applications, higher haptic refresh rates may become more feasible.

In contrast, just as with the visual channel, much lower update rates (rates at which the impedance provided to the user via the device is altered) of 10–20 Hz can be sufficient for realistic force display [Mark et al. 1996].[8] This can be accomplished by effectively decoupling the (fast) lower level device refresh from (slower) higher level algorithms that control changes in the value of the forces to be displayed [Adachi et al. 1995]. However, it works well only as long as the motion of the HIP is

---

[7]Note that, even if the haptic device is only designed to display forces to the user, the user's tactile receptors will still detect any vibrations in the device, even if these are not explicitly computed by the system but arise due, for example, to insufficiently rapid force refresh.

[8]As a result of the different refresh and rendering requirements, in the simulation engine, the haptic and other rendering channels are often run asynchronously (or decoupled) so as to perform their dedicated tasks at the required rate for each. This is discussed further in Section 7.7.

smooth and slow (relative to the 10–20-Hz update rate). If it is moved more quickly, then a sharp (and possibly quite large) change in force can result as the forces are updated for a different HIP location. This can be illustrated by considering the HIP moving toward a virtual object modeled as allowing very limited penetration (to account for some small deformability of the surface,[9] as, for example, one's thigh or forearm). If this action is performed slowly, the device will begin to display a resistive force as the HIP first makes contact. With the computed force rising rapidly with penetration distance, the HIP (and the corresponding position of the haptic device point) will be pushed back or held at a small penetration depth where the force applied by the user balances that displayed by the device. On the other hand, if the user pushes the device rapidly, the HIP could potentially be located quite far within the object before the force is updated. The displayed force will suddenly change from zero to a very high value corresponding to the large penetration depth, even if the force refresh rate was 1 kHz or greater. One way of avoiding effects such as this is to use simplified local models and interpolation schemes that ensure a smooth force transition even under decoupled high- and low-level control loops. We shall return to this shortly.

Another important issue with haptic feedback devices is stability [Adams et al. 1998]. The device position is sampled only at discrete time points, which means that the position of the virtual representation of the haptic device generally lags behind its "true" position; at best it will be coincident when the device is stationary. As a result, when pressing on a virtual object, the user in fact performs less work than they would in reality and in releasing receives more. Thus, pressing on a virtual object extracts energy from it [Colgate et al. 1993]! Another factor that impacts on stability is the presence of a human user within the haptic loop. Even if the virtual scene is modeled in such a way that the objects within it are passive (i.e., not exchanging energy with each other), the interaction with the user can potentially give rise to oscillations. Colgate and Brown [1994] write: "*Haptic display, however, makes the need for robustness more acute.*" They mention the human tactile response to frequencies up to $\sim$1 kHz (discussed above) and go on to add:

> ...*the human is also a dynamic system. Thus, even though a non-passive virtual environment may be stable, interaction with a human via a haptic interface may cause instability. In our studies of virtual walls, we have had many experiences with human operators adjusting their own behaviour until oscillations resulted.* [Colgate and Brown 1994, p. 3206]

They conclude their study by recommending the use of the highest spatial and temporal sampling resolutions possible and by maximizing the inherent damping in the device [Colgate and Brown 1994].

---

[9]For the purposes of this thought experiment, we assume that deformability of the object is not explicitly modeled, but a similar haptic response provided by allowing a very limited penetration. Deformable objects are discussed further in Section 7.5.5.

7.4   SINGLE-POINT HAPTIC INTERACTION

The simplest representation of a haptic interaction device is associated with the manipulation of a single point in the virtual space. This approach has been widely used with haptic devices capturing and returning to the user three degrees of freedom (3-DOF), usually three force components, in which the user controls the position of a thimble or the tip of a probe. As only the three components of the reaction force at the probe tip need to be calculated, this has also been a convenient simplification in enabling the development of real-time applications and the elucidation of fundamental issues related to haptic feedback [Salisbury 1999]. For our purposes, it also enables some key issues in haptic rendering to be elucidated and provides a foundation from which more complex interaction can be generalized. As Salisbury et al. [2004] write:

> *Arguably one of the most interesting events in haptics' history was the recognition, in the early 1990's, of the point interaction paradigm's usefulness.* [Salisbury et al. 2004, p. 28]

In this section, we briefly examine the algorithmic requirements of the various steps in the haptic interaction loop, introduced in Section 7.3.1, for the case of single-point interaction with virtual data represented as surfaces. We examine the situation with the common approach in computer graphics in which the virtual objects are defined as surfaces composed of polygons. We also cover problems and inconsistencies originating with this approach and refer to approaches that can circumvent difficulties.

As the HIP is moved within empty regions of the 3-D image space, no forces are applied and hence no resistance to motion of the device should be felt by the user. Indeed, this is often cited as a key desirable characteristic of haptic interaction devices: Free motion should feel free [Srinivasan and Basdogan 1997, Salisbury et al. 2004]. Whether or not the HIP encounters a part of the virtual scene is determined in the collision detection step. If a collision is detected, the appropriate haptic feedback is then calculated (rendered) and subsequently applied to the device. We now consider collision detection and haptic response computations in more detail.

7.4.1   Collision Detection

Collision detection represents a large research area in its own right, involving activities in areas such as computer graphics, CAD and robotics, as well as haptics, and a rich selection of algorithms and approaches exist [Jiménez et al. 2001]. In this subsection, we provide an introduction to the problem, especially as it applies to computer haptics, and outline some approaches that have been most widely used in this field. More general and complete overviews can be found in, for example, Foley et al. [1995], Lin and Gottschalk [1998], Watt [2000], Jiménez et al. [2001], and Lin et al. [2004].

If we assume that the HIP starts from a position in free space, the task of the collision detection algorithm is to determine when the HIP encounters a surface or passes from outside to within one of the virtual objects. If the objects are represented by simple analytic expressions, then collision detection can be achieved by evaluating a series of inequalities based on the HIP position relative to those of the objects. A simple example, presented by Basdogan and Srinivasan [2002], is the case of a single sphere of radius R centered at x_c. A collision is detected if the HIP position x_h satisfies the relation $|x_c - x_h| < R$. As discussed in more depth in Section 7.4.2, the extent of penetration into the object is often used to determine the strength of the force applied to the interaction device.

More usually, the virtual scene is represented as a collection of polygon surfaces. (For this discussion, we assume that each polygon has a surface normal associated with it, thus distinguishing "inside" from "outside" of the object.) For polygon data, collision detection approaches from fields such as computer graphics have provided a useful starting point for haptic collision detection. In haptic interaction with static scenes, the problem can be reduced to that of identifying collisions between the virtual representation of the interaction device and objects within the virtual scene [Ho et al. 1997]. This represents a slightly simpler problem than checking for collisions between any two objects within the virtual scene, as one of the potentially colliding objects is always the same (and often has a simple representation—a single point in the case of our current discussion). To seek collisions between the HIP and a number n_o of static objects within our virtual scene, a simple proximity detection procedure examines the position of the HIP relative to each object once, and thus it has an algorithmic complexity $O(n_o)$. However, in the more general case of haptic interaction with an evolving dynamic scene, collisions between arbitrary objects must also be sought. In this more general case, the resulting pairwise comparison has complexity $O(n_o^2)$ [Watt 2000].

One common approach to collision detection involves a two-pass procedure. The initial, "broad phase" part of the algorithm provides a rapid but coarse determination of whether two objects are in close proximity and hence are likely to collide. Only when this occurs is a more exact "narrow phase" collision detection algorithm employed, and the objects concerned are examined more precisely to determine whether a collision has in fact occurred [Hubbard 1993]. These two parts of the algorithm may be selected independently.

The broad phase part of the algorithm is often implemented by using simple bounding volumes around each of the individual objects. Because the object is entirely contained within the bounding volume, if the HIP does not intersect this volume, then by definition it is not in collision with the object itself. Conversely, if the bounding volume has been breached, then the second part of the algorithm is invoked to determine the existence and nature of the collision. Often, a hierarchy or "tree" of bounding volumes is computed for each object in the virtual scene [Cohen et al. 1995, Gottschalk et al. 1996]. In such hierarchies, at the top level, there is only one bounding volume that circumscribes the entire object. At levels of finer and finer spatial detail, a higher number of smaller volumes are used to describe the underlying shape more closely. A common example is the octree

[Hayward 1986, Watt 2000]. Here, the top-level bounding box is divided into eight equal sub-boxes at the next level. Those that contain part of the object are further divided and considered to "branch" from the box above them; this is continued recursively, creating a logical "tree" structure. Each node (box) is usually labeled "full," "empty" or "partially full." This recursion typically continues until either a predefined number of levels are reached or until all nodes are either empty or full [Jiménez et al. 2001].

Two popular forms of bounding volumes used in collision detection methods are spheres and parallelepipeds. Spherical bounding volumes are the simplest and offer advantages in the speed of computing overlaps or updating the hierarchy. However, unless the objects are reasonably isotropic, there will be a greater excess volume than with parallelepipeds, and hence a greater probability of detecting a "false alarm" collision proximity and needlessly invoking the more exact step. (We revisit a sphere-based approach shortly.) In the case of parallelepipeds, these "bounding boxes" may be aligned with the global coordinate system of the virtual space, known as "axis-aligned bounding boxes" (AABB's) [Cohen et al. 1995]. Alternatively, the bounding boxes can be oriented in the most optimal way for the shape and orientation of each object (or part thereof)—these are known as "oriented bounding boxes" (OBBs) [Gottschalk et al. 1996] and have proven particularly popular in haptics applications—(see Figure 7.2(a)). Each OBB includes a rotation matrix describing its orientation relative to the global (scene) axes and a vector whose components contain the size of the box in each direction. Gottschalk et al. [1996] also described an efficient algorithm to create a hierarchy of OBBs (known as an "OBBTree") and demonstrated that this approach was faster than an AABB representation. Although as they note, definitive comparisons are not straightforward as there are no accepted standard benchmarks.

As discussed by Zachmann [2002], the performance of broad-phase collision detection algorithms of this type in detecting collisions between two objects within the scene improves with the tightness of the fit of the bounding volumes to the underlying objects and with the simplicity of the bounding volume. The former affects the number of "true" broad-phase collision tests, whereas the second affects the efficiency of the overlap test. Latimer and Salisbury [1997] used an OBBTree approach to detect collisions both between the HIP and the objects within the scene and also collisions between the virtual objects themselves.

Another approach to the collision proximity problem involves a subdivision of the virtual space into smaller spatial units, with each of these cells linked to any object overlapping with it. The subdivision can be a hierarchical (for example, using an a octree structure, as described above [Smith et al. 1995]) or a nonhierarchical uniform or sparse grid [Held et al. 1995, Borro et al. 2004]. In the case of our single point interacting with virtual objects, the search space for haptic rendering is immediately limited to the cell containing the current HIP position [Raymaekers and Coninx 2003]. Indeed, if no other objects are present in the current cell, then the search stops immediately in the assurance that no collision has occurred.

Moreover, future collision detection tests can use the knowledge of prior HIP positions to narrow down the parts of the scene with which it might be in contact

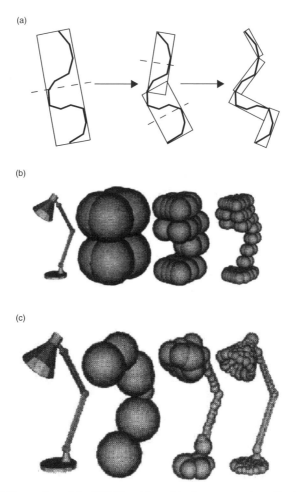

Figure 7.2: (a) Illustration of the OBBTree hierarchical representation of a simple object in two-dimensions. By allowing the orientation of the bounding boxes to follow the form of the object, the approximation is closer than methods in which the orientation of the bounding boxes is fixed. (b) Octree and (c) medial-axis hierarchical sphere representations of a desk lamp comprised 626 triangles. The medial axis representation yields a much tighter fit to the form of the object. [Figure (a) reproduced from Gottschalk, S., Lin, M.C., and Manocha, D., "OBB-tree: A Hierarchical Structure for Rapid Interference Detection," *Proc. SIGGRAPH '96*, (1996); © 1996 ACM. Figures (b) and (c) reproduced from Hubbard, P.M., "Approximating Polyhedra with Spheres for Time-Collision Detection," *ACM Transactions on Graphics*, **15**, (1996); © 1996 ACM.]

[Gregory et al. 2000]. A variation on this technique is the voxel-based approach of McNeely et al. [1999], in which the surfaces of static objects within the virtual scenes are replaced by a "voxelized" equivalent. Intersections between moving objects (considered as a collection of points) and these object "voxels" are then detected. Spatial subdivision approaches are sometimes used as a precursor to collision detection methods as outlined above; for example, Gregory et al. [1999, 2000] describe a hybrid algorithm in which both space partitioning and an OBBTree hierarchy are combined. They also deal with the potential to miss collisions because of the finite temporal sampling of the HIP position by testing for collisions between the bounding boxes and a line segment connecting the current and previously sampled HIP locations.

Having detected an overlap between bounding volumes, or between a bounding volume and the HIP, the second, "narrow phase" step is an exact determination of whether or not a collision has actually occurred. For objects represented as polygons, this amounts to a series of tests involving the vertex coordinates and polygon edges to determine whether they are in fact intersecting (see, for example, Möller [1997], Latimer and Salisbury [1997], Watt [2000]).

An interesting and flexible approach to detecting collisions between two virtual objects is described in an excellent article by Hubbard [1996]. Objects within the virtual space are again represented by surrounding volumes in a hierarchically increasing level of detail. In his method, collisions are first checked for at the coarsest scale for each object. If a collision is detected at this scale, then collisions are checked at the next level in the hierarchy (giving a finer spatial resolution), and so on, as above. This continues until either the full depth of the hierarchy has been traversed or (more likely) until the time available to the algorithm has been reached. The spatial accuracy of collision detection thus depends on how far in the hierarchy we have descended. This allows collisions to be detected with an increasing level of accuracy commensurate with the available computation time. This flexible tradeoff between accuracy and time is important for interactive scenarios. As Hubbard [1996] writes:

> The most promising way to make collision detection possible for more interactive applications is to use time-critical computing. The essence of this approach, which van Dam [1993] also calls negotiated graceful degradation, is trading accuracy for speed. [Hubbard 1996, p. 180]

In other words, for more complex virtual scenes, the collision detection phase need not slow down the application; the spatial accuracy of collision detection becomes more approximate, but interactivity is maintained. Clearly, the more tightly the bounding volumes fit the object at each level in the tree, the more accurate the collision detection for a given time budget. Hubbard also proposed an efficient sphere-tree creation algorithm, yielding a tighter fit than common alternative approaches (see Figures 7.2(b) and (c)). In both this approach and the broad-phase hierarchical methods discussed above, the problem of efficiently updating bounding volume hierarchies is critical in the interaction with dynamic scenes [Larsson and Akenine-Möller 2001].

7.4.2   The Computation of Reaction Forces

Once a collision between the HIP and a virtual object has occurred, the response force must be calculated; here we move to step 3 of the haptic interaction loop described in Section 7.3.1. When the virtual scene comprises objects defined in a surface representation, the force response may be calculated as proportional to the penetration depth of the HIP within the object. This widely used approach thus models the object as an elastic surface and has been reported to provide a quite realistic subjective feeling of rigid surfaces [Rosenberg and Adelstein 1993]. The force response F can thus be calculated according to Hooke's Law:[10]

$$F = -kD, \qquad (7.1)$$

where k is the stiffness coefficient and D represents the penetration distance into the virtual object [Sears and Zemansky 1964]. In haptic rendering, different values of k permit the modeling of objects of different rigidity in a straightforward manner; low values give the sensation of feeling a soft object, whereas higher values provide a more rigid rendering. The quality of the response when the HIP collides with a virtual rigid wall has become something of a benchmark for haptic interaction [Salisbury et al. 2004]. However, as there are limits to the forces that can be displayed by haptic interaction devices, considerable research has been carried out to analyze (heuristically) how the response to a rigid surface can be best modeled [Rosenberg and Adelstein 1993, Colgate and Brown 1994, Massie 1996]. One issue that arises relates to the fact that pushing and releasing a virtual spring creates energy due to the finite time resolution of the force update, leading to instability in the force response (as discussed in Section 7.3.2). This undesirable effect can be reduced, and the subjective sensation of a rigid surface can be improved, by adding to Eq. (7.1) a damping term proportional to the velocity when the HIP is inside the object ($|D| > 0$) [Salisbury et al. 1995]:

$$F = -kD - M\frac{dD}{dt}. \qquad (7.2)$$

Consider again the simple sphere example described previously; here, D can be determined analytically as $D = [R - |x_c - x_h|](x_h - x_c)/|x_h - x_c|$, i.e., proportional to the distance of the HIP from the nearest surface (see Figure 7.3(a)). For polyhedral objects, the distance to the geometrically closest surface point can also be used to determine the reaction force, an approach known as "geometrical minimization" (see Figure 7.3(b)). One issue with this method, pointed out by Ruspini et al. [1997], is that a potentially large number of polygons might need to be searched to determine the nearest surface point.

The fact that the coordinates of the haptic device are sampled at discrete time points can also lead to undetected collisions in the case of rapid user motion; for example, it could happen that the HIP passes completely through a small or thin object! What is missing is any record of the contact history or how the "collision" evolves over time. Moreover, this lack of a position history can also lead to problems in the form of "force discontinuities" when there is a direct mapping between

---

[10]Named after Robert Hooke (1635–1703). Hooke was a prodigious English scientist and contemporary of Isaac Newton.

(a)   (b)

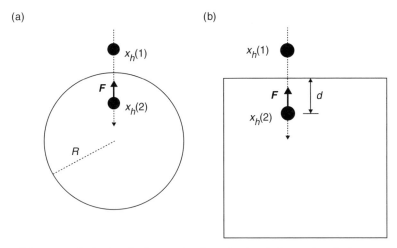

Figure 7.3: Due to limitations in the reaction force that haptic interaction devices can apply, the Haptic Interaction Point (HIP) often penetrates objects with which it is in contact. For interaction with objects defined as surfaces, the penetration depth of the HIP can be used to compute the reaction force applied to the device. Most commonly, a linear relationship between penetration depth and reaction force is computed, according to Hooke's Law (see text for details).

position (relative to the surface of an object) and the applied force and a thin object or a convex corner is encountered [see Figure 7.4]. To best understand this, consider an implementation in which the magnitude and direction of the applied force are governed by the nearest point on the surface to the HIP, i.e., a geometrical minimization approach. In the case of a thin object, when the HIP penetrates far enough to become closer to the other side of the object, the force suddenly becomes directed the other way, actively pushing the HIP out the other side of the object [Zilles and Salisbury 1994, Ruspini et al. 1997] (see Figure 7.4(b)). This occurs when there is not sufficient "depth" across the object to prevent the HIP approaching the other side. A similar phenomenon occurs at convex corners where the force suddenly switches direction as the HIP approaches too close to another edge [Ruspini et al. 1997, Basdogan and Srinivasan 2002] (see Figure 7.4(c)).

7.4.3   The Virtual Proxy

One approach to dealing with some of the above issues is to employ a "proxy" representation of the HIP within the virtual scene, a concept introduced by Zilles and Salisbury [1994], and Ruspini et al. [1997].[11] Whereas the HIP by definition tracks the interface device position exactly, the proxy is a second virtual copy of

---

[11]The term "proxy" is that used by Ruspini et al. [1997], and we follow that terminology here. Alternative terms found in the literature include "god-object" [Zilles and Salisbury 1994] or "Ideal Haptic Interaction Point" (IHIP) [Basdogan and Srinivasan 2002].

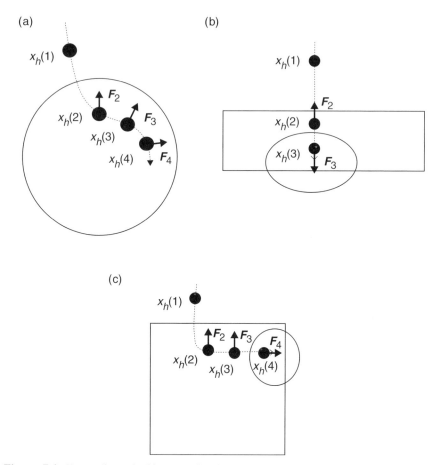

Figure 7.4: Force discontinuities can develop when the reaction force is computed as proportional to the distance from the HIP to nearest surface, without using contact history information. (a) For a smoothly varying surface such as the sphere, bringing the HIP into contact with the object and then moving it along the surface results in a smooth evolution of force direction. (b) For thin objects, if the HIP can penetrate far enough the force direction is reversed and the HIP is projected out the other side. (c) Corners of convex shapes can also give rise to force discontinuities.

the HIP that can be subjected to additional rules and constraints in order to render more physically realistic behavior to the user.

A key behavior that the proxy can provide is the nonpenetration of virtual objects. When the HIP is moving in unoccupied space within the virtual scene, the proxy tracks the HIP position exactly, and because no collisions have occurred, no force is applied to the user. However, when the HIP is in contact with or penetrating objects within the virtual scene, the proxy is constrained to follow rules designed to emulate ideal behavior relating to the object [Ruspini et al. 1997]. For example, in the case of a rigid surface, the proxy should remain on the surface even though the HIP may penetrate within the object (see Figure 7.5); in the case of a plastic or elastic surface, the proxy follows the deformation of the surface. The concept of a proxy provides more flexibility in computing reaction forces after

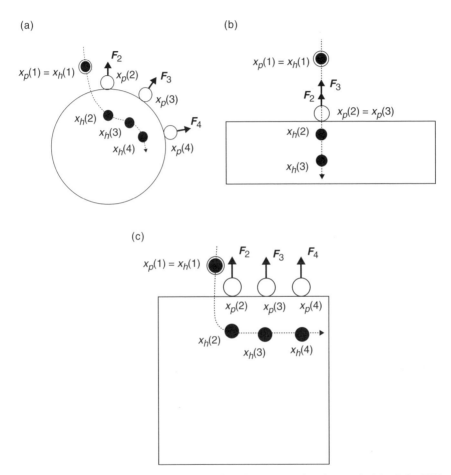

Figure 7.5: The use of a proxy or ideal virtual representation (open circle) of the HIP, constrained to physically realistic positions, is one way of avoiding some of the force discontinuities that can otherwise arise. Whilst in free space, no forces are applied and the proxy is spatially coincident with the HIP within the virtual model. When in contact with an object, however, the proxy remains in the physically realistic position (for example, on the surface of a rigid object) even though the HIP penetrates the object slightly due to limitations in device impedance. When a contact history of the proxy position is maintained, force discontinuities such as those illustrated in Figure 7.4 may be avoided. Although there is little difference in behavior for a smooth object such as a sphere (a), force discontinuities can be avoided when in contact with thin objects (b) or near convex corners (c).

collisions. Retaining a record of the previous proxy position at each iteration provides a computationally effective way of maintaining the contact history and hence of calculating the direction of reaction force more appropriately.

The position of the proxy on the object surface may be calculated by geometric minimization—the proxy being placed at the closest possible position to the HIP while remaining on the surface. The magnitude reaction force may then be calculated as being proportional to the distance between the HIP and the proxy [Zilles and Salisbury 1994]. This is similar to the method outlined above, where the distance between the HIP and the nearest surface point was used to determine the strength and direction of the reaction force. Indeed, in the case of contact with the center of a wide virtual wall (and using the same stiffness coefficient), the resulting force will be the same. However, the advantage with the proxy method is that it provides a convenient framework for tracking the contact history of the interface device with the object, namely the previous proxy position. In this example, rather than calculating a global geometric minimum distance to any surface in the object (as in Figure 7.4(b)), a local minimum is sought only on the parts of the surface that are currently constraining the proxy position [Zilles and Salisbury 1994].

Ruspini et al. [1997] describe an algorithm based on this approach that attempts to move the proxy along a straight line from its previous position to the new HIP position. Any collisions between this line segment and objects within the virtual scene are checked for by collision detection approaches, such as outlined in Section 7.4.1. When a collision is detected, the new proxy position is determined, taking into account the constraints provided by the object that has been encountered. If the metric to determine the proxy location is chosen to be the geometric minimum, the proxy is positioned at the closest location on the surface commensurate with the constraints provided by the object (assuming the HIP has penetrated the object). For example, in the case of a rigid (nondeformable) object, the proxy must remain on the surface. In a polygonal object representation, with the HIP position denoted by x_h and the proxy position by x_p, this is equivalent to minimizing the "geometric" cost function

$$C_{geom} = \|\mathbf{x}_h - \mathbf{x}_p\| \qquad (7.3)$$

subject to the geometrical constraint that the proxy must remain on the surface.

One innovative application of haptic interaction that illustrates some of the concepts discussed above is the "FeTouch" project,[12] illustrated in Figure 7.6, which allows the unborn child to be "touched" [Prattichizzo et al. 2004]. A static surface representation of the child's face is reconstructed from 3-D ultrasound scans and this can be felt by means of a single-point force feedback device. This application illustrates several of the issues we have discussed so far in this chapter. As explained further by La Torre et al. [2003], the collision detection algorithm operated within the 1 kHz haptic control loop, and so the number of polygons describing the surface was kept as low as possible, and combined with smoothing

---

[12]http://www.fetouch.org.

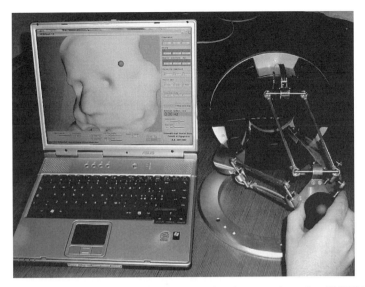

Figure 7.6: Illustration of the FeTouch application in operation. An OMEGA haptic interaction device is used to provide force feedback corresponding to the surface of the baby's face obtained from ultrasound scans. The face is rendered using standard graphics techniques and the user can explore the face haptically using the device, thus "feeling" as well as seeing the scan. (Image reproduced courtesy of D. Prattichizzo, scientific coordinator of the FeTouch project.)

procedures to avoid artefactual edges. Collision detection used an OBBTree representation of the data and a virtual proxy of the HIP. Haptic textures approximating the feel of human skin were added to the model, and the contact stiffness of the surface was set to different values to simulate "harder" or "softer" parts of the body (e.g., skull versus arm). Moreover, a heartbeat effect, based on recordings of the fetus' actual heartbeat, was also added to the model.

7.5 INCREASING THE REALISM OF FORCE FEEDBACK

In the previous section, we investigated some of the algorithmic issues concerned with rendering a response force vector to a haptic device, for the case of single-point interaction. As implementations of this paradigm were explored, however, it became apparent that the realism experienced by the user could be improved by addressing some limitations of the above approach [Salisbury et al. 1995]. One of these is the lack of friction; in real life, practically all touch interactions with surrounding objects involve friction. Interaction with a virtual scene using only the force feedback considerations discussed above gives an impression of touching a very slippery surface, with the probe tending to slip off convex surfaces into concave ones [Mark et al. 1996]. Moreover, any applications in which objects are to be grasped or moved rely upon friction to allow purchase of the virtual objects (unless they have some very specific shape). A related issue is that of providing surfaces with different textures to more accurately simulate different materials. Finally, when objects in the virtual scene are represented as polyhedra, the direction and magnitude of the reaction force is, unless corrected for, discontinuous at the polygon edges and so the polygon boundaries are clearly felt. In this section, we briefly discuss some of the methods that have been implemented to provide the impression of friction, texture, and smooth shape perception, while remaining within a single-point interaction paradigm.

7.5.1 Adding Frictional Forces

The incorporation of friction into the haptic feedback essentially involves the addition of static and dynamic friction forces tangential to the surface [Salisbury et al. 1995, Ho et al. 1999]. "Static friction" captures the resistance to motion along a surface for small values of the tangential component $\mathbf{F}_t$ of the applied force. Considering solid objects only, the threshold force required to move an object is approximately proportional to the force of the object onto the surface (e.g., the weight of the object in the case of an object resting on a horizontal surface) and hence to the reaction force $\mathbf{F}_n$ normal to the surface (see, for example, Sears and Zemansky [1964]). The constant of proportionality is the "coefficient of static friction" (μ_s), an empirical measure dependent upon the material comprising the object and the surface; some examples are given in Table 7.1. When $\|\mathbf{F}_t\| \leq \mu_s \|\mathbf{F}_n\|$, the applied force is not sufficient to overcome static friction, and no motion results (i.e., the proxy is not moved [Ruspini et al. 1997]). When $\|\mathbf{F}_t\| > \mu_s \|\mathbf{F}_n\|$, the object moves and the friction force decreases but still exerts a force opposing the motion. Analogous to static friction, this braking force is proportional to $\mathbf{F}_n$ by the "coefficient of dynamic friction" (μ_d), i.e., $\|\mathbf{F}_d\| = \mu_d \|\mathbf{F}_n\|$. The total force returned to the device is then the vector sum of the normal response

TABLE 7.1: Coefficients of friction.

Material	Static, μ_s	Dynamic, μ_d
Steel on steel	0.74	0.57
Aluminium on steel	0.61	0.47
Copper on steel	0.53	0.36
Brass on steel	0.51	0.44
Zinc on cast iron	0.85	0.21
Copper on cast iron	1.05	0.29
Glass on glass	0.94	0.40
Copper on glass	0.68	0.53
Teflon on teflon	0.04	0.04
Teflon on steel	0.04	0.04

Source: Sears, F.W., and Zemansky, M.W., *University Physics*, 3rd edn., Addison-Wesley (1964); © 2005 Pearson Education.

force due to contact with the object and the frictional force: $\mathbf{F}_{returned} = \mathbf{F}_f + \mathbf{F}_n$ (see Figure 7.7). Here $\mathbf{F}_f$ refers to $\mathbf{F}_t$ or $\mathbf{F}_d$, depending on whether the proxy or HIP is in the static or dynamic friction regime.

One approach to incorporating static and dynamic friction behavior into the haptic rendering algorithm has been to endow the proxy with a friction state, being either "sticking" or "sliding" [Salisbury et al. 1995, Ho et al. 1999]. When a collision of the HIP with an object in the scene first occurs, the friction state is set to "sticking." If the user then applies to the HIP a force whose component $\mathbf{F}_t$ parallel to the active surface is smaller in magnitude than the threshold force to overcome static friction ($\mathbf{F}_s = \mu_s \|\mathbf{F}_n\|$), then a reaction force—$\mathbf{F}_s$ is added to the feedback force and the proxy is not moved. If, however, the tangential component of the user's force ($\|\mathbf{F}_t\|$) exceeds the static friction threshold $\|\mathbf{F}_s\|$, then the proxy's friction state is changed to "sliding," and the smaller dynamic reaction force $\mathbf{F}_d$ is applied to the device. In the approach of Salisbury et al. [1995], the state was then set back to sticking for the next iteration, although Ho et al. [1999] report a more realistic sensation of dynamic friction if the sliding state is maintained until $\|\mathbf{F}_t\|$ decreases below the dynamic friction threshold, whereupon the state is switched back to "sticking" for the following iteration.

Ruspini et al. [1997] extended the dynamic friction model by adding a viscous damping term proportional to the velocity of the proxy. Adding such a term, with damping constant b, to the dynamic friction model above, the equation of motion becomes (assuming it is being modeled as having a mass of zero):

$$\mathbf{F}_t - \mu_d \mathbf{F}_n = b\dot{\mathbf{x}}_p, \qquad (7.4)$$

so that the velocity of the object in dynamic equilibrium, as the proxy is moving across the surface because of an applied force above the static friction

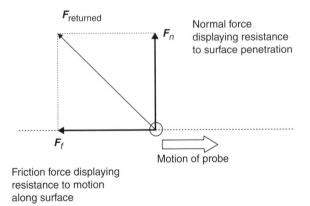

Figure 7.7: Components of the force rendered to the user in a point-based interaction paradigm. The normal force $\mathbf{F}_n$ is related to the elasticity or plasticity of the object and is often related to the depth of penetration of the HIP within the object. Friction effects can be incorporated by a tangential force component directed opposite to the direction of motion of the device.

threshold, is given by

$$\dot{\mathbf{x}}_p = \frac{\mathbf{F}_t - \mu_d \mathbf{F}_n}{b}. \tag{7.5}$$

The viscous damping term is useful in that it limits the maximum velocity, and hence the distance the proxy can move in a single iteration [Ruspini et al. 1997].

More complex friction behavior can be achieved by appropriately varying the friction coefficients over the surfaces of object [Ho et al. 1997]. Green and Salisbury [1997] investigated a series of real rigid planar surfaces and found that the value of the static friction coefficient is distributed randomly but according to a normal probability distribution. They then simulated surfaces of different roughnesses by mapping random, normally distributed, static friction coefficient values over a surface, with appropriate choices of the mean and standard deviation parameterizing the feel of the surface—rougher surfaces having a larger standard deviation.

7.5.2 Incorporating Haptic Texture

The variation in friction parameters over short length scales thus enables a sensation of *haptic texture* to be modeled. (Indeed, Minsky et al. [1990] demonstrated that convincing textures could be represented by perturbing the force vector in only two dimensions, as users explored a surface with a 2-DOF force feedback device.) Mark et al. [1996] describe a variation on the stick and slide model described above, where they model the HIP as a flexible tip with a certain flexing spring constant and populate the surface with a distribution of "dimples." When moved across the surface, the probe sticks in a dimple and a resistance force tangential to the surface is applied. This force is dependent on the spring constant associated with the probe and the distance of the probe from the dimple according to Hooke's Law and also proportional to the normal force into the surface, as above. As the user continues to push the probe (along the surface), this force increases until the probe has exceeded a threshold "escape" distance from the dimple. The probe then snaps free and only a dynamic friction force is applied, until another dimple is encountered. The nature of the surface modeled in this way is thus described by a slightly different set of parameters, namely the mean distance between dimples, a distance allowing a random variation about this position, the threshold escape distance of the tip from a dimple, and the flexing constant of the probe tip. These researchers found that by manipulating the values of these parameters, they could provide haptic sensations of substances as varied as concrete, rubber, skin, cloth, and sandpaper [Mark et al. 1996].

7.5.3 Smoothing Polygon Edges by Force Shading

One of the issues arising in haptic interaction with virtual surfaces represented as polygons is that the edges between adjacent elements are perceptible to the user;

the direction of the reaction force is discontinuous as the probe moves onto a plane with a different orientation, and the direction of the normal force vector suddenly changes. As in computer graphics, the lower the number of polygons, the lower the computational demand but the more marked are the boundaries. However, approaches similar to those used in computer graphics to smooth the visual appearance of polygon objects can be applied to smooth the reaction forces and render a more continuous shape to the user. In particular, "force shading" methods, analogous to Phong shading [Phong 1975], have been developed in computer haptics to reduce the perceived force discontinuities at edges of polyhedral objects [Zilles and Salisbury 1994, Morgenbesser and Srinivasan 1996].

In the force shading approach, rather than fixing the direction of the reaction force to that of the surface normal of the currently active polygon, the force vector at the proxy position can be interpolated between those of the current and the neighboring faces. For example, the shaded force vector F_S can be calculated as the weighted average of the normal vectors of the neighboring primitives. One example is the scheme of Ho et al. [1999], whose approach we now outline. In their algorithm, the polygonal object representations are reduced to a collection of triangles and the shaded force vector is calculated as the weighted average of the normals N^v at the three vertices of the currently active triangle. The weights are calculated from the areas A_i ($i = 1, \ldots, 3$) of the three subtriangles into which the proxy position divides the current triangle surface element:

$$\mathbf{F}_S = \frac{\sum_{i=1}^{3} A_i \mathbf{N}_i^v}{\sum_{i=1}^{3} A_i}. \tag{7.6}$$

The vertex normals N^v can be calculated *a priori* in the scene representation as the average of the normals N^p of their neighboring polygons, weighted by the angle subtended at the vertex.

As it stands, this approach ensures that the *direction* of the force vector is continuous at polygon edges, but not the *magnitude*. One heuristic approach to maintaining continuity of magnitude is to set it proportional to the geometric distance from the HIP to the active polygon surface along the direction of the shaded force vector. However, Ho et al. [1999] report that this is convincing only when the penetration distance of the HIP is small compared with the size of the polygon. Finally, we note that if an edge is actually a desirable feature of the virtual scene, force shading should not be applied to this particular discontinuity!

7.5.4 Intermediate Representations

As we discussed in Section 7.3.2, the haptic feedback channel needs to be refreshed at ~1 kHz, placing severe time constraints on the computation of the reaction forces, and a conflict between the complexity of the virtual scene and the accurate computation of the force response. Adachi et al. [1995] introduced the concept of an "intermediate representation" of the virtual scene to avoid this problem. The basic idea is to approximate the part of the object in contact with the HIP by a simple representation and calculate the force response within the high-frequency haptic loop with respect to this construct. For example, in the case of the HIP in collision with a stiff surface, the local tangent plane to the surface is often used. The intermediate representation is then modified (for example, in position) within the slower update loop of the virtual scene. However, if large changes have occurred, this relatively slow update can lead to force discontinuities. The rate of change of the intermediate representation within the update loop can be constrained to avoid such sharp changes in forces [Mark et al. 1996, Chen et al. 2000a].

Another approach to avoid sharp forces developing from unpredictable user motion is to delay the force update (within the slower loop) by one iteration, allowing the intermediate forces (within the fast haptic loop) to be interpolated between two known points [Zhuang and Canny 2000]. With such a method, the forces relayed to the user are delayed by one iteration cycle, but this constant delay of ~30 ms is not usually perceptible (or is less so than force discontinuities that might otherwise result).

7.5.5 More Complex Models, Torque, and Deformable Objects

In the above discussion, we have dealt exclusively with interactions that can be modeled by a single point, and with objects that are not altered because of the haptic interaction. Despite the utility of a simple point-based interaction paradigm, many situations exist in which more complex interaction is desirable. In particular, adding torque feedback to a 3-DOF interaction device—thereby providing 6-DOF—enables constraints on the orientation of the device to be modeled as well. This represents a slight generalization of point-based interaction, and we can consider tool-based paradigms in which the metaphor can be thought of as manipulating the handle of a more complex tool. Interaction with virtual objects is no longer accurately modeled by a single point. One example discussed by Reinig [1996] is the insertion of a needle into a virtual body (using the visible human data set[13]). Here, the tip provides a piercing action, but the shaft of the needle contributes frictional resistance (when pushed or pulled) and torque constraints that are stronger the further the needle is inserted. Reinig also discusses the slightly more complex case of a virtual scalpel; here the cutting action occurs along a *line* (the edge of the blade) and the rest of the blade provides drag and torque restrictions on movements of the tool handle. In the most general case, both needle shaft and scalpel blade can also deform the tissues when suitable pressure is applied. The haptic simulation of operations such as needle insertion and surgical cutting is an ongoing area of activity; see, for example, Gillespie and Rosenberg [1994], Gorman et al. [2000], Kyung et al. [2001], Mahvash and Hayward [2001], and DiMaio and Salcudean [2003].

---

[13]http://www.nlm.nih.gov/research/visible/visible_human.html.

A straightforward generalization of the point-based interaction scheme is one in which the probe is modeled as a line segment, or *ray*. This virtual probe thus has an explicit orientation in 3-D space. As it interacts with objects within the scene, response torques can be calculated, for example, using a damped spring model analogous to those commonly applied to force feedback [McNeely et al. 1999]. (That is, the angular orientation and angular velocity takes the place of the linear position and velocity in a relation of the form of Eq. (7.2).) Collision detection and calculation of the haptic response with 6-DOF becomes more complicated; for example, either the tip of the ray or its body might be in collision and moreover contact is possible with several objects within the scene simultaneously. The ray might even collide with an edge between two polygons. Ho et al. [1997] introduced a ray-based haptic interaction algorithm that detected collisions between a probe represented as a ray and convex objects—concave objects needing to be decomposed into a set of convex ones—and calculated response forces and torques for a 6-DOF interaction device. They generalized the concept of a proxy (introduced in Section 7.4.3) to a line segment representation and modeled the relationship between it and the direct mapping of the probe into the virtual space by two springs connecting the ends of each. Refinement of collision detection and haptic rendering for 6-DOF interaction is ongoing (see, for example, Kim et al. [2003b]), and as these methods become practical, interactions including torque feedback are likely to become more common.

The discussion so far in this chapter has dealt only with static virtual models; the objects do not change during the interaction. However, many applications require or can be enriched by enabling the virtual objects to be altered in response to haptic interaction. If the virtual scene is described in terms of polyhedral surfaces, objects can be deformed by altering the position of the vertex nearest to the contact point, for example, in response to a "push" by the interaction device. As the disruption becomes greater, neighboring vertices can also be moved. To keep computational costs down, it is clearly best to keep as few vertices involved as possible, generally only those directly local to the point of contact. If a virtual proxy is employed, this will move inward with the surface, while the HIP will typically be slightly inside the object. This sort of technique can however be extended to allow effects to propagate to further points, with intermediate representations of the local neighborhood, as discussed above.

An alternative surface representation is in terms of spline-based functions, such as NURBS.[14] These are specified in terms of a set of control points and associated weights and are particularly popular in CAD applications. Haptic interaction with surfaces defined in terms of NURBS has also been investigated. For example, Thompson et al. [1997] developed an algorithm that allowed single-point haptic interaction with such "implicitly defined" surfaces. They used a broad-phase collision detection algorithm based on bounding boxes, followed by (if one of the bounding boxes is breached) a method to determine the closest point to the HIP on the NURBS surface and hence the depth of penetration for computation of the response force.

---

[14]Standard abbreviation for "Non-Uniform Rational B-Splines." See, for example, Piegl [1991], Terzopoulos and Qin [1994], or Dimas and Briassoulis [1999].

As discussed in Section 7.2, and reviewed by Burdea [1996], "glove-based" inter-action devices have also been developed for use with virtual (or remote) environ-ments, and some of these are commercially available. These allow a more complex interaction than single-point- or line-based models[15] and are in particular targeted at "grasping" actions, being able to pick up and squeeze virtual objects. This represents a more direct "hands on" haptic contact, in comparison with 6-DOF tool-based procedures, and can allow more complex interaction. Typically, these devices provide a single point of force feedback at each fingertip, with the force being grounded on either the palm or the back of the hand [Springer and Ferrier 2002, Bouzit et al. 2002]. The simplest way to model five-finger interactions is to generalize the single-point approach we have discussed to comprise five HIPs, corresponding to the tip of each finger. Popescu et al. [1999] describe how elastic deformations of a convex object can then be modeled by five spring/damper models in such a scenario. However, they go on to discuss several further improve-ments to this model. They describe the use of a lower resolution version of the virtual object for the force response calculations, a similar philosophy to the inter-mediate representation described above, with force shading to smooth the effects of the polygon edges. They also generalize the interaction model further, using a cylindrical mesh around each fingertip, rather than a single point, in order to calcu-late more accurately the force based on the orientation of the fingertip [Popescu et al. 1999]. These calculations are based on the positions of the fingers relative to the hand—incorporating a 3-D position tracker in the glove allows the hand to be tracked through the virtual scene and absolute finger positions to be maintained [Burdea 1996].

7.6   HAPTIC INTERACTION WITH VOLUMETRIC DATA

In Sections 7.4 and 7.5, we have considered haptic interaction with scenes compris-ing data represented as surfaces, in particular polygonal meshes. Data represen-tations of this type have been standard in computer graphics for many years and form the basis of surface-rendering techniques for visual display. This has allowed us to look into some issues involved with haptic rendering, within the sim-plified (but useful) single-point interaction paradigm. It was also implicitly assumed that objects in the scene were hollow and could be modeled by haptic interaction with their surfaces. In this section, we move on to examine haptic interaction with volumetric data sets. We revisit the fundamental operations corresponding to collision detection and haptic rendering for the case of voxel-based data. In the case of a 3-DOF force feedback interaction, this requires determining whether a force needs to be computed and, if so, computing the direction and magnitude of the force vector. We initially discuss the case in which the user interacts with a static volumetric data set represented as a rectilinear 3-D array. Subsequently, we

---

[15]See also Wall and Harwin [2001] and Barbagli et al. [2003] for a discussion of single-point versus multi-point haptic interaction.

discuss data modification before generalizing to more general abstract data type (ADT) representations of volumetric data and consider strategies allowing for modification of the virtual scene. Scenarios corresponding to haptic exploration (where the user can explore throughout a volumetric image) and also the representation of surface properties are briefly discussed.

Certain types of data amenable to 3-D visualization are more naturally represented and in many cases acquired at source, in a "voxel-based" or "volumetric" representation (see Section 1.6.3). That is, the virtual objects are composed of collections of points extending over a volume and thus contain information on the interior structure of the objects.[16] Medical imaging data, such as those obtained from Magnetic Resonance Imaging (MRI), x-ray Computed Tomography (CT), or positron-emitted tomography (PET) modalities, represent an important class of such data. The physical source of the voxel intensity depends on the modality; in the case of CT data, for example, it reflects electron density, with higher voxel values corresponding to bone and soft tissues yielding lower intensities. In typical biomedical MRI scans, voxel intensities depend on local water concentration and the nature of its immediate environment; bone is often invisible, and the acquisition method is selected so that the pixel intensities reflect a desired contrast between different soft tissues. The acquisition can also be arranged to yield high intensities in regions of blood inflow to the imaging region and hence provide angiograms. Injection of contrast agents in both modalities can broaden even further the range of tissue contrasts available.

Although biomedical imaging data can be represented in its "raw" state, i.e., as it was acquired, several preprocessing steps are commonly used and can be beneficial for both visual and haptic rendering. One important step is to eliminate (or set to zero) background voxels containing only noise and corresponding to air. Another step is to "segment" the data into different tissue classes, enabling a more robust assignment of voxel properties than those based purely on voxel intensity alone (see, for example, Pham et al. [2000]). That is, voxels are assigned to one of several tissue classes, each of which can then *uniformly* portray the associated visual and/or haptic properties. One philosophy of haptic exploration is that the haptic and visual properties should be as closely matched as possible [Iwata and Noma 1993]. However, image segmentation can be useful when assigning haptic properties to MRI data, as there is often some variability in the voxel intensities within tissue of a given type, reflecting the specifics of the acquisition rather than the underlying tissue properties. An alternative approach, then, is to use tissue class identifiers to define haptic feedback, with the original data set used for visual display. That is, we can decouple the haptic and visual properties of the data.

---

[16]Volumetric data sets can be converted into a surface representation, for example, by identifying two-dimensional (2-D) contours corresponding to edges [Canny 1986, Kass et al. 1987] and then building up a mesh surface, or by determining polygonal surfaces using the Marching Cubes algorithm [Lorenson and Cline 1987]. The motivation for this has historically been that, for visual display, surface rendering algorithms were more tractable given the computing technology available. As computing power has increased in recent years, however, graphic volume rendering algorithms have become feasible for generating views of the virtual scene directly from voxel data, without the need for generating an intermediate surface representation [Chen et al. 2000b, Watt 2000].

With voxel-based representations, attributes of the data are encoded at the atomic level of each voxel, which naturally enables properties to be reflected on a local scale and object interiors as well as surfaces can be represented. This can be thought of as a "bottom-up" approach, with more global properties (such as resistance to applied force) developing from interactions at a local level. In addressing haptic interaction with volumetric data, however, we initially consider haptic exploration of a nondeformable, regularly sampled, 3-D volumetric array. This will allow us to introduce some key concepts regarding haptic interaction with voxel-based data, in particular the computation of the force vector. Subsequently, we set out a more general abstract data type (ADT) framework for the representation of volumetric data within the virtual space. Each voxel can then encode several non-binary physical properties.

7.6.1   Exploration of Volumetric Data

Probably the simplest representation for a volumetric object is a 3-D array of regularly spaced voxels, which we denote by V. This is the natural representation for many experimentally or computationally sampled volumetric data sets such as biomedical imaging data. In this case, each voxel simply encodes a single scalar quantity, often referred to as its intensity or density. The spatial positions of each voxel and its neighbors are explicit in the array representation (and thus do not need to be retrieved from within abstract data structures). This means that local regions of the data can be accessed rapidly and independently of the complexity of the scene [Avila and Sobierajski 1996b]. However, if each voxel encodes only a single intensity parameter, haptic and visual properties to be rendered for the user must be derived from the scalar intensity value. We consider initially a single-point 3-DOF haptic interaction with such a volumetric array and discuss methods for calculating the force vector.

For convenience, we can consider two possible paradigms for haptic interaction with volumetric scenes—those of "penetrable" and "nonpenetrable" data. In the former approach, the HIP is allowed to penetrate into regions of nonzero voxels, with the varying response force providing a haptic sensation reflecting the local object properties as the data set is explored. In this paradigm, identification (from the voxel data) and enforcement (by appropriately strong response forces) of impenetrable surfaces is not required. This enables the user to feel the inside of volumetric objects as bumps and hollows on a haptic landscape, taking advantage of the fact that the interiors of objects are also captured in voxel-based representations.[17]

---

[17]In this discussion, we only consider the virtual scene defined by the confines of the data array. More generally, the volumetric array might be embedded within a larger virtual scene space, which may also contain other (possibly nonvolumetric) objects. In this case, the voxel array could be considered as a rectilinear "object" within the scene. Penetration of the virtual representation by the haptic device (for example, the HIP) into the voxel array could then be detected by simple collision detection with its rectilinear envelope. While within the object, voxel-based interaction parameters could be determined as outlined above (with suitable coordinate transformations from the frame of the virtual scene to the frame of the voxel array). If the haptic transition into the voxel array is intended to be smooth, "background" voxels should be set to zero.

Later in this section we consider issues with implementing a nonpenetrable data model.

To return a plausible force **F** to the user, the magnitude and direction of the force vector must be calculated. A simple method for computing the magnitude of the force $|F|$ is simply based on the scalar intensity values local to the HIP position x_h:

$$|\mathbf{F}| = f(V, \mathbf{x}_h). \tag{7.7}$$

As it is likely that the spatial resolution of the voxel array will be lower than that at which the HIP is sampled [Mor et al. 1996], the intensity of the voxel closest to the HIP could be used, or an intensity value could be interpolated from those of surrounding voxels. In the former case, we can write:

$$f(V, \mathbf{x}_h) = aV([\mathbf{x}_h]), \tag{7.8}$$

where a is a constant of proportionality and $[\mathbf{x}_h]$ denotes rounding of the position of the HIP to the nearest voxel location within the array. A smoother change in force magnitude with changes in x_h can be achieved by interpolating an effective intensity value between voxel locations (see, for example, Marschner et al. [1994]).

To calculate the direction of the force vector, the intensities of voxels in the neighborhood of the current HIP position can be used to determine an *intensity gradient* denoted ∇V, usually interpolated between the discrete voxel locations by numerical methods. One approach is to use trilinear interpolation[18] to calculate estimated values of the scalar intensity field at locations one unit (inter-voxel spacing) either side of x_h and then use central differences to calculate the gradient at the current HIP position $\mathbf{x}_h = (x, y, z)^T$ [Gibson et al. 1998]. As illustrated in Figure 7.8, if we denote the inter-voxel spacing by δ, and compute interpolated scalar field values $V(x \pm \delta, y \pm \delta, z \pm \delta)$, the gradient can be calculated as

$$\nabla V = \left(\frac{\partial V}{\partial x}, \ \frac{\partial V}{\partial y}, \ \frac{\partial V}{\partial z} \right)^T, \tag{7.9}$$

where

$$\frac{\partial V}{\partial x} = \frac{V(x + \delta, y, z) - V(x - \delta, y, z)}{2\delta}, \tag{7.10}$$

$$\frac{\partial V}{\partial y} = \frac{V(x, y + \delta, z) - V(x, y - \delta, z)}{2\delta}, \tag{7.11}$$

$$\frac{\partial V}{\partial z} = \frac{V(x, y, z + \delta) - V(x, y, z - \delta)}{2\delta}. \tag{7.12}$$

---

[18]More sophisticated interpolation and gradient estimation schemes are possible; see, for example, Marschner et al. [1994] and Neumann et al. [2000].

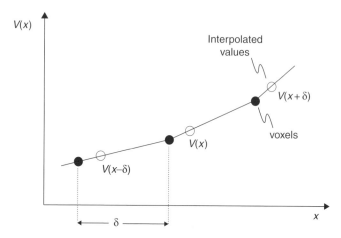

Figure 7.8: A one-dimensional illustration of one method of approximating the intensity gradient at a point V(x) within a discrete volumetric data set, with elements separated by a distance δ. First, the intensity at points offset by ± δ from V(x) is calculated from a linear interpolation between adjacent voxel values. The gradient between these two interpolated points, (V(x + δ) – V(x − δ))/2 δ, is then used as an approximation of the gradient at V(x).

The force, directed down the local intensity gradient, can then be written as

$$\mathbf{F}_{normal} = -\frac{\nabla V}{|\nabla V|} f(V, \mathbf{x}_h). \tag{7.13}$$

(Here the variables in brackets indicate that the force is calculated as a function of the local intensity value and position of the HIP only. This is not necessarily the case—for example, the local gradient itself can also be used to calculate the force magnitude, as we will discuss again shortly.) Assigning stronger reaction forces to image regions of higher intensity can be useful, for example, in exploring CT scans, in which bone appears bright. Bones would thus present greater resistance, requiring the user to "push through" until the force direction (if directed away from high-intensity regions) switches direction and the probe is pulled through the far surface. This is analogous to a "hill" in the haptic landscape. An alternative mapping of intensity to force is to invert the relationship, so that bright structures correspond to haptic "valleys" and therefore tend to attract the probe. In this way, haptic tracing of bright features is facilitated. Applications of this could include angiography, where the most intense signals are derived from blood vessels, which often trace complex 3-D forms. Avila and Sobierajski [1996a] described another application of this approach—the haptic exploration of a confocal microscopy image of an LGN[19] cell with many dendrites following, in a similar way to an angiogram, complex paths through space.

---

[19]Lateral Geniculate Nucleus—see Chapter 2.

7.6.2 Smoother Force Feedback

An undesirable feature of many medical imaging data sets is the presence of noise that creates local voxel-wise fluctuations in the image intensity that could perturb forces calculated based only on voxels immediately adjacent to the current HIP. Even in segmented data sets, the boundaries between one tissue class and another may contain irregularities.[20] One approach to reducing the effect of noise is to compute a locally smoothed version of the data that is used for haptic feedback. If the data are not altered by the interaction (as we assume in this section), then a smoothed version of the data can be pre-computed, for example, by convolution with a Gaussian kernel.[21] After such low-pass filtering operations, each voxel represents some weighted combination of its neighbors. In this way, smooth haptic feedback that reflects the object properties over a larger volume around the HIP can be calculated during the interaction loop based only on calculations on immediately adjacent voxels. This method requires a second voxel array to be stored (thus doubling the memory requirements). An alternative is to calculate the locally smoothed intensity value as the HIP is maneuvered through the array [Mor et al. 1996]—so saving memory but increasing computational cost during interaction.

Another approach is to model the HIP as a sphere rather than as a single point, and to calculate the response force based on the overlap between the sphere and the object (nonzero data values). Petersik et al. [2001] implemented such a scheme and calculated the force direction as the vector sum of radial vectors extending from those parts of the surface of the sphere lying within the object to either the surface of the object or the center of the sphere. This scheme thus emphasizes the *surfaces* of volumetric structures, an approach we discuss further shortly.

7.6.3 Additional Forces

Avila and Sobierajski [1996a] described a more general force calculation equation than that considered above, by including drag and ambient forces:

$$\mathbf{F} = \mathbf{F}_{gradient} + \mathbf{F}_{drag}(\dot{\mathbf{x}}_h) + \mathbf{F}_{ambient}. \tag{7.15}$$

Here, $\mathbf{F}_{gradient}$ is the force along the local intensity gradient that we discussed and $\mathbf{F}_{drag}(\dot{\mathbf{x}}_h)$ is a drag force whose magnitude increases with the velocity of the HIP, directed opposite to the direction of motion. $\mathbf{F}_{ambient}$ is another force that can be overlaid, for example, to specify the effect of gravity or provide a virtual plane that could help a user to cut a straight line. Mor et al. [1996] used a drag force dependent on the local intensity gradient to generate a friction effect at the surfaces of a

---

[20]This can arise, for example, from a segmentation procedure in which each voxel is classified independently. Near tissue boundaries, voxels may be near a transition point and their assignment to one class or the other can be determined by noise.

[21]It may be advantageous to re-mask the smoothed data set with a binary function in which "background" voxels are set to zero. This would prevent "bleeding" of intensities into "empty" regions of the array, preserving well-defined haptic boundaries.

TABLE 7.2: Example voxel attributes to be encoded in an abstract data type for each point.

Attribute	Type	Size (bytes)
Density	scalar	1
Gradient direction	Encoded unit vector	2
Gradient magnitude	scalar	1
Colour	R,G,B	3
Material properties	LUT index	1

Source: Avila, R.S., and Sobierajski, L.M., "A Haptic Interaction Method for Volume Visualization," *Proceedings of IEEE Visualization '96* (1996); 1996 IEEE.

segmented data set (where the gradient was large as the HIP passed from background to bone).

To enable more information pertaining to each voxel to be stored, a more general representation than just a single scalar field may be useful. For example, Avila and Sobierajski [1996a] employed an 8-byte data representation of each voxel, including properties for visual as well as haptic rendering (see Table 7.2). In this representation, the local intensity gradient may also be pre-computed and stored, at the expense of 3 bytes per voxel but speeding up force calculations based on the gradient during haptic interaction. This is best suited to volumetric data that is static, or altered only locally (thus making updated gradient calculations feasible during real-time operation).

7.6.4   The Impression of Surfaces Within Volumetric Images

So far in this section we have considered the scenario in which the HIP is allowed to penetrate into volumetric data sets, enabling an exploration of internal structures with the aid of force feedback, providing a 3-D landscape of haptic hills and valleys. However, it is sometimes desirable to represent surface-like properties within a voxel-based data set. In medical training applications, for example, realistic tissue properties are important. Consider a palpation simulation; clearly the fingers should not penetrate the patient's body but should feel the superficial tissues when pushed or squeezed. Another example is surgical simulations, in which the patient's body is not expected to be penetrated by the haptic device except where the tissue is explicitly penetrated (for example, by a needle) or cut (for example, by a scalpel). It might also be desirable to model bone as impenetrable. In this approach, force feedback must be implemented to realistically constrain the HIP position near the object surfaces.[22] We now briefly discuss computational strategies to identify and model surfaces within the data for force feedback. Subsequently, we move on to issues related to modeling deformations of the data.

[22]In the case of nondeformable objects, a fairly rigid force feedback is necessary to avoid gross discrepancy between the actual HIP penetration of the virtual object and the lack of visible deformation.

One approach that has been used to define surfaces within volumetric images has been simply to nominate an isosurface value from within the intensity range of the data. Voxels of this intensity then define the surface of interest; those with greater values are inside, and those with lower are outside. (For example, consider the case in which voxels within the objects of interest in the data have intensity values in the range 50–150. By setting an isosurface value of, say, 50, then if the HIP encounters a voxel of intensity 50 or greater, it has encountered the surface. In analogy with the surface-based approach, we could say that a "collision" has been detected.) Having defined the surface in this way, a surface-based representation of the data could be computed and haptic rendering proceeded using the surface-based techniques introduced previously. However, this is computationally expensive and so likely to be possible only as a pre-computed step, precluding data modification during interaction. An alternative is to calculate the force based on the local intensity value—for example, between a range of intensity values defining a thin shell at the isosurface [Avila and Sobierajski 1996a]—or based on the local intensity gradient [Gibson et al. 1998]. This is very similar to the approach we described for penetrable data, although in this case the mapping of data values to force would generate stronger response forces (although clearly within the range supported by the device) to convey the impression that a physical surface has been encountered. Applying haptic interaction with voxel-based data to arthroscopic knee surgery, Gibson et al. [1998] used a force whose magnitude as well as direction was determined by the local intensity gradient. They based the haptic response on a smoothed, segmented data set, and so in this way emphasized the surfaces of the segmented structures rather than their internal composition. However, in these approaches, the computed force is likely to provide an accurate impression only if the HIP remains very close to the surface. Moreover, in such schemes where the force is only based on local voxel values, it is possible to "push through" the surface, encountering reduced forces (or possibly force discontinuities). For example, in a CT scan of the head, the skull is relatively thin—it is possible the HIP may encounter the lower voxel values (or inverted gradient) inside the skull; in which case, the haptic rendering of an impenetrable surface breaks down.

Chen et al. [2000a] proposed the use of an intermediate representation of a plane tangential to the isosurface, similar to that discussed by Mark et al. [1996] for surface-based data. This enables a virtual proxy and contact history to be maintained, as with the surface-based approach [Zilles and Salisbury 1994, Ruspini et al. 1997]. They also implemented a "recovery time" constraint as introduced by Mark et al. [1996] to avoid sharp discontinuities. Lundin et al. [2002] describe a proxy-based method in which a virtual plane is not calculated explicitly, but the proxy is constrained to move perpendicular to the local gradient (i.e., along the surface). The location of the proxy relative to the HIP can then be used to calculate the force vector. The impedance force (in the absence of friction) can be calculated as a function of both the penetration distance of the HIP relative to the proxy and the local tissue properties (allowing, for example, certain tissues to feel "harder" than others). Typically the force will increase with HIP penetration (perhaps by a spring and damper model) to realistically render an impression of nonpenetrability.

7.6.5   Modification of Volumetric Data

In the foregoing discussion, we have considered volumetric data represented as a 3-D array of voxel values, with the possibility of associated arrays (or extended array elements) holding additional information. Modification of the image can be achieved simply by altering voxel values within the array(s). However, alternative representations of volumetric data can allow a more flexible and detailed description of voxel properties. For example, each voxel can be considered an independent "object" within the scene and be represented as an abstract data type containing a number of properties of the voxel. This can include an explicit statement of positional information, which allows a given voxel to move position but retain its other properties. This has advantages when considering applications in which the data are to be deformed. Furthermore, although many scanning modalities naturally yield a rectilinear 3-D data array, other data sources such as computational modeling in fluid dynamics, astrophysics, and geology may be sampled on irregular lattice or intrinsically comprise scattered data with explicit positions, and may be vector or scalar in nature [Gibson 1997b]. The data structure can also contain explicit links to nearest-neighbor voxels, allowing surfaces to be identified by the absence of a neighbor in one direction. Adding or removing links to other voxels enables material to be joined or cut. In a volumetric data set represented in this way, each voxel can encode several attributes, which are applicable to rendering for the various channels, as well as attributes governing their interaction with their neighbors.

One algorithm that has been implemented to provide real-time deformations of volumetric data sets, known as "3-D Chain-mail," was developed by Gibson [1997a]. In this scheme, voxels are linked to their six nearest neighbors. If one is moved, there is a displacement threshold to overcome before the deformation is propagated to the neighbors; in other words, there is "slack" in the system. This displacement threshold can be altered to provide more or less rigid response to haptic contact. If the threshold is violated, the neighboring voxel positions are altered until the separation is within the allowed range. It is repeated with all affected voxels until all inter-voxel separations are legal. Only if the system is in a state in which a large fraction of the inter-voxel distances are at their limit does a small local interaction propagate through the whole object. This approach permits object deformation in response to user interaction to be modeled in a computationally expedient fashion, with deformation times on a single processor implementation reported to rise linearly with the number of voxels [Gibson et al. 1998]. Material "tearing" can also be implemented by this algorithm by applying a second, larger, displacement threshold to the model. When this is violated, and cannot be resolved by moving neighboring voxels, a tear is implemented by breaking the connections between the appropriate voxels. In a similar way, *cutting* can be implemented by breaking the connections of neighboring voxels in response to appropriate contact from a virtual tool. These features of this approach have been demonstrated in an application to simulated arthroscopic knee surgery [Gibson et al. 1998]. By mapping the interaction device to different tools, ligaments could be cut, tacked in place, or sutured together.

This algorithm was extended by Park et al. [2002] to incorporate an elastic spring response between voxels when within the allowed separation range. In this way, the material returns to its initial state (in order to minimize the energy stored in the system) when the applied perturbation is removed. Moreover, the force displayed to the user was based on the total energy stored within the voxel array by the applied perturbation. In this voxel-based data philosophy, the response of the system to interaction thus originates from considering local interactions between voxels, rather than, for example, equations modeling global properties of the material.

When interacting with data represented in an ADT implementation, collision detection between the HIP and objects within the scene is no longer as simple as in the case of a rectilinear data array. One approach is to look for voxel-level overlap between objects mapped into the virtual space. Frisken-Gibson [1999] describes an "occupancy map" of the virtual space, maintained at a spatial resolution comparable with the intervoxel spacing. If a voxel lies within a certain occupancy cell, the cell contains a pointer to that voxel. If, when updating the virtual scene, a voxel is mapped into a cell that is already occupied, then both a collision is detected and the colliding voxels are identified for immediate calculation of the response. If two (or more) voxels from the same object are mapped to the same cell (due to compression of the material, for example), the collision can simply be ignored. Alternatively, the resolution of the occupancy map can be set to the minimum possible intervoxel spacing, ensuring there is at most one occupant of any cell. He and Kaufman [1997] presented an alternative approach to collision detection based on a hierarchical representation of "fuzzy" surfaces of volumetric objects (defined as being between two intensity thresholds) and pre-processed maps of the distance between each voxel and its object's surface.

7.7   MULTICHANNEL SOFTWARE ARCHITECTURES

As we discussed when considering the haptic interaction loop in Section 7.3.1, the haptic and visual display channels have quite different refresh requirements. Visual displays need only be refreshed at frequencies ~ 30 Hz, whereas realistic force feedback requires refresh frequencies of at least 1000 Hz. For both channels, the computational burden depends in general upon the amount of data in the scene and upon the level of sophistication of the rendering process. For haptic rendering of smooth, rigid objects, even with a host computer of modest performance by today's standards, Ho et al. [1999] found that high haptic refresh rates (approaching 10 kHz) could be sustained even for single-point interaction with scenes approaching 10^5 polygons. However, computing resources can still be stretched to the limit as the complexity of virtual scenes and models is increased—for example, employing finite element analysis techniques for more physically realistic simulations, or using a more complex model of the interaction device. As we discussed previously, even the step from 3-DOF to 6-DOF feedback incurs complications to the control software.

For these reasons, the haptic and visual (or other) rendering channels are often decoupled in the simulation engine so as to perform their dedicated tasks at the required rates. In particular, the time constraints of the haptic feedback loop are often decoupled from the rate at which the model of the virtual scene is updated—this latter is closer to the visual refresh rate, and so the graphic rendering and the full model update are often performed together. As we discussed in Section 7.5.4, a simplified intermediate representation of the virtual scene local to the interaction point can be used, this being able to be computed within the time constraints of the fast haptic loop. This simplified model is then in turn modified at the slower rate, following more accurate calculations.

As summarized by Ho et al. [1999], the architecture of such a system may be either "multiprocess" (cf. Mark et al. [1996]) or "multi-threaded" (cf. Chen et al. [1998]); see Figure 7.9. In a multiprocess approach, the computation for each channel is performed by a separate process and can thus be implemented on different computers [Burdea 1996, Mark et al. 1996]. In this case, each channel maintains its own copy of the virtual scene, and so efficient interprocess communication to maintain consistency in the virtual scenes held in memory in each computer is paramount. This solution is practical in the sense that machines particularly matched to the requirements of the different channels, or software developed on a particular platform, can be used, for example, using one machine with dedicated graphic rendering hardware for the visual display channel and a separate computer running the haptic algorithms and maintaining the force feedback loop. Implementations using standard network protocols such as TCP/IP have been employed [Mark et al. 1996]. However, the regular communication required between the processes to maintain consistency of the virtual scene can become a bottleneck depending on data transfer load; if large amounts of data must be transferred then a multi-threaded solution may be more appropriate [Ho et al. 1999]. The associated latency overhead is due to both data transfer *per se* and synchronization of the virtual scene.

7.8 DISCUSSION

In this chapter we have attempted to provide a background to some application areas in which haptic feedback is beginning to have an impact, introduced the key components of the haptic interaction loop, and discussed some of the underlying concepts concerned with haptic rendering. Our discussion centered on the basic steps of collision detection and the computation of the appropriate haptic feedback. The single-point interaction scenario has to date proven particularly fruitful in the field of computer haptics, and consideration of issues relating to force and torque feedback in this context provides a sound basis for understanding a number of applications and developing more complex interaction paradigms. For example, an application in which the user can grasp objects via feedback to three fingers can be considered as comprising three single-point interactions (although the modeling of the response of the virtual scene may be more complex than in a pure single-point case). Incorporating texture and friction effects can further enhance the realism of haptic interaction and by ensuring sensation of the constituent elements

(a)

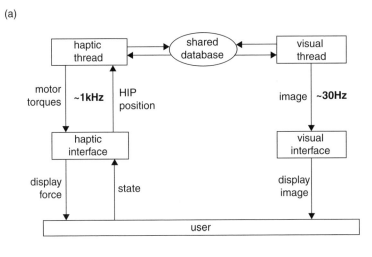

(b)

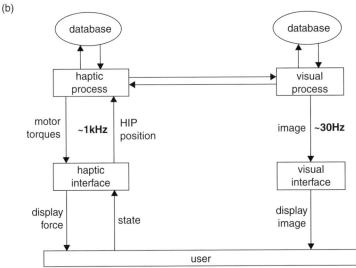

Figure 7.9: (a) Multi-threading and (b) multi-processor architectures for a visualization system employing haptic and visual channels. The visual channel as depicted here is unidirectional (for example, no head tracking input) and only renders the virtual scene for visual display. The required refresh rates of each channel are very different, $\sim$30 Hz for the visual channel but $\sim$1000 Hz for the haptic. [Reproduced by permission from Ho, C.H., Basdogan, C., and Srinivasan, M.A., "Efficient Point-Based Rendering Techniques for Haptic Display of Virtual Objects," *Presence*, 8, (1999); © 1999 MIT Press Journals.]

of the data themselves (polygons or voxels) does not override the intended impression of the object shape or other properties. To date, much of the modeling of the response of virtual objects to interaction has been based on simple models (such as the spring/damper relationship with penetration depth) that have been found empirically to provide a realistic sensation to the user. However, efforts toward haptic interaction with models following more accurate behavior based on physical laws (including the use of finite element methods) have also been undertaken and are likely to benefit from increases in computing power.

Haptic interaction with virtual images is now a vibrant field; we have touched on just a few of the exciting opportunities that have been explored. Commercial products are available—from haptic interaction devices and supporting software to integrated simulation systems incorporating haptic feedback. Research efforts in devices, software, and application evaluation and development are ongoing and new discoveries are continually being made. The addition of a fuller range of sensory inputs, satisfying the rich capabilities of our tactile input channels (such as the touch discrimination in our fingertips), is likely to greatly extend our haptic interaction capabilities in coming years. Although research into haptic interaction with virtual data dates back to the 1960s, activity in the field has taken off in the past 10–15 years, fuelled in large part by its association with developments in virtual reality. As we saw in Chapter 6, and will examine more closely in Chapter 8, there are numerous ways in which 3-D scenes can be visually presented to the user. Recently, haptic devices have also been coupled with other 3-D display techniques and are likely to play an important role in effective interaction with images depicted with creative display systems. Very many difficulties must still be overcome, and of course, we must never underestimate the complexities of the human haptic channel.

7.9   INVESTIGATIONS

1. Simulate the effect of single-point interaction with your real environment by exploring various objects with a pen, analogous to a haptic probe tool device. How much texture can you feel? How important is friction? How sensitive is this approach to edges and other "large" features in objects? How do the sensations compare with touching the same surfaces with your finger?

2. Specify three distinct tasks for which torque feedback is likely to be useful. How would the interaction be limited if only force feedback was supplied?

3. Draw a simple object (e.g., a car, a duck, a person, a cup, ...) on a sheet of graph paper. Now build a quadtree (octree in 2-D) hierarchy of at least three levels of bounding boxes (a) about the figure and (b) dividing the entire space. Denote each node as full, empty, or partly full. Discuss the computational steps required in each case to determine a collision (or possible collision) with a single HIP.

4. Consider a volumetric data set, in which the haptic rendering is based on a locally filtered version of that used for visual display. What are the relative advantages and disadvantages of performing this filtering on the fly, versus storing a pre-computed version of the data set? Consider storage requirements, computational cost, and the software architecture. In terms of commonly available computer equipment, how does this situation at the present time compare with that in, say, 1996?

8 The Visual Channel

At length did come an Albatross,
Through the fog it came;
As if it had been a Christian soul,
We hailed it in God's name.

8.1 INTRODUCTION

This chapter reviews a range of approaches that may be used in the implementation of creative three-dimensional (3-D) display systems. Although our focus is on general concepts and basic principles, where appropriate and to reinforce more abstract ideas, we will refer to particular past and current embodiments. As previously discussed, there are a wide variety of techniques that may be brought

Creative 3-D Display and Interaction Interfaces: A Trans-Disciplinary Approach, by Barry G. Blundell and Adam J. Schwarz

together for the implementation of creative 3-D displays. This results in systems that often offer significantly different visual characteristics, forms of image space, and that vary in their computational requirements. Furthermore, they range from readily portable technologies through to essentially fixed installations and provide a range of different interaction opportunities. By describing a number of these display paradigms within the context of a single chapter we hope to provide the reader with a clear insight into their diversity. As we work through various approaches (and our selection of techniques is simply intended to be indicative), we identify particular strengths and weaknesses and emphasize aspects that must be carefully considered during the design phase.

To describe techniques in depth would result in the chapter expanding to form a lengthy text in its own right. On the other hand, brevity risks oversimplification, the superficial treatment of important detail, and disregard for critical issues. Consequently we have attempted to strike a careful balance and trust that the interested reader will make use of the references that are cited throughout the chapter.

We begin this voyage by examining various forms of stereoscopic display in which different views of a 3-D scene are presented to each eye. Here we build on material previously introduced in Sections 6.3 and 6.4. Although the most common approaches rely on the viewer wearing special glasses, we also consider the implementation of "direct view" stereoscopic displays (in which headgear is not required). In Section 8.3, we discuss various multi-view techniques, in which stereoscopic views are provided for more than one viewing location, providing a limited degree of "look-around" capability. These approaches typically generate a range of different "viewing zones" in front of the display device. In the same section we also briefly describe computed holography (electroholography).

Section 8.4 introduces techniques that extend the basic stereoscopic approach by coupling it with hardware able to sense the direction of the user's viewpoint. In particular, we discuss immersive virtual reality (IVR) approaches, including personal (head-mounted) and room-based (CAVE) systems (and the Cybersphere). Subsequently, we briefly discuss augmented (or mixed) reality systems that explicitly mix real and virtual objects. Finally, in Section 8.5, we discuss AutoQ systems, specifically volumetric and varifocal approaches.

For various techniques, we allude to the associated computational requirements. We do this loosely in terms of the rate at which pixels must be rendered. Although this is indicative and provides a useful indicator, it is clearly important to remember that aspects of the computational requirements of some systems may lend themselves (to a greater or lesser extent) to parallel computation. Consequently, for example, two systems having the same computational cost may be quite dissimilar in terms of their ability to make efficient use of parallel processing facilities, and naturally this impacts on the actual speed at which image scenes may be rendered.

This chapter is intended to review the basic elements of a range of creative 3-D display technologies. In addition to the references cited throughout the chapter, we recommend to the reader the following works. Valyus [1962] and Lipton [1982] provide a thorough coverage of stereoscopic display principles and historical material. Okoshi [1976] covers lenticular sheet and holography in some detail (see also Saleh and Teich [1991] regarding the latter). McAllister [1993] provides an excellent collection of chapters dedicated to a wide range of different 3-D display techniques. Blundell and Schwarz [2000] provide an history of volumetric display systems and discuss many underlying principles. For an in-depth discussion on virtual reality, see Burdea and Coiffet [2003]. Recent review articles that provide an overview of 3-D display research include Halle [1997], Pastoor and Wopking [1997] and Sexton and Surman [1999].

8.2 STEREOSCOPIC DISPLAY TECHNIQUES

> Once more the gate behind me falls;
> Once more before my face
> I see the moulder'd Abbey-walls
> That stand within the chace.[1]

Images rendered for a single viewpoint simulate only the pictorial depth cues (see Section 2.6.1) and are designed for viewing on conventional flat-screen display devices. However, as we have previously discussed, a far more compelling sensation of depth can be achieved by providing each eye with a slightly different view of the virtual 3-D scene. In this way, the depth cue of binocular parallax (stereopsis) is satisfied (see Section 2.6.2). Technologies based on supporting the binocular parallax cue are known as stereoscopic systems, and these were previously introduced in Section 6.3.1. The most commonly found stereoscopic systems employed for the human–computer interaction process are designed to augment the conventional display paradigm by permitting operation in both "normal" and "stereo" modes.

In this section, we briefly consider some of the techniques that may be used in the implementation of stereoscopic displays within the context of the human–computer interface.

8.2.1 Temporally Coded Systems

As described in Section 6.3.1, one way of providing distinct views to each eye is to display the left and right views alternately on a conventional 2-D screen; in other words, the views for display are "temporally coded." These views are then decoded for correct stereoscopic viewing by additional hardware which ensures that each eye sees only the designated series of images. We now examine some approaches to the implementation of displays operating on this general principle.

1. *Decoding by Means of Mechanical Occlusion*: Early temporally coded stereoscopic displays employed various types of mechanical shutter arrangement. For example, as illustrated in Figure 8.1(a), one embodiment used the mechanical

---

[1]Alfred Lord Tennyson, "The Talking Oak." From *The Works of Alfred Lord Tennyson*, Wordsworth Poetry Library (1994).

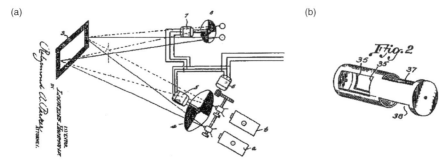

Figure 8.1: Early approaches to temporally coded stereoscopic displays, using mechanical occlusion. (a) The Teleview stereoscopic system proposed by Hammond [1924, 1928]. (b) The "rotating beer can" shutter component used in the electromechanical goggles originally proposed by Caldwell. [Reproduced from Caldwell, G.D., and Hathorn, G.M., *Viewing Instrument for Stereoscopic Pictures and the Like*, U.S. Patent 2,273,512 (1942).]

motion of synchronized rotating wheels—one located in front of separate left and right eye image projectors and a second positioned in front of each viewer. The occluding wheel in front of the projector allowed only one of the views to be projected at any time, and the other wheel ensures that each that each eye received only the designated view [Hammond 1924, 1928]. A later approach used the somewhat unusual headgear illustrated in Figure 8.1(b). This comprised a cylinder with windows cut out such that one eye's view was occluded, whereas the other's was not. The device was rapidly rotated about its main axis in synchronism with the sequential display of the left and right eye views [Caldwell and Hathorn 1942].

For further related reading we recommend the excellent summaries of past and recent approaches to stereoscopic display implementation provided by Lipton [1982, 1991, 2001].

2. *Decoding by Means of Electro-optical Devices*: As indicated in Section 6.3.1, modern approaches to the "temporal coding" of stereoscopic images use electro-optical rather than mechanical action to code and decode the two views. Liquid crystal devices (LCDs) are most commonly used at the present time (see, for example, Lipton [2001], and Philip Bos writing in [McAllister 1993]). To achieve synchronization between display and filter switching, the glasses (re-imaging subsystem) need to be linked to the display hardware either via a cable or a wireless connection.

An alternative approach to the implementation of the temporally coded stereoscopic display is to alternately polarize the light from the left and right eye views into orthogonal components, for example, by a switchable filter covering the screen. This can then be decoded by "passive filtering" glasses containing static orthogonally polarized filters in front of the corresponding eyes. Clearly, as no synchronization is required between the display pipeline and the viewing glasses, they are more economical to produce than their LCD-based counterpart. Historically, linearly polarized filters were more readily available, but these suffer from the drawback that tilting the head can result in cross-talk (see below). However, circularly polarized filtering provides stereoscopic viewing that is much more robust to small changes in the viewer's head [Walworth 1984].

Two important issues that must be considered in the implementation of stereoscopic displays employing the temporal coding techniques outlined above relate to "flicker" and "cross-talk." These are briefly described as follows:

1. *Image Flicker*: As we have seen, in the case of a temporally coded stereoscopic display system, each eye receives only alternate frames. Consequently, when a display is switched from "mono" to "stereo" mode, the effective image refresh rate available to each eye falls by a factor of two. The display refresh rate must therefore be sufficiently high to avoid image flicker becoming apparent when the display is operating in stereoscopic mode. As discussed in Section 2.7, although 25–30 Hz is sufficient to enable comfortable perception of "continuity of presence" (temporal fusing) for occasional viewing, 60 Hz or higher refresh rates are required to preclude more subtle eyestrain arising during prolonged usage. Current computer graphics hardware and monitors often support frame rates of up to 120 Hz, enabling undesirable flicker to be minimized even in stereoscopic mode. See Carl Machover writing in [MacDonald and Lowe 1997] for discussion.

2. *Image Cross-Talk (Ghosting)*: This arises when either view within the stereoscopic pair is visible to both eyes (either in part or for some duration of time). In the case of temporally coded systems based on Cathode Ray Tube (CRT) technology, this may arise due to the finite persistence (decay) of the light intensity from the phosphor used to generate the screen pixels (the image element generation subsystem, see Section 1.7). This can also arise in passively filtered systems due to deviations from an optimal viewing geometry—for example, head tilting when using linearly polarized filter glasses. The perceived severity of cross-talk also depends upon factors such as the image content, including contrast, color, and degree of parallax. The recent advent of digital projectors, in which temporal persistence between image frames is greatly reduced, promises to render the cross-talk problem negligible for displays in which these devices are used [Lipton 2001].

8.2.2 Chromatically Coded Systems

As indicated in Section 6.3.1, another approach to stereoscopic display implementation involves the simultaneous presentation of both views depicted on a conventional two-dimensional (2-D) screen. In this case, coding of the left and right views can be achieved by use of color.[2] Appropriate passive filters in front of

---

[2]Another way of *simultaneously* coding two images on a single display screen is to orthogonally polarize the light from each view, as discussed above in the context of temporally coded displays. The difference here is that each view is displayed simultaneously. This is more suited to projection-based systems than to conventional computer-based displays. This technique was patented by Anderton in 1891, but it was not until the availability of good quality linear polarizing filters in the 1930s that it was applied to stereoscopic cinema.

each eye then transmit only the correct view to each eye. Stereoscopic systems using this technique are commonly referred to as "anaglyph displays,"[3] where the left and right eye images are displayed in complementary colors, typically red and either green, blue, or cyan. As such, this represents a "chromatically encoded" technique (see Section 6.3.1). Images are viewed through glasses with corresponding filters. In a pure anaglyph approach the images must be single color (color is used only for encoding the two views).

The anaglyph technique is by no means new, and it appears to have been discovered by Joseph D'Almeida and Louis Du Hauron in the 1850s and used for 3-D magic lantern slide shows and printed stereograms. It has since been used for comics and advertisements, and has a particularly long heritage in 3-D cinema. The first 3-D anaglyph movie was apparently created by William Friese-Green in 1889 and was popularized by the stereo movies of the 1950s.

Despite using color to encode the left and right eye images, a certain degree of color may nevertheless be incorporated by the intelligent use of colors that survive both filters:

> *Although essentially a black and white system, a certain amount of colour can be introduced into the anaglyph. Colours other than red, blue and green pass through both filters and successfully combine in the 3-D image, e.g., white, yellow, brown, gold, bronze, silver.* [Girling 1990]

8.2.3   Spatially Coded Systems

An alternative approach to the systems discussed above (and which generally require the user to don special viewing glasses) is a technique employing "spatial coding." In this case, the two views of the 3-D scene are visible from spatially distinct "viewing zones" in front of the display. Figure 8.2 illustrates the general principle: The right-eye view is visible from a zone to the right of center, and the left-eye view is visible from the left. An advantage of this approach is that it provides stereoscopic viewing without the need for viewing glasses to be used. However, the viewing position is often closely constrained, and the basic technique provides a 3-D view from only one viewpoint (cf. Baird's stereoscopic television display system outlined in Section 6.3.1).

Typically, the viewing zones are designed to have a width approximately equal to the average interocular distance (around 6.5 cm). Thus, if the viewer's head deviates more than $\sim$3 cm (half the interocular distance) laterally from the ideal central viewing position, then both eyes may lie within the same zone and the stereoscopic effect will be lost. Furthermore, in the case of some approaches of this type, the views repeat adjacent to the ideal viewing zones. Thus, as the viewer moves sideways away from the screen center, the right eye can see the left-eye view and vice versa, resulting in a "pseudoscopic" image.[4] In such

---

[3]The word *anaglyph* comes from the Greek *anagluphein*, which means "to carve in relief."
[4]See also the reference to Wheatstone's "pseudoscope" in Section 6.3.1.

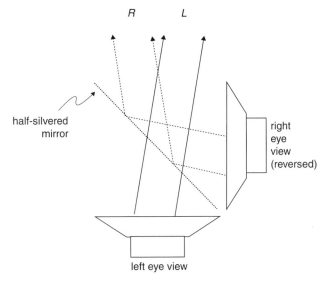

Figure 8.2: The principle of operation of a half-silvered mirror used to provide spatially coded stereo views, via two separate viewing zones, one for each eye. Although a half-silvered mirror may be used, other partially transmissive, partially reflective surfaces can be employed. (For example, Swan's Cube, implemented in the mid-nineteenth century, used the interface between two prisms.)

situations, the binocular parallax cue is in conflict with depth information due to shading, occlusion, etc.

The most common spatially coded stereoscopic approaches are specific (two-view) cases of autostereoscopic multi-view systems, such as the parallax barrier or lenticular sheet techniques (see Section 8.3). However, alternative approaches are also possible, such as the use of a half-silvered mirror, or an optical equivalent. This is a surface that reflects light incident from one side but also transmits light incident from the other. When placed at an appropriate angle, stereoscopic views can be directed to different spatial viewing zones, as illustrated in Figure 8.2. This technique in fact dates back to "Swan's Cube," a device invented by H. Swan in the nineteenth century [Sexton and Surman 1999]. We will meet the half-silvered mirror again in Section 8.4.4 where it is used to enable the combination of virtual and real objects, rather than the combination of stereoscopic views.

8.2.4 Computation for Stereoscopic Views

In Section 1.6.1 we introduced the perspective projection for mapping a single viewpoint of a 3-D scene onto a conventional 2-D display. Typically, for complex scenes, this is combined with a rendering procedure to provide a realistic image containing a

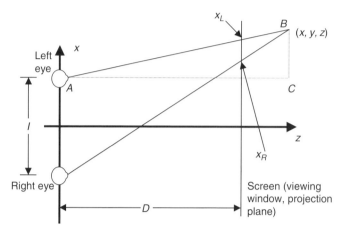

Figure 8.3: A plan view of a projection from a point (x,y,z) to the two eyes. This projection cuts the viewing window at points (x_R, y_R) and (x_L, x_L). See text for details. (Diagram © 2005 Q.S. Blundell.)

full range of pictorial depth cues. A stereoscopic display must depict two such scenes, one for each eye's view, and so the most straightforward approach to the computation of stereo views is simply to separately render the two images. This entails performing the projection twice, from viewing positions offset $\pm I/2$ (I represents the interocular distance[5]) laterally from the $y = 0$ plane (see Figure 8.3). This illustration shows the plan view geometry of the projection from a point $(x.y.z)$ to the two eyes. We assume that the projection for the left eye intersects the viewing window at (x_L, y_L) and for the right eye at (x_R, y_R). Consider the triangle ABC, from which it is apparent that for $x \geq I/2$,

$$\frac{z}{D} = \frac{\left(x - \dfrac{I}{2}\right)}{\left(x_L - \dfrac{I}{2}\right)}.$$

Thus,

$$x_L = \frac{Dx}{z} - \frac{DI}{2z} + \frac{I}{2}. \tag{8.1}$$

[5]However, in practice, a physically realistic value of I and viewing distance D may not be the best choice unless the objects or scene being depicted are to be viewed at their actual size [Lipton 1997]. In effect, when very large or very small objects (e.g., buildings, mountains, molecules) are to be depicted, the scale of the viewer should be decoupled from that of the scene in order to create an appropriate depth effect.

And for y_L we may simply use Eq. (1.1):

$$y_L = \frac{yD}{z}. \tag{8.2}$$

Similarly, for the right eye view, we have

$$x_R = \frac{Dx}{z} + \frac{DI}{2z} - \frac{I}{2}, \quad y_R = \frac{yD}{z}. \tag{8.3}$$

In a temporally coded system, the number of pixels to be rendered is clearly

$$Number\ of\ pixels\ per\ stereo\ refresh = 2 \times N_x \times N_y, \tag{8.4}$$

where N_x and N_y denote the number of pixels located horizontally and vertically on the display. Thus, in a simplistic approach where each view is rendered independently, the computation time for the stereoscopic pair is $t_{stereo} = 2t_{mono}$, where t_{mono} is the time required to render a single monoscopic view.

However, this approach does not take advantage of the fact that many aspects of the two views are likely to be the same or can be inferred. By doing so, significant increases in stereoscopic rendering speed may be achieved. Consider the two projection transformations given above. It can be seen that, for a given point, the y-projection is the same for both views, whereas the x-projection in the right-eye view is related to that in the left-eye view as

$$x_R = x_L + I\left(\frac{D}{z} - 1\right). \tag{8.5}$$

Thus:

> ...the point moves horizontally between the views by a distance dependent on the depth of the point to be projected, the distance from the viewing position to the projection plane, and the distance between the two viewing positions.[6] [Adelson and Hodges 1993]

Consequently, given a rendering for the left eye view, then, the x-projection for the right eye view can be analytically calculated based on the known parameters of the interocular separation and the viewing distance. However, Eq. (8.5) only works completely under certain circumstances and the interested reader is referred to the more detailed discussion offered by Adelson and Hodges [1993]. Nevertheless, coherence between stereoscopic views forms the basis of algorithms developed to enable ray-traced stereoscopic pairs to be computed rapidly. The stereoscopic

---

[6]For clarity, symbols used by the authors are omitted.

computation requirements are therefore more generally represented as $t_{stereo} = \alpha t_{mono}$, where α is a factor of between 1 and 2. For example, by targeting and recalculating for the right-eye view only those pixels that are not robustly estimated from the left eye view, Adelson and Hodges [1993] achieved stereoscopic ray-traced computation times with α in the range 1.05 to 1.3. Unfortunately, the advantages offered by this approach vary with scene content.

Details of several publications that have not been specifically cited in the above text are provided in the General Bibliography. The books by MacDonald and Lowe (eds.) [1997] and by McAllister [1993] provide a wealth of information—as do Lipton [1982] and Valyus [1962].

8.3   MULTI-VIEW SYSTEMS AND ELECTROHOLOGRAPHY

> Philosophy is like the mother who gave birth to and endowed
> all the other sciences. Therefore, one should not scorn her
> in her nakedness and poverty, but should hope, rather, that
> part of her Don Quixote ideal will live on in her
> children so that they do not sink into philistinism.[7]

In this section we briefly review techniques that provide a range of views to the user and do not require special glasses or headgear to be worn. Display techniques discussed here are characterized by providing differing degrees of viewing freedom without recourse to tracking a viewer's location (systems that track the viewing location are discussed in the next section). Displays in this and the next section are commonly termed "autostereoscopic" (see Section 6.2), in that they permit a limited degree of motion parallax ("look-around" capability).

8.3.1   Lenticular and Parallax Barrier Techniques

A popular class of 3-D display techniques makes use of a static mask or optical element placed in front of a conventional 2-D display to provide multiple views of a 3-D scene from different positions (viewing zones). In this way, the viewer sees a 3-D image space without the need for glasses or headgear. When each eye falls into a different viewing zone, binocular parallax is satisfied and the viewer perceives a stereoscopic image. If more than two views are provided, the viewpoints change with lateral head position. Since these techniques generate spatially separate viewing zones, they can be thought of as spatially coded displays (see also the discussion in Section 6.3.1). A vertically striped mask (parallax barrier) or a sheet of cylindrical lenses (lenticular sheet) may, for example, be used in the implementation of displays of this type and represent the re-imaging projection sub-system introduced in Section 1.7. We now consider each of these approaches in turn.

---

[7]Attributed to Albert Einstein, 1932 Quoted from P.S. Churchland, *Neurophilosophy* (1988).

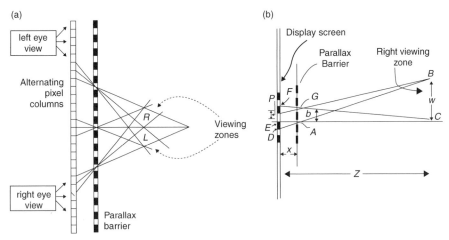

Figure 8.4: The principle of operation of the parallax barrier technique for providing spatially coded stereoscopic views. In (a) the two views are interleaved in alternating columns of pixels on a flat screen, and the barrier (representing the re-imaging projection sub-system discussed in Chapter 1) ensures that from the correct viewing zones each eye sees only the corresponding view. Diagram (b) shows the basic geometry discussed in the text. Note that this diagram is simplified and for clarity partially constructs only the right viewing zone. Neither diagram is drawn to scale, and the optical paths have been simplified.

1. *The Parallax Barrier Technique*: The principle of the parallax barrier approach is illustrated in Figure 8.4.[8] A mask of thin vertical strips is positioned in front of a conventional 2-D display. The two are aligned so that from each of several specified viewing zones in front of the screen, only a specific subset of pixel columns is seen; the barrier blocks the light from the others. In this way, different perspective views of a 3-D scene can be calculated and depicted in the appropriate pixel columns corresponding to that view. The number of views can vary, from two, providing a simple stereoscopic display (see Figure 8.4(a)), to many more, providing an autostereoscopic display with a degree of look-around capability. This approach creates specific viewing zones in front of the display that correspond to each of the different perspectives. The user is located so that eyes are positioned in the different zones and so see a different perspective.

Figure 8.4(b) illustrates the basic geometry governing the 2-D screen, the barrier, and the right viewing zone in the case of a two-view display (note that the left viewing zone has been omitted for clarity). The distance between adjacent dark strips (pitch) of the barrier is such that from each of the two viewing zones the correct pixel columns are seen. Examination of similar triangles ACG and CEF shown in the geometry illustrated in Figure 8.4(b) yields a relationship relating

[8]The parallax barrier technique was originally devised for two views by F.E. Ives in 1903, and extended to multiple views by Kanolt in 1918.

the barrier pitch (b), the pixel pitch (p), the viewing distance (z), and the spacing (x) between the screen and the barrier. From the necessity that rays from adjacent left/right pixel boundaries converge at the transition between the two viewing zones, we obtain

$$b = 2p\left(\frac{z-x}{z}\right) = 2p\left(\frac{1-x}{z}\right).$$ (8.6)

The fraction in brackets that originates from the spacing between the barrier and the screen is known as the "viewpoint correction." From this equation we can see that for a two-view display, the barrier pitch is just *less* than twice the pixel dimension. The difference between the two is determined by the separation of the barrier from the screen and the viewing distance. The relationship between the viewing distance and the lateral width w of the viewing windows can also be deduced from the examination of the similar triangles ABC and ADE shown in Figure 8.4(b). This yields

$$z = x\left(\frac{w+p}{p}\right).$$ (8.7)

In the more general case of N_v views, Eq. (8.6), governing the required barrier pitch, generalizes to

$$b = N_V p\left(\frac{z-x}{z}\right).$$ (8.8)

One problem with parallax barrier techniques concerns degradation due to light diffraction as the barrier pitch is reduced [Okoshi 1976]. However, recent work has shown that the resulting cross-talk can be substantially reduced by optimizing the cross-sectional profile of the barrier strips [Holliman 2005].

   In the case of the parallax barrier approach, the pixels on the 2-D screen must be assigned to one or the other of the different 3-D views. The number of pixels contained in each view is thus reduced by a factor equal to the number of views. Comparing with the 2-D screen resolution of $N_x \times N_y$, for N_v views, we have

$$\textit{Number of pixels per view} = \frac{N_x \times N_y}{N_v}.$$ (8.9)

The result is a loss in horizontal resolution by a factor equal to the number of views. However, the pixel bandwidth per refresh is maintained at the same level as in the 2-D case:

$$\textit{Number of pixels per refresh} = N_x \times N_y.$$ (8.10)

Another potential problem of the parallax barrier approach concerns the loss of image brightness caused by the physical presence of the barrier. As the number of views increases, the ratio of the slit width to slit spacing decreases accordingly. For example, for ten views, only one tenth of the light is transmitted, requiring high brightness illumination of the 2-D display (specifically the image element generation sub-system).[9]

A practical advantage of the parallax barrier approach is that the barrier may be switched electronically, opening the way to switchable 2-D/3-D displays. The use of electronically programmable Spatial Light Modulators (SLMs) as barrier filters allow a subset of the 2-D screen to be three-dimensional (i.e., a "3-D window(s)" within an otherwise 2-D environment). This allows full horizontal resolution in the 2-D portions of the screen. Consumer electronics companies (see for example, Inoue et al. [2000], Hamagishi et al. [2001]), have recently developed systems that allow the user to switch between 2-D and 3-D modes, effectively by toggling on and off an electronic parallax barrier mask. More sophisticated variants use head tracking information to electronically update the pitch and position of the barrier strips to ensure that the two viewing zones follow the user's eyes [Hamagishi et al. 2001, Perlin et al. 2000, 2001]. It supports an increased degree of movement by the viewer, toward and away from the screen as well as laterally.

The parallax barrier technique supports horizontal parallax only. Furthermore, as with stereoscopic displays, convergence/occlusion conflict can be problematic.

2. *The Lenticular Sheet Technique*: A related approach uses a sheet of vertical column "lenses," rather than vertical slits. These are located in front of the screen, and such a re-imaging projection sub-system is known as a lenticular sheet. As illustrated in Figure 6.13, the basic idea is similar to the parallax barrier approach, with the light being directed to the different viewing zones, in this case by refraction. This approach is attributed to Lippmann [1908], who proposed using a "fly's eye" lens sheet to provide full parallax.

One advantage of this technique over the parallax barrier method is that the passage of light is not obstructed by the re-imaging projection sub-system, and so image brightness is not an issue. Generally, efforts using this technique have concentrated on horizontal-parallax-only images, in which an array of cylindrical lenses is used. In recent years this technique has frequently been employed on 3-D postcards, often the different views being used to encode an animation of a scene rather than to provide different perspectives.

For the lenticular sheet technique, the geometry governing the formation of the viewing zones is directly analogous to the parallax barrier case described above, with a viewpoint correction ensuring the correct views are seen for all pixels across the screen. For a two-view system, Eqs. (8.6–8.8) continue to apply. However, in this case, the parameter s refers to the focal length of the lenslets.

One disadvantage associated with static spatially coded techniques is that if the viewer moves away from the assumed viewing position, the image distorts.

---

[9]See Eichenlaub [1993] for one particular solution to this problem.

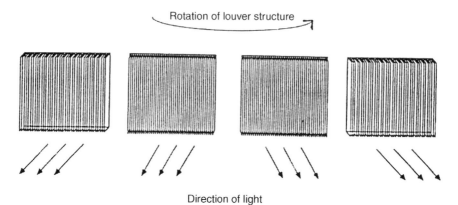

Direction of light

Figure 8.5: Principle of operation of the time-varying collimated view filter. The orientation of the louvers directs each view to the appropriate viewing direction. [Reproduced by permission from Kollin, J.S., "Collimated View Multiplexing: A New Approach to 3-D", *Proc. SPIE 902*, (1988); © 1988 SPIE.]

Furthermore, it is possible for each eye to receive the "wrong" view and a pseudo-scopic image results. As with the stereoscopic displays discussed previously (see Section 8.2), cross-talk between different views remains an important issue.[10]

8.3.2 Dynamic Multi-View Systems

Multi-view techniques of the type described above use a static re-imaging sub-system (filter element) to form the viewing zones. An alternative approach is to sweep out the viewing zones sequentially in time, using a dynamic re-imaging sub-system (time-varying filter) located in front of the 2-D screen. Of course, for this to work, these views must all be generated with sufficient rapidity. In this sub-section, we briefly review several approaches to the creation of creative 3-D displays of this type and discuss some general issues.

1. *Collimated Views*: One approach to sequentially generating a range of per-spective views is to use a re-imaging sub-system that acts like an array of vertical louvers or Venetian blinds [Kollin 1988]. These are angled such that a given 2-D image is visible only from its corresponding viewing direction. The louvers are then rotated slightly, and the adjacent perspective view is displayed; this is repeated for the full range of views, as illustrated in Figure 8.5.

In contrast to the systems outlined in the previous subsection, all pixels in the 2-D display can now (in principle) contribute to each view.[11] If the 2-D display comprises $N_x \times N_y$ pixels, a collimated view system essentially maintains the same

---

[10]A novel innovation is the use of an angled lenticular sheet [van Berkel et al. 1996, van Berkel and Clarke 1997].

[11]To an approximation.

amount of information in each view:

$$Number\ of\ pixels\ per\ view \approx N_x \times N_y\ . \tag{8.11}$$

However, this is at the cost of needing to display these pixels N_v times in each refresh cycle. Consequently, the number of pixels that need be transmitted to the display and physically activated during each refresh becomes

$$Number\ of\ pixels\ per\ refresh = N_x \times N_y \times N_v\ . \tag{8.12}$$

In the case of the approach described above, only horizontal parallax is supported (as indeed is the case with most multi-view techniques). Vertical parallax could be included simply by adding a second filter oriented at right angles to the first. However, this is impractical as the number of image frames that must be displayed in each refresh is increased further—by a factor equal to the number of vertical views.

2. *The Moving Slit Approach*: Another approach uses a rapidly moving single vertical slit positioned in front of a 2-D display to deliver a range of viewing perspectives of a 3-D scene [Collender 1967, Tilton 1988]. At a single instantaneous position, the slit acts like one of the slits in the parallax barrier technique, different columns of pixels on the screen are visible from different positions in front of the display. By moving the slit across the face of the display, and updating the image information in the pixel columns in accordance with the slit position, different perspective views on the 3-D scene are provided for each of a range of viewing positions.

During a single cycle of the slit across the display screen, this approach can be thought of as sequentially building up a number of slit positions, in a manner analogous to the parallax barrier approach described previously. However, an important difference concerns the contributions made by each pixel. Here, essentially all pixels across the width of the 2-D screen can contribute to a perspective view, so that Eq. (8.11) applies. However, this means that the 2-D screen must be driven at a higher refresh rate—a factor of N_v times greater than a standard 2-D case—so that the entire 3-D scene is updated at a refresh rate higher than the flicker fusion frequency.

In keeping with our focus on the computer interface, we have discussed this technique implicitly assuming a pixel-based display. However, it is interesting to note that 3-D displays of this type (employing a non-pixel-based image element generation sub-system) were demonstrated by Robert Collender in the 1960s. In this system, a continually (smoothly) moving strip[12] was used, as described in his fascinating publication [Collender 1967]. In fact, the moving strip followed a cylindrical path and the display was visible through 360°. Later, the moving slit approach was used with a CRT to display synthetic 3-D images [Tilton 1988].[13]

---

[12]This type of moving slit mask is often referred to as a Collender filter.
[13]The Collender display was termed the "stereoptiplexer." Tilton's display was called the "*parallactiscope*."

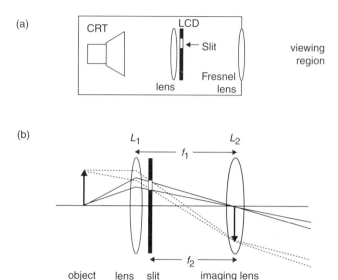

Figure 8.6: The dynamic (temporally coded) multi-view display. An overview of this approach is shown in (a). A CRT with a rapid frame rate is used to display sequential perspective views of the 3-D scene. The two lenses and moving slit filter serve to direct each perspective only into the appropriate viewing zone. By rapidly displaying a range of perspective views while the slit is moved, an autostereoscopic view is provided in the viewing region. Geometrical optics of the imaging arrangement are given in (b). Lens L_1 creates a real image of the object in the plane of the imaging lens L_2. The slit, located in the focal plane of L_2, serves to collimate the image only through a small viewing angle. These diagrams are plan views (the slit is vertical, providing horizontal parallax only). [Reproduced by permission from Lang, S.R., Travis, A.R.L., Castle, O.M., and Moore, J.R., "A 2nd Generation Autostereoscopic 3-D Display", in Lister, P.F., (ed.), *Proc. 7th Eurographics Workshop on Graphics Hardware*, (1992); © 1992 Eurographics Association.]

An alternative time-varying filter approach employing a vertical slit that is rapidly scanned across the display screen during each refresh cycle was developed at the University of Cambridge during the 1990s [Travis 1990, Lang et al. 1992, Travis et al. 1995, Dodgson et al. 1999]. It is illustrated schematically in Figure 8.6. Referring to this diagram, the system consists of two lenses and a moving slit filter, arranged such that lens L_2 lies in the focal plane of lens L_1, whereas the slit filter lies in the focal plane of lens L_2. With this arrangement, L_1 creates an image of the 2-D display screen in the plane of L_2, while the slit serves to collimate the image into a single direction only. The instantaneous position of the slit thus determines the angle of view transmitted to an observer. A 3-D image space is built up from N_v perspectives by the correct set of combinations of 2-D view and slit position. As with the collimated view approach described above, this system requires an increase in the number of 2-D frames displayed per refresh cycle by a factor N_v, but it enables the full 2-D image resolution to be retained; Eqs. (8.11) and (8.12) apply.

8.3.3 Electroholography

Electroholography is also known as "computed holography" or "holographic video," and refers to display systems that depict digital holograms in real time (i.e., are refreshed at, approximately, video rates). A hologram stores its 3-D information in an interference or fringe pattern created by the interference of light from the 3-D object with light from a reference source. When re-illuminated, the hologram modulates the light and reconstructs a replica of the wavefronts scattered from the original object. All depth cues are satisfied, including the parallax cues, occlusion, and accommodation. In this sense, holography promises an ideal 3-D display technique. A brief account of some basic aspects of standard holographic image generation is provided in Appendix B.

In fact, computational holography is by no means a new concept and dates back to the 1960s. Research conducted at IBM provides us with an example of the types of approach that have been adopted [Lesem et al. 1969]. In the case of this technique, the phase of the wavefront emanating from a virtual object was computed, neglecting entirely amplitude variations [Okoshi 1976]. Thus it was assumed that each sample of the object's surface emitted light of the same amplitude and with the same phase. The wavefront containing the essential phase information was then computed across a planar surface.

The results were then plotted (using grayscale) and the resulting copy was photographically reduced to generate the "Kinoform." Clearly this does not represent a pure holography technique since amplitude variations of reflectance from the virtual object are neglected. However, as we will discuss, many of the computed holographic techniques make various approximations mainly in order to reduce the computational cost associated with the process. In fact, the vast amount of information that must be computed and displayed per image frame (coupled with the computationally expensive calculations) has made the development of a dynamic electroholographic 3-D graphics display extremely challenging. (Methods to try to reduce the information required in the interference fringe pattern were devised in the 1960s [Burkhardt 1968]. For more recent work, see, for example, Benton [1991] and Lucente [1997].)

The direct approach to producing an electronic hologram of a virtual object is to digitally create the fringe pattern that would normally be generated by optical methods. As outlined in Appendix B, the intensity pattern $I(x,y)$ recorded by an optical hologram is a function of the object and reference waves [$U_o(x,y)$ and $U_r(x, y)$, respectively]. In the case of computer-generated holograms, only components of Eq. (B.3) (for example) that capture the interference pattern of interest need be computed. So, for each point of the object, complex-valued light waves are traced to the hologram plane, where the interference with the reference wavefront is calculated and sampled at the hologram resolution. A key issue with computational holograms is that, in order to diffract visible light, the fringe pattern needs a resolution on the order of the wavelength of light ($\sim$400–700 nm). The digital fringe pattern must therefore be displayed at a spatial resolution of around 2000 pixels/mm! A ray-tracing method based on the physics of hologram creation is much too slow to generate digital holograms at real time rates.

A more accurate calculation of the number of digital samples N_{FP} required in a full-parallax hologram of height h, width w gives

$$N_{FP} = \frac{4wh \sin^2 \theta}{\lambda^2}, \qquad (8.13)$$

where θ is the viewing angle and λ is the light wavelength [St. Hilaire et al. 1992]. As an example, a 100-mm square hologram with a maximum diffraction (viewing) angle of 30° both horizontally and vertically requires $N_{FP} \sim 33 \times 10^9$ pixels for a single frame. If each pixel is displayed at an 8-bit resolution and for a refresh rate of 30 Hz, the required bandwidth is $\sim 10^{12}$ bytes/s or 1 TB/s.

The prospects for interactive holography appear daunting, but consideration of Eq. (8.13) leads to a number of shortcuts that can be taken to reduce the required number of pixels and hence the hologram computation time [St. Hilaire et al. 1992]:

1. Vertical parallax can be removed, by constructing the hologram as a vertical stack of horizontal 1-D holographic strips or "hololines." The total number of samples in a horizontal-parallax only (HPO) hologram is given by

$$N_{HPO} = \frac{2wl \sin \theta}{\lambda}. \qquad (8.14)$$

Continuing with the numerical example used above, and $l = 100$ lines vertically, the required number of pixels falls to $N_{HPO} \sim 18 \times 10^6$, a reduction by a factor of approximately 2000.

2. The viewing angle θ can be reduced. However, reducing θ from 30° to, say, 15° gains only a factor of two and begins to limit the viewing zone to a single position: At a viewing distance of 50 cm, the lateral viewing zone would be reduced from 58 cm to 27 cm.

3. The physical size of the hologram can be reduced. For example, shrinking by a factor of two in each dimension reduces the number of pixels by a factor of four (keeping other factors unchanged).

More subtle methods relating to hologram formation and display have also enabled faster hologram calculation. Three such approaches are indicated as follows:

1. *Algorithmic*: For example, alternatives to the ray-tracing algorithm for calculation of the fringe pattern can be devised. One approach is to construct the hologram from a linear combination of "basis interference patterns" [Lucente 1993]. Each basis pattern corresponds to the interference fringe that would result from a point source in the object space. Component fringes for all possible locations can thus

be precomputed and stored in a look-up table. In this way, the fringe pattern corresponding to an object made up of an arbitrary collection of voxels can be rapidly calculated. It is reported as increasing performance by a factor of 50, and in 1990, it allowed interactive display[14] of small holographic images on the first MIT Holovideo display. Note that this approach is based on a collection of self-luminous sources and thus generates translucent images; no occlusion is incorporated into the computation. However, a graphics front-end is reported to have been implemented that enabled polygon objects to be displayed. Polygons at the rear of the object were culled before the visible polygons were populated with voxels for hologram fringe calculation. This polygon culling is possible due to the well-defined, restricted viewing range. This approach also permitted shading, as the brightness of the voxels in a given polygon could be determined by its orientation relative to an ambient light source. Related methods for computing the hologram fringe pattern from objects composed of line segments or texture-mapped rectangles, compatible with much of standard computer graphics, have also been investigated [Ritter et al. 1997, 1998].

2. *Resolution*: A further approach to enhancing computational performance is to reduce image resolution. A full hologram reconstructs the light that is observed with greater resolution than may be necessary for the human visual system. The information in the fringe can be reduced by subsampling the fringe, spatially and spectrally, effectively providing a compression of the fringe pattern [Lucente 1996]. This may give rise to a loss of sharpness in the image, but the compression parameters can be selected so that the image degradation is imperceptible. In one reported example, encoding the fringe pattern in this way enabled a compression ratio of 16, and the associated computation time was reduced by a factor of 3000 [Lucente 1994, 1996].

3. *Multi-view*: An alternative to computing a full hologram is to depict "holographic stereograms." This is more like a multi-view approach in that a discrete set of views of the 3-D scene are calculated and then displayed using holographic methods. The rendered views can then be converted into a fringe pattern using basis fringes similar to those mentioned above. Unfortunately, holographic stereograms do not support the accommodation depth cue and provide only a finite number of views of the 3-D scene. However they are faster to calculate and for this reason have been an attractive alternative for electroholography researchers. In Subsection 8.2.4, we mentioned that similarities, or coherence, between the two images in a stereopair can be used to speed up the calculation of the two views required for stereoscopic depiction. This concept can in fact be generalized to multiple views, where the smoothly varying aspects of the 3-D scene when viewed from a horizontally moving viewpoint enable a reduction in the number of computations that need to be performed for each viewpoint (see [Halle 1996]).

---

[14]However, the "real-time" hologram computations at MIT in the early-1990s nevertheless required a supercomputer. More recently standard workstations have been used for the task [Plesniak et al. 2002].

Electrohologram displays include one or more SLMs and additional optical components that reconstruct the wavefronts corresponding to the computed 3-D scene and direct them to the viewing zone.[15] Light must be modulated at video refresh rates and at the very high spatial resolution present in the hologram. Generally the SLM does not support the pixel resolution required of the hologram, so some optical demagnification must be incorporated into the display unit.

8.4   VIRTUAL REALITY SYSTEMS

A limitation of the basic stereoscopic display approach (see Sections 6.3 and 8.2) is the lack of "look-around" capability; the image does not change as the viewer's head moves. As we have seen in Section 8.3, one way of adding this functionality is to provide more than two viewing zones in a spatially coded multi-view system. An alternative is to add head-tracking to a stereoscopic display system. As discussed in Section 6.5, this approach uses hardware to monitor the viewer's head position, and the display software recalculates the binocular views to correspond to the new viewing perspective. In this way, the perspective of the scene changes (in principle) naturally with viewing angle—as with objects in the physical world. Such a system presents "autostereoscopic" images. Systems that incorporate hardware able to track physical body position and orientation (such as viewing perspective and the position of limbs) and which use the information derived from such measurements to provide sensory feedback, are loosely considered to fall under the virtual reality classification. However, as we discussed in Section 6.5.1, there is as yet no formal and generally agreed definition of this title.

In this section, we briefly discuss a number of general approaches that illustrate different facets of virtual reality. These have been selected to be indicative of the general VR paradigm.

We may loosely distinguish between the rich diversity of VR techniques according to two criteria:

1. The extent to which the user is "decoupled" (detached) from the physical world.
2. The extent to which the user is "decoupled" from visual cues that support the human somatosensory processes.

Both relate to the degree of "immersion" offered by the technique, but may be viewed separately. In relation to the first of these, consider for example the task of donning the conventional type of headgear used in a fully immersive VR application (together with special-purpose gloves, etc.). Since the user cannot switch between real and virtual worlds instantaneously, this adds to the degree to which

---

[15]For an introduction to acousto-optic modulation, see, for example, Wilson and Hawkes [1998]. See also interesting background reading on the Scophony Light Valve [Johnson 1979, Robinson 1939, Sieger 1939, Mortensen (ed.) 1992].

a user may feel "decoupled" from their physical surroundings. On the other hand, if a user needs simply hold a display system to the eyes (in the same manner as binoculars), then switching between real and virtual worlds is simple and effectively instantaneous; the user may experience a sense of being less decoupled. As indicated in (2) above, an aspect of the decoupling process concerns the degree to which the VR paradigm impacts upon the sense of body position and poise. Systems that are fully immersive remove our ability to view ourselves, and when we are to perform dexterous tasks within a virtual space, it may be necessary to create, for example, a virtual rendition of our hand(s). This is by no means a simple exercise, and human dexterity can easily be eroded if we have to become accustomed to an artificial and approximate rendition of the hand, especially if this is associated with positioning error and movement latency. Furthermore, the VR paradigm may decouple the user with respect to their location in physical space and orientation in relation to the vertical! Certainly, dexterity is supported by our ability to directly view limb position, and in the case that we feel any sense of imbalance, it is convenient to be able to view, contact, and gain momentary support from physical stable objects. Various VR paradigms that we will refer to as being "spatially immersive," support an immersive sensory experience and allow a user to view their limbs, interaction tools etc. directly. We will briefly discuss such systems in Section 8.4.2.

As mentioned above, fully immersive VR represents an extreme embodiment in which all image artifacts are processed within the digital domain and depicted by some form of electronic display screen(s). Various other VR techniques enable computer-generated imagery to be overlaid onto a direct view of the physical world. Alternatively, support may be provided to enable views of objects captured electronically from the real world to be overlaid on a digital scene. Generally these types of approach that permit the synthesis of real and virtual objects are referred to as "mixed" or "augmented" reality. In principle, mixed reality systems present information in a way that is visually consistent. This contrasts with the spatially immersive systems mentioned above which, under certain circumstances, present information in a visually inconsistent manner.

An enormous wealth of literature covers the field of virtual reality. In the following pages, we lay various foundations and recommend the text by Burdea and Coiffet [2003] as a starting point for the reader seeking detailed discussion. This book provides excellent and extensive coverage of not only the underlying principles, but also it examines many current technologies. It also presents a significant bibliography. The texts by Sherman and Craig [2003] and Vince [1995] are also recommended.

8.4.1 Immersive Virtual Reality

In Section 1.6.1 we referred to some pioneering work carried out in the 1940s in relation to the depiction of 3-D perspective views from computed[16] data, and in Section 6.3.1, we discussed the history of the stereoscope. It appears that Otto Schmitt (who submitted an excellent paper early in 1947 [Schmitt 1947]) may have been the first to merge these techniques, presenting electronically generated

---

[16]In this context, we refer to analog computation.

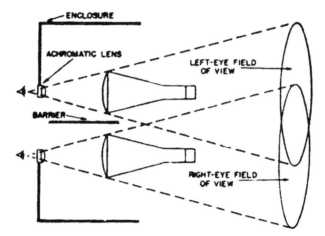

Figure 8.7: An immersive stereoscopic display described by Otto Schmitt in his 1947 publication. The stereopair is depicted on two CRTs. The diagram is reproduced from the original publication in which various other display configurations are presented [Reproduced by permission from Schmitt, O.H., "Cathode-Ray Presentation of Three-Dimensional Data", *J. Appl. Phys.*, **18**, (1947); © 1947 IOP Publishing Ltd.]

perspective views by means of a form of stereoscope. One embodiment described by Schmitt is shown in Figure 8.7. This perhaps represents the first immersive electronic 3-D display. Schmitt writes:

> *In addition, two cathode-ray pictures, properly interlaced, can yield a real three-dimensional view if eye accommodation and comparison with surroundings are properly suppressed so that the eyes will be forced to rely on convergence and object shape for depth perception.*
>
> *It is the purpose of this report to point out how easily the underlying principles of projective and perspective drawings and of stereoscopic photography can be applied to cathode-ray presentation so as to convert raw electrical data directly into vividly recognizable three-dimensional pictures.* [Schmitt 1947]

As indicated in Section 6.5.1, Ivan Sutherland and Morton Heilig are credited for advancing IVR in the 1960s. Interestingly, the display technique described by Sutherland in his 1968 publication [Sutherland 1968] represents a mixed reality paradigm. Despite the passage of time, this paper retains much of its relevance and is well worth perusal. In connection with the head-mounted display (HMD), he writes:

> *Half-silvered mirrors in the prisms through which the user looks allow him to see both the images from the cathode-ray tubes and objects in the room simultaneously. Thus displayed material can be made either to hang disembodied in space or coincide with maps, desk tops, walls, or the keys of a typewriter.*

This is, of course an excellent description of the mixed (augmented) reality technique (see Section 8.4.3). He also describes two approaches to position

(a) 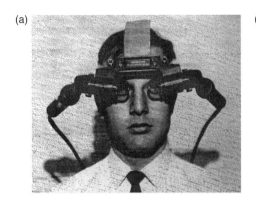   (b)

Figure 8.8: Reproduced from Sutherland's publication showing (a) the HMD and (b) a position-sensing system employing a set of linkages and position encoders. At one end, this is attached to the HMD, and at the other end, it is fixed to the ceiling [Reproduced from Sutherland, I.E., "A Head-Mounted Three Dimensional Display," *AFIPS Conf. Proc.* **33**, (1968), with kind permission of Professor I. Sutherland.]

sensing—one using a set of mechanical linkages fixed at one end to the HMD and attached at the other end to the ceiling.[17] This permitted both rotational and translational motion of the user, and digital position sensors were used to enable movement to be accurately measured (see Figure 8.8). A second approach employing three ultrasonic transmitters (attached to the HMD), and four receivers located in a square array in the ceiling, is also described. Each transmitter operated at a different frequency, and each receiver was equipped with suitable filters enabling the signals received from the transmitters to be distinguished. Movement of the user therefore resulted in changes in signal phase in the 12 signals passed to the computer.

Ideally, any tracking system should provide position and orientation information with sufficient speed and accuracy so that the user is not aware of any delay or positional mismatch. In practice there is likely to be some inaccuracy (real vs. reported position), jitter (random variations or noise in repeated reports of the same position), drift (gradual change in reported position with time), and latency (delay in reporting changes in position). Ultrasound continues to provide a convenient technique for position sensing—see discussion in Burdea and Coiffet [2003, chap. 2] concerning the use of ultrasound, magnetic fields, and optical position-tracking techniques.

The development and continual refinement of simulators for use in areas such as avionics has spanned some decades and represents a key aspect of the progress made in the implementation of VR systems. (For interesting reading, see Ellis [1991].) Generally, such systems are highly specialized and represent a significant

---

[17]Parker & Wallis [1948] mention the use of head-tracking as a means of updating 3-D images in accordance with changes in viewing position.

investment. In fact it was not until the 1980s that interest in VR techniques became widespread. Increases in computer performance (both in terms of processing power and raster graphics capabilities) coupled with relatively low-cost display and position sensing hardware are factors that are likely to have been chief catalysts. The VR concept attracted interest from a very diverse audience, and media speculation played a pivotal part in dissociating VR from achievable reality. Articles describing the impact that VR systems were likely to have on practically every aspect of human activity abounded; total sensory immersion within cyberspace offered boundless opportunities. In an article that appeared in 1991 (entitled "Reality Check"), Dwight Davis wrote:

> *Indeed, despite the intrigue and anticipation, virtual reality is not without its critics, many of whom contend that the field's proponents spend more time fantasizing about how to transport people into simulated, virtual worlds than they do figuring out how to bring the necessary technology into the real world.* [Davis 1991]

However, real applications that could derive benefit from plausible VR techniques gradually began to emerge and speculative reporting has found other areas on which to feed (look out ubiquitous computing and nanotechnology). Real progress made during the 1980s and 1990s (not only in terms of techniques, but also in our acceptance of the complexity of the human sensory interface) has provided the foundations for current activities, and a rich diversity of techniques are now the subject of research activity. Furthermore, systems are now finding useful employment across a range of applications.

The fully immersive VR technique supports only the transferred interaction paradigm—all objects within the image space are computer generated. The completely synthetic nature of the virtual world provides great flexibility, but as image scenes become increasingly complex and detailed, computational cost rises and ultimately limits performance. In an excellent article previously quoted in Chapter 6, Steve Bryson discusses various aspects of VR and considers the application of this general 3-D display technique to scientific visualization [Bryson 1996]. In this context, he discusses the scale of data sets generated in, for example, computational fluid dynamics applications and the impact that this has upon opportunities to visualize and interact in real time with such data. Naturally we can assume that continued increases in computer performance will eventually ameliorate latencies that we may currently experience when visualizing and interacting with huge, complex data sets. However, as Bryson writes:

> *... the problems addressed in real-time scientific visualization will far outstrip the advances in technology. Increased computational capacity will be used to perform simulations that produce far larger data sets and contain far more phenomena.* [Bryson 1996]

In short it is likely that for many interactive visualization applications, we will always be working at the limits of system performance, and compromises will have to be accepted.

Interestingly, the underlying display technique associated with the IVR approach is the converse of that associated with other creative display systems. Generally, a creative 3-D display permits a computer-generated image to be viewed within the context of the physical world [i.e., the virtual object is placed (or appears to be placed) within our physical space]. However, when the IVR technique is used, the user must exit the physical world and enter a space apparently occupied by the image (i.e., the user is placed within the virtual world).

The headset employed for IVR applications usually contains an optical arrangement between each display screen and the eye. This is so that the eye sees, and thus focuses on, a magnified and more distant virtual image of the screen (the displays are located closer to the eyes than the near point distance (see Section 2.3.1)). This approach was in fact first used in the Oliver Wendell-Holmes stereoscope viewer developed in the mid-nineteenth century. The optical arrangement usually projects the image between 1 and 5 m in front of the user. In this way, the image can occupy a field-of-view of up to 100–140° horizontally and 40–60° vertically. However, a drawback to magnifying the image in this way is that the "pixellation" of the 2-D displays can become more apparent. To counter this, a diffusing sheet is sometimes used to slightly blur the image. Another solution possible with HMDs is to optically direct more of the pixels toward the center of the visual field, where visual acuity is the highest (recall Section 2.5.2). In this case the displayed images must be specially predistorted, and this is likely to increase the computation cost [Cruz-Niera et al. 1992].

A disadvantage of the conventional HMD is that the headgear can, when used for protracted periods, be uncomfortable to wear, and as indicated, previously its attachment and removal can cause the user to experience an increased sense detachment (decoupling) from the physical world. Furthermore, although in principle the HMD enables the user freedom of movement (e.g., the ability to walk around), sensory conflict may cause the user to experience difficulty in maintaining balance. A related approach uses similar stereoscopic displays that are not worn by the user but are held in the manner of binoculars. Various approaches may be used in the implementation of such systems; these include "hand-supported systems" (which are held in the same way as are binoculars), and "floor-supported displays".[18] These are supported by linkages anchored to the floor, and a counterweight conveniently offsets the weight of the display device. Although this approach reduces freedom of movement, it is possible to constrain the speed of user motion and this helps maintain a consistent update[19] of the visual display with changes in position [Cruz-Niera et al. 1992]. Sensors in the linkages are able to accurately track motion (this is equivalent to the position sensing technique described earlier

---

[18]Frequently referred to by the acronym "BOOM" (Binocular Omni-Oriented Monitor).

[19]Overshoot provides an example of a potential inconsistency. In this case, the visually computed scene can continue to move after the viewer has suddenly stopped moving. Image lag provides a further example and is particularly critical for head-tracked VR as the continual user motion requires that the new perspectives are calculated and displayed quickly enough so that users do not perceive delay between their own motion and the visual response. In fact, lag and other inconsistencies between the various sensory inputs can lead to ill-effects during and after immersive VR sessions.

in connection with Sutherland's research, although his system was supported from the ceiling rather than by the floor). See Burdea and Coiffet [2003] for further discussion and also the review of various forms of VR system provided by Buxton and Fitzmaurice [1998].

8.4.2   The CAVE and Cybersphere

The CAVE is a projection-based VR system that may be considered to represent a "spatially immersive" technique and provides a remarkable 3-D experience. Here, one or more users enter a cubic "room" (with, in the case of the classic CAVE, sides of approximately 3 m in length). Temporally coded stereoscopic images are projected (via externally located projectors) onto the walls, floor, and possibly ceiling (also see Section 6.5.1). Users within the room are thus immersed in a virtual world that now occupies virtually the entire visual field of view (see Figure 8.9).

Each user wears active shutter glasses, and one viewer is also equipped with a head-tracking device by means of which the viewing perspective is calculated and updated. Consequently, the images are displayed on the basis of a single head position, and other viewers therefore see an inferior, although generally acceptable, 3-D experience.

The CAVE (a recursive acronym for "CAVE Automatic Virtual Environment") was the brain-child of Dan Sandin, Thomas DeFanti, and coworkers at the Electronic Visualization Laboratory (University of Illinois at Chicago). The initial impetus for this work was the development of a system able to assist in the process of scientific visualization. An early publication [DeFanti et al. 1992] features a prototype implementation of the CAVE comprising only two walls, and in this informative article, the authors discuss factors that impact upon "suspension of disbelief" (their use of this term is slightly different to that discussed in Chapter 1 and used in this book). It is instructive to briefly review the five factors that they summarize as impacting on the suspension of disbelief. These are as follows:

1. *The Field of View*: This concerns the extent of the visual angle occupied by an image (without head rotation) (see also Section 2.5.1). For a display of width W, viewed at a distance D, the horizontal visual angle (θ) is simply

$$\theta = 2\arctan\left(\frac{W}{2D}\right). \tag{8.15}$$

 In the case of the CAVE, the field of view is essentially limited only by the stereoscopic glasses that must be worn.

2. *Panorama*: This relates to a display's ability to "wrap" the observer within the image scene and differs from the field of view as head/body movement is used to view the "panorama." (Field of view assumes a stationary viewing position.)

(a)

(b)

Figure 8.9: Image (a) shows an artist's rendering of the CAVE Automatic Virtual Environment (CAVE), a four-wall, rear-projected, immersive virtual reality system invented at University of Illinois at Chicago's (UIC) Electronic Visualization Laboratory (EVL). Image courtesy Milana Huang, UIC/EVL. Image (b) are EVL students Brenda Lopez Silva, Chris Scharver, and Ka-Leung Jark in EVL's CAVE. CAVE was the first VR technology to allow multiple users to be immersed in the same virtual environment at the same time. It is widely used for research, industrial prototyping, and networked art exhibition. (Images courtesy of UIC/EVL.)

In supporting "panorama," issues such as image lag and overshoot must be considered carefully. In the context of lag, DeFanti et al. [1992] write:

> *The CAVE solves this problem by showing all views from a fixed location simultaneously. Users of the Cave experience the same viewing location and head rotation delays as do users of the HMD, but since rotations only require a small alteration to the stereo projections the effect is less noticeable.*

3. *Viewer−Centered Perspective*: As discussed in Chapter 4, the concept of a viewer-centered perspective was a critical feature of Renaissance art. Naturally, in a system such as the CAVE, the hardware and software responsible for locating

(and tracking) user position impacts upon how well the "viewer-centered perspective" is achieved.

4. Body and Physical Position: As we have previously discussed, the ability to directly view limbs, finger positions, etc. may be of considerable importance in various interactive display applications. Furthermore, in the case of, for example, creative design and visualization activities, interaction between users is often pivotal. In the case of the IVR approach discussed previously in this section, for users to share a VR experience, each must be provided with their own display and interaction hardware. In the case of the CAVE, viewers are able to naturally view[20] their own bodies and can interact with others (located in the same CAVE directly. (Clearly in the case of two or more CAVE facilities linked across a network, user interaction is less natural.)

The creation of the perspective views and their update in real time in response to user motion or interactive operations is computationally demanding. Consequently, when the cost of the necessary computer systems is added to those of the display hardware and the space needed to house the installation, the total system cost is considerable. However, the visualization experience is impressive (despite effects such as aliasing and slight image mismatches between walls). As an aid to both teaching and research, BGB has viewed at first hand the benefits that can be derived from the technology when properly used. However, on two occasions, he has witnessed CAVE facilities within universities that remained largely unused. In both cases, and despite the significant capital investment in the hardware and software systems, little account was taken of the need for skilled staff able to develop the facilities and especially promote their trans-disciplinary use. Rapidly such systems simply become showpieces, generally turned on to run demonstration software when visitors are to be impressed.

The RAVE (Reconfigurable Virtual Environment) represents a more flexible CAVE technique as the walls may be rearranged so as to be positioned at different orientations. Various other CAVE-like systems are available—see Burdea and Coiffet [2003], and for more technical discussion on the CAVE, a good starting point is the publication by Carolina Cruz-Neira [1993].

The Cybersphere represents a radical approach to the implementation of a projection-based display [Fernandes et al. 2003]. Here a single user enters a translucent sphere (3.5 m in diameter) onto the surface of which images are projected. The sphere rests on a low-pressure air bearing, and so friction is minimized. Thus, as the occupant walks, the sphere rotates cf. a hamster in a ball—but without physical translational motion). The system is illustrated schematically in Figure 8.10, and as may be seen from this illustration, below the main spherical chamber is a smaller sphere. Rotation of the large sphere causes this smaller sphere to rotate, and this motion is sensed and passed to the host computer. Images projected onto the sphere can then be updated accordingly.

---

[20]Although since the CAVE is operated in a darkened room, illumination is provided by the image scenes cast onto the surfaces.

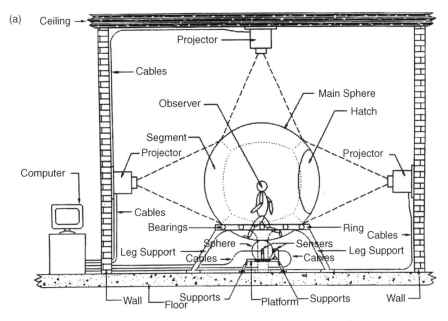

Figure 8.10: The Cybersphere shown schematically in (a). This diagram illustrates the main sphere and lower position-sensing sphere. Projectors are used to case images onto the translucent sphere. See text for details. A photograph of the sphere is presented in (b). [(a) Images kindly provided by Professor Vinesh Raja and thanks also to Julian Eyre of VR Systems. (b) Reproduced by permission from Fernandes, K.J., Raja, V., and Eyre, J., "Cybersphere: The Fully Immersive Spherical Projection System," *Communications of the ACM*, **46**, (2003); © 2003 ACM.]

Clearly, this approach enables a user to walk in a natural manner in any direction and over any distance without being hampered by the boundaries imposed by, for example, the CAVE walls or by the range over which the position-sensing hardware associated with HMD-based systems will operate.

A variation on the CAVE approach is to project stereoscopic images onto a single planar or curved surface. This can be more suitable for certain applications such as presentations, where participants are likely to be seated. Clearly, although this reduces the field of view and panorama provided to the viewer, the former is usually large enough for impressive effects to be achieved. Moreover, if the viewers are seated, then head-tracking is no longer problematic. Projecting a finite number of pixels onto a large screen can lead to visible pixellation of the images. In some systems, this is overcome by using several projectors (projections) "tiled" together to form a larger image. Here, as at the wall boundaries in CAVE type systems, accurate spatial and temporal synchronization between the different projectors is critical in order that the image areas may be appropriately blended.

Fakespace Systems manufacture various projection systems offering a wide field of view. These include CURV, which as the name implies employs a curved screen onto which images are projected from either the front or rear; PowerWall, which provides large-screen stereoscopic (temporally coded) image projection (using active shutter glasses), and ImmersaDesk. This latter system provides a large desktop (the angle of which can be adjusted) onto which stereoscopic images are projected (from below). This system can incorporate head tracking (for further details, see, for example, Czernuszenko et al. [1997]).

In fact, the ImmersaDesk and the InfinityWall (a version of the PowerWall system referred to above) were developed at the Electronic Visualization Laboratory (University of Illinois at Chicago), pioneers of the CAVE along with PARIS (Personal Augmented Reality Immersive System), which particularly supports interaction (including haptics).

8.4.3   Mixed Reality Techniques

A key restriction of the HMD-based IVR techniques is that the user is completely immersed within a synthetic world in which all visible imagery must be graphically rendered to be visible; without the computer, cyberspace is void! The CAVE is of course one exception. Here the user's own body, other participants, and physical interaction tools remain visible.[21] However, the real and virtual objects are not necessarily viewed consistently; for example, a real hand can occlude a virtual object that is perceived as being closer to the viewer.

Another approach that can be adopted and which generally reduces the degree to which the user is decoupled from the physical world is known as "augmented" or "mixed reality." Techniques of this sort may involve the use of some form of HMD but with the crucial difference that they explicitly combine a view of the

---

[21]In the case of the Cybersphere, the operator's own body remains visible—but of course the sphere houses only a single user.

real world with superimposed graphics. Importantly, this allows (in principle) a consistent visual representation of real and virtual objects. Thomas Furness III [1988] wrote in this context:

> *Virtual space is transparent. Since virtual information can be projected into the eye/ ears and presented to the hands through mechanisms which do not occult the normal ambient, it is possible to superimpose the virtually synthesized information over the real world sights and sounds. This aspect of the virtual world opens whole new possibilities for information display...*

Naturally the overlay of information on real-world imagery has many potential benefits, although various technical criteria must be met. For example, if we assume that the virtual scene or information is to map to specific items within the real-world image, then:

1. The synthetic overlay must be located with sufficient positional accuracy relative to the real-world scene under observation. In some applications, it may be necessary to provide the user with an interaction tool via which it is possible to indicate to the host computer a particular object of interest within the real-world scene.

2. The synthetic image should be stable relative to real-world image components, and any update of the latter as a consequence of user motion should maintain stability (e.g., in terms of latency and overshoot).

3. In some applications, it may be necessary for portions of the synthetic overlay to occlude the observers view of the real-world scene.

4. Real-world and synthetic imagery must be simultaneously in focus—despite the fact that overlaid imagery will probably be created closer to the observer's eyes (i.e., in the case that a HMD is used)

5. For some applications, a color pallet should be supported in the overlay.

6. In the case of a system employing some form of HMD, the hardware should not negatively impact on a user's view of the real-world scene.

7. The overlay will need to maintain visibility across a range of real-world lighting conditions.

In order to combine graphics with a view of the real world in front of the user, various techniques can be used. For example, graphics may be overlaid on video images; e.g., video streams from two cameras (stereoscopic) or one camera (monoscopic) mounted on a headset may be presented to the viewer. Additionally, computed views of virtual objects (or text) may be added to the video image. Since the real-world image is in electronic (digital) form, this approach has certain clear advantages in terms of the processing and the combination of this image stream with the virtual imagery. Certainly, support for the issues raised above are facilitated by this paradigm, with the exception of (6). Clearly the use of a video camera system will degrade image quality of the real-world scene (impacting on spatial and temporal resolution, focus and depth of field, etc.). Furthermore, for some applications, the use of the camera system is likely to result in a loss of immediacy—the degree to which the user experiences a sense of being decoupled increases. However, this approach facilitates issue (3) listed above—consistent occlusion can be presented, assuming accurate position information of the real objects is available.

The use of some form of HMD is not an essential requirement for this general technique. For example, augmented reality may be achieved via a conventional flat-screen display (perhaps supporting the depiction of temporally coded stereo-scopic imagery). In, for example, an architectural design application, a proposed structure (e.g., a virtual building) can be superimposed onto real landscape images.

In an alternative approach, a see-through form of HMD display may be used (as discussed previously in the context of the display described by Sutherland [1968]). Displays of this type allow the user to view the surrounding environment directly by looking through transparent displays. The real world is thus seen in a more natural way, and computer-generated images are overlaid upon it. This can, for example, be achieved by means of viewing real-world scenes through LCD panels, or by means of a half-silvered mirror which combines real-world and synthetic images. Clearly, to obtain proper occlusion of real-world objects when using see-through displays (see issue (3) listed above), a means must be found to completely block (in selected regions) the light incoming from the real environment (Kiyokawa et al. [2000]).[22]

Kiyokawa et al. [2000] describe a mixed-reality display system, known as ELMO,[23] that is able to completely block light from selected viewpoints on the real world. Here a half-silvered mirror is used to combine the optical paths from synthetic and real images, whereas an LCD panel is used as a filter able to selectively occlude portions of the real-world scene (on a pixel-by-pixel basis). However, the LCD filter (the occlusion mask) is located close to a viewer's eyes. Consequently, it will be out of focus when the observer is viewing more distant objects in the 3-D scene. In their publication, Kiyokawa et al. describe a simple optical method for overcoming this difficulty. The ELMO system provides an example of an arrangement that (in principle) allows full occlusion of real-world objects. However, an accurate knowledge of the position of the objects relative to the virtual scene is pivotal to the correct operation of such a system.

8.4.4   Pepper's Ghost Revisited

In Section 6.8.1 we described the Pepper's Ghost theatrical illusion. This technique can also be used to provide an image space in which real and synthetic objects can coexist. As illustrated in Figure 8.11, images from a conventional 2-D screen are reflected in a glass plate (or half-silvered mirror). The result is that the image scene appears to occupy an image space lying *behind* the glass. In some implementations, temporally coded stereoscopic images are projected, with the user wearing glasses to resolve the stereo information. The space behind the mirror is accessible

---

[22]Kiyokawa et al. also summarize various other techniques that may be employed.
[23]"Enhanced optical see-through display using an LCD for Mutual Occlusion" [Kiyokawa et al. 2000].

Figure 8.11: A practical solution to the implementation of a display system supporting the direct interaction paradigm. Here the image and interaction spaces are coincident. However, since light from which the image is formed only appears to emanate from behind the glass plate (but does not in fact do so), the presence of the interaction device cannot interfere with image formation [Reproduced from Schmandt, C., "Spatial Input/Display Correspondence in a Stereoscopic Computer Graphics Work Station," *Computer Graphics*, **17**, (1983); © 1983 ACM.]

to the user (by reaching around or under the plate), and so hands or interaction tools may coexist in the same space as the virtual objects. This approach supports the use of direct interaction tools which may be equipped to provide haptic feedback. Since a virtual image is created, the presence of hands or interaction tools within the image space cannot cause inconsistent image occlusion. For further reading, see, for example, the informative article by Christopher Schmandt [1983] and also Mulder et al. [2003] (this latter publication focuses on head tracking for application with this type of display paradigm).

8.5 THE VOLUMETRIC APPROACH

> Once you have flown, you will walk the earth
> with your eyes turned skyward;
> for there you will have been,
> there you long to return.[24]

[24]Attributed to Leonardo da Vinci (1452–1519).

As indicated in Section 6.5.3, volumetric display systems enable images to be created within a transparent volume, and so they occupy a physically 3-D image space. Displays of this class may be characterized as follows:

> *A volumetric display device permits the generation, absorption or scattering of visible radiation from a set of localized and specified regions within a physical volume.*
> [Blundell and Schwarz 2000]

Since the elements from which the images are formed (voxels—see Section 1.6.3) are dispersed within a physical volume, most near-field depth cues are automatically satisfied in a consistent manner, rather than being simulated by the system. In particular, accommodation and convergence are not in conflict, and binocular and motion parallax arise naturally. However, the extent of the image space determines the depth of field, and so the maximum degree to which the convergence and accommodation cues can vary when one's gaze shifts from the closest part of an image to that which is the furthest away.

In the case of practically all of the many approaches that have been proposed or adopted in the implementation of volumetric systems, the occlusion depth cue is not satisfied and images are translucent.[25] For some applications, this may be advantageous (as internal structures are visible), especially as the accommodation and convergence cues appear to compensate—enabling us to naturally direct our visual system to a particular image component of interest. On the other hand, the lack of opacity makes it very difficult to photograph more complex volumetric images (see Figures 8.12 and 8.13). Furthermore, the "all-round" view offered by many volumetric implementations precludes the use of standard graphics techniques, such as hidden-line removal.

From the point of view of the user, and of the applications software, the volumetric image space is generally considered to be represented as a rectilinear 3-D coordinate system. However, in the majority of embodiments, this is an approximation as there is usually a lack of isotropy and homogeneity with respect to both voxel placement and to the propagation of light through the image space. Naturally, given the nature of the image space, displays of this type are best suited to the depiction of volumetric (voluminous) data sets (see Section 1.6.3).

Many volumetric techniques have been proposed and implemented over the past century. These have basically followed one of two schemes: either activation of visible points or lines on a surface that rapidly sweeps out the image volume (referred to as "swept-volume" systems)—or effecting changes in the visual characteristics of selected regions within a static transparent medium or matrix (known as "static-volume" systems).[26] It is not intended that this section should provide a comprehensive treatment of volumetric systems: indeed given the diversity

---

[25]Translucency is not, however, an inherent characteristic of volumetric display systems; see, for example, U.S. Patents 3,609,706 and 3,609,707. These are discussed in Blundell and Schwarz [2000 pp. 178–182].

[26]This is a simplification as various hybrid techniques may also be used; see Blundell and Schwarz [2000].

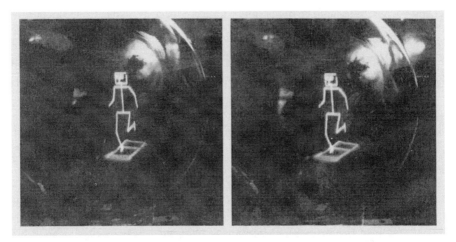

Figure 8.12: A simple stick figure able to run naturally around an image space is readily photographed, and the sense of inherent three-dimensionality is retained by means of stereo photography. The image is depicted on the Cathode Ray Sphere (CRS) and should be viewed via a stereoscope; see text for details. (Original image © 2005 B.G. Blundell.)

Figure 8.13: Here a more complex wire-frame image is shown depicted on the Cathode Ray Sphere (CRS) (the "Stealth" aircraft). The lack of opacity (which is offset by accommodation and convergence cues when the image is viewed directly) and the absence of binocular parallax in the photographed image detracts greatly from the photographic rendition. (Original image © 2005 B.G. Blundell.)

of approaches, this would be impossible within the space available. Consequently, in the following pages, we limit discussion to a small number of indicative example techniques. The interested reader is encouraged to refer to the Blundell and Schwarz [2000] text as this provides detailed discussion on a wide range of approaches and implementations. See also [Blundell 2006].

8.5.1   Swept Volume Systems

One approach to volumetric display implementation has been to use a rapidly moving surface, on which voxels (points of light) are created in synchronism with its motion. Thus, the surface sweeps out the 3-D image space during the course of its periodic movement (and so defines its extent). Typically the motion takes the form of a rotation about an axis lying along the surface or a back-and-forth reciprocating action. In both cases, visible voxels are created at appropriate locations on the surface as it passes through the desired position in the space. Naturally, it is crucial that each voxel should remain visible only briefly; otherwise the motion of the surface would result in the formation of "trails" rather than point-form voxels.

Visible voxels may be created on the moving surface through the use of electron or laser beam(s) which address the surface as it sweeps out the image space (known as the "swept volume beam addressed approach"). This technique places requirements on the nature of the target surface. For example, if electron beams are used, the surface must be coated with short persistence phosphor(s) that are stimulated to emit light by the incidence of the electron beam(s). If laser or other light beams are used, the surface needs to scatter the light from the beam. In either case, the beam must be rapidly deflected between successive voxel locations, and be either blanked off or directed outside the image space during periods when no voxels are being activated. Two approaches to implementing such "beam addressed" displays are as follows:

1. *Laser Addressing*: Laser beams continue to be used to generate visible voxels on a moving target screen—typically helical in shape. This approach was pioneered by Rüdiger Hartwig [1984] and represents a popular volumetric display configuration See, for example, research by several groups: Texas Instruments [Williams and Garcia 1988, Clifton and Wefer 1993], U.S. Navy Research Laboratories in San Diego [Soltan et al. 1994, Lasher et al. 1996], and the Felix group in Germany [Bahr et al. 1996, Langhans et al. 2002].

2. *Electron Beam Addressing*: Electron beam-based volumetric displays continue to be the subject of research. Despite the popularity of lasers, electron beams offer rapid deflection. Several systems collectively denoted the CRS have been developed by the author since work began in 1989 [Blundell and King 1991]. The design of the display vessel for one of the early prototypes is shown in Figure 6.14. It incorporates a rotating planar screen, addressed by two electron beams positioned $120°$ apart perpendicular to the rotation axis [Blundell et al. 1993, 1994, Blundell and Schwarz 1995a and b, Schwarz and Blundell 1997].

The vacuum vessel of this prototype is spherical, allowing a wide range of viewing angles, interrupted only by the electron guns. Coating the target surface with different phosphors on each side (and on each side of the axis of rotation) enables color image generation. Color mixing has also been demonstrated.

The number of voxels that can be created during an image refresh period (generally corresponding to a full (or half) cycle of the motion of the surface) is referred to as the voxel activation capacity (N_A). This may be expressed as

$$N_A = \frac{P}{Tf}, \tag{8.16}$$

where T denotes the time required to activate each voxel, f denotes the frequency of motion of the surface, and P expresses the number of voxels that can be activated simultaneously (i.e., the degree of parallelism supported by the image element generation and activation sub-systems—see Figure 1.10). In the case of the beam addressed systems mentioned (i.e., the conventional laser addressing technique and the Cathode Ray Sphere), P generally tends to be limited to 1–2 (i.e., essentially sequential voxel activation). Therefore for $T = 0.1$ μs and $f = 25$ Hz, N_A is approximately 400,000. However, it is important to note that this value is much less than the possible number of potential voxel locations within an image space (N_L). Consequently, during an image refresh, it is possible to activate only a proportion of the available voxel sites. This proportion is referred to as the "fill factor" (η), where

$$\eta(\%) = \frac{N_A}{N_L} \cdot 100. \tag{8.17}$$

Beam addressed systems such as those described above have fill factors which are significantly less than 1%.[27] An alternative technique is to use a surface that contains a matrix of "active" voxel elements that can be made to emit light under electronic control. For example, Berlin [1979] suggested the use of a planar surface fitted with an array of light emitting diodes. Such an approach tends to support parallelism in voxel activation and therefore enables a much larger fill factor to be achieved than do the beam addressed systems outlined. Unfortunately, the physical presence of the array may impact on the optical properties of the image space.

A display known as the Perspecta [Favalora 2001], employs beams for voxel creation and exhibits a high degree of parallelism in the image element generation and activation sub-systems. This is achieved by making use of spatial light

---

[27]A small fill factor value is not necessarily disadvantageous. Should all voxels be activated during a refresh, then the display becomes a bright light source! Further activation of many voxels during a refresh results in a cluttered image space (and spatial clarity is lost). More important than the absolute fill factor value is the combination of voxels that can be activated in a refresh. *It should be possible to select any combination from the set of possible voxel sites.*

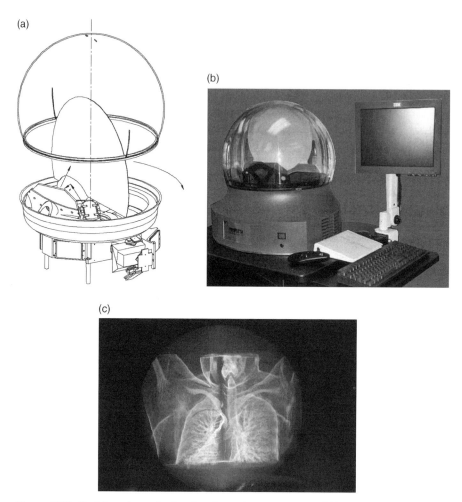

Figure 8.14: In (a) a schematic showing the main components within an Actuality Systems Perspecta display. The display system is illustrated in (b), and a spatial depiction of a data set acquired via a Computed Tomography scan is depicted in (c) (this image is actually displayed in color on the Perspecta system) and comprises 11,599,872 voxels. (Images kindly supplied by Gregg Favalora of Actuality Systems.)

modulators. In this system, digital micro-mirrors (one for each primary colour) are used to modulate a 768×768 pixel array at 5 kHz. This enables 198 radial image slices to be projected onto the rotating planar screen at a volume refresh rate of 25 Hz. A schematic of this display system is provided in Figure 8.14 together with photographs of the display itself and an image depicted by it. Unlike the CRS, this display exhibits a high degree of parallelism and can exhibit a 100% fill factor.

8.5.2 Static Volume Systems

In the case of static volume volumetric displays, the image space is not created by the periodic motion of a surface but consists of a transparent solid, liquid, or gaseous medium, within which individual points or lines can be made visible.[28] Over the years, a number of static volume methods have been investigated. One approach employs the stepwise excitation of fluorescence. In this scheme, two beams (usually infrared) are directed into the image space. Where they intersect, the material is excited to a fluorescent state and emits visible light (a voxel is formed).[29]

In principle, this approach provides a very elegant volumetric display paradigm.[30] However, systems employing a non-gaseous medium suffer from optical distortion at the image space boundary (due to the difference in refractive index between the medium and its surroundings), and with gaseous approaches, voxel intensity can be an issue. One has to continually remember that even the "perfectly" formed image may not appear as such—for before reaching the observer, light has to traverse the image space and emerge from it—indeed a hazardous journey! Failure to take this into consideration results in displays that have preferential viewing directions; an image may appear best when located in a particular region of the image space and viewed from a particular orientation.

8.5.3 Varifocal Mirror Systems

The basic concept of the varifocal mirror technique is illustrated in Figure 6.15. Here a flexible reflective surface is mounted on a loudspeaker that is driven at a frequency of around 30 Hz. The ensuing pressure variation creates a curved mirror that has a continually changing focal length. Image sequences depicted on a flat-screen display may then be projected onto the mirror in synchronization with its motion. An advantage of the varifocal mirror approach is its relative simplicity and the fact that a relatively small amplitude of motion of the mirror provides a much larger (15–30 times) apparent image space [Rawson 1969]. For additional reading, see, for example, Traub [1967]; Rawson [1968, 1969], Fuchs et al. [1982], Harris et al. [1988], Harris [1986], Kennedy and Nelson [1987], Sher [1988, 1993], Udupa [1983].

The image space created by the varifocal mirror technique suffers from various problems such as varying image magnification and a nonlinear variation of image plane depth with mirror position. Fortunately, such problems may be corrected by the control and image processing systems. The generation of acoustic noise as

---

[28]A 3-D array of light emitting elements may also be used. However, it is clearly critical that they should not impact on the transparency of the volume or on the uniformity of its refractive index.

[29]For further related reading, see Zito and Schraeder [1963], Lewis et al. [1971], Verber [1977], Kim et al. [1996], Downing [1996], Ebert et al. [1999], Langhans et al. [2003], Blundell and Schwarz [2000], or Blundell [2006], which provide an overview and detailed references.

[30]An alternative approach uses a stack of static planar screens that can be individually modulated to be either in a transparent or a light emissive (or light scattering) state. Voxels in each depth plane are activated, whereas all those planes in front are transparent. Optical modulation rather than physical motion thus selects the depth plane in which voxels are activated. See Sullivan [2003].

a consequence of loudspeaker vibrations at ~30 Hz or greater [Sher 1993] must, of course, be considered. For details of more recent work in this area, see McKay et al. [1999a,b] and Blundell [2006].

8.6   DISCUSSION

A key issue with all 3-D display technologies is the increased bandwidth needed to support the extra dimension of visual information. As the component technologies are usually pushed to their limits, this has generally led to tradeoffs being made in terms of reduced image resolution, a smaller image space, or a lower refresh rate. Figure 8.15 broadly summarizes the flow of image data into a creative 3-D display system. For a given 3-D scene, the data must first be rendered or converted into inputs suitable for the display device itself. Then, once the data are prepared for display, the associated pixels or voxels must be physically activated by the display device so as to create the visible image. This depiction step is constrained by the requirements of the human visual system; the image must be refreshed with

Generalized Display Pipeline

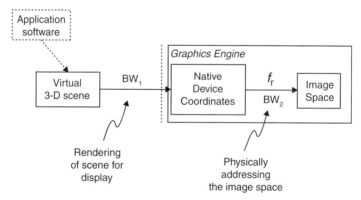

Figure 8.15: Generalized schematic of the 3-D display data pipeline. For a given 3-D scene, the data must be rendered into a form suitable for input to the display device. This computational stage will have an associated bandwidth (BW_1). Typically, the rendering algorithms are adjusted so that with limitations in computing performance, real-time rendering rates can be achieved. This might involve limiting the number of points in the image to ensure fast enough rendering. In general, BW_1 increases with improvements in computing power. Once rendered, the 3-D image data must be generated within the image space. This physical image formation stage also has an associated bandwidth (BW_2). This must usually be achieved at a refresh frequency sufficient to avoid flicker. This part of the system usually involves customized interface cards and data buffers as well as the physical image activation mechanism. Limitations here constrain the total number of points that can be displayed.

sufficient rapidity to minimize flicker. We can associate bandwidths BW_1 and BW_2 with the two phases.

For example, in the case of a temporally coded stereoscopic system, the two views on the 3-D scene must be calculated at the rendering phase. The number of pixels to be rendered is (in principle) twice that of a corresponding monocular display system. However, as discussed in Section 8.2.4, similarity between the two scenes can be exploited to reduce the rendering time. In the display phase, each 2-D view must be depicted in turn on the 2-D monitor. In this case, BW_2 is set by the refresh rate and the resolution of the monitor and graphics card; however, the refresh rate perceived by each eye will be half that of the standard 2-D operation, due to the temporal interleaving of the views.

In the case of spatially coded multi-view systems, the bottleneck tends to be in the depiction step, with the number of views being limited by how rapidly the 2-D display component of the system can depict the consecutive views. Systems of this type must be able to depict N_{views} 2-D images in each image space refresh period. In contrast, static multi-view systems, such as the parallax barrier approach, display all views at once, with the number of pixels in each view being reduced relative to the 2-D situation.

In the case of electroholographic systems, the rendering step involves calculation of the interference fringe pattern at a resolution of thousands of points per millimeter (computationally demanding) and conversion into signals for input into the SLMs. The holographic data pipeline is illustrated in Figure 8.16. As discussed in Section 8.3.3, tradeoffs can be made (such as eliminating vertical parallax) to make the computation time feasible for close to real-time interaction. The depiction step is also challenging, as available SLMs have generally not satisfied the combination of

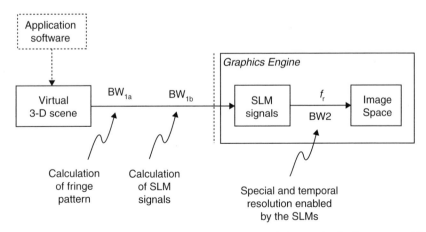

Figure 8.16: Example of the data pipeline for an electroholographic display system. The rendering process must calculate both the fringe pattern corresponding to the virtual scene content and the corresponding SLM signals for the image element activation sub-system.

high spatial and temporal resolutions required for real-time holographic display. However, in recent years, innovative hardware configurations along with advances in SLM technologies have enabled prototype electroholography systems to be implemented.

Volumetric display systems with low degrees of parallelism have often been limited by BW_2, with not all possible voxel locations able to be addressed in each image space refresh [Blundell 2006]. As a result, only the visible voxels (typically a small fraction of the full set) are activated. This fraction (generally expressed as a percentage) is referred to as the "fill factor."

Putting to one side interaction issues, we can consider the conventional flat-screen display (providing only monocular cues) as an electronic equivalent to the traditional artist's canvas. The stereoscopic and multi-view techniques provide additional non-pictorial cues and therefore represent an extension of this paradigm. These approaches provide considerable flexibility because, as with traditional painting techniques, depth cues are synthetically created. Volumetric systems provide a 3-D tableau for image depiction, and various depth cues are inherently associated with the image. Consequently, the volumetric image may be used to depict spatial relationships or the geometrical form of objects. In this latter case, the display technique equates more closely to the creation of sculptures than to the traditional painted rendition on a 2-D tableau. This comparison is valid if we assume that the lack of opacity associated with volumetric images is not an inherent facet of the display paradigm. The introduction of opacity (and thereby support for the occlusion depth cue) relies on the formation of voxels able to scatter ambient light (rather than the emissive voxels usually employed for volumetric image formation). Once this goal has been achieved, the volumetric system will be able to provide a 3-D space that may be used for the creation and depiction, of objects that are the virtual equivalent of the sculpted object. Natural shading and shadows will be inherently associated with such images.

This chapter has briefly described a range of approaches to the implementation of creative 3-D display systems. It is the very diversity of possible techniques that may be brought to bear in the creation of 3-D displays that makes this a truly fascinating area of research. On the other hand, this has perhaps hampered commercial development—making it difficult to bring one approach to the fore—especially in the case of desktop systems. During the presentation of a paper[31] before the Radio Section of the IEE on March 24, 1948, various discussions took place. One participant (R.A. Smith, speaking in the context of the diversity of volumetric techniques (other approaches were not discussed)) stated:

This paper gave me the impression that we are suffering from an embarrass de richesse; anyone coming into this field finds so many possible displays that he may be in doubt about which line to investigate... [Parker and Wallis 1949]

[31]The original publication [Parker and Wallis 1948] is highly recommended. The research reported denoted a major advance in 3-D display technology. Photographs of early perspective images are included.

Nearly 60 years later, many additional techniques have been prototyped, and as we have discussed, volumetric systems represent only one class of display paradigm. Consequently, the comment made by this speaker is perhaps now even more relevant than ever. This discussion ended with a response from Parker and Wallis, and it is perhaps appropriate to conclude this chapter with an extract from their closing remarks:

> It is difficult to treat the problem theoretically, and detailed comparisons between different displays for different applications must await actual experience. We have no doubt about the fundamental possibility of usefully presenting three dimensions, but we are still sounding the problem before setting the course.

8.7 INVESTIGATIONS

1. The classic versions of the spatially coded (lenticular sheet or parallax barrier) and temporally coded (moving slit) multi-view techniques provide horizontal parallax only. How could these be modified to provide vertical parallax as well? What are the issues to be overcome in each case?

2. Consider a beam addressed swept volume volumetric display, with a planar screen and a vertical rotation axis. Why is more than a single beam source used? What issues must be considered if the beam sources are re-located so as to lie below the equator of the sphere (as may be desirable in order to maximize viewing freedom)? What are the advantages and disadvantages of having corotating beam sources (see, for example, U.S. Patent 2,967,905)?

3. Using a glass plate or half-silvered mirror together with a monitor that can depict stereoscopic images, implement the display paradigm discussed in Section 8.4.4. Investigate the interaction opportunities.

4. What major problems would you expect to encounter in the prototyping of the Cybersphere? In each case, identify possible solutions.

5. Consider the single-view parallax barrier technique. Assuming a pixel pitch of 0.1 mm and barrier-screen separation of 1 mm, calculate the approximate distance of the viewing zones from the screen (you may assume that the zones are separated by the interocular distance). How does this value compare with the distance at which a conventional computer monitor is viewed? Suggest ways of reducing the distance.

9 Adopting a Creative Approach

Farewell, farewell! But this I tell
To thee, thou Wedding-Guest!
He prayeth well who loveth well
Both man and bird and beast.

9.1 INTRODUCTION

In this brief and concluding chapter we draw on and extend material presented previously. We begin by considering aspects of two-handed (bi-manual) activity. As we know only too well, should one of our arms or hands be injured and put out of action for even a short period, our interactions with the physical world are greatly hampered and even the simplest of tasks such as unscrewing the top from a bottle of ketchup or

Creative 3-D Display and Interaction Interfaces: A Trans-Disciplinary Approach, by Barry G. Blundell and Adam J. Schwarz
Copyright © 2006 John Wiley & Sons, Inc.

uncorking a bottle of wine poses almost insurmountable problems. Immediately apparent from such an experience is the remarkable synergy that is derived from bi-manual interaction, the sense of great frustration that we feel if this interaction modality is impaired, and the increased reliance we must then place on the visual sense so as to successfully carry out even the most minor of tasks. Consider that mysterious and seemingly impossible feat of knitting. Those skilled at that craft seem to exercise rapid and complex control over their hands and fingers at the same time as being engrossed by a television program or involved in conversation. In fact they give the impression that this "asymmetric" bi-manual activity is effortless and only occasionally is there a need for them to glance at their work.

Given the importance of the synergy that we derive from the cooperation between the two hands in our daily lives (and the frustration we experience when this is impaired), it is perhaps surprising that very few computer users have access to interfaces that properly support parallel two-handed activity. Certainly the keyboard enables two-handed operation, but the input is essentially sequential and (with the exception of certain keys such as "Shift" and "Ctrl") the actions of one hand/ finger do not directly impact upon those of the other. Researchers involved in the modeling and evaluation of bi-manual activity have repeatedly demonstrated that its incorporation within the human–computer interface can (for many operations) be advantageous. This parallels the work of researchers who have investigated forms of creative three-dimensional (3-D) display technologies and have readily perceived the benefits that can be derived from their use. However, in both cases, the computer industry has failed to advance the manner in which the majority of users interact with their computer systems, and the interface has not significantly progressed.

In the next section we consider aspects of bi-manual interaction relevant to the computer interface. We restrict our discussions to interaction opportunities involving some forms of physical tool, since this in itself is a major topic. We hope that the reader exploring this area for the first time will be encouraged to research elsewhere the fascinating subject of free-handed, gesture-based interaction whereby the natural methods that we use in conversation are directed toward our communication with the digital world. Having briefly considered aspects of bi-manual interaction and referred to some of the trials conducted in the evaluation of this modality, we discuss issues relating to its implementation. Here we make reference to a small number of systems that support forms of two-handed interaction and which illustrate the general usage of this paradigm.

In Section 9.3 we turn our attention toward the desktop computer and consider the desirability of incorporating (within its architecture) support for stereoscopic and (limited) motion parallax image depiction. As we have discussed previously, a number of approaches may be adopted in the implementation of a display system able to switch between mono and stereo modes of operation—the various technologies that may be used are well understood, and systems need not necessarily denote a major investment for the end user. However, support for these additional cues is not routinely provided. We discuss possible reasons for this, building upon discussion presented previously in Chapter 1.

Finally, in Section 9.4, we turn our attention to several creative 3-D display and interaction systems that have been researched and used. Here we refer the reader to several exemplar systems and provide brief discussion together with appropriate references for further reading.

9.2 TWO-HANDED INTERACTION

In Chapter 1, we discussed some of the inherent constraints imposed by the conventional display paradigm, and to readily contrast aspects of two-dimensional (2-D) and 3-D space, we made reference to the works of Edwin Abbott in his tales of "Flatlands." We proposed that certain tasks that are inherently 3-D in nature cannot be carried out intuitively within the confines of a 2-D space and suggested the need to adopt creative 3-D display techniques so as to provide an interface able to advance the human–computer interaction process. Furthermore, we indicated that creative display systems may enable new and advanced interaction opportunities, and this therefore represents a major reason for display research. We have discussed a variety of display techniques, considered interaction paradigms (such as direct and transferred interaction), and have briefly made reference to various creative interaction tools. Although we may easily recognize (albeit subjectively) the benefits that may ultimately be derived by making major advances to the interaction feedback loop, it is readily apparent that for certain tasks (particularly, for example, those requiring a greater degree of dexterity), a lack of support for two-handed (bi-manual) manipulation will cause the interaction process to continue to fall short of its real-world equivalent.

Of course, the conventional keyboard supports two-handed input. However, although this device requires a considerable degree of cooperation between the hands the keyboard is, in essence, a device that supports sequential hand activity (in the main only one key is pressed at any instant). Thus, the use of both hands simply serves to increase the bandwidth of this input channel. Of course, there are exceptions—such as when the "shift," "ctrl," or "alt" keys are used. In these cases the actions of one hand modify the task performed by the other. Sutherland's Sketchpad system [Sutherland 1963] and the Xerox 8010 Star Information System (see Section 1.3) provide us with examples of interfaces able to support a limited form of bi-manual input. For example, in the case of the Sketchpad a light pen held in one hand was used in conjunction with buttons operated by the other. A simple example of the type of operation facilitated by this approach is as follows:

> *To draw the circle we place the light pen where the circle is to be and press the button "circle center," leaving behind a center point. Now, choosing a point on the circle (which fixes the radius) we press the button "draw" again . . .* [Sutherland 1963]

Similarly the Xerox system provided additional function keys located on the left-hand side of the keyboard, so permitting a degree of bi-manual interaction. These

Figure 9.1: In the top photograph we illustrate the layout of the standard keyboard most commonly in use today. This compares with early approaches that supported a degree of bi-manual input through the provision of special-purpose keys on the left side of the keyboard. Such a keyboard is shown in the lower illustration and was standard for Apollo systems. The vertical black line shows that the character key "q" of each keyboard is approximately in line. From this it is apparent that today's keyboards have shifted their layout to the right so as to more strongly support right-hand (preferred hand) input. Since the right-hand must also navigate the mouse, this layout places a considerable burden on the preferred hand and relegates the non-preferred hand to typing-only activity. (Image © 2005 Q.S. Blundell.)

buttons could be conveniently operated by the left hand, leaving the right free to navigate the mouse. A similar approach was subsequently adopted for keyboard layout in the Apollo computer systems that were widely used in the 1980s. In the case of these high-end workstations,[1] a set of special-purpose keys was provided for the left hand and supported mouse activity with the right (see Figure 9.1). Such systems provide examples of the use of basic bi-manual cooperation within the human–computer interface, and since these pioneering innovations,

---

[1]These machines were most frequently interconnected using a token passing ring network topology and provided an extremely advanced graphical user interface via the Aegis operating system. Early Apollo workstations such as the DN300 had a small touch pad on the right-hand-side of the keyboard. However, the mouse was more commonly used for cursor navigation.

considerable research has been undertaken in investigating not only more complex bi-manual interaction but also the way in which the hands work together in task performance. Unfortunately, this research appears to have been largely disregarded for, as may be seen from a cursory comparison of the standard conventional keyboard shown in Figure 9.1 and the superior layout provided by, for example, Apollo some 20 years ago; vendors appear to have disregarded the obvious advantages associated with properly supporting left-hand (non-preferred) input. Furthermore, today's widely adopted layout makes the right hand responsible for both mouse navigation and for the operation of other special purpose keys.

The Toolglass computer interface provides us with an example of a novel approach to human–computer interaction where the need to support bi-manual interaction was central to its design [Bier et al. 1993]. This interface provides a set of tools that are semi-transparent and appear to lie on a transparent surface ("glass") interposed between the application and the cursor. The Toolglass sheet could be moved with an interaction device operated by the non-preferred hand whilst the cursor is positioned with the other. Thus:

> *The user can position the sheet with the non-dominant hand, using a device such as a trackball, at the same time as the dominant hand positions a cursor (e.g., with a mouse or stylus). The user can line up a widget, a cursor, and an application object in a single two-handed gesture.* [Bier et al. 1993]

Here we note that the non-preferred hand is made responsible for coarse movements (i.e., the positioning of the Toolglass sheet) and the preferred hand carries out the cursor positioning task, so identifying objects beneath the sheet which are to be acted upon. Naturally this latter task requires greater positioning accuracy. This reflects a characteristic described by Guiard [1987] in his development of the "kinematic chain theory" (which we refer to again in the next sub-section). Within this context, Leganchuk et al. [1998] summarizes four basic characteristics, one of which is referred to as "left-right scale differentiation" in respect of which, they write:

> *...the granularity of action of the left hand is coarser than the right; the left-hand movement is macrometric; and the right-hand movement is micrometric.*

In Section 1.5.3 (in the context of the conventional display), we referred to the erosion of the area of screen available for creative tasks (such as drawing) by the presence of the event-driven menu system. It is interesting to note that the Toolglass approach provides an effective solution to this problem:

> *In most applications, a control panel competes for screen space with the work area of the application. Toolglass sheets exist on a layer above the work area. With proper management of the sheets, they can provide an unlimited space for tools. The widgets in use can take up the entire work area. Then, they can be scrolled entirely off the screen to provide an unobstructed view of the application or space for a different set of widgets.* [Bier et al. 1993]

In the next subsection we briefly discuss a small sample of the work undertaken in this interesting area, and in Section 9.2.2, we consider several exemplar systems that support types of bi-manual interaction.

9.2.1 Bi-manual Task Performance

> In a Wonderland they lie,
> Dreaming as the days go by,
> Dreaming as the summers die:
> Even drifting down the stream-
> Lingering in a golden gleam-
> Life, what is it but a dream?[2]

We are all aware of the difficulty of undertaking simple tasks such as rubbing the stomach with one hand while patting the head with the other or simultaneously sweeping out in space two different shapes, such as a square and a circle. Even causing the hands to trace a circular path (in, for example, a vertical plane) in opposite directions can take effort. Considerably greater difficulty is experienced when we attempt to tap a separate rhythm with each hand. *"a polyrhythm: two conflicting but isochronous sequences. Most people have great difficulty in coordinating the two hands in such tasks in which the two rhythms are not integer multiples of each other."* [Leganchuk et al. 1998]. The problem that we experience is linked to the independent nature of the two tasks and their asymmetry. However, when the hands are brought to bear on a common task, they demonstrate a remarkable degree of cooperative action. Consider for a moment some simple real-world tasks requiring a high degree of dexterity such as treading a small nut onto a bolt, threading cotton through the "eye" of a fine needle or even tasks requiring less dexterity, such as pressing the keys on a calculator. Although it may initially appear that the tasks would be facilitated by fixing either the bolt or the needle in a clamp or by placing the calculator on a stable surface (to ensure that the "targets" do not move during execution of the task), in reality our performance is enhanced by making use of both hands. In this way we utilize a natural synergy that exists between the hands and hold, for example, the needle or calculator in our non-preferred hand whilst leaving our preferred hand to make more dextrous movements. Aspects of two-handed manipulation are discussed at length in an excellent publication by Ken Hinckley and co-workers (which we will discuss in Section 9.2.2) [Hinckley et al. 1998]. In this context, he writes:[3]

> *This input mapping has another subtle effect on user behaviour: since the non-preferred hand now defines a dynamic frame of reference relative to which all manipulation occurs, this means that the user is not forced to work relative to the screen itself or relative to some center point within the environment, as required by one-handed desktop VR interfaces that employ free-space input devices [Deering 1992; Liang*

---

[2]Lewis Carroll, *Through the Looking Glass.*
[3]Reproduced with permission from Hinckley et al. [1998].

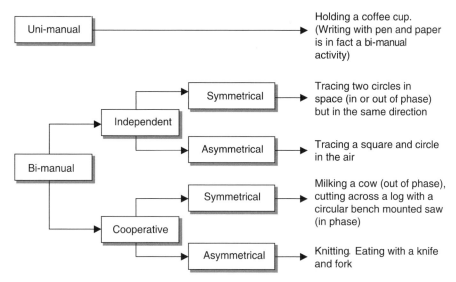

Figure 9.2: Bi-manual activities can be either cooperative or independent. In each case, tasks can be viewed as being either symmetrical or asymmetrical. On the right of the illustration, we provide simple examples of associated activities. See text for further discussion. (Image © 2005 Q.S. Blundell.)

and Green 1993]. Users are at liberty to shift their body posture, to hold their hands at a comfortable position on the desk surface, or even to hold them in their lap.

Bi-manual activity can be classified as either symmetric or asymmetric (see Figure 9.2). The former refers to situations in which each hand is assigned an identical role, such as the tracking of separate (and similarly moving) targets by each hand. This is in fact the basis for trials conducted by Balakrishnan and Hinckley [2000]. In one scenario, two targets moved around the screen—each target covering the same distance (horizontally and vertically) at each image update, so maintaining constant separation. The participants tracked the targets by means of two cursors— one of which was controlled by each hand. Hence the cursor movement required to track each of the targets was identical—providing a symmetric bi-manual activity. The trials conducted also considered the impact of the visual process on motor function and examined the effect of having a smaller or larger separation between the targets.[4] Of particular interest to our current discussions is the impact of the visual stimulus on the parallelism of the bi-manual activity. In the case of a larger target separation, participants were forced to switch attention between the targets, leading to a greater degree of sequential tracking activity. Naturally this suggests that bi-manual tracking is best achieved when both targets are close together; however, these trials also indicated that when the targets were interconnected, this reinforced the perception of a single tracking task and promoted parallel activity.

[4]In further trials, the targets were effectively interconnected; see publication for details.

In the case of an asymmetric cooperative bi-manual activity, the actions of one hand are dependent on those of the other (e.g., using a knife and fork). Of course many asymmetric activities do not require cooperation of the hands and we mentioned several relatively simple tasks of this type at the beginning of this subsection (see also Figure 9.2). It is perhaps surprising that seemingly trivial tasks such as simultaneously outlining two different shapes in the air can be problematic when we carry out far more complex bi-manual tasks such as reaching for, and taking hold of, a cup of coffee and pen simultaneously, without any conscious effort. This is a matter discussed by Diedrichsen et al. [2004]. Their paper is well worth perusal as it covers considerable ground in connection with bi-manual reaching. One set of trials concerns reaching toward two targets whose positions change during the reaching process. Thus the participant must make trajectory corrections. Previous researchers have considered this for uni-manual movements, and as summarized by Jörn Diedrichsen et al.:

> *When a target stimulus is displaced during the initial phase of a reaching movement, an adjustment in movement trajectory can be detected within 150 ms [Pelisson et al. 1986, Prablanc and Martin 1992]. Moreover, these adjustments can occur without awareness of target displacement [Goodale et al. 1986] and sometimes occur involuntarily despite task instructions [Pisella et al. 2000].*

Interestingly, one aspect of the results reported in this publication indicates that the motor system can support both uni-manual and simultaneous bi-manual reaching with equal accuracy "... *participants were able to readily modify movement trajectories, regardless of whether one or both targets were displaced.*" [Diedrichsen et al. 2004]. Naturally this suggests the parallel control of the two movement activities. The publication includes investigation into the role of the point of fixation. When participants fixed there gaze on a nontarget location, the speed and efficiency with which they made trajectory adjustments decreased in comparison with when they were permitted to freely move their eyes.

Hinckley et al. [1997] provide insight into cooperative bi-manual activity including consideration of the respective roles played by the two hands. Interestingly, physical rather than computer-generated objects were used in the trials. As indicated:[5]

> *Since the purpose of the experiment is to look at some basic aspects of bi-manual motor control, we felt that by using physical objects we could be certain that we were measuring the human, and not artefacts caused by the particular depth cues employed, the display frame rate, device latency, or other possible confounds associated with virtual manipulation.*

Hinckley et al. report the use of several targets (such as a cube) into which a slot was cut. This was held in one hand and the other held, for example, a stylus. The

---

[5]This is an important consideration and such issues may have added to the discrepancies of the results reported for some Fitts' Model trials (see Section 5.3).

aim was to insert the tool into the slot machined into the target and make contact with a small conductive pad located at the bottom of the slot. This process completed an electrical circuit which was used for timing operations. Two classes of trial are reported. In the easier case, the participant could use the sides of the slot to guide the insertion of the stylus. In these trials, no error was possible. However, in a set of more challenging trials, should the stylus (or other tool) miss the small target area, an error was logged. Thus, the easier trials focused on speed of operation, and in the more difficult trials, both speed and error frequency were measured. Trials were carried out with the target held in the left hand and the tool in the right and vice versa. The results reported confirm that for more demanding operations (i.e., the more difficult trials mentioned above), the preferred hand works best when operating relative to the non-preferred hand and that holding the heavier object in the non-preferred hand can assist in damping motor tremors. Furthermore, in the simpler trials, the participant benefited from the haptic feedback provided by using the sides of the slot to guide the tool, as the authors of this work indicate "*... the motor control required for the Easy conditions, where there was plentiful haptic feedback in the form of physical constraints, fundamentally differed from the Hard conditions.*"

In the previous subsection we referred to the "kinematic chain theory" and have mentioned two characteristics of this model. Firstly, as indicated in the quotation taken from Hinckley et al. [1998] earlier in this subsection, the non-preferred hand provides a dynamic frame of reference for the non-preferred hand. A second characteristic was quoted from Leganchuk et al. [1998] in connection with the non-preferred hand being responsible for coarser movements. A third characteristic refers to the precedence of action—the non-preferred hand leads the preferred hand. In essence, the "kinematic chain theory" assumes that the arm may be viewed as a series of abstract motors interconnected by linkages. As indicated by Hinckley et al. [1998]:

> *For example, the shoulder, elbow, wrist and fingers form a kinematic chain representing the arm. For each link (e.g. the forearm), there is a proximal element (the elbow) and a distal element (the wrist). The (distal) wrist must organise its movements relative to the output of the (proximal) elbow, since the two are physically attached.*

The model proposes that the preferred and non-preferred hands form a functional kinematic chain with the preferred hand lying at the end of this chain.[6] Thus, the preferred hand forms the distal element and the non-preferred hand the proximal element (see the excellent paper by Yves Guiard who proposed this model

---

[6]As indicated by Guiard [1987] the preferred hand need not necessarily end the chain, "*there is no reason to eliminate the possibility that what the left and right hands do together form the input to another more distal motor organ: The mouth represents the most obvious candidate for occupying a still higher rank in the chain.*"

[Guiard 1987][7]). Consequently we can see that this structure possesses the characteristics that we have mentioned above and which are summarized below:

1. The non-preferred hand provides a dynamic frame of reference for the preferred hand.[8]
2. Finer granularity of motion is achieved with the preferred hand—the two hands exhibit "asymmetric temporal-spatial scales of motion."
3. The non-preferred hand leads the sequence of actions.

From the various trials that have been conducted, it is apparent that bi-manual activity increases the speed of completion for various tasks, and in an interesting and detailed study by Leganchuk et al. [1998], the results obtained indicate that in certain cases, as task complexity is increased, bi-manual activity becomes more efficient. In this respect, they write:

> *For the cognitively less demanding tasks . . . we see the performance of the two-handed technique was similar or even inferior to that of the one-handed technique. However as the tasks become more cognitively demanding, . . . we see that two-handed [interaction] has a significant performance gain.*

Increased task performance is of course only one criterion against which we need to assess the benefits of bi-manual interaction, and factors such as cognitive load and additional demands that may be placed on the human visual system are of equal importance. Furthermore, as we have indicated previously, simply increasing the number of "channels" via which a user may interface with the digital world is certainly not in itself necessarily advantageous. The major gains are brought about by the synergy that can exist when we bring these "channels" together and permit natural human actions, thereby reducing mental effort. This is well demonstrated by the bi-manual interaction paradigm.

9.2.2   The Potential Benefits of Bi-manual Interaction

Experimental trials such as those outlined in the previous section often tend to simply confirm in a quantitative manner our personal experience. It is derived from the knowledge that we acquire of our own bodies and in our day-to-day observations of those around us. Furthermore, when conducting such trials, it is generally necessary to focus on one particular type of task. Thus, in the case of, for example,

---

[7]See also Guiard and Ferrand [1996] for discussion on asymmetry in bi-manual activities.

[8]This can be easily demonstrated by means of a simple trial described by Guiard. Writing is a bi-manual activity with the non-preferred hand providing a frame of reference and regularly adjusting the position of the paper. Guiard placed a carbon sheet beneath the writing paper so enabling the participants writing to appear not only on the paper but also (unbeknown to the participant) on the static surface (the desk top). The results clearly indicate that "*the motion of the pen is executed, not with reference to the environment, but with reference to landmarks located on the sheet of paper, a mobile object manipulated by the non-preferred hand.*" ([Guiard 1987] citing earlier work).

asymmetric bi-manual activity, a trial provides an indication of performance in one (or a small number) of tasks and we are left to consider (somewhat subjectively) whether or not this is a valid performance indicator that can be extrapolated across a range of interface tasks. Certainly, some tasks lend themselves more readily to parallelism than do others. On the other hand, parallelism represents only one of the potential advantages that can be derived from bi-manual activity. Here it is important to remember that the hands do not simply represent output devices via which we are able to effect controlled action, but are also input devices and supply us with a rich variety of haptic stimuli. Thus, the use of two hands influences the manner in which we undertake interactive operations and may in fact (and under certain circumstances) reduce the reliance that we place upon the visual sense (recall from Chapter 3 discussion on proprioception—our subconscious awareness of the position of our limbs in absolute and relative terms without the requirement for visual cues). Hinckley et al. [1998] write:[9]

> *... two hands do more than just save time over one hand. Users have a keen sense of where their hands are relative to one another, and this can be used to develop interaction techniques which are potentially less demanding of visual attention. Using both hands helps users to ground themselves in a body-relative interaction space as opposed to requiring consciously calculated action in an abstract environment-relative space .... Using both hands alters the syntax of the manual tasks which must be performed, which influences a user's problem-solving behaviour and therefore has a direct influence on how users think about a task.*

Of course, trials such as those briefly mentioned in the last subsection represent basic research supporting the development and verification of models that approximate human behavior. As our confidence in such models increases, we can cautiously apply them across a broader set of tasks; ultimately, they influence (or should influence) interface design. Perhaps an even more important aspect of such work is that it focuses attention upon the complex nature of the human motor and sensory systems, and reinforces understanding of the benefits that can be derived by developing interfaces that exploit and extend human skills rather than interfaces that force the operator to adapt to the restricted ways of the machine.

Certainly the ultimate benefits that may be derived from, for example, bi-manual interaction, can only be properly understood through the experience gained by observing such systems in use. This is of particular importance because new interaction modalities are likely to influence the manner in which an interface is used, in ways that we are unlikely to be able to envisage in advance. A publication by Cutler et al. [1997] reinforces this point. This describes a bi-manual interaction paradigm used in conjunction with the "Responsive Workbench" display system. In brief this display projects high-quality temporally coded stereoscopic images onto the table-top. Head tracking is supported, and a user is able to move around the table and "touch" the images that appear above its surface. Interaction is reported as being

---

[9]Reproduced with permission from Hinckley et al. [1998].

effected via Fakespace's PINCH gloves (equipped with six-degrees-of-freedom (DOF) position sensors) that can detect the pinching together of different fingers and a Polhemus stylus (being pen-like in form and tracked by a 6-DOF position sensing system and having a single interaction button). Here the stylus represents the more accurate interaction tool, and the user is free to either use the gloves (continually worn) for interaction or pick up and use the stylus. By providing this flexibility, it is possible for the operator to naturally select the most intuitively appropriate manipulator. A set of tools are described, these being categorized as either uni-manual (e.g., "one-handed grab"—pick up and move a single object), bi-manual symmetric (e.g., "turntable"—enabling an object to be rotated about a fixed axis), or bi-manual asymmetric (e.g., "zoom"). The researchers report:

> *During our observations we also found that users often picked up two seemingly independent one-handed tools and used them together in a coordinated fashion . . . One of the more surprising results was that the asymmetric combination of a PINCH glove for the left hand and stylus for the right hand worked much better in many situations than the two PINCH gloves, especially for asymmetric tasks.*

In their summary, they add:

> *When beginning this work we thought that all the two-handed input techniques would need to be explicitly designed and programmed. However, when using the system we found that perhaps the most interesting tasks emerged when the user combined two otherwise independent uni-manual tools.* [Cutler et al. 1997]

Consequently, it is generally not possible to decide in advance the manner in which users will choose to perform tasks, and best experience is derived through the provision of flexible interaction opportunities and observation (gained visually or by recording user activities via the underlying software systems).[10]

Although considerable work has been undertaken in investigating the use of bi-manual interaction trials in conjunction with creative 3-D display paradigms (such as that just described), formal trials have focused upon the conventional display screen and so a great amount of research remains to be done in this area. Many interesting issues and technical obstacles need to be overcome if we are to enable the hands to simultaneously and "directly" manipulate a virtual object (e.g., a virtual clay). Accurately tracking the movement of the hands and fingers is in itself a major exercise as parts of one hand may in some way occlude parts of the other. Consequently, systems supporting bi-manual activity tend to support a separate interface channel for each hand and facilitate interactions that do not bring the hands into contact. Furthermore, in the case of immersive VR applications, even given a correct measurement of the spatial characteristics of the hands and fingers, creating an accurate (and realistic) virtual rendition of the hand based on

---

[10]A range of publications exists in connection with the Responsive Workbench. See also, for example, de Haan et al. [2002], which discusses alternative interaction tools.

this data without introducing unacceptable latency is fraught with difficulty (this is sufficiently challenging for a single hand). Consequently, bi-manual approaches are likely to continue for some time to employ display paradigms in which the physical hands may be viewed directly.

Ken Hinckley and co-workers produced an extremely interesting publication (from which we have already quoted) describing a bi-manual interface designed for use in neurosurgical visualization [Hinckley et al. 1998]. This represents an interface paradigm developed specifically for use with a particular application but which could be applied to others. In discussing the traditional approach and so providing the context for work undertaken, Hinckley et al. write:[11]

> *In order to view a model of the brain or position a cutting plane with respect to the brain, the surgeon had to specify a set of six values with sliders labeled Yaw, Pitch, Roll, X, Y, and Z. As we talked, the surgeon picked up a full-scale model of a skull from a table next to his chair and said 'When I'm thinking about surgery, I'll often pick up one of these to help focus my thinking. Do you think you could do something like that? I want a skull I can hold in my hand.*

The interface that was developed employed an interaction device in the form of a doll's head that could be held in the non-preferred hand. Rotation of this head caused the image of the brain depicted on a conventional computer display system to corotate. Similarly, moving the head toward or away from the computer screen allowed the user to zoom. The use of a doll's head gives (through passive haptic sensation) an immediate sense of the orientation of the displayed cranial image relative to the skull. A cutting tool was also used (see Figure 9.3) and held in the preferred hand:[12]

> *The cutting-plane prop is used in concert with the head prop rather than as a separate tool. The user holds the cutting-plane prop against the head to indicate a slice through the brain data. The computer shows a corresponding virtual plane intersecting the virtual head, along with a cross section of the volumetric head data.* [Hinckley et al. 1998]

This type of bi-manual interaction loosely parallels much earlier work discussed by Cyrus Levinthal [1966]. Here, software enabled complex molecular structures to be depicted on a Cathode Ray Tube (CRT) display and interaction was achieved not only via the keyboard, but also via a light pen. Furthermore, rotation (direction and speed) was obtained via a gimbaled control. Interestingly, the light pen supported interaction by the non-preferred hand—rotation being controlled by the preferred hand—see Figure 9.4.

A display paradigm called the "Escritoire" is briefly described by Mark Ashdown and Peter Robinson [2004]. The approach adopted is illustrated in Figure 9.5. Here two projectors are used; one projects a low-resolution image over the surface of a desktop. The second projector casts a high-resolution image immediately in front

---

[11]Reproduced with permission from Hinckley et al. [1998].
[12]Reproduced with permission from Hinckley et al. [1998].

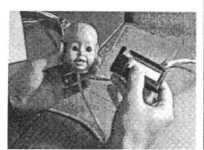
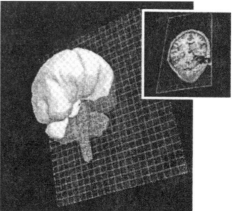

Figure 9.3: The use of the doll's head and cutting tool in neurosurgical visualization. The doll's head allows the operator to intuitively perform rotation and zoom operations on a cranial image. A cutting tool is held in the preferred hand. This is used in conjunction with the doll's head and allows the user to specify the orientation of a cross-section. [Reproduced from Hinckley, K. and Pausch, R., "Two-Handed Virtual Manipulation," *ACM Transactions on Computer-Human Interaction*, **5**, (1998); © 1998 ACM.]

of the user. Thus, an operator can move virtual objects (such as "paper") around the desktop and position them within the high-resolution imaging region when they are to be perused in detail. This creates a so-called "foveal display" mimicking the action of the eye (see Section 2.3.2). From the perspective of our current discussions,

(a)
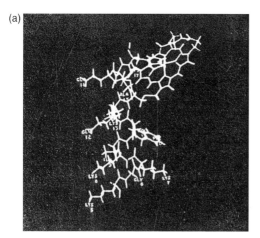

(b)

Figure 9.4: An early bi-manual interactive display system for the depiction and manipulation of complex molecular structures, as shown in (a). In (b), the display is illustrated together with bi-manual interaction tools. [Reproduced from Levinthal, C., "Molecular Model-Building by Computer," *Scientific American*, **214/6**, (1996).]

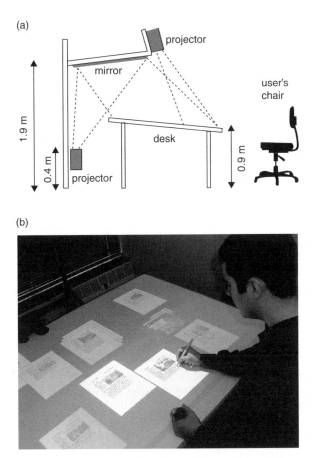

Figure 9.5: The "Escritoire" dual projection display. Image (a) provides an overview of the projection system, and in (b), the virtual paper is depicted. Bi-manual interaction is supported—see text for brief discussion. (Images kindly supplied by Dr. Mark Ashdown and Dr. Peter Robinson.)

it is interesting to note that bi-manual user interaction is supported. An ultrasonic white board pen is used by the non-preferred hand, whilst the preferred hand achieves finer interaction via a desk-sized digitizer and associated stylus.

9.3 AUGMENTING THE DESKTOP INTERFACE

As previously discussed, a variety of approaches may be adopted in the implementation of a display able to support binocular and motion parallax (although in many embodiments, this latter cue is supported only to a limited extent). In most cases, the technologies are standard and are typically inexpensive. Furthermore, as we have shown, various facets of the visualization experience can be significantly advanced through the provision of these non-pictorial cues. In fact, a display system unable to provide these cues to our visual sense is akin to an audio system providing only a mono rather than a stereo auditory experience. In Section 1.8, we briefly considered various factors that may have prevented the widespread adoption of creative 3-D display systems, and certainly the diversity of techniques that may be employed in their implementation has negatively impacted upon widespread commercialization. Furthermore, no single approach is without flaws, particularly when we consider not only a display's visual characteristics but also the interaction opportunities that it offers to efficiently support.

Unfortunately the benefits that may be derived from a creative 3-D display are dependent on the infrastructure underpinning the operation of such systems. For example, although the Internet provides multimedia support, visual opportunities tend in the main to center on the standard monocular image. Of course, this is because creative systems are not in general use. On the other hand, given the lack of suitable image content and applications software, the purchase of a creative system would not necessarily benefit the user wishing to augment the Internet experience. Interestingly, early stereoscopes were often used to support the "armchair" traveler, enhancing the view of distant locations through the augmented sense of realism offered by this technique. We can certainly imagine the advantages of using a low-cost desktop version of a creative 3-D display for such an application, particularly as ever-increasing network bandwidth and image compression techniques are now able support the requirements of animated stereoscopic image transmission. Unfortunately, today's "armchair" traveler would find that the creative display was largely confined to providing monocular imagery, not as a consequence of technical problems, but simply because the infrastructure is currently configured for this *modus operandi*. However, this represents a real, affordable application for existing creative 3-D technologies.

In the 1970s and early 1980s, there were those who questioned the need for computer monitors able to support full-color image depiction, and similarly when stereo radio transmission was proposed, many questioned whether the increased electronic complexity was justified when considered in terms of the benefits which would ensue. In both cases, the technical challenges were met and undoubtedly progress was made. The ability of the desktop computer monitor to usefully support (as a matter of routine) binocular and motion parallax requires not only the refinement and marketing of an affordable creative display paradigm, but also the creation and adoption of appropriate applications software and interaction tools. Without doubt, the technology will be imperfect (but, for example, so too are the VHS cassette and the CD) and the scale of benefits cannot be known with certainty in advance. However, once systems are in widespread use, no doubt we will no longer understand why there was any procrastination in connection with the necessary investment and potential.

Introducing haptic feedback to the desktop machine is more challenging. As we have already discussed in this context, we must particularly consider the extent to which the interface is to interact with the human sensory systems, the type of interaction opportunities that are to be accommodated by the system, and of course their integration with the display paradigm. However, an active hand-held pointer able to convey a degree of haptic sensation, or an active glove able to provide haptic feedback to restricted parts of the hand, can readily be coupled to an appropriate display technology, and advantages could (at least in principle) be gained by the end user from a small hardware investment. By way of example, consider the use of such a system in an application permitting the virtual tour of a museum. Certainly, the ability of the display to support the binocular and motion parallax cues would add to our visual perception of artifacts by augmenting both realism and information content. If our creative 3-D display and interaction interface enables us to hold and "touch" virtual artifacts, then it is likely that we would feel more closely connected with the physical objects that they represent. In a most interesting publication, Doron Swade [2003] discusses our perception of the significance of physical objects that in some way relate to our own personal history (or to more general historical events) and considers the role that may be played by both physical and virtual replicas. From one perspective, such objects may be perceived as "messengers from the past," and in this context, Swade writes:

> *Family heirlooms are imbued with associations and personal significance. We populate our lives with them. When we notice them, encounter or contemplate them they trigger internal dialogues with past owners and stimulate trains of thought as we visit memory, embroider and elaborate, explore and speculate . . . The issue is a deep one and despite our efforts at analysis, our relationships with things remain an enduring puzzle.*

If we view artifacts as messengers from the past, then it is apparent that however excellent the visual, haptic, and interaction channels are in their support for our interfacing with an object's virtual rendition, it will never equal direct sensory contact with the real article. Of course, in practice, the physical object may not be accessible to the touch (as is often the case when artifacts are exhibited), and so contact with the virtual rendition may be an acceptable compromise. Furthermore, the virtual rendition (or graphical animation) of entities may provide us with a greater insight into either the usage or the operation of a physical system (in this latter case, see discussion in relation to the animation of Babbage's Difference Engine provided in Swade [2003]).

9.4   READINGS ON IMPLEMENTATIONS AND APPLICATIONS

A great number of scientific publications discuss a broad spectrum of creative 3-D display and interaction systems. Furthermore, there are many papers that focus not only on the hardware and software systems but also describe in detail the development of solutions intended to address particular applications. Given the volume and diversity of the available literature, we decided when originally planning this book that, in view of the space available, an exhaustive overview would not be possible (such a review could easily span a book in its own right). Consequently we have mainly focused discussion on the introduction of general concepts (drawn from a range of traditional subject disciplines) and have used specific examples of either system implementation or system application to reinforce broader principles. Thus, the example systems introduced in the book have been selected as being indicative and we hope that they will give the reader new to this area an impression of the sheer diversity of techniques that may be used in the creation of systems.

In this brief section, we provide references to sample literature that may provide a convenient starting point for the reader wishing to find out more about the implementation and application of creative systems. These references have generally not been cited elsewhere in the text, and therefore, they are additional to those quoted in other parts of the book.

The *Communications of the ACM* [August 2004] provides an excellent starting point. A range of interesting articles are presented covering aspects of both display and haptic systems. The articles concerning the design of cranial implants (see also Vannier et al. 1983] using an augmented reality technique, and on adopting a "painterly" approach to virtual painting are particularly interesting. The application of the Responsive Workbench (see Section 9.2.2) is discussed in three excellent publications by Gerold Wesche and co-workers [Wesche and Droske 2000, Wesche and Seidel 2001, Wesche 2003]. They discuss support for stylus-type interaction permitting free-form drawing (i.e., the direct creation of lines and curves within free space) that forms the basis of an intuitive design process.

Many excellent publications have been written concerning the application of creative 3-D design and interaction interfaces for medical applications. See reference to the FeTouch project provided in Section 7.4 and Bajura et al. [1992] and Stephenson et al. [2003] provide useful discussion on interesting work.

In connection with collaborative work opportunities, see, for example, Kauff and Schreer [2002], Raskar et al. [1998], and Gross et al. [2003].

In relation to interaction devices, Frohlich and Plate [2000] describe the "Cubic Mouse," Iwata [1990] discusses a force feedback system (although this is an older publication, it is still well worth perusal), and Wormell and Foxlin [2003] review a range of interaction tools. Plesniak and Pappu [1999] discuss the incorporation of haptic systems with holographic displays.

9.5 DISCUSSION

And so we come to the end of our voyage of exploration. We have covered a considerable distance and visited a number of remote lands. It is a pity that our visits have often been brief, and therefore, we have only made a cursory investigation of geography, history, and culture. Indeed it would have been pleasant to have stayed in those distant places for longer and so have gained a greater knowledge. However, that was not the goal of our quest—we sought to highlight diversity. This diversity arises from the range of skills and the scope of the knowledge base that must be brought to bear in the development of systems that will radically impact on our interaction with the digital world. Approaches that are not based upon such broad foundations are unlikely to provide optimal solutions—solutions that demonstrate the synergy that may be catalysed when interaction "channels" are properly supported and which exhibit suitability for usage across a broad range of applications.

Interacting with the digital world should be a positive, natural experience in which the operator is empowered, rather than the machine. Today, this is certainly not always the case. The challenge is to change this situation for the better ...

"I don't see much sense in that," said Rabbit.
"No." said Pooh humbly, "there isn't. But there was going to be when I began it. It's just that something happened to it along the way.". . .

"Pooh," said Rabbit kindly, "you haven't any brain."
"I know," said Pooh humbly.[13]

---

[13]From *The Complete Tales and Poems of Winnie-the-Pooh* by A.A. Milne and E.H. Shepard, Dutton Books (2001).

APPENDIX A
The Chimenti Drawings

The fair breeze blew, the white foam flew.
The furrow followed free;
We were the first that ever burst
Into that silent sea.

As we have seen, the underlying principle of the stereoscope underpins many creative 3-D display techniques, and in Section 6.3.1, we briefly reviewed the origins of this device. In this context, we referred to the controversy that arose between Charles Wheatstone and David Brewster. As we have seen, and for whatever reason, the latter appears to have been intent upon denying the former credit for his insight into stereopsis and for the invention of the stereoscope. Among other claims, Brewster suggested that Jacopo Chimenti da Empoli had understood the process of stereoscopic vision nearly 300 years earlier. Central to this assertion were two drawings attributed to Chimenti (see Figure A.1). In the brief account provided below, we draw on the publication by Professor Nicholas Wade [2003]. His excellent and well-referenced article is recommended to the interested reader.

A student, Alexander Crum Brown, played a pivotal role in catalyzing the intense debate that took place in connection with the Chimenti drawings. During a visit in 1859 to the Musée Wicar in Lille, he viewed these two re-discovered sketches hung side by side and was convinced that they formed a stereopair from which a sense of *relief* could readily be derived by appropriately converging the eyes [Wade 2003]. He reported his observations by letter to the Principal of the University of St. Andrews–James Forbes. In turn, Forbes passed the letter to David Brewster, and in view of his efforts to discredit Charles Wheatstone's claim, Brewster must have perused it with great joy. Unfortunately, it appears that in his enthusiasm, Brewster promoted Browns observations without having first viewed the sketches! In fact, it seems that he did not obtain photographs of the drawings until 1862 when he presented them to a meeting of the members of the Photographic Society of Scotland. Here, Wade [2003] quotes Brewster as having indicated that *"The*

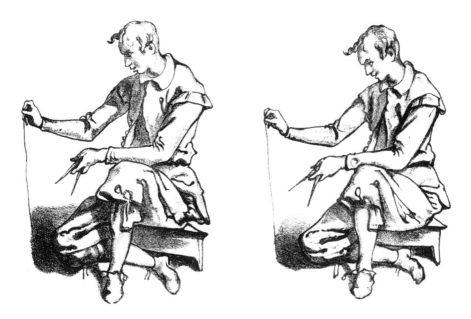

Figure A.1: The Chimenti drawings, published in *The Photographic Journal* in April 1862. These are based upon woodcut copies of the original Chimenti drawings. Wade [2003] reports the originals as each measuring approximately 30 by 22 cm, and Alexander Crum Brown indicated that for optimal effect they were best viewed at a distance of 4 or 5 yards. (Images kindly supplied in digital form by Professor Nicholas Wade.)

full stereoscopic relief of Chimenti's pictures was seen and acknowledged by all." In fact, it appears that Brewster also sought to form a link between the sketches and the possible invention of the stereoscope by Giovanni Battista della Porta. However, the following passage, which is provided in English by Wade, and which is taken from Porta's *De Refractione* treatise [Porta 1593] provides us with a clear insight into Porta's understanding of the binocular visual process:

> *Nature has given us two eyes, one on the right and the other on the left, so that if we are to see something on the right we use the right eye, and on the left the left eye. It follows that we always see with one eye, even if we think both are open and that we see with both. We may prove it by these arguments: To separate the two eyes, let us place a book before the right eye and read it; then if someone shows another book to the left eye, it is impossible to read it or even see the pages, unless for a short moment of time the power of seeing is taken from the right eye and borrowed by the left. We observe the same thing happening in other senses: if we hear someone talking with the right ear we cannot listen to another with the left ear; and if we wish to hear both we shall hear neither, or indeed if we hear something with the right we lose the same amount from the left. Similarly, if we write with one hand we cannot play a lyre with the other, nor count out coins. There is another argument. If someone places a staff in front of himself and sets it against some obvious crack in the wall opposite, and notices the place, then when he shuts the left eye he will not see the staff to have moved from the crack opposite. The reason is that one sees with the right eye, just as one uses the right hand and foot and someone using the left eye or hand or foot is considered a monster. But if the observer closes the right eye, the staff immediately shifts to the right side. There is a third argument – that nature made two eyes, one beside the other, so that one may defend a man from attackers from the right and the other from the left. This is more obvious in animals, for their eyes are separated by half a foot, as is seen in cattle, horses and lions. In birds one eye is opposite the other, consequently, if things must be seen both on the right and on the left, the power of seeing must be engaged very quickly for the mind to be able to accomplish its function. For these reasons the two eyes cannot see the same thing at the same time.* (Reproduced by the kind permission of Professor Nicholas Wade, and with thanks to Helen Ross who translated this passage from Porta [1593].)

Although relief may be observed in small parts of the Chimenti drawings, the overall effect is not convincing and Brewster failed to impress his peers.

In Section 4.3, we alluded to the debate concerning the painting made by Filippo Brunelleschi of the Florentine Baptistery. It is unlikely that we will ever know for sure of the method that he used in obtaining accurate perspective—nor of his reasons for requiring the viewer to observe the mirrored reflection of the painted scene. Similarly we are unlikely to ever know why Chimenti created these two images from different perspectives. It would seem that had he been experimenting with the stereoscopic drawing, a far simpler scene would have been chosen. However, in both cases, it is likely that the actual reasons are far simpler than we might imagine after the passage of years.

APPENDIX B
Holographic Images

The loud wind never reached the ship,
Yet now the ship moved on!
Beneath the lightning and the Moon
The dead men gave a groan.

Denis Gabor first elucidated the principle of holography[1] in a remarkable one-page article which appeared in *Nature* in the late 1940s [Gabor 1948]. At that time,

---

[1]Gabor coined the term "hologram" from the Greek *holos*—to see. There is some uncertainty as to who first used the term "holography" (bringing together *holo*gram and photo*graphy*), but it may have been George Stoke [Kock 1981].

Gabor's interests centered upon limitations of the electron microscopy techniques then in use. Consequently, the holographic technique that he described was intended to significantly advance electron microscopy, and his interests in holograms created by means of visible light were secondary. Writing in the early 1970s Gabor recalled that "*After pondering this problem* [the limitations of electron microscopy techniques] *for a long time, a solution suddenly dawned on me, one fine day at Easter 1947.*"

In fact, Gabor's development of an holography technique employing visible light was intended to verify basic principles prior to its application to complex electron microscopes. One of his early two-dimensional (2-D) holographic images is illustrated in Figure B.1. The basic principle of holography can be readily understood by reference to one of Gabor's diagrams, which is reproduced in Figure B.2. Although this shows the use of electron beams, this need not be a source of concern as such a beam can be regarded as a wave; in which case, the wavelength (λ) is given by

$$\lambda = \frac{h}{\sqrt{2\ meV}},$$

where h represents Planck's constant, m is the mass of the electron, e is the charge of an electron, and V is the voltage used to accelerate the electron beam [Okoshi 1976].

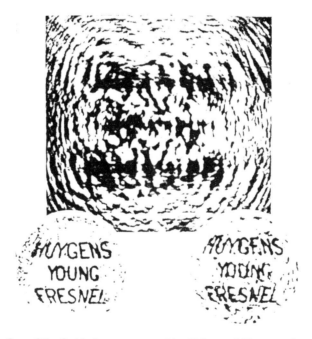

Figure B.1: One of the first holograms created by Gabor and his co-workers in 1948. The original 2-D object is shown on the left, and the reconstructed image is on the right. Central, the actual hologram is shown. [Reproduced by permission from Gabor, D., "Holography, 1948–1971," *Proc. IEEE* (June 1972); © 1972 IEEE.]

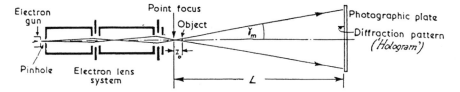

Figure B.2: The basic holographic recording technique. Gabor first sought to dramatically advance electron microscopy by means of holography—consequently this diagram shows the use of an electron beam rather than visible radiation. A portion of the beam (electron or light) passes through a small object. The photographic plate captures the interference pattern created by that portion of the beam that passed through the object, and that which travelled directly to the screen. This is the in-line ('coherent background') holographic technique. [Reproduced by permission from Gabor, D., "Holography, 1948–1971," *Proc. IEEE* (June 1972); © 1972 IEEE.]

Thus, for a value of V of 60,000 V, we obtain a wavelength of approximately 0.005 nm.

Returning to Figure B.2, the electron beam passes through a point of focus before subsequently diverging whilst in transit to the screen (this takes the form of a photographic plate). A part of this beam (or wave) impinges upon a small thin object, and in passing through this, the beam is scattered. Thus, the photographic plate records the "interference pattern" generated by the portions of the beam that did not impinge upon the object, and those that did. Here we reach the fundamental concept of holography; namely that when waves are incident on, and scattered by an object, the scattering process is described by the amplitude and phase of the emergent waves (we assume that there is no difference in the frequency of the incident and scattered waves). Conventional photographs record only amplitude information and consequently do not store a complete representation of the form of an object (for example a conventional photograph does not support the accommodation depth cue—a holographic image does).

The photographic image takes the form of an interference pattern (which as we will discuss shortly acts as a diffraction grating). Naturally, the recording of phase information needs to be undertaken relative to some stable reference, and for this, the portions of the unscattered beam are used. Gabor's early experiments employed a high-pressure mercury arc lamp as a source of illumination rather than the electron beam source depicted in Figure B.2. His work was hampered by the poor coherence characteristics of such lamps (in terms of the requirements of the holographic method), and to achieve the required spatial coherence, he was only able to use light emanating from a small region of the source. Consequently, since he was not able to utilize the overall light output from the lamp, he had to cope with very low energy object illumination. However, despite this difficulty, once the interference pattern generated by a small transparent object was produced (as a photographic transparency) and re-irradiated, an image of the original object became visible, and appeared to be located at the same location as the physical object.

The technique described above has various weaknesses, one of which is that the object must be transparent to the radiation. A second difficulty relates to the appearance of a second image—visibly in line with the first. These two images are referred to as the "real" (conjugate) and "virtual" (true) images. The real image is located in front of the photographic recording, whereas the latter is positioned at the same location as was occupied by the original physical object during the holographic recording phase. As we will discuss shortly, the development of the laser permitted this original "in-line" holographic technique (originally termed the "coherent background" method) to be superseded by a "two beam" technique (sometimes referred to as the "carrier frequency" method). This enables the real and virtual images to be separated so that the virtual image can be observed in isolation. The approach is illustrated schematically in Figure B.3 (these diagrams are reproduced from Gabor's 1972 publication which was referred to previously).

Some years passed between Gabor's original work and the implementation of the two-beam technique by Emmett Leith and Juris Upatnieks [Leith and Upatnieks 1962, 1963, 1964; Hariharan 2002]. The publication of Gabor's 1948 article catalysed some interest in the holographic technique (see, for example, the brief text by Winston Kock [1981] where he refers to the generation of a microwave hologram by himself and Floyd Harvey (reported in 1951) and which is illustrated in Figure B.4). However, as indicated by Gabor, "*Around 1955 holography went into a long hibernation.*" [Gabor 1972]. The development of the laser in the early 1960s played a pivotal role in reawakening interest in holography as it offered appropriate spatial coherence, together with high-intensity monochromatic illumination. No longer was it necessary for objects to be transparent; three-dimensional (3-D) holographic images could be formed from light scattered from object surfaces.

The holographic image obtained by, for example, the two-beam approach acts as a diffraction grating generating a central beam undeviated beam and two first-order diffracted beams created by the interference pattern in the photographic image. One of these represents the virtual image, and the other represents the real (conjugate) image.

Mathematical descriptions describing holographic image formation abound. Below we adopt an elementary approach following writers such as Smith and Thomson [1973] and Wilson and Hawkes [1998] as this is sufficient to provide an insight into the creation of the holographic storage and reconstruction processes. However, this is not intended to represent by any means a rigorous analysis and the interested reader should consult, for example, Hecht and Zajac [1974] or Saleh and Teich [1991] for a more detailed discussion.

Let us begin by assuming that a photographic plate lies in the (x, y) plane as illustrated in Figure B.5. In this plane, we represent at time t the complex amplitude of the wavefront propagating from the object as $U_o (x, y)$. We will similarly denote the complex amplitude of the reference wave by $U_r (x, y)$. As illustrated in Figure B.5, the reference beam does propagate parallel to the z axis but is inclined at an angle θ to it. For simplicity, we will assume that this tilt is relative the x axis—there being no tilt with respect to the y axis. This results in a linear phase change (φ)

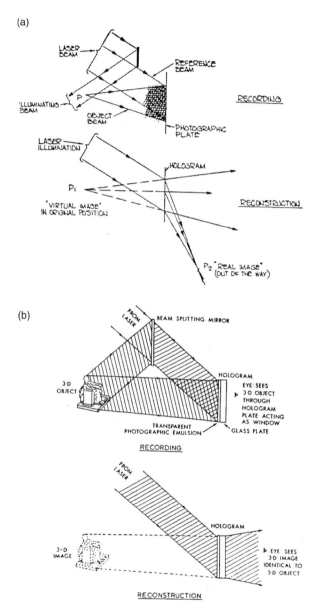

Figure B.3: Describing the two-beam technique ("carrier frequency" method) for both recording and reconstruction. Using this approach, the real and virtual images may be separated, and so the virtual image [which is located at the same location as was occupied by the physical object during the recording process (see (b))] may be viewed in isolation. [Reproduced by permission from Gabor, D., "Holography, 1948–1971," *Proc. IEEE* (June 1972); © 1972 IEEE.]

(a)

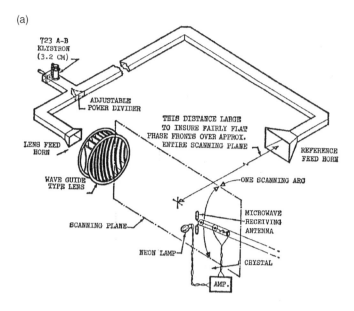

(b)

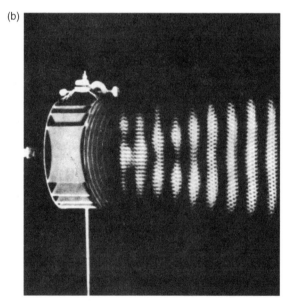

Figure B.4: In (a), a microwave source is used to generate an interference hologram. This experiment by Winston Kock and Floyd Harvey was reported in 1951 and represents an example of the interest catalysed by Gabor's original publication. The interference pattern (b) was captured with the help of a neon lamp whose level of illumination provided a measure the local radiation strength. [Reproduced from Kock, W.E., *Lasers and Holography: An Introduction to Coherent Optics*, 2nd edn., Dover Publications (1981); © 1981 Dover Publications.]

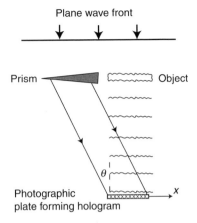

Plane wave front

Prism — Object

Photographic
plate forming hologram

θ

x

Figure B.5: The reference beam impinges upon the photographic plate at an angle θ with respect to the z axis. Its phase (in the plane of the photographic plate) varies linearly with x. [Reproduced by permission from Smith, F.G., and Thomson, J.H., *Optics*, John Wiley (1975); © 1975 John Wiley & Sons.]

across the surface of the plate that may be expressed as

$$\varphi = \frac{2\pi x \sin \theta}{\lambda}.$$

This phase change is important in the separation of the real and virtual images. Since the wave emanating from the object and the reference beams are coherent (in fact for holography we require a coherence length which is greater than the distance traversed by the light as it travels to the photographic film), the irradiance as recorded photographically [$I(x, y)$] can be expressed as

$$I(x, y) = |U_o + U_r|^2 = (U_o + U_r)(U_o^* + U_r^*). \tag{B.1}$$

Here we note that the irradiance is represented by the square of the wave amplitude[2] and use the relation $Z.Z^* = |Z|^2$ (the '*' represents the complex conjugate). This may be expanded to give

$$I(x, y) = (U_o U_o^* + U_r U_r^*) + (U_r U_o^* + U_o U_r^*). \tag{B.2}$$

The left-hand bracket in this expression contains the sum of the individual irradiencies, and the second bracket encapsulates information relating to the interference process—and is therefore of particular relevence. Turning now to the reconstruction process, we assume (following Wilson and Hawkes [1998]) that the transmission of

[2]More correctly we should express the irradience as $I(x, y) = \langle (U_o + U_r)^2 \rangle$, where $\langle \rangle$ denotes the average over time.

the photographic transparency is proportional to $I(x, y)$—let the constant of proportionality be denoted as T. The photographic image is illuminated by the original reference beam with complex amplitude U_r (and the transmitted light has a complex amplitude denoted $U_T(x, y)$). Thus,

$$U_T(x, y) = TU_r I(x, y).$$

Using Eq. (B.2), we may write

$$U_T(x, y) = T[U_r(U_o U_o^* + U_r U_r^*) + U_r^2 U_o^* + U_r U_r^* U_o]. \tag{B.3}$$

As indicated previously, the hologram acts as a diffraction grating. The undeviated "central beam" is described by the first term in the above expression. The middle term describes the "real" image. The right-hand term is the most important—representing the "virtual" image which appears at the same location as that occupied by the physical object during the recording process. Clearly, in the case of a computational holographic technique, we only have to compute the essential portion of this equation.

A holographic recording possesses a number of remarkable features. For example, the information scattered from a "point" on the surface of the object is distributed across a wide area of the hologram. Consequently, if a region of the holographic image is damaged (or even removed), this does not mean that a particular corresponding area of the reconstructed image will also be destroyed "... *since each small fragment of it* [the hologram] *contains information about the entire object, at least as seen from that vantage point, and can reproduce, albeit with diminishing resolution, the entire image.*" [Hecht and Zajac 1974]. For information on the creation of white light (volume) holograms, see, for example, Saleh and Teich [1991].

FURTHER READING

The short but well-informed book by Kock [1981] provides a sound nonmathematical introduction to holography. More advanced and wide-ranging discussion (including coverage of white-light and color holography) is presented in Okoshi [1976]. All of Gabor's holography related publications are well worth accessing—Gabor [1948–1972] provide an excellent starting point. Most optics texts contain useful standard discussion—for example, Hecht and Zajac [1974].

General Bibliography

Details of references specifically cited within the chapters may be found in the References section. Below are details of additional publications of relevance to readers who are seeking further background information.

CHAPTER 1

1. The following texts provide basic and interesting introductions to computer graphics (the Cooley and Egerton books being particularly welcoming to those who do not have a strong mathematical background).

Burger, P., and Gillies, D. *Interactive Computer Graphics: Functional, Procedural and Device-Level Methods*, Addison-Wesley.

Cooley, P., *The Essence of Computer Graphics*, Prentice-Hall (2001).

Egerton, P.A., and Hall, W.S., *Computer Graphics: Mathematical First Steps*, Prentice Hall (1999).

Hearn, D., and Baker, M.P., *Computer Graphics*, Prentice-Hall (1986).

Hill, F.S., *Computer Graphics*, Macmillan (1990).

Krouse, J.K., *What Every Engineer Should Know About Computer-Aided Design and Computer-Aided Manufacturing: The CAD/CAM Revolution*, Marcel Dekker (1982).

2. For those interested in historical aspects of computing, the following citations are well worth reading. (The book by Dahl is particularly recommended for a history of the CRT. So, too, is the Von Ardenne text, which provides outstanding reading in connection with basic experimental development work in Germany in the pre-WWII era.)

Dahl, P.F., *Flash of the Cathode Rays: A History of J J Thomson's Electron*, IOP Publishing Ltd. (1997).

Von Ardenne, M., *Cathode Ray Tubes*, Pitman (1939).

Williams, F.C., "Early Computers at Manchester University," *The Radio and Electronic Engineer*, **45** (7), pp. 327–331 (July 1975).

3. Aspects of human–computer interaction and user interface design are explored in the following:

Dix, A., Finlay, J., Abowd, G., and Beale, R., *Human-Computer Interaction*, 2nd edn., Prentice-Hall (1998).

Marcus, A., and van Dam, A., "User-Interface Developments for the Nineties," *Computer*, pp. 49–57 (September 1991).

Roufs, J.A.J. (ed.), *The Man-Machine Interface*, Macmillan (1991).

Shneiderman, B., *Designing the User Interface: Strategies for Effective Human-Computer Interaction*, 3rd edn., Addison-Wesley (1998).

4. For those wishing to read further in connection with approaches to the visualization of data, the following is recommended:

Spence, R., *Information Visualization*, Addison-Wesley (2001).

CHAPTER 2

Cobb, P.W., "Some Comments on the Ives Theory of Flicker," *J. Opt. Soc. Am.*, **24**, pp. 91–98 (1934).

De Lange Dzn, H., "Research into the Dynamic Nature of the Human Fovea → Cortex Systems with Intermittent and Modulated Light. I. Attenuation Characteristics with White and Colored Light," *J. Opt. Soc. Am.*, **48** (11), pp. 777–784 (1958).

De Lange Dzn, H., "Research into the Dynamic Nature of the Human Fovea → Cortex Systems with Intermittent and Modulated Light. II. Phase Shift in Brightness and Delay in Color Perception," *J. Opt. Soc. Am.*, **48** (11), pp. 785–789 (1958).

Farrell, J.E., "Fitting Physical Screen Parameters to the Human Eye," in Roufs, J.A.J. (ed.), *The Man-Machine Interface*, Vision and Visual Dysfunction **15**, pp. 7–23, Macmillan (1991).

Hartridge, H., "Chromatic Aberration and Resolving Power of the Eye," *J. Physiol.*, **52**, pp. 175–246 (1918).

Levinson, J.Z., "Flicker Fusion Phenomena," *Science*, **160** (3823), pp. 21–28 (1968).

Lowry, E.M., "The Photometric Sensibility of the Eye and the Precision of Photometric Observations," *J. Opt. Soc. Am.*, **21** (3), pp. 132–136 (1931).

Masland, R.H., "The Functional Architecture of the Retina," *Scientific American*, pp. 90–99 (December 1986).

Roufs, J.A.J., "Dynamic Properties of Vision—I. Experimental Relationships between Flicker and Flash Thresholds," *Vision Res.*, **12**, pp. 261–278 (1972).

Shimojo, S., and Nakajima, Y., "Adaptation to the Reversal of Binocular Depth Cues: Effects of Wearing Left-Right Reversing Spectacles on Stereoscopic Depth Perception," *Perception*, **10**, pp. 391–402 (1981).

Shioiri, S., and Cavanagh, P., "Achromatic Form Perception is Based on Luminance, not Brightness," *J. Opt. Soc. Am.*, **9** (10), (1992).

Stockman, A., Sharpe, L.T., Zrenner, E., and Nordby, K., "Slow and Fast Pathways in the Human Rod Visual System: Electrophysiology and Psychophysics," *J. Opt. Soc. Am.*, **8** (10), pp. 1657–1665 (1991).

CHAPTER 3

Sherrington, Sir C.S., *The Integrative Action of the Nervous System*, Yale University Press (1961).

CHAPTER 4

Banchoff, T.F., *Beyond the Third Dimension: Geometry, Computer Graphics and Higher Dimensions*, Scientific American Library (1996).

Berger, J., *Ways of Seeing*, BBC and Penguin (1977).

Gips, J., Olivieri, P., and Tecce, J., "Direct Control of the Computer through Electrodes Placed Around the Eyes," in Smith, M.J., and Salvendy, G. (eds.), *Human-Computer Interaction: Application and Case Studies*, pp. 630–635, Elsevier (1993).

Gold, M.Y., *Multidimensional Input Devices and Interaction Techniques for a Modeler-Animator*, Masters Thesis, Brown University (1990).

Henry, T.R., Yeatts, A.K., Hudson, S.E., Myers, B.A., and Feiner, S., "A Nose Gesture Interface Device: Extending Virtual Realities," *Presence*, **1**, pp. 258–261 (1992).

Hong, T.Z., Pang, X.D., and Duriach, N.I., "Manual Resolution of Length, Force, and Compliance," *Advances in Robotics*, DSC **49** ASME, New York, pp. 13–18 (1992).

King, R., *Michelangelo and the Pope's Ceiling*, Pimlico (2003).

Spalter, A.M., *The Computer in the Visual Arts*, Addison-Wesley (1999).

Stevens, J.C., and Green, B.G., "Temperature-Touch Interaction: Weber's Phenomenon Revisited," *Sensory Processes*, **2**, pp. 206–219 (1978).

Stone, R.J., "Haptic Feedback: A Potted History, From Telepresence to Virtual Reality," *Proc. First International Workshop on Haptic Human-Computer Interaction*, Glasgow, 31 August–1 September, pp. 1–7 (2000).

Tan, B.T., "Sensor Application to the Space-Suit Glove," in Webster, J. (ed.), *Tactile Sensors for Robotics and Medicine*, pp. 331–340, John Wiley (1988).

Tan, H.Z., Eberman, B., Srinivasan, R.A., and Cheng, B., "Human Factors for the Design of Force-Reflecting Haptic Interfaces," *Dynamic Systems and Control*, **1**, DSC **55–1** ASME, pp. 353–360 (1994).

CHAPTER 5

Dickinson, J., *Proprioceptive Control of Human Movement*, Lepus Books (1974).

Mackenzie, I.S., and Ware, C., "Lag as a Determinant of Human Performance in Interactive Systems," *Proc. ACM Conference on Human Factors in Computer Systems—INTERCHI '93*, pp. 488–493, NY ACM (1993).

McGuigan, F.J., *Experimental Psychology: A Methodological Approach*, 2nd edn., Prentice-Hall (1968).

CHAPTER 6

Akamatsu, M., Sato, S., and MacKenzie, I.S., "Multimodal Mouse: A MouseType Device with Tactile and Force Display," *Presence*, **3** (1), pp. 73–80 (Winter 1994).

Bach, M., Schmitt, C., Kromeler, M., and Kommerell, G., "The Freiburg Stereoacuity Test: Automatic Measurement of Stereo Threshold," *Graefe's Arch. Clin. Exp. Ophthalmol.*, **239**, pp. 562–566 (2001).

Bauer, W., and Riedel, O., "New Techniques for Interaction in Virtual Worlds—Contents of Development and Examples," in Smith, M.J., and Salvendy, O. (eds.), *Human-Computer Interaction: Software and Hardware Interfaces*, pp. 687–692, Elsevier (1993).

Clarke, J., and Vines, J., "What's All This Reality Sandwich Stuff, Anyhow?" http://www.arl.hpc.mil/outreach/eLink_Spring03/flatworld.html (accessed June 2004).

Hodges, L.F., "Tutorial: Time-Multiplexed Stereoscopic Computer Graphics," *IEEE Computer Graphics & Applications*, pp. 20–30 (March 1992).

Hodges, L.F., and McAllister, D.F., "Stereo and Alternating-Pair Techniques for Display of Computer-Generated Images," *IEEE Computer Graphics & Applications*, **5**, pp. 38–45 (September 1985).

Lam, A.K.C., Chau, A.S.Y., Lam, W.Y., Leung, G.Y.O., and Man, B.S.H., "Effect of Naturally Occurring Visual Acuity Differences between Two Eyes in Stereoacuity," *Ophthal. Physiol. Opt.*, **16** (3), pp. 189–195 (1996).

Kamm, A., and Baird, M., *John Logie Baird: A Life*, National Museums of Scotland (2002).

Okoshi, T., "Three-Dimensional Displays," *Proc. IEEE*, **68** (5), pp. 548–564 (May 1980).

Pommeray, M., Gazalet, J.G., Kastelik, J.-C., and Camus, L., "Stereo-Pair Processing in a Three-Dimensional Laser Display System," *Journal of Electronic Imaging*, **7** (3), pp. 677–683 (July 1998).

Rule, J.T., "Stereoscopic Drawings," *J. Opt. Soc. Am.*, **28** (August 1938).

Wade, N.J., "Guest Editorial," *Perception*, **31**, pp. 265–271 (2002).

Wong, B.P.H., Wong, O.D., Woods, R.L., and Peli, E., "Stereoacuity at Distance and Near," *Optometry and Vision Science*, **79** (12), pp. 771–778 (December 2002).

Zaroff, C.M., Knutelska, M., and Frumkes, T.E., "Variation in Stereoacuity: Normative Description, Fixation Disparity, and the Roles of Aging and Gender," *Investigative Ophthalmology & Vision Science*, **44** (2) (February 2003).

CHAPTER 7

Bier, E.A., "Skitters and Jacks: Interactive 3D Positioning Tools," *ACM Proc. Workshop on Interactive 3D Graphics, Oct. 1986*, pp. 183–196 (1986).

Bier, E.A., and Stone, M.C., "Snap-Dragging," *ACM Computer Graphics*, **20** (4), pp. 233–240 (1986).

Bordegoni, M., and Hemmje, M., "A Dynamic Gesture Language and Graphical Feedback for Interaction in a 3D User Interface," in Hubbold, R.J., and Juan, R. (eds.), *Computer Graphics Forum*, **12** (3), pp. C1–C11 (September 1993).

Eglowstein, H., "Reach Out and Touch Your Data," *BYTE*, pp. 283–290 (July 1990).

Rovetta, A., and Sala, R., "Robotics and Telerobotics Applied to a Prostatic Biopsy on a Human Patient," *Annual Int. Symp. on Medical Robotics and Computer Assisted Surgery*, **2**, pp. 104–110 (November 1995).

CHAPTER 8

Bryson, S., and Levit, C., "The Virtual Wind Tunnel," *IEEE Computer Graphics & Applications*, **12**, pp. 25–34 (July 1992).

Codella, C., Jalili, R., Koved, L., Lewis, J.B., Ling, D.T., Lipscomb, J.S., Rabenhorst, D.A., Wang, C.P., Norton, A., Sweeney, P., and Turk, G., "Interactive Simulation in a Multi-Person Virtual World," *CHI '92 Conf. Proc.*, pp. 329–334 (1992).

Cruz-Neira, C., Sandin, D.J., and DeFanti, T.A., "Surround-Screen Projection-Based Virtual Reality: The Design and Implementation of the CAVE," *Computer Graphics Proc., Annual Conf. Series*, pp. 135–142 (1993).

Cutchen, J.T., Harris Jr., J.O., and Laguna, G.R., "PLZT Electrooptic Shutters: Applications," *Appl. Opt.*, **14** (8), pp. 1866–1873 (August 1975).

Deering, M., "High Resolution Virtual Reality," *Computer Graphics*, **26** (2), pp. 195–202 (July 1992).

Fisher, S.S., and Tazelaar, J.M., "Living in a Virtual World," *Byte*, pp. 215–220 (July 1990).

Foley, J.D., "Interfaces for Advanced Computing," *Scientific American*, pp. 83–86 (October 1987).

Hartwig, R., "Appatus for Three Dimensional Imaging in a Cylindrical Space," German Patent DE 2622802, applied May 21, 1976.

Hartwig, R., "A Three Dimensional Computer Display," invited presentation and demonstration, TELI—European Union of Science Journalists, German Study Tour, University of Heidelberg, Germany, November 5, 1982.

Hartwig, R., and Soltan, P., "The Volumetric-3D-Display and its Applications," Presentation, Technical University, Berlin, Germany, July 12, 1996.

Hartwig, R., "Apparatus and Method for Producing Picture Element Groups in Space," German Patent DE 100 47 695, applied September 25, 2000.

Hartwig, R., "Apparatus and Method for Producing Picture Element Groups in Space," European Patent pending, EP 01 969 758, applied September 25, 2000.

Hartwig, R., "Apparatus and Method for Producing Picture Element Groups in Space," US-Patent Pending, US 10/381 538, March 21, 2003.

Hartwig, R., "A Volumetric 3D Display for Air Traffic Visualisation," AVIGEN04 Conference, Linkoping University, Sweden, September 9–10, 2004.

Hirose, M., and Hirota, K., "Surface Display and Synthetic Force Sensation," in Smith, M.J., and Salvendy, G. (eds.), *Human-Computer Interaction: Software and Hardware Interfaces*, pp. 645–650, Elsevier (1993).

Hodges, L.F., and McAllister, D.F., "Stereo and Alternating-Pair Techniques for Display of Computer-Generated Images," *IEEE CGM*, pp. 38–45 (September 1985).

Jachimowicz, K.E., and Gold, R.S., "Stereoscopic (3-D) Projection Display Using Polarized Color Multiplexing," *Optical Engineering*, **29** (8), pp. 838–842 (August 1990).

Lantz, E., "Future Directions in Visual Display Systems," *Computer Graphics*, pp. 38–45 (May 1997).

Lipton, L., "Coming Attraction: Stereo Vision on your Workstation," *Mechanical Engineering*, pp. 36–39 (March 1990).

Lipton, L., "The Future of Autostereoscopic Electronic Displays," *SPIE 1669 Stereoscopic Displays and Applications III*, pp. 156–162 (1992).

Mackinlay, J.D., Card, S.K., and Robertson, G.D., "Rapid Controlled Movement Through a Virtual 3D Workspace," *Computer Graphics*, **24** (4), (August 1990).

McCormick, M., and Davies, N., "3-D Worlds," *Physics World*, pp. 42–46 (June 1992).

Meacham, G.B.K., "Autostereoscopic Displays—Past and Future," *SPIE **624** Advances in Display Technology VI*, pp. 90–101 (1986).

Okoshi, T., "Three-Dimensional Displays," *Proc. IEEE*, **68** (5), pp. 548–564 (May 1980).

Owczarczyk, J., and Owczarczyk, B., "Evaluation of True 3D Display Systems for Visualizing Medical Volume Data," *The Visual Computer*, **6** (4), pp. 219–226 (1990).

Pausch, R., "Three Views of Virtual Reality," *Computer*, pp. 79–83 (February 1993).

Starks, M., "Stereoscopic Video and the Quest for Virtual Reality: An Annotated Bibliography of Selected Topics—Part II," *SPIE **1669** Stereoscopic Displays and Applications III*, pp. 216–227 (1992).

Wann, J.P., and Mon-Williams, M., "Health Issues with Virtual Reality Displays: What We Do Know and What We Don't," *Computer Graphics*, pp. 53–57 (May 1997).

Ware, C., and Balakrishnan, R., "Reaching for Objects in VR Displays: Lag and Frame Rate," *ACM Transactions on Computer-Human Interaction*, **1** (4), pp. 331–356 (December 1994).

1. Specifically relating to stereoscopic and multiview displays:

Azuma, R., and Bishop, G., "Improving Static and Dynamic Registration in an Optical See-through HMD," *ACM Computer Graphics*, **28**, SIGGRAPH Proc., pp. 197–204 (1994).

Burckhardt, C.B., "Optimum Parameters and Resolution Limitation of Integral Photography," *J. Opt. Soc. Am.*, **58** (1), (January 1968).

Caudell, T.P., and Mizell, D.W., "Augmented Reality: An Application of Heads-Up Display Technology in Manual Manufacturing Processes," *Proc. IEEE HICSS '92*, pp. 659–669 (1992).

Chung, J.C., Harns, M.R., Brooks, F.P., Fuchs, H., Kelley, M.T., Hughes, J., Ouh-young, M., Cheung, C., Holioway, R.L., and Pique, M., "Exploring Virtual Worlds with Head-Mounted Displays," *Proc. SPIE, **1083**, Three-Dimensional Visualization and Display Technology*, pp. 42–52 (1989).

Collender, R.B., "3-D Display System Permits Viewing without Special Glasses," *Information Display*, pp. 19–20 (March 1986).

Hodges, L.F., and McAllister, D.F., "Chromostereoscopic CRT-Based Display," *SPIE Vol 902 Three-Dimensional Imaging and Remote Sensing Imaging*, pp. 37–44 (1988).

Holliman, N., "Mapping Perceived Depth to Regions of Interest in Stereoscopic Images," *Stereoscopic Displays and Applications XV, San Jose, California* (2004).

Okoshi, T., "Optimum Design and Depth Resolution of Lens-Sheet and Projection-Type Three-Dimensional Displays," *Appl. Opt.*, **10** (10), pp. 2284–2291 (October 1971).

Pommeray, M., Gazalet, M.G., Kastelik, J.-C., and Camus, L., "Stereo-Pair Processing in a Three-Dimensional Laser Display System," *Journal of Electronic Imaging*, **7** (3), pp. 677–683 (1998).

Starks, M., "Stereoscopic Video and the Quest for Virtual Reality," *SPIE, **1669**, Stereoscopic Displays and Applications III*, pp. 216–227 (1992).

Travis, A.R.L., "The Display of Three-Dimensional Video Images," *Proc. IEEE*, **85** (11), (November 1997).

Travis, A.R.L., and Lang, S.R., "A CRT Based Autostereoscopic Display," *Eurodisplay '90* (September 25–27, 1990).

Vince, J., "Virtual Reality Techniques in Flight Simulation," *Proc. Virtual Reality Systems, BCS, London* (May 1992).

2. Specifically relating to holography

Andrews, J.R., Haas, W.E., and Rainsdon, M.D., "Holographic Displays for the Man-Machine Interface," *Optical Engineering*, **28** (6), pp. 643–649 (June 1989).

Andrews, J.R., Tuttle, B., Rainsdon, M., Damm, R., Thomas, K., and Haas, W.E., "Holographic Stereograms Generated with a Liquid Crystal Spatial Light Modulator," *SPIE 902 Three-Dimensional Imaging and Remote Sensing Imaging*, pp. 92–94 (1988).

Bartelt, H., and Streibl, N., "Three Dimensional Display Based on Thick Holographic Phase Components," *Optical Engineering*, **24** (6), pp. 1038–1041 (November/December 1985).

Benton, S.A., "Holographic Displays—A Review," *Optical Engineering*, **14** (5), pp. 402–407 (September/October 1975).

Benton, S.A., "Holographic Displays: 1975–1980," *Optical Engineering*, **19** (5), pp. 686–695 (September/October 1980).

Benton, S.A., "Holographic Imaging Research at the M.I.T. Media Lab," *IEE 3rd Int. Conf. on Holographic Systems, Components & Applications, Conference Publication 342, 16–18 September* (1991).

Cameron, C.D., Pain, D.A., Stanley, M., and Slinger, C.W., "Computational Challenges of Emerging Novel True 3D Holographic Displays," *Proc. SPIE 4109 (Critical Technologies for the Future of computing)*, pp. 129–140 (2001).

Denisyuk, Y.N., "Three-Dimensional and Pseudodeep Holograms," *Opt. Soc. Am. A.*, **9** (7), pp. 1141–1147 (July 1992).

Enloe, L.H., Murphy, J.A., and Rubinstein, C.B., "Hologram Transmission via Television," *The Bell System Technical Journal*, **45** (2), pp. 335–339 (February 1966).

Glaser, I., and Frisem, A.A., "Imaging Properties of Holographic Stereograms," *SPIE 120 Three-Dimensional Imaging*, pp. 150–162 (1977).

Halle, M.W., "The Ultragram: A Generalized Holographic Stereogram," *SPIE 1461 Practical Holography V*, pp. 142–155 (1991).

Hart, S.J., and Dalton, M.N., "Display Holography for Medical Tomography," *SPIE 1212 Practical Holography IV*, pp. 116–135 (1990).

Jeong, T.H., "Cylindrical Holography and Some Proposed Applications," *J. Opt. Soc. Am.*, **57**, pp. 1396–1398 (November 1967).

Jeong, T.H., Rudolf, P., and Luckett, A., "360° Holography," *J. Opt. Soc. Am.*, **56**, pp. 1263–1263 (September 1966).

King, M.C., Noll, A.M., and Berry, D.H., "A New Approach to Computer-Generated Holography," *Appl. Opt.*, **9** (2), pp. 471–475 (February 1970).

Kuo, C.J., and Tsai, M.H., *Three-Dimensional Holographic Imaging*, John Wiley (2002).

Leith, E.N., "Coherence Relaxation Methods for Holography," *SPIE 120 Three-Dimensional Imaging*, pp. 145–149 (1977).

Leith, E.N., "White-Light Holograms," *Scientific American*, **235**, pp. 80–95 (October 1976).

Lin, L.H., and LoBianco, C.V., "Experimental Techniques in Making Multicolor White Light Reconstructed Holograms," *Appl. Opt.*, **6** (7), pp. 1255–1259 (July 1967).

Lunazzi, J.J., "Holophotography with a Diffraction Grating," *Optical Engineering*, **29** (1), pp. 15–18 (January 1990).

McDonnell, M.M., "Holographic Terrain Displays," *SPIE 120 Three-Dimensional Imaging*, pp. 163–173 (1977).

Okoshi, T., "Projection-Type Holographic Displays," *SPIE 120 Three-Dimensional Imaging*, pp. 102–108 (1977).

Onurai, L., Bozdaği, G., and Atalar, A., "A New Approach to Holographic Video Imaging: Principles and Simulations," *SPIE 1667 Practical Holography VI*, pp. 63–72 (1992).

Onurai, L., Bozdaği, G., and Atalar, A., "New High-Resolution Display Device for Holographic Three-Dimensional Video: Principles and Simulations," *Optical Engineering*, **33** (3), pp. 835–844 (March 1994).

Pappu, R., Kropp, A., Sparrell, C., Underkoffler, J., Chen, B., and Plesniak, W., "A Generalized Pipeline for Preview and Rendering of Synthetic Holograms," in Benton, S.A. (ed.), *Proceedings of the IS&T/SPIE's Symposium on Electronic Imaging, Practical Holography XI* (1997).

Pole, R.V., "3-D Imagery and Holograms of Objects Illuminated in White Light," *Appl. Phys. Letts.*, **10** (1), pp. 20–23 (January 1967).

Stanley, M., Bannister, R.W., Cameron, C.D., Coomber, S.D., Cresswell, I.G., Hughes, J.R., Hui, V., Jackson, P.O., Milham, K.A., Miller, R.J., Payne, D.A., Quarrel, J., Scattergood, D.C., Smith, A.P., Smith, M.A.G., Tipton, D.L., Watson, P.J., Webber, P.J., and Slinger, C.W., "100 Mega-Pixel Computer Generated Holographic Images from Active Tiling™—a Dynamic and Scalable Electro-Optic Modulator System," in *Practical Holography XVII and Holographic Materials IX*, Jeong, T.H. (ed.), Proc. SPIE-IS&T Electronic Imaging, SPIE **5005**, pp. 247–258 (2003).

Trayner, D., and Orr, E., "Autostereoscopic Display using Holographic Optical Elements," *Proc. SPIE*, **2653**, pp. 65–74 (1996).

Tsunoda, Y., and Takeda, Y., "Three-Dimensional Color Display by Projection-Type Composite Holography," *IEEE Transactions on Electron Devices*, **ED-22** (9), pp. 784–789 (1975).

Upatnieks, J., and Embach, J.T., "360-Degree Holograph Displays," *Optical Engineering*, **19** (5), pp. 696–704 (September/October 1980).

CHAPTER 9

Buxton, W., "Touch, Gesture and Marking," in Baecker, R.M., Grudin, J., Buxton, W., and Greenberg, S., (eds.), *Readings in Human Computer Interaction: Toward the Year 2000*, Ch.7, Morgan Kaufman (1995).

Galyean, T.A., and Hughes, J.F., "Sculpting: An Interactive Volumetric Modeling Techniques," *Computer Graphics*, **25** (4), pp. 267–274 (July 1991).

Guiard, Y., "Failure to Sing the Left-Hand Part of the Score during Piano Performance: Loss of the Pitch and Stroop Vocalizations," *Music Perception*, **6** (3), pp. 299–314 (Spring 1989).

Hinckley, K., Pausch, R., Goble, J.C., and Kassell, N.F., "A Survey of Design Issues in Spatial Input," *UIST '94*, Marina del Rey, CA, 2–4 November, pp. 213–222 (1994).

Kitamura, Y., Konishi, T., Yamamoto, S., and Kishino, F., "Interactive Stereoscopic Display for Three or More Users," *ACM SIGGRAPH 2001*, Los Angeles, CA, 12–17 August, pp. 231–239 (2001).

Tan, H.Z., Durlach, N.I., Shao, Y., and Wei, M., "Manual Resolution of Compliance when Work and Force Cues are Minimized," DSC-Vol. **49**, *Advances in Robotics, Mechatronics, and Haptic Interfaces*, ASME 1993, pp. 99–104 (1993).

References

Abbott, E.A., *Flatland: A Romance of Many Dimensions*, Seeley (1884).

Abramson, A., *The History of Television, 1880 to 1941*, McFarland and Co. (1987).

Adachi, Y., Kumano, T., and Ogino, K., "Intermediate Representation for Stiff Virtual Objects," *Proc. IEEE Virtual Reality Annual International Symposium*, pp. 203–210 (1995).

Adams, R.A., *Calculus: A Complete Course*, Addison-Wesley (1991).

Adams, R.J., Moreyra, M.R., and Hannaford, B., "Stability and Performance of Haptic Displays: Theory and Experiments," *Proc. ASME International Mechanical Engineering Congress and Exhibition, (Anaheim, CA)*, pp. 227–234 (1998).

Adelson, S.J., and Hodges, L.F., "Stereoscopic Ray-Tracing," *The Visual Computer*, **10** (3), pp. 127–144 (1993).

Anon, *Encyclopaedia Britannica*, 9th edn, Vol. IV, Adam and Charles Black, Edinburgh (1876).

Anon, "Stereoscopic Colour Television," *Wireless World* (February 1942).

Arsenault, R., and Ware, C., "Eye-Hand Co-ordination with Force Feedback," *CHI Lett.*, **2** (1), pp. 408–414 (2000).

Asamura, N., Yokoyama, N., and Shinoda, H., "Selectively Stimulating Skin Receptors for Tactile Display," *IEEE Computer Graphics and Applications*, **18** (6), pp. 32–37 (1998).

Ashdown, M., and Robinson, P., "A Personal Projected Display," *ACM Multimedia '04, October 10–16 2004, New York, NY* (2004).

Avila, R.S., and Sobierajski, L.M., "A Haptic Interaction Method for Volume Visualisation," *Proc. IEEE Visualization '96*, pp. 197–204 (1996a).

Avila, R.S., and Sobierajski, L.M., "Haptic Interaction Utilizing a Volumetric Representation," *Proc. First PHANToM User's Group Workshop (Sept. 27–30)* (1996b).

Bahr, D., Langhans, K., Gerken, M., Vogt, C., Bezecny, D., and Homann, D., "Felix—A Volumetric 3DLaser Display," *Projection Displays II: SPIE Proceedings*, **2650**, pp. 265–273 (1996).

Bajura, M., Fuchs, H., and Ohbuchi, R., "Merging Virtual Objects with the Real World," *Computer Graphics* **26** (2), pp. 203–210 (July 1992).

Balakrishnan, R., and Hinckley, K., "Symmetric Bimanual Interaction," *CHI Lett.*, **2** (1), pp. 33–40 (2000).

Balakrishnan, R., Ware, C., and Smith, T., "Virtual Hand Tool with Force Feedback," *Proc. ACM Conference on Human Factors in Computing Systems (CHI'94)*, pp. 83–84 (1994).

Barbagli, F., Prattichizzo, D., and Salisbury, K., "Dynamic Local Models for Stable Multi-Contact Haptic Interaction with Deformable Objects," *Proc. Symposium on Haptic Interfaces for Virtual Environment and Teleoperator Systems*, pp. 109–116 (2003).

Basdogan, C., and Srinivasan, M.A., "Haptic Rendering in Virtual Environments," in Stanney, K.M. (ed.), *"Handbook of Virtual Environments: Design, Implementation, and Applications (Human Factors and Ergonomics),"* pp. 117–134, Lawrence Erlbaum Associates (2002).

Basdogan, C., Lum, M., Sacedo, J., Chow, E., Kupiec, S.A., and Kostrewski, A., "Autostereoscopic and Haptic Visualization for Space Exploration and Mission Design," *Proc. 10th Symposium on Haptic Interfaces for Virtual Environment and Teleoperator Systems (March 24–25, Orlando, FL)*, pp. 271–276 (2002).

Beatty, S., Good, P.A., McLaughlin, J., and O'Neill, E.C., "Echographic Measurements of the Retrobulbar Optic Nerve in Normal and Glaucomatous eyes," *Brit. J. Ophthalmol.*, **82**, pp. 43–47 (1998).

Benton, S.A., "Experiments in Holographic Video Imaging," *SPIE Institute Series* **IS8**, pp. 247–267 (1991).

Berkley, C., "Three-Dimensional Representation on Cathode-Ray Tubes," *Proc. IRE—Waves and Electrons Section*, pp. 1530–1535 (December 1948).

Berlin, E.P., Three-Dimensional Display, U.S. Patent 4,160,973 (1979).

Bibermanm, L.M. (ed.), *"Perception of Displayed Information,"* Plenum Press, New York (1973).

Bier, E.A., Stone, M., Pier, K., Buxton, W., and DeRose, T., "Toolglass and Magic Lenses: The See-Through Interface," *Proc. SIGGRAPH '93*, pp. 73–80 (1993).

Birmanns, S., and Wriggers, W., "Interactive Fitting Augmented by Force-Feedback and Virtual Reality," *Journal of Structural Biology*, **144**, pp. 123–131 (2003).

Bishop, P.O., "Vertical Disparity, Egocentric Distance and Stereoscopic Depth Constancy: A New Interpretation," *Proceedings R. Soc. London Ser. B*, **237**, pp. 445–469 (1989).

Blake, D.T., Hsaio, S.S., and Johnson, K.O., "Neural Coding Mechanisms in Tactile Pattern Recognition: The Relative Contributions of Slowly and Rapidly Adapting Mechanoreceptors to Perceived Roughness," *Journal of Neuroscience*, **17** (19), pp. 7480–7489 (1997).

Blundell B.G., *"Computer Interaction in a 3-D Space: The Volumetric Approach"* John Wiley (2006).

Blundell, B.G., and King, W., "Outline of a Low-Cost Prototype System to Display Three-Dimensional Images," *IEEE Transactions on Instrumentation and Measurement*, **40** (4), pp. 792–793 (1991).

Blundell, B.G., and Schwarz, A.J., "A Graphics Hierarchy for the Visualisation of 3D Images by means of a Volumetric Display System," *Proc. IEEE Tencon '94*, pp. 1–5 (1994).

Blundell, B.G., and Schwarz, A.J., "Volumetric Three-Dimensional Displays," *McGraw-Hill Yearbook of Science and Technology*, pp. 95–97 (1995a).

Blundell, B.G., and Schwarz, A.J., "Visualisation of Complex System Dynamics on a Volumetric 3D Display Device," *Proceedings "Visualisierung—Dynamik und Komplexität,"* Bremen 24–26 September (1995b).

Blundell, B.G., and Schwarz, A.J., "*Volumetric Three-Dimensional Display Systems,*" Wiley Interscience (2000).

Blundell, B.G., Schwarz, A.J., and Horrell, D.K., "The Cathode Ray Sphere: A Prototype Volumetric Display System," *Proceedings Eurodisplay '93 (Late News Papers),* pp. 593–596 (1993).

Blundell, B.G., Schwarz, A.J., and Horrell, D.K., "The Cathode Ray Sphere: A Prototype System to Display Volumetric Three-Dimensional Images," *Optical Engineering,* **33** (1) pp. 180–186 (1994).

Boff, K.R., Kaufman, L., and Thomas, J.P., (eds.), *Handbook of Perception and Human Performance, Volume I, Sensory Processes and Perception,* John Wiley (1986).

Boring, E.G., Langfeld, H.S., and Weld, H.P., *Psychology: A Factual Textbook,* John Wiley (1935).

Born, M., and Wolf, E., *Principles of Optics,* Pergamon Press (1959).

Borro, D., Garcia-Alonso, A., and Matey, L., "Approximation of Optimal Voxel Size for Collision Detection in Maintainability Simulations within Massive Virtual Environments," *Computer Graphics Forum,* **23** (1), pp. 13–23 (2004).

Bostrom, M., Singh, S., and Wiley, C., "Design of an Interactive Lumbar Simulator with Tactile Feedback," *Proc. IEEE Virtual Reality Annual international Symposium (VRAIS),* pp. 280–286 (1993).

Bouzit, M., Burdea, G., Popescu, G., and Boian, R., "The Rutgers Master II-New Design Force Feedback Glove," *IEEE/ASME Transactions on Mechatronics,* **7** (2), pp. 256–263 (2002).

Boyer, C.B. (Revised by Merzbach U.C.), *A History of Mathematics,* 2nd edn., John Wiley (1991).

Brenner, E., Smeets, J.B.J., and Landy, M.S., "How Vertical Disparities Assist Judgements of Distance," *Vision Research,* **41**, pp. 3455–3465 (2001).

Brooks, F.P., Ouh-Young, M., Batter, J.J., and Kilpatrick, P.J., "Project GROPE: Haptic Displays for Scientific Visualization," *Computer Graphics,* **24** (4), pp. 177–185 (August 1990).

Bruce, V., Green P.R., and Georgeson M.A., *Visual Perception: Physiology, Psychology and Ecology,* 4th edn., Psychology Press (2003).

Bryson, S., "Virtual Reality in Scientific Visualization," *Communications of the ACM,* **39** (5), (May 1996).

Bumsted, K., and Hendrickson, A., "Distribution and Development of Short-Wavelength Cones Differ Between Macaca Monkey and Human Fovea," *J. Comp. Neurol.,* **403**, pp. 502–516 (1999).

Burckhardt, C.B., "Information Reduction in Holograms for Visual Display," *J. Opt. Soc. Am.,* **58** (2), pp. 241–246 (1968).

Burdea, G.C., *Force and Touch Feedback for Virtual Reality,* John Wiley (1996).

Burdea, G.C., and Coiffet, P., *Virtual Reality Technology,* 2nd edn., John Wiley (2003).

Burgess, P.R., and Clark, F.J., "Characteristics of Knee Joint Receptors in the Cat," *Journal of Physiology,* **203**, pp. 317–335 (1969).

Burke, R.B., *Opus Majus of Roger Bacon*, Vol. 1, Philadelphia (1928).

Burton, H.E., "The Optics of Euclid," *J. Opt. Soc. Am.*, **35** (5), pp. 357–372 (1945).

Buxton, B., and Fitzmaurice, G.W., "HMD's, Caves & Chameleon: A Human-Centric Analysis of Interaction in Virtual Space," *Computer Graphics*, pp. 69–76 (November 1998).

Caldwell, G.D., and Hathorn, G.M., *Viewing Instrument for Stereoscopic Pictures and the Like*, U.S. Patent 2,273,512 (1942).

Cameron, J.R., Skofronick, J.G., and Grant, R.M., *Physics of the Body*, 2nd edn., Medical Physics Publishing (1999).

Canny, J., "A Computational Approach to Edge Detection," *IEEE Transactions on Pattern Analysis and Machine Intelligence*, **8**, pp. 679–698 (1986).

Card, S.K., and Moran, T.P., *User Technology: From Pointing to Pondering*, ACM (1986).

Card, S.K., English, W.K., and Burr, B.J., "Evaluation of Mouse, Rate-Controlled Isometric Joystick, Step Keys and Text Keys for Text Selection on a CRT," *Ergonomics*, **21** (8), pp. 601–613 (1978).

Card, S.K, Moran, T.P., and Newell, A., *The Psychology of Human Computer Interaction*, Lawrence Erlbaum Associates (1983).

Carpenter, R.H.S. (ed.), "Eye Movements," in *Vision and Visual Disfunction*, Vol. 8, Macmillan (1991).

Champion, H.R., and Gallagher, A.G., "Surgical Simulation—A Good Idea Whose Time Has Come," *British Journal of Surgery*, **90**, pp. 767–768 (2003).

Chapanis, A., Garner, W.R., and Morgan, C.T., *Applied Experimental Psychology*, John Wiley (1949).

Charman, W.N., and Chateau, N., "The Prospects for Super-Acuity: Limits to Visual Performance After Correction of Monochromatic Ocular Aberration," *Ophth. Physiol. Opt.*, **23**, pp. 479–493 (2003).

Chen, H., and Sun, H., "Real-Time Haptic Sculpting in Virtual Volume Space," *Proc. ACM Symposium on Virtual Reality Software and Technology (VRST'02)* (2002).

Chen, K.W., Heng, P.A., and Sun, H., "Direct Haptic Rendering of Isosurface by Intermediate Representation," *Proc. ACM Symposium on Virtual Reality Software and Technology (VRST'00)* (2000a).

Chen, M., Kaufman, A., and Yagel, R. (eds.), *Volume Graphics*, Springer-Verlag (2000b).

Chen, T., Anderson, D., and Nagata, S., "On Integrating Multi-Sensory Components in Virtual Environments," *Proc. Fourth International Conference on Virtual Systems and Multimedia (Gifu, Japan, Nov 18–20)* (1998).

Chu, W-S., Napoli, J., Cossairt, O.S., Dorval, R.K., Hall, D.M., Purtell II, T.J., Schooler, J.F., Banker, Y., and Favalora, G.E., "Spatial 3D Infrastructure: Display-Independent Software Framework, High-Speed Rendering Electronics, and Several New Displays," *Proc. SPIE (Stereoscopic Displays and Virtual Reality Systems XII)*, 5664, pp. 302–312 (2005).

Churchland, P.S., "*Neurophilosophy: Toward a Unified Science of the Mind-Brain*," Massachusetts Institute of Technology (1986).

Clark, J.H., "Designing Surfaces in 3-D," *Communications of the ACM*, **19** (8), pp. 454–460 (1976).

Clement, R.A., *Introduction to Vision Science*, Lawrence Erlbaum Associates Ltd. (1993).

Clifton, T.E., and Wefer, F.L., "Direct Volume Display Devices," *IEEE Computer Graphics and Applications*, **13** (4), pp. 57–65 (1993).

Cobb, S.V.G., Nichols, S., Ramsey, A., and Wilson, J.R., "Virtual Reality-Induced Symptoms and Effects (VRISE)," *Presence*, **8** (2), pp. 169–186 (1999).

Cohen, J.D., Lin, M.C., Manocha, D., and Ponamgi, M., "I-COLLIDE: An Interactive and Exact Collision Detection System for Large Scale Environments," *Proc. 1995 Symposium on Interactive 3-D Graphics (Monterrey, CA)*, pp. 291–302 (1995).

Cohn, M.B., Lam, M., and Fearing, R.S., "Tactile Feedback for Teleoperation," *Proc. SPIE (Conference on Telemanipulator Technology)*, **1833**, pp. 240–254 (1993).

Coleridge, S.T., *Biographia Literaria: Biographical Sketches of my Literary Life and Opinions*, Princeton University Press (1985).

Colgate, J.E., and Brown, J.M., "Factors Affecting the Z-Width of a Haptic Display," *Proc. IEEE International Conference on Robotics and Automation (San Diego, CA)*, pp. 3205–3210 (1994).

Colgate, J.E., Grafing, P., Stanley, M., and Schenkel, G., "Implementation of Stiff Virtual Walls in Force-Reflecting Interfaces," *Proc. IEEE Virtual Reality Annual Symposium (VRAIS'93)*, pp. 202–208 (1993).

Collender, R.B., "The Stereoptiplexer: Competition for the Hologram," *Information Display*, **4** (6), pp. 27–31 (1967).

Coren, S., Ward, L.M., and Enns, J.T., "*Sensation and Perception*," 4th edn., Harcourt Brace & Company (1994).

Cosman, P.H., Cregan, P.C., Martin, C.J., and Cartmill, J.A., "Virtual Reality Simulators: Current Status in Acquisition and Assessment of Surgical Skills," *Australian and New Zealand Journal of Surgery*, **72**, pp. 30–34 (2002).

Costello, P.J., "Health and Safety Issues Associated with Virtual Reality—A Review of Current Literature," *JISC Advisory Group on Computer Graphics, Technical Report* (1997).

Cronly-Dillon, J.R., and Gregory, R.L., (eds.), "Evolution of the Eye and Visual System," in *Vision and Visual Disfunction*, Vol. 2, Macmillan (1991).

Crossman, E.R.F.W., and Goodeve, P.J., "Feedback Control of Hand Movement and Fitts' Law," reprinted in *Quarterly Journal of Experimental Psychology*, **35A**, pp. 251–278 (Originally presented as a paper at the meeting of the Experimental Psychology Society, Oxford, England) (July 1963).

Cruz-Neira, C., Sandin, D.J., and DeFanti, T.A., "Virtual Reality: The Design and Implementation of the CAVE," *Proc. SIGGRAPH 93 Computer Graphics Conference, ACM SIGGRAPH*, pp. 135–142 (1993).

Cruz-Neira, C., Sandin, D.J., DeFanti, T.J., Kenyon, R.V., and Hart, J.C., "The Cave: Audio Visual Experience Automatic Virtual Environment," *Communications of the ACM*, **35** (6), pp. 65–72 (1992).

Cruz-Neira, C., Sandin, D.J., DeFanti, T.A., Kenyon, R.V., and Hart, J.C., "The CAVE: audio Visual Experience Automatic Virtual Environment," *Communications of the ACM*, **35** (6) (June 1992).

Cutler, L.D., Froehlich, B., and Hanrahan, P., "Two-Handed Direct Manipulation on the Responsive Workbench," *1997 Symp. on Interactive 3D Graphics, Providence RI, USA*, ACM, pp. 107–114 (1997).

Cutting, J.E., "How the Eye Measures Reality and Virtual Reality," *Behav. Res. Meth. Instr.*, **29** (1), pp. 27–36 (1997).

Czernuszenko, D.P., Sandin, D., DeFanti, T., Dawe, G.L., and Brown, M.D., "The Immer-saDesk and Infinity Wall Projection-Based Virtual Reality Displays," *Computer Graphics*, pp. 46–49 (May 1997).

Da Vinci, L., and Richter, I.A. (eds.), *The Notebooks of Leonardo da Vinci*, Oxford University Press (1952).

Darwin, C., *Origin of the Species*, Gramercy Books (1998).

Davies, A.G.J., *Solid Geometry in 3-D*, Chatto and Windus (1967).

Davis, D.B., "Reality Check," *Computer Graphics World*, pp. 49–52 (June 1991).

Davis, M.R., and Ellis, T.O., "The Rand Tablet: A Man Machine Graphical Communication Device," *Fall Joint Computer Conference, AFIPS Conference Proceedings*, Vol. 26 (1964).

Dayal, R., Faries, P.L., Lin, S.C., Bernheim, J., Hollenbeck, S., DeRubertis, B., Trocciola, S., Rhee, J., McKinsey, J., Morrissey, N.J., and Kent, K.C., "Computer Simulation as a Component of Catheter-Based Training," *Journal of Vascular Surgery*, **40** (6), pp. 1112–1117 (2004).

De Boeck, J., Raymaekers, C., and Coninx, K., "Aspects of Haptic Feedback in a Multi-Modal Interface for Object Modelling," *Virtual Reality*, **6**, pp. 257–270 (2003).

De Jong, J.R., "The Effects of Increasing Skill on Cycle Time and its Consequences for Time Standards," *Ergonomics*, **1**, pp. 51–60 (1957).

DeAngelis, G.C., "Seeing in Three Dimensions: the Neurobiology of Stereopsis," *Trends Cogn. Sci.*, **4** (3), pp. 80–90 (2000).

DeAngelis, G.C., Cumming, B.G., and Newsome, W.T., "Cortical Area MT and the Percep-tion of Stereoscopic Depth," *Nature*, **394**, pp. 677–680 (1998).

Deisinger, J., Blach, R., Wesche, G., Breining, R., and Simon, A., "Towards Immersive Modelling—Challenges and Recommendations: A Workshop Analyzing the Needs of Designers," *Eurographics Workshop on Virtual Environments 2000*, pp. 145–156 (2000).

Dember, W.N., *The Psychology of Perception*, Holt, Rinehart and Winston (1960).

Demel, J.T., and Miller, M.J., *Introduction to Computer Graphics*, Wadsworth (Brooks/Cole Engineering Division) (1984).

Diedrichsen, J., Namibsan, R., Kennerley, S.W., and Ivry, R.B., "Independent On-Line Control of the Two Hands During Bimanual Reaching," *European Journal of Neuroscience*, **19**, pp. 1643–1652 (2004).

DiMaio, S.P., and Salcudean, S.E., "Needle Insertion Modelling and Simulation," *IEEE Transactions on Robotics and Automation*, **19** (5), pp. 864–875 (2003).

Dimas, E., and Briassoulis, D., "3D Geometric Modelling Based on NURBS: A Reeview," *Advances in Engineering Software*, **30** (9–11), pp. 741–751 (1999).

Dodgson, N.A., Moore, J.R., and Lang, S.R., "Multi-View Autostereoscopic 3D Display," *Proc. International Broadcasting Convention* (September 10–14, Amsterdam), pp. 497–502 (1999).

Dodgson, N., "Variation and Extrema of Human Interpupillary Distance," *Proc. SPIE (Stereoscopic Displays and VR Systems XI)*, **5291-A**, pp. 36–46 (2004).

Doerrer, C., and Wertschuetzky, R., "Simulating Push-Buttons using a Haptic Display: Requirements on Force Resolution and Force-Displacement Curve," *Proc. Eurohaptics* (2002).

Downing, E., Hesselink, L., Ralston, J., and Macfarlane, R., "A Three-Color, Solid-State Three-Dimensional Display," *Science*, **273**, pp. 1185–1189 (1996).

Drascic, D., and Milgram, P., "Perceptual Issues in Augmented Reality," *Proc. SPIE (Stereoscopic Displays and Virtual Reality Systems III, San Jose, California)*, **2653**, pp. 123–134 (1996).

Ebert, D., Bedwell, E., Maher, S., Smoliar, L., and Downing, E., "Realizing 3D Visualization using Crossed-Beam Volumetric Displays," *Communications of the ACM*, **42** (8), pp. 101–107 (1999).

Eco, U., *Foucault's Pendulum*, Vintage (2001).

Edgerton, S.Y., *The Renaissance Rediscovery Of Linear Perspective*, Harper and Row (1976).

Edgerton, S.Y., *The Heritage Of Giotto's Geometry—Art And Science On The Eve Of The Scientific Revolution*, Cornell University Press (1991).

Eichenlaub, J., "The Parallax Illumination Autostereoscopic Method," in McAllister, D.F. (ed.), *Stereo Computer Graphics and Other True 3D Technologies*, pp. 166–182, Princeton University Press (1993).

Ellis, S., "Nature and Origins of Virtual Environments: A Bibliographical Essay," *Computing Systems in Engineering*, **2** (4), pp. 321–347 (1991).

Ellis, S. (ed.), *Pictorial Communication in Virtual and Real Environments*, 2nd edn., Taylor & Francis Ltd. (1993).

English, W.K., Engelbart, D.C., and Berman, M.L., "Display-Selection Techniques for Text Manipulation," *IEEE Transactions on Human Factors in Electronics*, **HFE-8** (1), (March 1967).

Enoch, J.M., and Lakshminarayanan, V., "Duplication of Unique Optical Effects of Ancient Egyptian Lenses from the IV/V Dynasties: Lenses Fabricated ca 2620–2400 BC or Roughly 4600 Years Ago," *Ophthal. Physiol. Opt.*, **20** (2), pp. 126–130 (2000).

Epps, B.W., "Comparison of Six Cursor Control Devices Based on Fitts' Law Models," *Proc. 30th Annual Meeting of the Human Factors Society, Santa Monica, CA: Human Factors Society*, pp. 327–331 (1986).

Favalora, G.E., Dorval, R.K., Hall, D.M., Giovinco, M., and Napoli, J., "Volumetric three-dimensional display system with rasterization hardware," in Woods, A.J., Bolas, M.T., Merritt, J.O., and Benton, S.A., *Proc. SPIE Vol 4297 Stereoscopic Display and Virtual Reality System VII*, p.227 (2001).

Favalora, G.E., Napoli, J., Hall, D.M., Dorval, R.K., Giovinco, M.G., Richmond, M.J., and Chun, W.S., "100 Million Voxels Volumetric Display," *Proc. SPIE* **4712** *(Cockpit Displays IX: Displays for Defense Applications)*, pp. 300–312 (2002).

Faw, B., "Pre-frontal Executive Committee for Perception, Working Memory, Attention, Long-term Memory, Motor Control, and Thinking: A Tutorial Review," *Conscious and Cognition*, **12** (1), pp. 83–139 (2003).

Feggin, D., Keehner, M., and Tendick, F., "Haptic Guidance: Experimental Evaluation of a Haptic Training Method for a Perceptual Motor Skill," *Proc. 10th Symposium on Haptic Interfaces for Virtual Environments and Teleoperator Systems*, pp. 40–50 (2002).

Fernandes, K.J., Raja, V., and Eyre, J., "Cybersphere: The Fully Immersive Spherical Projection System," *Communications of the ACM*, **46** (9ve), pp. 141–146 (September 2003).

Feynman, R.P., Leighton, R.B., and Sands, M., *The Feynman Lectures on Physics: Mainly Mechanics, Radiation, and Heat*, Addison-Wesley (1963).

Fitts, P.M., "The Information Capacity of the Human Motor System in Controlling the Amplitude of Movement," *Journal of Experimental Psychology*, **47** (6), (June 1954).

Fitts, P.M., "Information Capacity of Discrete Motor Responses," *Journal of Experimental Psychology*, **67** (2), (February 1964).

Fitts, P.M., and Radford, B.K., "Information Capacity of Discrete Motor Responses Under Different Cognitive Sets," *Journal of Experimental Psychology*, **71** (4), (April 1966).

Flanagan, D., *Java Foundation Classes in a Nutshell*, O'Reilly (1999).

Foley, J., van Dam, A., Feiner, S., and Hughes, J., *Computer Graphics*, 2nd edn., Addison-Wesley (1995).

Foley, J.D., van Dam, A., Feiner, S.K., Hughes, J.F., and Phillips, R.L., *Introduction to Computer Graphics*, Addison-Wesley (1994).

Foley, J.D., van Dam, A., Feiner, S.K., Hughes, J.F., and Phillips, R.L., *Introduction to Computer Graphics*, Addison-Wesley (1997).

Foskey, M., Otaduy, M.A., and Lin, M.C., "ArtNova: Touch-Enabled 3D Model Design," *Proc. IEEE Virtual Reality Conference 2002*, pp. 119–126 (2002).

Freund, H.J., "Somatosensory and Motor Disturbances in Patients with Parietal Lobe Lesions," *Advances in Neurology*, **93**, pp. 179–193 (2003).

Frisken-Gibson, S.F., "Using Linked Volumes to Model Object Collisions, Deformation, Cutting, Carving, and Joining," *IEEE Transactions on Visualization and Computer Graphics*, **5** (4), pp. 333–348 (1999).

Fröhlich, B., and Plate, J., "The Cubic Mouse: A New Device for Three-Dimensional Input," *CHI Lett.*, **2** (1), pp. 526–531 (April 2000).

Fuchs, H., Pizer, S.M., Tsai, L.C., Bloomberg, S.H., and Heinz, E.R., "Adding a True 3-D Display to a Raster Graphics System," *IEEE Computer Graphics and Applications*, **2** (5), pp. 73–78 (1982).

Furness III, T.A., "Harnessing Virtual Space," *SID '88 International Symp. Digest of Technical Papers*, pp. 4–7, SID (1988).

Gabor, D., "A New Microscopic Principle," *Nature*, **161**, pp. 777–778 (May 1948).

Gabor, D., "Holography, 1948–1971," *Proc. IEEE*, **60** (6) (June 1972).

Geldard, F.A., *Fundamentals of Psychology*, John Wiley (1962).

Gibson, J.J., *The Perception of the Visual World*, Houghton Mifflin (1950).

Gibson, J.J., "Observations on Active Touch," *Psychological Review*, **69** (6), pp. 477–491 (November 1962).

Gibson, S., "3D ChainMail: A Fast Algorithm for Deforming Volumetric Objects," *Proc. 1997 Symposium on Interactive 3D Graphics*, pp. 149–154 (1997a).

Gibson, S., "Linked Volumetric Objects for Physics-Based Modelling," *Mitsubishi Electric Research Laboratories (MERL), Technical Report TR97–20* (1997b).

Gibson, S., Fyock, C., Grimson, E., Kanade, T., Kikinis, R., Lauer, H., McKenzie, N., Mor, A., Nakajima, S., Ohkammi, H., Osborne, R., Samosky, J., and Sawada, A., "Volumetric

Object Modelling for Surgical Simulation," *Medical Image Analysis*, **2** (2), pp. 121–132 (1998).

Gildenberg, P., and Tasker, R., *Textbook of Stereotactic and Functional Neurosurgery*, McGraw-Hill (1998).

Gillespie, B., and Rosenberg, L.B., "Design of High-Fidelity Haptic Display for One-Dimensional Force Reflection Applications," *Proc. SPIE East Coast Conference on Telemanipulators and Telepresence (Boston)*, pp. 44–54 (1994).

Gilson, M.K., "Theory of Electrostatic Interactions in Macromolecules," *Current Opinion in Structural Biology*, **5** (2), pp. 216–223 (1995).

Gilson, M.K., Given, J.A., Bush, B.L., and McCammon, J.A., "The Statistical-Thermodynamic Basis for Computation of Binding Affinities: A Critical Review," *Biophysical Journal*, **72** (3), pp. 1047–1069 (1997).

Girling, A.N., *Stereoscopic Drawing: A Theory of 3-D Vision and its Application to Stereoscopic Drawing*, Arthur Girling (1990).

Gleitman, H., *Psychology*, W.W. Norton and Company (1981).

Goble, J., Hinckley, K., Pausch, R., and Kassell, N., "Two-handed spatial interface tools for neurosurgical planning," *IEEE Computer*, **28** (7), pp. 20–26 (1995).

Goodale, M.A., Pelisson, D., and Prablanc, C., "Large Adjustments in Visually Guided Reaching Do Not Depend on Vision of the Hand or Perception of Target Displacement," *Nature*, **320**, pp. 748–750.

Goodwin, N.C., "Cursor Positioning on an Electronic Display using Lightpen, Lightgun or Keyboard for Three Basic Tasks," *Human Factors*, **17**, pp. 289–295 (1975).

Gordon, G. (ed.), *Active Touch: The Mechanism of Recognition of Objects by Manipulation: A Multi-Disciplinary Approach*, Pergamon Press (1977).

Gorman, P., Krummel, T., Webster, R., Smith, M., and Hutchens, D., "A Prototype Lumbar Puncture Simulator, *Proc. Medicine Meets Virtual Reality 2000*, pp. 106–109 (2000).

Gottschalk, S., Lin, M.C., and Manocha, D., "OBB-tree: A Hierarchical Structure for Rapid Interference Detection," *Proc. SIGGRAPH '96*, pp. 171–180 (1996).

Grant, B., Helser, A., and Taylor, R.M., "Adding Force Feedback to a Stereoscopic Head-Tracked Projection Display," *Proc. IEEE VRAIS'98 (Atlanta)*, pp. 81–88 (1998).

Green, D.F., and Salisbury, J.K., "Texture Sensing and Simulation using the PHANToM: Towards Remote Sensing of Soil Properties," *Proc. Second PHANToM User's Group Workshop (Oct. 19–22)*, (1997).

Gregory, A., Lin, M.C., Gottschalk, S., and Taylor, R., "H-COLLIDE: A Framework for Fast and Accurate Collision Detection for Haptic Interaction," *Proc. Virtual Reality Conference*, (1999).

Gregory, A., Lin, M.C., Gottschalk, S., and Taylor, R., "Fast and Accurate Collision Detection for Haptic Interaction using a Three Degree-Of-Freedom Force-Feedback Device," *Computational Geometry: Theory and Applications*, **15** (1–3), pp. 69–89 (2000).

Gross, M., Würmlin, S., Naef, M., Lamboray, E., Spagno, C., Kunz, A., Koller-Meier, E., Svoboda, T., Van Gool, L., Lang, S., Strehlke, K., Vande Moere, A., and Staadt, O., "blue-c: A Spatially Immersive Display and 3D Video Portal for Telepresence," *ACM Transactions on Graphics*, **22** (3), pp. 819–827 (July 2003).

Guiard, Y., "Asymmetric Division of Labor in Human Skilled Bimanual Action: The Kinematic Chain as a Model," *J. of Motor Behavior*, **19** (4), pp. 486–517 (1987).

Guiard, Y., and Ferrand, T., "Asymmetry in Bimanual Skills," in *Manual Asymmetries in Motor Performance*, Elliott, D., and Roy, E.A. (eds.), pp. 175–195, CRC Press (1996).

Guthold, M., Falvo, M., Matthews, W.G., Paulson, S., Mullin, J., Lord, S., Erie, D., Washburn, S., Superfine, R., Brooks, F.P., and Taylor, R.M., "Investigation and Modification of Molecular Structures with the NanoManipulator," *Journal of Molecular Graphics and Modeling*, **17** (3–4), pp. 187–197 (1999).

Halle, M., "Multiple Viewpoint Rendering," *Proceedings SIGGRAPH '96* (1996).

Halle, M., "Autostereoscopic Displays and Computer Graphics," *Computer Graphics (ACM SIGGRAPH)*, **31** (2) pp. 58–62 (1997).

Hamagishi, G., Sakata, M., Yamashita, A., Mashitani, K., Inoue, M., and Shimizu, E., "15" High-Resolution Non-Glasses 3-D Display with Head-Tracking System," *Transactions of the IEE (Japan)*, **121-C** (5), (May 2001).

Hammond, J.H., *The Camera Obscura: A Chronicle*, Adam Hilger (1981).

Hammond, J.H., and Austin, J., *The Camera Lucida in Art and Science*, Adam Hilger (1984).

Hammond, L., *Stereoscopic Motion Picture Device*, U.S. Patent 1,506,524 (August 26, 1924).

Hammond, L., *Stereoscopic Picture Viewing Apparatus*, U.S. Patent 1,658,439 (February 7, 1928).

Hariharan, P., *Basics of Holography*, Cambridge University Press (2002).

Harris, L.D., "A Varifocal Mirror Display Integrated into a High-Speed Image Processor," *SPIE* **902** *Three-Dimensional Imaging and Remote Sensing Imaging*, pp. 2–9 (1988).

Harris, L.D., Camp, J.J., Ritman, E.L., and Robb, R.A., "Three-Dimensional Display and Analysis of Tomographic Volume Images using a Varifocal Mirror," *IEEE Transactions on Medical Imaging*, **MI-5** (2), pp. 67–72 (June 1986).

Hartridge, H., "Visual Acuity and the Resolving Power of the Eye," *J. Physiol.*, **57**, pp. 52–67 (1922).

Hartwig, R., German Patent DE 26 22 802 C2 (1984).

Haykin, S., *Communication Systems*, 4th edn., John Wiley (2001).

Hayward, V., "Fast Collision Detection Scheme by Recursive Decomposition of a Manipulator Workspace," *Proc. IEEE International Conference on Robotics and Automation*, **2**, pp. 1044–1049 (1986).

Hayward, V., and Astley, O.R., "Performance Measures for Haptic Interfaces," in Giralt, G., and Hirzinger, G. (eds.), *Robotics Research: The 7th Int. Symposium*, pp. 195–297, Springer-Verlag (1996).

Hayward, V., Astley, O.R., Cruz-Hernandez, M., Grant, D., and Robles-De-La-Torre, G., "Haptic Interfaces and Devices," *Sensor Review*, **24** (1), pp. 16–29 (2004).

He, T., and Kaufman, A., "Collision Detection for Volumetric Objects," *Proc. IEEE Visualization*, pp. 27–34 (1997).

Hecht, S., and Mintz, E.U., "The Visibility of Single Lines at Various Illuminations and the Retinal Basis of Visual Resolution," *Journal of General Physiology*, pp. 593–612 (1939).

Hecht, E., and Zajac, A., *Optics*, Addison-Wesley (1974).

Hecht, S., Shlaer, S., and Pirenne, M.H., "Energy Quanta and Vision," *Journal of General Physiology*, **25**, pp. 819–840 (1942).

Heilig, M., *Sensorama Simulator*, U.S. Patent 3,050,870 (1962).

Held, M., Klosowski, J.T., and Mitchell, J.S.B., "Evaluation of Collision Detection Methods for Virtual Reality Fly-Throughs," *Proc. Seventh Canadian Conference on Computer Geometry*, **3**, pp. 205–210 (1995).

Helmholtz, H.H., *Popular Lectures on Scientific Subjects* (English Translation by Atkinson, E.), Longmans, Green, and Co. (1873).

Hill, J.W., "The Perception of Multiple Tactile Stimuli," *Stanford Electronics Laboratory Technical Report No. 4823–1*, Stanford University (1967).

Hillis, J.M., Ernst, M.O., Banks, M.S., and Landy, M.S., "Combining Sensory Information: Mandatory Fusion Within, But Not Between, Senses," *Science*, **298**, pp. 1627–1630 (2002).

Hinckley, K., Pausch, R., Proggitt, D., and Kassell, N.F., "Two-Handed Virtual Manipulation," *ACM Transactions on Computer-Human Interaction*, **5** (3), pp. 260–302 (September 1998).

Ho, C.-H., Basdogan, C., and Srinivasan, M.A., "Haptic Rendering: Point- and Ray-Based Interactions," *Proc. Second PHANToM User's Group Workshop (Oct. 19–22)* (1997).

Ho, C.-H., Basdogan, C., and Srinivasan, M.A., "Efficient Point-Based Rendering Techniques for Haptic Display of Virtual Objects," *Presence*, **8** (5), pp. 477–491 (1999).

Holliman, N.S., http://www.dur.ac.uk/n.s.holliman/(accessed April 2005).

Houghton, J.T., *The Physics of Atmospheres*, Cambridge University Press (1977).

Howard, I.P., *Seeing in Depth*, Vol. I Basic Mechanisms, I. Porteous (2002).

Howard, I.P., and Rogers, B.J., *Binocular Vision and Stereopsis*, Oxford University Press, Oxford (1995).

Howard, I.P., and Rogers, B.J., *Seeing in Depth*, Vol. II Depth Perception, I. Porteous (2002).

Howard, I.P., and Templeton, W.B., *Human Spatial Orientation*, John Wiley (1966).

Huang, C., Qu, H., and Kaufman, A.E., "Volume Rendering with Haptic Interaction," *Proc. Third PHANToM User's Group Workshop (Oct. 3–6)*, (1998).

Hubbard, P.M., "Interactive Collision Detection," *Proc. IEEE Symposium on Research Frontiers in Virtual Reality*, pp. 24–31 (1993).

Hubbard, P.M., "Approximating Polyhedra with Spheres for Time-Critical Collision Detection," *ACM Transactions on Graphics*, **15** (3), pp. 179–210 (1996).

Hutchins, E.L., Hollan, J.D., and Norman, D.A., "Direct Manipulation Interfaces," in Norman, D., and Draper, S. (eds.), *User Centered System Design*, pp. 87–124, Erlbaum (1986).

Ikei, Y., Wakamatsu, K., and Fukuda, S., "Vibratory Tactile Display of Image-Based Textures," *IEEE Computer Graphics and Applications*, **17** (6), pp. 53–61 (1997).

Inoue, M., Hamagishi, G., Sakata, M., Yamashita, A., and Mahitani, K., "Non-Glasses 3-D Displays by Shift-Image Splitter Technology," *Proceedings 3D Image Conf. 2000, Tokyo* (2000).

Ishii, M., and Sato, M., "A 3D Spatial Interface Device using Tensed Strings," *Presence*, **3** (1), pp. 81–86 (1994).

Ivins, W.M., *On The Rationalization Of Sight—With An Examination Of Three Renaissance Texts On Perspective*, Da Capo Press (1973).

Iwata, H., "Artificial Reality with Force-Feedback: Development of Desktop Virtual Space with Compact Master Manipulator," *Computer Graphics*, **24** (4), pp. 165–170 (August 1990).

Iwata, H., and Noma, H., "Volume Haptization," *Proc. IEEE 1993 Symposium on Research Frontiers in Virtual Reality (San Jose)*, pp. 16–23 (1993).

Jackson, M.J. (ed.), "*Engineering a Cathedral*," Thomas Telford (1993).

Jamot, J., "*Chambon-sur-Voueize: A Travers les Ages*," Editions Verso (1995).

Jeannerod, M., Arbib, M.A., Rizzolatti, G., and Sakata, H., "Grasping Objects: The Cortical Mechanisms of Visuomotor Transformation," *Trends in Neuroscience*, **18** (7), pp. 314–320 (1995).

Jenkins, F.A., and White, H.E., *Fundamentals of Optics*, 3rd edn., McGraw-Hill (1957).

Jiang, J., and Williams, D.R., "Aberrations and Retinal Image Quality of the Normal Human Eye," *J. Opt. Soc. Am. A*, **14** (11), pp. 2873–2883 (1997).

Jiménez, P., Thomas, F., and Torras, C., "3D Collision Detection: A Survey," *Computers and Graphics*, **25**, pp. 269–285 (2001).

Johnson, J., Roberts, T.L., Verplank, W., Smith, D., Irby, C.H., and Beard, M., "The Xerox Star: A Retrospective," *IEEE Computer*, **22** (9), pp. 11–29 (September 1989).

Johnson, J., Roberts, T.L., Verplank, W., Smith, D.C., Irby, C.H., Beard, M., and Mackey, K., "The Emergence of Graphical User Interfaces," in Baecker, R.M., Grudin, J., Buxton, W.A.S., and Greenberg, S. (eds.), *Readings in Human-Computer Interaction: Toward the Year 2000*, 2nd edn., pp. 53–69, Morgan Kaufman (1995).

Johnson, R.V., "Scophony Light Valve," *Appl. Opt.*, **18** (23), pp. 4030–4038 (December 1979).

Jones, G., Lee, D., Holliman, N., and Ezra, D., "Controlling Perceived Depth in Stereoscopic Images," *Proc. SPIE (Stereoscopic Displays and Virtual Reality Systems VIII)*, **4297**, pp. 42–53 (2001).

Jones, O., *Introduction to the X Window System*, Prentice-Hall (1989).

Judd, D.B., *Colour in Business, Science and Industry*, John Wiley (1952).

Julesz, B., *Foundations of Cyclopean Perception*, University of Chicago Press (1971).

Kaczmarek, K.A., Tyler, M.E., and Bach-y-Rita, P., "Electrotactile Haptic Display on the Fingertips: Preliminary Results," *Proc. 6th Annual Conference of the IEEE Engineering in Medicine and Biology Society*, pp. 940–941 (1994).

Kaczmarek, K.A., Webster, J.G., Bach-y-Rita, P., and Tompkins, W.J., "Electrotactile and Vibrotactile Displays for Sensory Substitution Systems," *IEEE Transactions on Biomedical Engineering*, **38** (1), pp. 1–16 (1991).

Kajimoto, H., Kawakami, N., Maeda, T., and Tachi, S., "Electrocutaneous Display as an Interface to a Virtual Tactile World," *Proc. IEEE Conference on Virtual Reality (VR'2001)*, pp. 289–290 (2001).

Kameyama, K., and Ohtomi, K., "A Shape Modelling System with a Volume Scanning Display and Multisensory Input Device," *Presence*, **2** (2), pp. 104–111 (1993).

Kameyama, K., Ohtomi, K., and Fukui, Y., "Interactive Volume Scanning 3-D Display with an Optical Relay System and Multidimensional Input Devices," *Stereoscopic Displays and Applications IV: SPIE Proceedings*, **1915**, pp. 12–20 (1993).

Kandel, E.R., Schwartz, J.H., and Jessell, T.M., *Principles of Neural Science*, 4th edn., McGraw-Hill (2000).

Kapadia, M.K., Westheimer, G., and Gilbert, C.D., "Spatial Distribution of Contextual Interactions in Primary Visual Cortex and Visual Perception," *J. Neurophysiol.*, **84**, pp. 2048–2062 (2000).

Karim, S., Clark, R.A., Poukens, V., and Demer, J.L., "Demonstration of Systematic Variation in Human Intracortical Optic Verve Size by Quantitative Magnetic Resonance Imaging and Histology," *Invest. Ophth. Vis. Sci.*, **45** (4), pp. 1047–1051 (2004).

Kass, M., Witkin, A., and Terzopoulos, D., "Snakes: Active Contour Models," *International Journal of Computer Vision*, **1** (4), pp. 321–331 (1987).

Katz, D., *The World of Touch* (ed. and trans. by Krueger, L.E., from original German version 1925), Lawrence Erlbaum Associates (1989).

Kauff, P., and Schreer, O., "An Immersive 3D Video-Conferencing System using Shared Virtual Team User Environments," *ACM CVE '02, Sept.30-Oct.2, Bonn, Germany* (2002).

Kemp, M., "Science, Non-Science and Nonsense: the Interpretation of Brunelleschi's Perspective," *Art History*, **1** (2), pp. 134–161 (1978).

Kennedy, D.N., and Nelson, A.C., "Three-Dimensional Display from Cross-Sectional Tomographic Images: An Application to Magnetic Resonance Imaging," *IEEE Transactions on Medical Imaging*, **MI-6** (2), pp. 134–140 (1993).

Kerstner, W., Pigel, G., and Tscheligi, M., "The FeelMouse: Making Computer Screens Feelable," *Proc. Computers for Handicapped Persons (ICCHP'94)* (1994).

Ketchpel, R.D., "CRT Provides Three-Dimensional Display," *Electronics*, pp. 54–57 (November 1962).

Ketchpel, R.D., "Direct-View Three-Dimensional Display Tube," *IEEE Trans. on Electron. Devices*, **10**, pp. 324–328 (1963).

Kim, I.I., Korevaar, E., and Hakakha, H., "Three-Dimensional Volumetric Display in Rubidium Vapour," *Proc. SPIE (Projection Displays II)*, **2650**, pp. 274–284 (1996).

Kim, S., Berkley, J.J., and Sato, M., "A Novel Seven Degree of Freedom Haptic Device for Engineering Design," *Virtual Reality*, **6** (4), pp. 217–228 (2003a).

Kim, Y.J., Otaday, M.A., Lin, M.C., and Manocha, D., "Six-Degree-of-Freedom Haptic Rendering using Incremental and Localised Computations," *Presence*, **12** (3), pp. 277–295 (2003b).

King, A.J., "The Superior Colliculus," *Curr. Biol.*, **14** (9) pp. R335–R338 (2004).

King, A.J., and Calvert, G.A., "Multisensory Integration: Perceptual Grouping By Eye and Ear," *Current Biology*, **11**, pp. R322–R325 (2001).

Kingsley, R.E., *Concise Text of Neuroscience*, 2nd edn., Lippincott Williams and Wilkins (2000).

Kiyokawa, K., Kurata, Y., and Ohno, H., "An Optical See-Through Display for Mutual Occlusion of Real and Virtual Environments," *IEEE and ACM Symp. on Augmented Reality (ISAR '00)*, pp. 60–67 (2000).

Kock, W.E., *Lasers and Holography: An Introduction to Coherent Optics*, 2nd edn., Dover Publications (1981).

Koenderink, J.J., "Pictorial Relief," *Phil. Trans. Roy. Soc. Lond. A*, **356**, pp. 1071–1086 (1998).

Kollin, J.S., "Collimated View Multiplexing: A New Approach to 3-D," *Proc. SPIE **902** (Three Dimensional Imaging and Remote Sensing Imaging)*, pp. 24–30 (1988).

Komerska, R., and Ware, C., "Haptic Task Constraints for 3D Interaction," *Proc. 2003 IEEE Virtual Reality and Haptics Symposium (Los Angeles)*, pp. 270–277 (2003).

Komerska, R., and Ware, C., "A Study of Haptic Linear and Pie Menus in a 3D Fish Tank VR Environment," *Proc. 12th International Symposium on Haptic Interfaces for Virtual Environment and Teleoperator Systems (HAPTICS '04)*, pp. 224–231 (2004).

Kovacs, I., "Gestalten of Today: Early Processing of Visual Contours and Surfaces," *Behav. Brain Res.*, **82**, pp. 1–11 (1996).

Kovacs, I., and Julesz, B., "A Closed Curve is Much More than an Incomplete One: Effect of Closure in Figure-Ground Segmentation," *P. Natl. Acad. Sci. USA*, **90**, pp. 7495–7497 (1993).

Kovacs, I., and Julesz, B., "Perceptual Sensitivity Maps Within Globally Defined Visual Shapes," *Nature*, **370**, pp. 644–646 (1994).

Künnapas, T., "Distance Perception as a Function of Available Visual Cues," *J. Exp. Psych.*, **77** (4), pp. 523–529 (1968).

Kyung, K.U., Kwon, D.S., Kwon, S.M., Kang, H.S., and Ra, J.B., "Force Feedback for a Spine Biopsy Simulator with Volume Graphic Model," *Proc. 2001 IEEE/RSJ International Conference on Intelligent Robots and Systems (Hawaii)*, pp. 1732–1737 (2001).

la Torre, B., Prattichizzo, D., Barbagli, F., and Vicino, A., "The FeTouch Project," *Proc. IEEE International Conference on Robotics and Automation (ICRA2003, Taipei, Taiwan, May 2003)*, pp. 1259–1263 (2003).

Land, M.F., and Nilsson, D.-E., *Animal Eyes*, Oxford University Press (2002).

Landy, M.S., Maloney, L.T., Johnston, E.B., and Young, M., "Measurement and Modeling of Depth Cue Combination: In Defense of Weak Fusion," *Vision Research*, **35** (3), pp. 389–412 (1995).

Lang, S.R., Travis, A.R.L., Castle, O.M., and Moore, J.R., "A 2nd Generation Autostereo-scopic 3-D Display," Lister, P.F. (ed.), in *Proc. 7th Eurographics Workshop on Graphics Hardware (Cambridge, UK, 5–6 Septemeber 1992)*, pp. 53–63 (1992).

Langhans, K., Bahr, D., Bezecny, D., Homann, D., Oltmann, K., Guill, C., Rieper, E., and Ardey, G., "FELIX 3D Display: An Interactive Tool for Volumetric Imaging," *Proc. SPIE **4660** (Stereoscopic Displays and Virtual Reality Systems IX)* (2002).

Langhans, K., Guill, C., Rieper, E., Oltmann, K., and Bahr, D., "SOLID FELIX: A Static Volume 3D-Laser Display," *Proc. SPIE **5006** (Stereoscopic Displays and Applications XIV)* (2003).

Larsson, T., and Akenine-Möller, T., "Collision Detection for Continuously Deforming Bodies," *Proc. Eurographics*, pp. 325–333 (2001).

Lasher, M., Soltan, P., Dahlke, W., Acantilado, N., and MacDonald, M., "Laser Projected 3-D Volumetric Displays," *Proc. SPIE **2650** (Projection Displays II)*, pp. 285–295 (1996).

Latimer, C., and Salisbury, J.K., "A Unified Approach to Haptic Rendering and Collision Detection," *Proc. Second PHANToM User's Group Workshop (Oct. 19–22)* (1997).

Leganchuk, A., Zhai, S., and Buxton, W., "Manual and Cognitive Benefits of Two-Handed Input: An Experimental Study," *ACM Trans. On Computer-Human Interaction*, **5** (4), pp. 326–359 (December 1998).

Leith, E.N., "Dennis Gabor, Holography, and the Nobel Prize," *Proc. IEEE*, **60** (6), (1972).

Leith, E.N., and Upatnieks, J., "Reconstructed Wavefronts and Communication Theory," *J. Opt. Soc. Am.*, **52**, pp. 1123–1130 (1962).

Leith, E.N., and Upatnieks, J., "Wavefront Reconstruction with Continuous-Tone Objects," *J. Opt. Soc. Am.*, **53**, pp. 1377–1381 (1963).

Leith, E.N., and Upatnieks, J., "Wavefront Reconstruction with Diffused Illumination and Three-Dimensional Objects," *J. Opt. Soc. Am.*, **54**, pp. 1295–1301 (1964).

Lesem, L.B., Hirsch, P., and Jordan, J.P. Jr., "The Kinoform: A New Wavefront Reconstruction Device," *IBM Res. Develop.*, **13** (3), pp. 150–155 (March 1969).

Levinthal, C., "Molecular Model-Building by Computer," *Scientific American*, **214/6**, pp. 42–52 (June 1966).

Lewis, J.D., Verber, C.M., and McGhee, R.B., "A True Three-Dimensional Display," *IEEE Transactions on Electron Devices*, **ED-18**, pp. 724–732 (1971).

Liebowitz, S., and Margolis, S.E., *Typing Errors*, Reasononline, http://reason.com (June 1996) (accessed 13 October 2004).

Lin, M.C., and Gottschalk, S., "Collision Detection Between Geometrical Models: A Survey," *Proc. IMA Conference on Mathematics of Surfaces* (1998).

Lin, M.C., and Manocha, D., "Collision and Proximity Queries," in O'Rourke, J., Goodman, E. (eds.), *Handbook of Discrete and Computational Geometries*, 2nd edn., pp. 787–808, CRC Press (2004).

Lindberg, D.C., "Alhazen's Theory of Vision and its Reception in the West," *Isis*, **58**, pp. 321–341 (1967).

Lindberg, D.C., "Al-kindi's Critique of Euclid's Theory of Vision," *Isis*, **62**, pp. 469–489 (1971).

Lindberg, D.C., *Theories of Vision from Al-Kindi to Kepler*, University of Chicago Press (1976).

Lindberg, D.C., *Roger Bacon and the Origins of Perspectiva in the Middle Ages*, Clarendon Press, Oxford (1996).

Lindemann, R., and Tesar, D., "Construction and Demonstration of a 9-string 6-DOF Force Reflecting Joystick for Telerobotics," *Proc. NASA International Conference on Space Telerobotics*, **4**, pp. 55–63 (1989).

Lindsay, P.H., and Norman, D.A., *Human Information Processing: An Introduction to Psychology*, Academic Press (1972).

Lippmann, G., "Epreuves Reversibles Donnant la Sensation du Relief," *Journal of Physics* **7** (4th series), pp. 821–825 (November 1908).

Lipton, L., *Foundations of Stereoscopic Cinema*, van Nostrand-Reinhold, NY (1982). [Also available from http://www.stereographics.com/whitepapers].

Lipton, L., "Selection Devices for Field-Sequential Stereoscopic Displays: A Brief History," *Proc. SPIE 1457 (Stereoscopic Displays and Applications II)*, pp. 274–282 (1991). [Also available from http://www.stereographics.com/whitepapers].

Lipton, L., *Stereographics Developers' Handbook*, Stereographics Corp., San Francisco (1997). [Also available from http://www.stereographics.com].

Lipton, L., "The Stereoscopic Cinema: from Film to Digital Projection," *SMPTE Journal*, pp. 586–593 (September 2001). [Also available from http://www.stereographics.com].

Livingstone, M.S., and Hubel, D.H., "Psychophysical Evidence for Separate Channels for the Perception of Form, Colour, Movement and Depth," *J. Neurosci.*, **7** (11), pp. 3416–3468 (1987).

Lorensen, W.E., and Cline, H.E., "Marching Cubes: A High-Resolution 3D Surface Construction Algorithm," *Computer Graphics (Proceedings SIGGRAPH '87)*, **21** (4), pp. 163–169 (1987).

Low, A.M., *Popular Scientific Recreations*, Ward, Lock and Co. (1933).

Lucente, M., "Interactive Computation of Holograms using a Look-Up Table," *Journal of Electronic Imaging*, **2** (1), pp. 28–34 (1993).

Lucente, M., *Diffraction-Specific Fringe Computation for Electro-Holography*, Ph.D. Thesis, Massachussetts Institute of Technology (1994).

Lucente, M., "Holographic Bandwidth Compression using Spatial Subsampling," *Optical Engineering*, **35** (6), pp. 1529–1537 (1996).

Lucente, M., "Interactive Three-Dimensional Holographic Displays: Seeing the Future in Depth," *Computer Graphics (SIGGRAPH)*, pp. 63–67 (May 1997).

Lucente, M., Benton, S.A., and St. Hilaire, P., "Electronic Holography: The Newest," *International Symp. on 3-D Imaging and Holography*, Osaka, Japan (November 1994).

Lundin, K., Ynnerman, A., and Gudmundsson, B., "Proxy-Based Feedback from Volumetric Density Data," *Proc. Eurohaptics* (2002).

Lynes, J.A., "Brunelleschi's Perspectives Reconsidered," *Perception*, **9**, pp. 87–99 (1980).

MacDonald, L.W., and Lowe, A.C., *Display Systems Design and Applications*, John Wiley (1997).

MacDonald, R.I., "Three-Dimensional Television by Texture Parallax," *Appl. Opt.*, **17** (2), (January 1978).

MacKay, D.M., "Projective Three-Dimensional Displays, Part I," *Electronic Engineering* July 1949 (1949a).

MacKay, D.M., "Projective Three-Dimensional Displays, Part II," *Electronic Engineering*, August 1949 (1949b).

MacKay, D.M., "A Simple Multi-Dimensional CRT Display Unit," *Electronic Engineering*, pp. 344–347 (June 1960).

MacKenzie, I.S., "Fitts' Law as a Research and Design Tool in Human-Computer Interaction," *Human Computer Interaction*, **7**, pp. 91–139 (1992).

MacKenzie, I.S., Kauppinen, T., and Silfverberg, M., "Accuracy Measures for Evaluating Computer Pointing Devices," *SIGCHI '01*, March 31–April 4, Seattle, WA (2001).

Mahvash, M., and Hayward, V., "Haptic Rendering of Cutting: A Fracture Mechanics Approach," *Haptics-e*, http://www.haptics-e.org, **2** (3), (2001).

Mark, W., Randolph, S., Finch, M., van Verth, J., and Taylor, R., "Adding Force Feedback to Graphics Systems: Issues and Solutions," *Proc. SIGGRAPH '96 (New Orleans)*, pp. 447–452 (1996).

Marschner, S.R., Lobb, R.J., Bergerson, R.D., and Kaufman, A.E., "An Evaluation of Reconstruction Filters for Volume Rendering," *Proc. Visualization '94*, pp. 100–107 (1994).

Parker, M.J., and Wallis, P.A., "Three-Dimensional Cathode-Ray Tube Displays," *Journal of the IEE*, **95**, pp. 371–390 (September 1948).

Parker, M.J., and Wallis, P.A., "Discussion on 'Three-Dimensional Cathode-Ray Tube Displays,'" *Journal of the IEE*, **96(III)** (42), pp. 291–294 (1949).

Pasquero, J., and Hayward, V., "STReSS: A Practical Tactile Display System with One Millimetre Spatial Resolution and 700 Hz Refresh Rate," *Proc. Eurohaptics* (2003).

Pastoor, S., and Wopking, M., "3-D Displays: A Review of Current Technologies," *Displays*, **17**, pp. 100–110 (1997).

Pastore, N., *Selective History of Theories of Visual Perception: 1650–1950*, Oxford University Press (1972).

Patterson, R., and Martin, W.L., "Human Stereopsis," *Human Factors*, **34** (6), pp. 669–692 (1992).

Peli, E., "The Visual Effects of Head-Mounted Display (HMD) Are Not Distinguishable From Those of a Desk-Top Computer Display," *Vision Res.*, **38**, pp. 2053–2066 (1998).

Pelisson, D., Prablanc, C., Goodale, M.A., and Jeannerod, M., "Visual Control of Reaching Movements without Vision of the Limb. II. Evidence of Fast Unconscious Processes Correcting the Trajectory of the Hand to the Final Position of a Double-Step Stimulus," *Exp. Brain Res.*, **62**, pp. 303–311 (1986).

Perlin, K., Paxia, S., and Kollin, J.S., "An Autostereoscopic Display," *Proc. ACM SIGGRAPH* (July 2000).

Perlin, K., Poultney, C., Kollin, J.S., Kristjansson, D.T., and Paxia, S., "Recent Advances in the NYU Autostereoscopic Display," *Proc. SPIE*, **4297** (2001).

Petersik, A., Pflesser, B., Tiede, U., and Höhne, K.H., "Haptic Rendering of Volumetric Anatomic Models at Sub-Voxel Resolution," *Proc. Eurohaptics* (2001).

Pham, D.L., Xu, C., and Prince, J.L., "Current Methods in Medical Image Segmentation," *Annual Reviews: Biomedical Engineering*, **2**, pp. 315–337 (2000).

Phong, B.T., "Illumination for Computer Generated Pictures," *Communications of the ACM*, **18** (6), pp. 311–317 (1975).

Piegl, L., "On NURBS: A Survey," *IEEE Transactions on Computer Graphics and Applications*, **11** (1), pp. 55–71 (1991).

Pierce, J.R., and Karlin, J.E., "Reading Rates and the Information Rate of the Human Channel," *Bell System Technical Journal*, **36**, pp. 497–516 (1957).

Pisella, L., Grea, H., Tilikete, C., Vighetto, A., Desmurget, H., Rode, G., Boisson, D., and Rossetti, Y., "An 'Automatic Pilot' for the Hand in Human Posterior Parietal Cortex: Toward Reinterpreting Optic Ataxia," *Nat. Neurosci.*, **3**, pp. 729–736 (2000).

Plesniak, W., and Pappu, R., "Spatial Interaction with Haptic Holograms," *Proc. IEEE International Conf. on Multimedia Computing and Systems* (June 1999).

Plesniak, W., Pappu, R., and Benton, S., "Tangible, Dynamic Holographic Images," in Kuo, C.J., and Tsai, M.H. (eds.), *Three Dimensional Holographic Imaging*, pp. 77–98, John Wiley (2002).

Poole, H.H., *Fundamentals of Display Systems*, Macmillan and Co (1966).

Popescu, V., Burdea, G., and Bouzit, M., "Virtual Reality Simulation Modeling for a Haptic Glove," *Proceedings IEEE Computer Animation '99 (Geneva)* (1999).

Prablanc, C., and Martin, O., "Automatic Control During Hand Reaching at Undetected Two-Dimensional Target Displacement," *J. Neurophysiol.*, **67**, pp. 455–469 (1992).

Prager, F.D., and Scaglia, G., *Brunelleschi, Studies of His Technology and Inventions*, MIT Press (1970).

Prattichizzo, D., la Torre, B., Barbagli, F., Vicino, A., Severi, F.M., and Petraglia, F., "The FeTouch Project: An Application of Haptic Technologies to Obstetrics and Gynaecology," *International Journal of Medical Robotics and Computer Assisted Surgery*, **1** (1), pp. 83–87 (2004).

Purves, D., and Lotto, R.B., "*Why We See What We Do: An Empirical Theory of Vision*," Sinauer Associates Inc (2003).

Ramachandran, V.S., "Perceiving Shape from Shading," *Sci. Am.*, **259**, pp. 58–65 (1988).

Ramachandran, V.S., and Hirstein, W., "The Perception of Phantom Limbs," *Brain*, **121**, pp. 1603–1630 (1998).

Raskar, R., Welch, G., Cutts, M., Lake, A., Stesin, L., and Fuchs, H., "The Office of the Future: A Unified Approach to Image-Based Modeling and Spatially Immersive Displays," *SIGGRAPH '98, Computer Graphics Proc., Annual Conference Series*, pp. 1–10 (1998).

Raskin, J., *The Humane Interface*, ACM Press (2000).

Rawson, E.G., "3D Computer-Generated Movies using a Varifocal Mirror," *Appl. Opt.*, **7** (8), pp. 1505–1511 (1968).

Rawson, E.G., "Vibrating Varifocal Mirrors for 3D Imaging," *IEEE Spectrum*, pp. 37–43 (September 1969).

Raymaekers, C., and Coninx, K., "Improving Haptic Rendering of Complex Scenes using Spatial Partitioning," *Proc. Eurohaptics* (2003).

Reinig, K.D., "Haptic Interaction with the Visible Human," *Proc. First PHANToM User's Group Workshop (Sept. 27–30)* (1996).

Richter, I.A., *The Notebooks of Leonardo da Vinci*, Oxford University Press (1998).

Ritter, A.O., Bottger, J., Deussen, O., and Strothotte, T., "*Fast Texture-Based Interference for Synthetic Holography*," Technical Report 3/98, Fakultät für Informatik, Otto-von-Guericke-Universität Magdeburg, Germany (1998).

Ritter, A.O., Wagener, H., and Strothotte, T., "Holographic Imaging of Lines: a Texture Based Approach," *Proc. International Conference on Information Visualization IV'97*, London, August, pp. 272–278 (1997).

Roberts, D. (ed.), *Signals and Perception: The Fundamentals of Human Sensation*, Palgrave Macmillan (2002).

Robinson, D.M., "The Supersonic Light Control and Its Application to Television With Special Reference to the Scophony Television Receiver," *Proc. I.R.E.*, pp. 483–486 (August 1939).

Rooney, J., and Steadman, P., *Principles of Computer-Aided Design*, Pitman (1993).

Roorda, A., and Williams, D.R., "The Arrangement of the Three Cone Classes in the Living Human Eye," *Nature*, **397**, pp. 520–521 (1999).

Rosenberg, L.B., and Adelstein, B.D., "Perceptual Decomposition of Virtual Haptic Surfaces," *Proc. IEEE 1993 Symposium on Research Frontiers in Virtual Reality*, pp. 46–53 (1993).

ocal Mirror Oscillations," *Appl. Opt.*,

Appl. Opt., **29** (29), pp. 4341–4342

son, N.A., "Time-Multiplexed Three-
, **3/4**, pp. 203–205 (1995).

Van Nostrand (1930).

s (1990).

kosky, M.R., "Preliminary Tests of an
manipulation," *Proc. ASME IMECE*

(ed.), *Binocular Vision*, Macmillan

in Regan, D. (ed.), *Binocular Vision*,

3D Scenes Produced by Computerized
(March 1983).

roc. SPIE, **3639**, pp. 84–91 (1999).

nd Optimisation of 3D-LCD Design,"

Multi-View LCD," *Proc. SPIE*, **2653**

mplications of a New Paradigm," *Proc.*
Virtual Reality, pp. 5–8 (1993).

g System of the Fast-Intelligent-Track-
).

Tactile Displays in Human Computer

ree Dimensional Computer Graphics
ation," *Computer Graphics*, **17** (3),

Readings from Scientific American,

of Three-Dimensional Displays using
IE, **120**, pp. 62–67 (1977).

Spotlight: Parietal Guiding the Tem-
).

Perception Within Near Visual Space,"

(1995).

s, G., "An Example of Task Oriented
," *Journal of Universal Computer*

Ruspini, D.C., Kolarov, K., and Khatib, O., "The Haptic Display of Complex Graphical Environments," *Proc. 24th Annual Conference on Computer Graphics and Interactive Techniques (SIGGRAPH'97, Los Angeles)*, pp. 345–352 (1997).

Sakata, H., Taira, M., Kusunoki, M., Murata, A., and Takaka, Y., "The Parietal Association Cortex In Depth Perception And Visual Control Of Hand Action," *Trends Neurosci.*, **20** (8), pp. 350–357 (1997).

Saleh, B.E.A., and Teich, M.C., *Fundamental of Photonics*, John Wiley (1991).

Salisbury, J.K., "Making Graphics Physically Tangible," *Communications of the ACM*, **42** (8), pp. 75–81 (1999).

Salisbury, J.K., Brock, D., Massie, T., Swarup, N., and Zilles, C., "Haptic Rendering: Programming Touch Interaction with Virtual Objects," *Proc. ACM Symposium on Interactive 3D Graphics*, pp. 123–130 (1995).

Salisbury, J.K., Conti, F., and Barbagli, F., "Haptic Rendering: Introductory Concepts," *IEEE Computer Graphics and Applications*, **24** (2), pp. 24–32 (2004).

Salmon, R., and Slater, M., *Computer Graphics Systems and Concepts*, Addison-Wesley (1987).

Sankaranarayanan, G., Weghorst, S., Sanner, M., Gillet, A., and Olson, A., "Role of Haptics in Teaching Structural Molecular Biology," *Proc. 11th Symposium on Haptic Interfaces for Virtual Environment and Teleoperator Systems (HAPTICS'03)* (2003).

Saper, C.B., "The Central Autonomic Nervous System: Conscious Visceral Perception and Autonomic Pattern Generation," *Annual Reviews of Neuroscience*, **25**, pp. 433–469 (2002).

Satava, R.M., "Surgical Education and Surgical Simulation," *World Journal of Surgery*, **25**, pp. 1484–1489 (2001a).

Satava, R.M., "Accomplishments and Challenges of Surgical Simulation: Dawnng of the Next-Generation Surgical Education," *Surgical Endoscopy*, **15**, pp. 232–241 (2001b).

Satava, R., and Sackier, J.M., *Cybersurgery: Advanced Technologies for Surgical Practice*, John Wiley (1998).

Scharf, B. (ed.), *Experimental Sensory Psychology*, Scott, Foresman and Company (1975).

Schieber, M.H., "Constraints on Somatotopic Organization in the Primary Motor Cortex," *Journal of Neurophysiology*, **86**, pp. 2125–2143 (2001).

Schiffman, H.R., *Sensation and Perception*, John Wiley (1976).

Schiffman, H.R., *Sensation and Perception*, 2nd edn., John Wiley (1982).

Schiffman, H.R., *Sensation and Perception*, 3rd edn., John Wiley (1990).

Schijven, M., and Jakimowicz, J., "Virtual Reality Surgical Laparoscopic Simulators," *Surgical Endoscopy*, **17**, pp. 1943–1950 (2003).

Schmandt, C., "Spatial Input/Display Correspondence in a Stereoscopic Computer Graphic Work Station," *Computer Graphics*, **17** (3), pp. 253–259 (July 1983).

Schmitt, O.H., "Cathode-Ray Presentation of Three-Dimensional Data," *J. Appl. Phys.*, **18**, pp. 819–829 (September 1947).

Schwarz, A.J., and Blundell, B.G., "Optimising Dot-Graphics for Volumetric Displays," *IEEE Trans. on Computer Graphics and Applications*, pp. 72–78 (1997).

Sears, F.W., and Zemansky, M.W., *University Physics*, 3rd edn., Addison-Wesley (1964).

Sedgwick, H.A., "Space Perception," in Boff, K.R., Kaufman, L., and Thomas, J.P., (eds.), *Handbook of Perception and Visual Performance*, John Wiley (1986).

Sener, B., Pedgley, O., Wormald, P., and Campbell, I., "Incorporating the Free! Haptic Modelling System into New Product Development," *Proc. Euroha* (2003).

Sener, B., Wormald, P., and Campbell, I., "Towards 'Virtual Clay' Modelling—Challe and Recommendations: A Brief Summary of the Literature," *Proc. DESIGN 200 International Design Conference*, **1**, pp. 545–550 (2002).

Sexton, I., and Surman, P., "Stereoscopic and Autostereoscopic Display Systems," *Signal Processing Magazine*, pp. 85–99 (May 1999).

Seymour, N.E., Gallagher, A.G., Roman, S.A., O'Brien, M.K., Bansal, V.K., Ande D.K., and Satava, R.M., "Virtual Reality Training Improves Operating Room Perf ance: Results of a Randomized, Double-Blinded Study," *Annals of Surgery*, **23** pp. 458–464 (2002).

Shannon, C.E., "A Mathematical Theory of Communication," *Bell Sys. Tech. J* pp. 379–423 (1948).

Shannon, C.E., and Weaver, W., *The Mathematical Theory of Communications*, The versity of Illinois Press (1949).

Sher, L.D., "SpaceGraph, a True 3-D PC Peripheral," *SPIE* **902** *Three-Dimen. Imaging and Remote Sensing Imaging*, pp. 10–17 (1988).

Sher, L.D., "The Oscillating Mirror Technique for Realizing True 3D," in McA! D. (ed.), *Stereo Computer Graphics and Other True 3D Technologies*, pp. 196 Princeton University Press (1993).

Sherman, W.R., and Craig, A.B., *Understanding Virtual Reality: Interface, Applicatic Design*, Morgan Kaufmann (2003).

Sherrington, C.S., "The Muscular Sense," in Schaefer, E.A. (ed.), *Textbook on Physi* Macmillan (1900).

Siegel, M., Tobinaga, Y., and Akiya, T., "Kinder Gentler Stereo," *Proc. SPIE* pp. 18–27 (1998).

Sieger, J., "The Design and Development of Television Receivers Using the Scc Optical Scanning System," *Proc. I.R.E.*, pp. 487–492 (August 1939).

Sigman, M., Cecchi, G.A., Gilbert, C.D., and Magnasco, M.O., "On A Common Natural Scenes and Gestalt Rules," *Proc. Natl. Acad. Sci. USA*, **98** (4), pp. 1940 (2001).

Smith, A., Kitamura, Y., Takemura, H., and Kishino, F., "A Simple and Efficient Met Accurate Collision Detection among Deformable Polyhedral Objects in A! Motion," *Proc. Virtual Reality Annual International Symposium (VRAIS'9* 136–145 (1995).

Smith, D.K., and Alexander, R.C., *Fumbling the Future: How Xerox Invented Ignored, the First Personal Computer*, toExcel (1999).

Smith, F.G., and Thomson, J.H., *Optics*, John Wiley (1975).

Snibbe, S., Anderson, S., and Verplank, B., "Springs and Constraints for 3D Dr; *Proc. Third PHANToM User's Group Workshop (Oct. 3–6)* (1998).

Soltan, P., Trias, J., Dahlke, W., Lasher, M., and MacDonald, M., "Laser-Ba Volumetric Display System (2nd generation)," *SID'94 Proc.* (1994).

Spillmann, L., and Dresp, B., "Phenomena of Illusory Form: Can We Bridge t between Levels of Explanation?" *Perception*, **24** pp. 1333–1364 (1995).

Traub, C., "Stereoscopic Display using Rapid Vari **6** (6), pp. 1085–1087 (1967).

Travis, A.R.L., "Autostereoscopic 3-D Display," (1990).

Travis, A.R.L., Lang, S.R., Moore, J.R., and Dod; Dimensional Video Display," *Journal of the SII*

Troland, L.T., *The Principles of Psychophysiology,*

Tufte, E.R., *Envisioning Information*, Graphics Pre:

Turner, M.L., Gomez, D.H., Tremblay, M.R., and C Arm-Grounded Haptic Feedback Fevice in Te *Haptics Symposium (Anaheim)* (1998).

Tyler, C.W., "Cyclopean Vision," in Regan, D. (1991).

Tyler, C.W., "The Horopter and Binocular Fusion," Macmillan (1991).

Udupa, J.K., "Display of 3D Information in Discrete Tomography," *Proc. IEEE*, **71** (3), pp. 420–43!

Valyus, N., *Stereoscopy*, Focal Press (1962).

van Berkel, C., "Image Preparation for 3D-LCD,"

van Berkel, C., and Clarke, J.A., "Characterisation *Proc. SPIE*, **3012** (1997).

van Berkel, C., Parker, D.W., and Franklin, A.R., (1996).

Van Dam, A., "VR as a Forcing Function: Software I *1993 IEEE Symposium on Research Frontiers in*

van den Brink, H.B., and Willemsen, O.H., "Trackir ing (F!T) Tube," *Journal of the SID*, **11/3** (200:

van Erp, J.B.F, "Guidelines For The Use of Vibro Interaction," *Proc. Eurohaptics* (2002).

Vannier, M.W., Marsh, J.L., and Warren, J.O., " for Craniofacial Surgical Planning and Eval! pp. 263–273 (July 1983).

Various, *Mathematics in the Modern World:* W.H. Freeman and Company (1968).

Verber, C.M., "Present and Potential Capabilities Sequential Excitation of Fluorescence," *Proc. S*

Vidyasagar, T.R., "A Neuronal Model of Attention poral," *Brain Res. Rev.*, **30** (1), pp. 66–76 (199

Viguier, A., Clement, G., and Trotter, Y., "Distance *Perception*, **30**, pp. 115–124 (2001).

Vince, J., *Virtual Reality Systems*, Addison-Wesley

Volbracht, S., Domik, G., Shahrbabaki, K., and Fe Empirical Evaluations of 3D-Display Mode *Science*, **4** (5), pp. 534–546 (1998).

von Senden, M., *Space And Sight: The Perception of Space And Shape in Congenitally Blind Patients Before and After Operation*, Methuen (1960).

Wade, N.J. (ed.), *Brewster and Wheatstone on Vision*, Academic Press (1983).

Wade, N.J., "On the Late Invention of the Stereoscope," *Perception*, **16**, pp. 785–818 (1987).

Wade, N.J., "The Chimenti Controversy," *Perception*, **32**, pp. 185–200 (2003).

Wade, N.J., *Visual Allusions: Pictures of Perception*, Lawrence Erlbaum Associates Ltd (1990).

Wagner, C.R., Howe, R.D., and Stylopoulos, N., "The Role of Force Feedback in Surgery: Analysis of Blunt Dissection," *Proc. 10th Symposium on Haptic Interfaces for Virtual Environments and Telepresence*, pp. 73–79 (2002).

Walker, J., "The Amateur Scientist: Visual Illusions that Can Be Achieved by Putting a Dark Filter over One Eye," *Scientific American*, **238**, pp. 142–153 (1978).

Wall, S.A., and Harwin, W.S., "Design of a Multiple Contact-Point Haptic Interface," *Proc. Eurohaptics* (2001).

Wall, S.A., Paynter, K., Shillito, A.M., Wright, M., and Scali, S., "The Effect of Haptic Feedback and Stereo Graphics in a 3D Target Acquisition Task," *Proc. Eurohaptics* (2002).

Wallace, M.T., "The Development of Multisensory Processes," *Cognitive Proc*, **5**, pp. 69–83 (2004).

Walworth, V., "Three-Dimensional Projection with Circular Polarizers," *Proc. SPIE 462 (Optics in Entertainment II)* (1984).

Wanger, L., "Haptically Enhanced Molecular Modelling: A Case Study," *Proc. Third PHANToM User's Group Workshop (Oct. 3–6)* (1998).

Wann, J.P., Rushton, S., and Mon-Williams, M., "Natural Problems for Stereoscopic Depth Perception in Virtual Environments," *Vision Res.*, **35** (19), pp. 2731–2736 (1995).

Ware, C., *Information Visualization: Perception for Design*, Morgan Kaufman (2000).

Warren, R.M., and Warren, R.P. (eds.), *Helmholtz on Perception: Its Physiology and Development*, John Wiley (1968).

Watt, A., *3D Computer Graphics*, Addison-Wesley (2000).

Welford, A.T., *Fundamentals of Skill*, Methuen (1968).

Wertheim, E., *Ueber die Durchführbarkeit und den Werth der mikroskopischen Untersuchung des Eiters entzündlicher Adnexentumoren während der Laparotomie*, (1894).

Wesche, G., "The ToolFinger: Supporting Complex Direct Manipulation in Virtual Environments," in Deisinger, J., and Kunz, A. (eds.), *International Immersive Projection Technologies Workshop, Eurographics Workshop on Virtual Environments (2003)*, pp. 39–45, The Eurographics Association (2003).

Wesche, G., and Droske, M., "Conceptual Free-Form Styling on the Responsive Work-bench," *Proc. VRST2000 (Seoul, Korea)*, pp. 83–91 (2000).

Wesche, G., and Seidel, H.-P., "FreeDrawer—a Free-Form Sketching System on the Responsive Workbench," *Proc. VRST2001 (Banff, Canada)*, pp. 83–91 (2001).

Westheimer, G., "Image Quality in the Human Eye," *Optica Acta*, **17** (9), pp. 641–658 (1970).

Wheatstone, C., "Contributions to the Theory of Vision—Part the First, On Some Remarkable, and Hitherto Unobserved, Phenomena of Binocular Vision," *Phil. Trans. Roy. Soc. (London)*, **128**, pp. 371–394 (1838).

Williams, R.D., and Garcia, F., "A Real Time Autostereoscopic Multiplanar 3D Display System," *SID'88 Digest*, **19**, pp. 91–94 (1988).

Williams, R.L., "Cable-Suspended Haptic Interface," *International Journal of Virtual Reality*, **3** (3), pp. 13–21 (1998).

Wilson, J., and Hawkes, J., *Optoelectronics: An Introduction*, 3rd edn., Prentice-Hall (1998).

Woods, A., Docherty, T., and Koch, R., "Image Distortions in Stereoscopic Video Systems," *Proc. SPIE (Stereoscopic Displays and Applications IV)*, **1915** (1993).

Wormell, D., and Foxlin, E., "Advancements in 3D Interactive Devices for Virtual Environments," *International Immersive Projection Technologies Workshop, Eurographics Workshop on Virtual Environments*, pp. 47–56 (2003).

Yarbus, A.L., *Eye Movements and Vision*, Plenum Press (1967).

Young, P., Chen, T., Anderson, D., and Yu, J., "LEGOLAND: A Multi-Sensory Environment for Virtual Prototyping," *Proc. Second PHANToM User's Group Workshop (Oct. 19–22)*, (1997).

Zachmann, G., "Minimal Hierarchical Collision Detection," *Proc. ACM Conference on Virtual Reality Systems and Technology (VRST'02)* (2002).

Zhuang, Y., and Canny, J., "Haptic Interaction with Global Deformations," *Proc. IEEE International Conference on Robotics and Automation (San Francisco)* (2000).

Zilles, C.B., and Salisbury, J.K., "A Constraint-Based God-Object Method for Haptic Display," *Proc. ASME Haptic Interfaces for Virtual Environment and Teleoperator Systems, Dynamic Systems and Control 1994 (Chicago)*, **1**, pp. 146–150 (1994).

Zito, R., and Schraeder, A.E., "Optical Excitation of Mercury Vapour for the Production of Isolated Fluorescence," *Appl. Opt.*, **2** (12), pp. 1323–1328 (1963).

INDEX

Creative 3-D Display and Interaction Interfaces: A Trans-Disciplinary Approach, by Barry G. Blundell and Adam J. Schwarz
Copyright © 2006 John Wiley & Sons, Inc.

Wheatstone, C., "Contributions to the Theory of Vision—Part the First, On Some Remarkable, and Hitherto Unobserved, Phenomena of Binocular Vision," *Phil. Trans. Roy. Soc. (London)*, **128**, pp. 371–394 (1838).

Williams, R.D., and Garcia, F., "A Real Time Autostereoscopic Multiplanar 3D Display System," *SID'88 Digest*, **19**, pp. 91–94 (1988).

Williams, R.L., "Cable-Suspended Haptic Interface," *International Journal of Virtual Reality*, **3** (3), pp. 13–21 (1998).

Wilson, J., and Hawkes, J., *Optoelectronics: An Introduction*, 3rd edn., Prentice-Hall (1998).

Woods, A., Docherty, T., and Koch, R., "Image Distortions in Stereoscopic Video Systems," *Proc. SPIE (Stereoscopic Displays and Applications IV)*, **1915** (1993).

Wormell, D., and Foxlin, E., "Advancements in 3D Interactive Devices for Virtual Environments," *International Immersive Projection Technologies Workshop, Eurographics Workshop on Virtual Environments*, pp. 47–56 (2003).

Yarbus, A.L., *Eye Movements and Vision*, Plenum Press (1967).

Young, P., Chen, T., Anderson, D., and Yu, J., "LEGOLAND: A Multi-Sensory Environment for Virtual Prototyping," *Proc. Second PHANToM User's Group Workshop (Oct. 19–22)*, (1997).

Zachmann, G., "Minimal Hierarchical Collision Detection," *Proc. ACM Conference on Virtual Reality Systems and Technology (VRST'02)* (2002).

Zhuang, Y., and Canny, J., "Haptic Interaction with Global Deformations," *Proc. IEEE International Conference on Robotics and Automation (San Francisco)* (2000).

Zilles, C.B., and Salisbury, J.K., "A Constraint-Based God-Object Method for Haptic Display," *Proc. ASME Haptic Interfaces for Virtual Environment and Teleoperator Systems, Dynamic Systems and Control 1994 (Chicago)*, **1**, pp. 146–150 (1994).

Zito, R., and Schraeder, A.E., "Optical Excitation of Mercury Vapour for the Production of Isolated Fluorescence," *Appl. Opt.*, **2** (12), pp. 1323–1328 (1963).

von Senden, M., *Space And Sight: The Perception of Space And Shape in Congenitally Blind Patients Before and After Operation*, Methuen (1960).

Wade, N.J. (ed.), *Brewster and Wheatstone on Vision*, Academic Press (1983).

Wade, N.J., "On the Late Invention of the Stereoscope," *Perception*, **16**, pp. 785–818 (1987).

Wade, N.J., "The Chimenti Controversy," *Perception*, **32**, pp. 185–200 (2003).

Wade, N.J., *Visual Allusions: Pictures of Perception*, Lawrence Erlbaum Associates Ltd (1990).

Wagner, C.R., Howe, R.D., and Stylopoulos, N., "The Role of Force Feedback in Surgery: Analysis of Blunt Dissection," *Proc. 10th Symposium on Haptic Interfaces for Virtual Environments and Telepresence*, pp. 73–79 (2002).

Walker, J., "The Amateur Scientist: Visual Illusions that Can Be Achieved by Putting a Dark Filter over One Eye," *Scientific American*, **238**, pp. 142–153 (1978).

Wall, S.A., and Harwin, W.S., "Design of a Multiple Contact-Point Haptic Interface," *Proc. Eurohaptics* (2001).

Wall, S.A., Paynter, K., Shillito, A.M., Wright, M., and Scali, S., "The Effect of Haptic Feedback and Stereo Graphics in a 3D Target Acquisition Task," *Proc. Eurohaptics* (2002).

Wallace, M.T., "The Development of Multisensory Processes," *Cognitive Proc*, **5**, pp. 69–83 (2004).

Walworth, V., "Three-Dimensional Projection with Circular Polarizers," *Proc. SPIE 462 (Optics in Entertainment II)* (1984).

Wanger, L., "Haptically Enhanced Molecular Modelling: A Case Study," *Proc. Third PHANToM User's Group Workshop (Oct. 3–6)* (1998).

Wann, J.P., Rushton, S., and Mon-Williams, M., "Natural Problems for Stereoscopic Depth Perception in Virtual Environments," *Vision Res.*, **35** (19), pp. 2731–2736 (1995).

Ware, C., *Information Visualization: Perception for Design*, Morgan Kaufman (2000).

Warren, R.M., and Warren, R.P. (eds.), *Helmholtz on Perception: Its Physiology and Development*, John Wiley (1968).

Watt, A., *3D Computer Graphics*, Addison-Wesley (2000).

Welford, A.T., *Fundamentals of Skill*, Methuen (1968).

Wertheim, E., *Ueber die Durchführbarkeit und den Werth der mikroskopischen Untersuchung des Eiters entzündlicher Adnexentumoren während der Laparotomie*, (1894).

Wesche, G., "The ToolFinger: Supporting Complex Direct Manipulation in Virtual Environments," in Deisinger, J., and Kunz, A. (eds.), *International Immersive Projection Technologies Workshop, Eurographics Workshop on Virtual Environments (2003)*, pp. 39–45, The Eurographics Association (2003).

Wesche, G., and Droske, M., "Conceptual Free-Form Styling on the Responsive Workbench," *Proc. VRST2000 (Seoul, Korea)*, pp. 83–91 (2000).

Wesche, G., and Seidel, H.-P., "FreeDrawer—a Free-Form Sketching System on the Responsive Workbench," *Proc. VRST2001 (Banff, Canada)*, pp. 83–91 (2001).

Westheimer, G., "Image Quality in the Human Eye," *Optica Acta*, **17** (9), pp. 641–658 (1970).

Sener, B., Pedgley, O., Wormald, P., and Campbell, I., "Incorporating the FreeForm Haptic Modelling System into New Product Development," *Proc. Eurohaptics* (2003).

Sener, B., Wormald, P., and Campbell, I., "Towards 'Virtual Clay' Modelling—Challenges and Recommendations: A Brief Summary of the Literature," *Proc. DESIGN 2002 7th International Design Conference*, **1**, pp. 545–550 (2002).

Sexton, I., and Surman, P., "Stereoscopic and Autostereoscopic Display Systems," *IEEE Signal Processing Magazine*, pp. 85–99 (May 1999).

Seymour, N.E., Gallagher, A.G., Roman, S.A., O'Brien, M.K., Bansal, V.K., Andersen, D.K., and Satava, R.M., "Virtual Reality Training Improves Operating Room Performance: Results of a Randomized, Double-Blinded Study," *Annals of Surgery*, **236** (4), pp. 458–464 (2002).

Shannon, C.E., "A Mathematical Theory of Communication," *Bell Sys. Tech. J.*, **27** pp. 379–423 (1948).

Shannon, C.E., and Weaver, W., *The Mathematical Theory of Communications*, The University of Illinois Press (1949).

Sher, L.D., "SpaceGraph, a True 3-D PC Peripheral," *SPIE* **902** *Three-Dimensional Imaging and Remote Sensing Imaging*, pp. 10–17 (1988).

Sher, L.D., "The Oscillating Mirror Technique for Realizing True 3D," in McAllister, D. (ed.), *Stereo Computer Graphics and Other True 3D Technologies*, pp. 196–213, Princeton University Press (1993).

Sherman, W.R., and Craig, A.B., *Understanding Virtual Reality: Interface, Application and Design*, Morgan Kaufmann (2003).

Sherrington, C.S., "The Muscular Sense," in Schaefer, E.A. (ed.), *Textbook on Physiology*, Macmillan (1900).

Siegel, M., Tobinaga, Y., and Akiya, T., "Kinder Gentler Stereo," *Proc. SPIE* **3639**, pp. 18–27 (1998).

Sieger, J., "The Design and Development of Television Receivers Using the Scophony Optical Scanning System," *Proc. I.R.E.*, pp. 487–492 (August 1939).

Sigman, M., Cecchi, G.A., Gilbert, C.D., and Magnasco, M.O., "On A Common Circle: Natural Scenes and Gestalt Rules," *Proc. Natl. Acad. Sci. USA*, **98** (4), pp. 1935–1940 (2001).

Smith, A., Kitamura, Y., Takemura, H., and Kishino, F., "A Simple and Efficient Method for Accurate Collision Detection among Deformable Polyhedral Objects in Arbitrary Motion," *Proc. Virtual Reality Annual International Symposium (VRAIS'95)*, pp. 136–145 (1995).

Smith, D.K., and Alexander, R.C., *Fumbling the Future: How Xerox Invented, Then Ignored, the First Personal Computer*, toExcel (1999).

Smith, F.G., and Thomson, J.H., *Optics*, John Wiley (1975).

Snibbe, S., Anderson, S., and Verplank, B., "Springs and Constraints for 3D Drawing," *Proc. Third PHANToM User's Group Workshop (Oct. 3–6)* (1998).

Soltan, P., Trias, J., Dahlke, W., Lasher, M., and MacDonald, M., "Laser-Based 3D Volumetric Display System (2nd generation)," *SID'94 Proc.* (1994).

Spillmann, L., and Dresp, B., "Phenomena of Illusory Form: Can We Bridge the Gap between Levels of Explanation?" *Perception*, **24** pp. 1333–1364 (1995).

Ruspini, D.C., Kolarov, K., and Khatib, O., "The Haptic Display of Complex Graphical Environments," *Proc. 24th Annual Conference on Computer Graphics and Interactive Techniques (SIGGRAPH'97, Los Angeles)*, pp. 345–352 (1997).

Sakata, H., Taira, M., Kusunoki, M., Murata, A., and Takaka, Y., "The Parietal Association Cortex In Depth Perception And Visual Control Of Hand Action," *Trends Neurosci.*, **20** (8), pp. 350–357 (1997).

Saleh, B.E.A., and Teich, M.C., *Fundamental of Photonics*, John Wiley (1991).

Salisbury, J.K., "Making Graphics Physically Tangible," *Communications of the ACM*, **42** (8), pp. 75–81 (1999).

Salisbury, J.K., Brock, D., Massie, T., Swarup, N., and Zilles, C., "Haptic Rendering: Programming Touch Interaction with Virtual Objects," *Proc. ACM Symposium on Interactive 3D Graphics*, pp. 123–130 (1995).

Salisbury, J.K., Conti, F., and Barbagli, F., "Haptic Rendering: Introductory Concepts," *IEEE Computer Graphics and Applications*, **24** (2), pp. 24–32 (2004).

Salmon, R., and Slater, M., *Computer Graphics Systems and Concepts*, Addison-Wesley (1987).

Sankaranarayanan, G., Weghorst, S., Sanner, M., Gillet, A., and Olson, A., "Role of Haptics in Teaching Structural Molecular Biology," *Proc. 11th Symposium on Haptic Interfaces for Virtual Environment and Teleoperator Systems (HAPTICS'03)* (2003).

Saper, C.B., "The Central Autonomic Nervous System: Conscious Visceral Perception and Autonomic Pattern Generation," *Annual Reviews of Neuroscience*, **25**, pp. 433–469 (2002).

Satava, R.M., "Surgical Education and Surgical Simulation," *World Journal of Surgery*, **25**, pp. 1484–1489 (2001a).

Satava, R.M., "Accomplishments and Challenges of Surgical Simulation: Dawnng of the Next-Generation Surgical Education," *Surgical Endoscopy*, **15**, pp. 232–241 (2001b).

Satava, R., and Sackier, J.M., *Cybersurgery: Advanced Technologies for Surgical Practice*, John Wiley (1998).

Scharf, B. (ed.), *Experimental Sensory Psychology*, Scott, Foresman and Company (1975).

Schieber, M.H., "Constraints on Somatotopic Organization in the Primary Motor Cortex," *Journal of Neurophysiology*, **86**, pp. 2125–2143 (2001).

Schiffman, H.R., *Sensation and Perception*, John Wiley (1976).

Schiffman, H.R., *Sensation and Perception*, 2nd edn., John Wiley (1982).

Schiffman, H.R., *Sensation and Perception*, 3rd edn., John Wiley (1990).

Schijven, M., and Jakimowicz, J., "Virtual Reality Surgical Laparoscopic Simulators," *Surgical Endoscopy*, **17**, pp. 1943–1950 (2003).

Schmandt, C., "Spatial Input/Display Correspondence in a Stereoscopic Computer Graphic Work Station," *Computer Graphics*, **17** (3), pp. 253–259 (July 1983).

Schmitt, O.H., "Cathode-Ray Presentation of Three-Dimensional Data," *J. Appl. Phys.*, **18**, pp. 819–829 (September 1947).

Schwarz, A.J., and Blundell, B.G., "Optimising Dot-Graphics for Volumetric Displays," *IEEE Trans. on Computer Graphics and Applications*, pp. 72–78 (1997).

Sears, F.W., and Zemansky, M.W., *University Physics*, 3rd edn., Addison-Wesley (1964).

Sedgwick, H.A., "Space Perception," in Boff, K.R., Kaufman, L., and Thomas, J.P., (eds.), *Handbook of Perception and Visual Performance*, John Wiley (1986).

Traub, C., "Stereoscopic Display using Rapid Varifocal Mirror Oscillations," *Appl. Opt.*, **6** (6), pp. 1085–1087 (1967).

Travis, A.R.L., "Autostereoscopic 3-D Display," *Appl. Opt.*, **29** (29), pp. 4341–4342 (1990).

Travis, A.R.L., Lang, S.R., Moore, J.R., and Dodgson, N.A., "Time-Multiplexed Three-Dimensional Video Display," *Journal of the SID*, **3/4**, pp. 203–205 (1995).

Troland, L.T., *The Principles of Psychophysiology*, Van Nostrand (1930).

Tufte, E.R., *Envisioning Information*, Graphics Press (1990).

Turner, M.L., Gomez, D.H., Tremblay, M.R., and Cutkosky, M.R., "Preliminary Tests of an Arm-Grounded Haptic Feedback Fevice in Telemanipulation," *Proc. ASME IMECE Haptics Symposium (Anaheim)* (1998).

Tyler, C.W., "Cyclopean Vision," in Regan, D. (ed.), *Binocular Vision*, Macmillan (1991).

Tyler, C.W., "The Horopter and Binocular Fusion," in Regan, D. (ed.), *Binocular Vision*, Macmillan (1991).

Udupa, J.K., "Display of 3D Information in Discrete 3D Scenes Produced by Computerized Tomography," *Proc. IEEE*, **71** (3), pp. 420–431 (March 1983).

Valyus, N., *Stereoscopy*, Focal Press (1962).

van Berkel, C., "Image Preparation for 3D-LCD," *Proc. SPIE*, **3639**, pp. 84–91 (1999).

van Berkel, C., and Clarke, J.A., "Characterisation and Optimisation of 3D-LCD Design," *Proc. SPIE*, **3012** (1997).

van Berkel, C., Parker, D.W., and Franklin, A.R., "Multi-View LCD," *Proc. SPIE*, **2653** (1996).

Van Dam, A., "VR as a Forcing Function: Software Implications of a New Paradigm," *Proc. 1993 IEEE Symposium on Research Frontiers in Virtual Reality*, pp. 5–8 (1993).

van den Brink, H.B., and Willemsen, O.H., "Tracking System of the Fast-Intelligent-Tracking (F!T) Tube," *Journal of the SID*, **11/3** (2003).

van Erp, J.B.F, "Guidelines For The Use of Vibro-Tactile Displays in Human Computer Interaction," *Proc. Eurohaptics* (2002).

Vannier, M.W., Marsh, J.L., and Warren, J.O., "Three Dimensional Computer Graphics for Craniofacial Surgical Planning and Evaluation," *Computer Graphics*, **17** (3), pp. 263–273 (July 1983).

Various, *Mathematics in the Modern World: Readings from Scientific American*, W.H. Freeman and Company (1968).

Verber, C.M., "Present and Potential Capabilities of Three-Dimensional Displays using Sequential Excitation of Fluorescence," *Proc. SPIE*, **120**, pp. 62–67 (1977).

Vidyasagar, T.R., "A Neuronal Model of Attentional Spotlight: Parietal Guiding the Temporal," *Brain Res. Rev.*, **30** (1), pp. 66–76 (1999).

Viguier, A., Clement, G., and Trotter, Y., "Distance Perception Within Near Visual Space," *Perception*, **30**, pp. 115–124 (2001).

Vince, J., *Virtual Reality Systems*, Addison-Wesley (1995).

Volbracht, S., Domik, G., Shahrbabaki, K., and Fels, G., "An Example of Task Oriented Empirical Evaluations of 3D-Display Modes," *Journal of Universal Computer Science*, **4** (5), pp. 534–546 (1998).

Springer, S., and Ferrier, N.J., "Design and Control of a Force-Reflecting Haptic Interface for Teleoperational Grasping," *Journal of Mechanical Design*, **124** (2), pp. 277–283 (2002).

Srinivasan, M.A., and Basdogan, C., "Haptics in Virtual Environments: Taxonomy, Research Status and Challenges," *Computers and Graphics*, **21** (4), pp. 393–404 (1997).

Stephenson, P., Encarnação, L.M., Branco, P., Tesch, J., and Zeltzer, D., "StudyDesk—Semi-Immersive Volumetric Data Analysis," *ACM Proc. 1st Int.Conf.on Computer Graphics and Interactive Techniques in Australasia and South East Asia*, pp. 251–252 (2003).

St. Hilaire, P., Benton, S., and Lucente, M., "Synthetic Aperture Holography: a Novel Approach to Three-Dimensional Displays," *J. Opt. Soc. Am. A.*, **9** (11), pp. 1969–1977 (1992).

Stratton, G.M., "Some Preliminary Experiments On Vision without Inversion of the Retinal Image," *Psychol. Rev.*, **3**, pp. 611–617 (1896).

Stratton, G.M., "Vision without Inversion of the Retinal Image," *Psychol. Rev.*, **4** (4), pp. 341–360 (1897).

Sullivan, A., "A Solid-State Multiplanar Volumetric Display," *Proc. SID'03 Digest* (2003).

Sutherland, I.E., "Sketchpad: A Man-Machine Graphical Communication System," in *SJCC*, Spartan Books, Baltimore, MD (1963).

Sutherland, I.E., "A Head-Mounted Three Dimensional Display," *AFIPS Conf. Proc.*, **33**, pp. 757–764 (1968).

Swade, D., *The Cogwheel Brain*, Abacus (2000).

Swade, D., "Virtual Objects: The End of the Real?" *Interdisciplinary Science Reviews*, **28** (4), pp. 273–279 (2003).

Tarrin, N., Coquillart, S., Hasegawa, S., Bouguila, L., and Sato, M., "The Stringed Haptic Workbench: A New Haptic Workbench Solution," *Computer Graphics Forum*, **22** (3), pp. 583–589 (2003).

Taylor, R.D., Jewsbury, P.J., and Essex, J.W., "A Review of Protein-Small Molecule Docking Methods," *Journal of Computer-Aided Molecular Design*, **16**, pp. 151–166 (2002).

Taylor, R.M., "Scientific Applications of Force Feedback: Molecular Simulation and Microscope Control," in *Haptics: From Basic Principles to Advanced Applications, SIGGRAPH'99* (1999).

Terzopoulos, D., and Qin, H., "Dynamic NURBS with Geometric Constraints for Interactive Sculpting," *ACM Transactions on Graphics*, **13** (2), pp. 103–136 (1994).

Tholey, G., Desai, J.P., and Castellanos, A.E., "Force Feedback Plays a Significant Role in Minimally Invasive Surgery," *Annals of Surgery*, **241** (1), pp. 102–109 (2005).

Thompson, T.V., Johnson, D.E., and Cohen, E., "Direct Haptic Rendering of Sculptured Models," *Proc. 1997 Symposium on Interactive 3D Graphics*, pp. 167–176 (1997).

Tilton, H.B., "Nineteen-Inch Parallactiscope," *Proc. SPIE* **902** *(Three-Dimensional Imaging and Remote Sensing Imaging)*, pp. 17–23 (1988).

Toomer, G.J., "Ptolemy," in Gillespie, C.C. (ed.), *Dictionary of Scientific Biography*, pp. 186–206, vol. XI, Charles Scribner's Sons, New York (1970).

Tovée, M.J., *An Introduction to the Visual System*, Cambridge University Press (1996).

angles, 72
characteristics, 70
Volumetric data, 27
exploration of, 244
Volumetric display, 186, 194, 287
addressing, 290
Volumetric image projection, 199
Voxel, 27
activation capacity, 291
attributes, additional, 29

Weber
fraction, 108
illusion, 96
Wheatstone, Charles,
165, 320
Wordsworth, William, xiv, 15

Xerox 8010 Star, 301
Xerox Alto, 9
Xerox PARC, 8